ARTISAN | NEW YORK

WHERE GOLF IS GREAT

The Finest Courses of SCOTLAND and IRELAND

JAMES W. FINEGAN

Photography by LAURENCE C. LAMBRECHT *and* TIM THOMPSON

Golf-course photographs copyright © 2006 by Laurence C. Lambrecht
Other photographs copyright © 2006 by Tim Thompson
For other photography credits, see page 527.

Published by Artisan
A Division of Workman Publishing, Inc.
225 Varick Street
New York, New York 10014
www.artisanbooks.com

Library of Congress Cataloging-in-Publication Data

Finegan, James W.
    Where golf is great: the finest courses of Scotland and Ireland/James W. Finegan;
photography by Laurence C. Lambrecht and Tim Thompson.
        p. cm.
Includes index.
ISBN-13: 978-1-57965-271-5
ISBN-10: 1-57965-271-9
    1. Golf courses—Scotland—Guidebooks. 2. Golf courses—Ireland—
Guidebooks. I. Lambrecht, Laurence Casey. II. Thompson, Tim 1942– . III. Title.

GV984.F545 2006
796.352'06841—dc22   2006045867

10 9 8 7 6 5 4 3 2 1

Printed in China

Book design by Susi Oberhelman

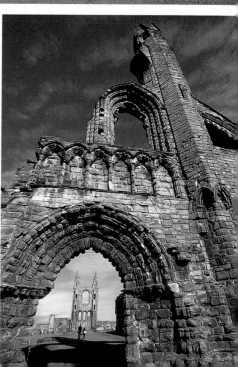

CONTENTS

INTRODUCTION

Over the years, many friends aiming to play golf in the British Isles have asked me the same simple question: Scotland or Ireland? The answer is also simple: both. I've made more than forty visits since 1971, and I still cannot choose one splendid land over the other—both offer the grand game in all its glory.

As does this book, which, at first glance, is a classically handsome picture book. But it is so much more. With essentially all the information a traveler will need on more than 150 golf courses in Scotland and Ireland—plus lodging, dining, and sightseeing advice—and an unparalleled selection of photographs, this is a golfer's best friend. Virtually all of the notable courses are here, including many unheralded venues. Are you familiar, for instance, with the Scotland gems Edzell, Moray, Brora, Lanark, and the 12-hole Shiskine links? Or the blessedly uncrowded Irish courses at Ardglass, Narin & Portnoo, Strandhill, and Carlow?

Many of the courses in this book—about half—are links. Among the more than 32,000 golf courses in the world, no more than 170 are authentic links, the great majority of which are in the U.K. and Ireland. The game played on linksland—along the rumpled ground almost as much as through the air—is exhilarating. Generally speaking, a links course is seaside, sea level, and routed over quick-draining, sand-based terrain. Dunes, whether modest (St. Andrews Old Course) or magnificent (Ballybunion), are almost always present. Over tens of thousands of years, this linksland evolved as the sea receded, leaving behind sandy wastes that the winds fashioned into ripples and knobs and knolls, into gullies and swales and hollows and hummocks. Then grass began to grow in the hollows, and other vegetation—gorse, heather, broom—took root. The golf holes laid out over this terrain are more truly natural than those on inland courses. There is an appealing spaciousness, an invigorating sense of openness and freedom about seaside courses; the beauty is severe, sometimes even stark.

The types of shots executed over this land set links golf apart. On a links, with its ever-present seaside breezes (and sometimes gales), we hit low and piercing drives, take three clubs more than we first thought, and knock our iron shots down under the wind. In the green complexes, we manufacture shut-face little 6-iron run-ups that skip and skate. Or we may choose to putt from 40 yards off the green—or maybe even 80. What it all adds up to is an irresistible challenge that calls for imagination and ingenuity, finesse and feel. It is the game as it was in the beginning, as it was meant to be, and as it still can be, if only on a links course.

It is also the game as it so rarely is in the United States: open to visitors. Of all the clubs and courses covered in this book, there is only one, Loch Lomond, that does not welcome the stranger. This is rather different from what we're accustomed to at home, where private clubs are by definition private. But in Scotland and Ireland, even the most prestigious clubs accept the unaccompanied visitor. And no course is closed to women. Also worth keeping in mind: golf carts are frequently available.

Some courses (Royal Portrush, Royal County Down, and the Old Course at St. Andrews) have a policy requiring visitors to present a current handicap card or a letter of introduction with handicap confirmation. Also, in all likelihood you will be playing from the daily or regular markers. Only very rarely will you use the back tees; they are almost always reserved for competitions. So in this book, it is the yardages from the regular markers that I consistently provide.

Tee times in season will often be more difficult to pin down than hotel reservations. You may have to contact the club or course far in advance—say, eight months, a year, even more. In some cases, nearby hotels may have special relationships that facilitate getting tee times. Accommodations range here from country inns to grand resorts, virtually all with very good food. As for the sightseeing opportunities, in both Scotland and Ireland they are even more rewarding than one could imagine.

In certain locales—those where the combination of golf, hotel, dining, and non-golf attractions is remarkably outstanding—I found myself instinctively wanting to call special attention to them. The result is the couple dozen boxes scattered throughout the text, a rundown of the very best of the best, the greatest golf-vacation experiences in these two lands, where much more than merely the golf is, undeniably, superlative.

Opposite: St. Andrews Bay Torrance Course, 17th. Previous spread: The K Club, 16th.

It was in Scotland, over 550 years ago, that golf was born. For the first 400 years, the game stayed right there. It could scarcely be said to have thrived: by 1850 there were fewer than 20 courses. But by 1909 there were 275, and today, in a land that is a bit smaller than the state of Maine, there are more than 550 courses. • The embryonic game was first played beside the sea. In this book 44 Scottish links courses are examined. Some are bona fide shrines, such as the Old Course at St. Andrews, Muirfield, Carnoustie, Turnberry's Ailsa, and Royal Troon. These five Open Championship venues

S C O T L A N D

provide marvelous opportunities to play in the very footsteps of the game's towering figures, such as Vardon, Braid, Taylor, Hagen, Jones, Armour, Snead, Hogan, Palmer, Nicklaus, Player, Ballesteros, Watson, and Woods—all of whom triumphed in Scotland. • And then there are the unsung seaside jewels—Montrose, Murcar, The Machrie—not to mention such excellent inland layouts as the altogether splendid trio at Gleneagles; the Duke's Course, at St. Andrews; the Rosemount eighteen at Blairgowrie; and Belleisle, in Ayr. • As the Scots are wont to say, "The golf traveler is spoilt for choice."

ANCIENT ST. ANDREWS
AND THE KINGDOM OF FIFE

ST. ANDREWS

The first of my more than thirty visits to Scotland took place in mid-September 1952. I was twenty-one, a lowly ensign on the aircraft carrier USS *Wasp*, which had anchored in the Firth of Clyde, several miles below Glasgow. At liberty for a day, a shipmate and I took the train to St. Andrews, lightweight golf bags over our shoulders. We walked directly from the terminal to the Royal and Ancient clubhouse, blithely assuming that this was where we would change our clothes. The porter politely informed us that unless we were guests of a member, we could not be admitted. Suggesting we try the St. Andrews Golf Club, he pointed to a building just beyond the 18th green. Here, in a plain room at the top of the clubhouse, we hung our uniforms on pegs—there were no lockers—donned golf clothes, then clattered down the uncarpeted stairs in our spikes, crossed Links Road and the 18th fairway, and paid our green fee, 25 pence, at the kiosk. There were no other players about on this pretty afternoon, a brisk breeze driving high clouds out over St. Andrews Bay.

From the outset I loved this ancient links, but it baffled me. I had grown up caddieing and playing in suburban Philadelphia, so the Old Course did not resemble any golf course I had seen before: treeless, only two fairways wide, unimaginably vast greens serving two holes, corresponding "double fairways," sand bunkers with steep, stacked-sod faces that looked as though a bricklayer must have fashioned them. Not to mention gorse and heather and, above all, the rippling, heaving, hummocky terrain. After the round we took high tea in the town. From our window table we watched the university students in their traditional red robes going back to their lodgings, and the townspeople, putters in hand, trooping down to the wildly undulating putting green (it is not called the "Himalayas" for nothing) between the 2nd hole and the beach.

For a dozen years my wife, Harriet, and I spent most of the summer in St. Andrews, in a rented flat overlooking the 1st and 18th holes of the Old Course and providing a view of the R&A clubhouse, the beach, the bay, and the coastline. I would write in the morning and play in the afternoon or evening, on the New Course or the Jubilee or the Eden or on what seems to me the most complex great course in the world, the Old.

By now I have played the Old Course more than a hundred times and can report that it is shamelessly deceitful (just where *are* those hidden bunkers in the center of the 12th fairway?) and capricious (George Duncan, 1920 British Open champion, once said, "You can play a damned good shot there and find the ball in a damned bad place") and frustrating, from the gathering Swilcan Burn that fronts the 1st green to the gathering Valley of Sin in the forepart of the 18th green.

Some form of golf, however primitive in the beginning, has been played over this ground for close to six hundred years. Virtually every great champion—Ben Hogan is the glaring exception—has competed on this links. The British Open (properly called the Open Championship) has been contested here twenty-seven times, the Amateur Championship fifteen times, the Walker Cup eight times, and the British Ladies' Amateur four times. The R&A does not own the Old Course. Ownership of it, as well as of the other five St. Andrews links, is vested in the Northeast Fife District Council. The game upon these courses belongs to the world.

The design of the Old Course cannot be attributed to any single golf architect; the layout simply evolved over time. However, certain features were introduced and certain revisions were effected by Allan Robertson, Old Tom Morris, Alister MacKenzie, James Braid, and Donald Steel.

ON THE OLD COURSE

The most useful tip I can provide about playing the Old Course is one you won't get from a caddie (for obvious reasons): roughly 80 percent of the putts are straight, whether from 40 feet or 4 feet. So unless you are faced with a putt that unequivocally proclaims a break, don't borrow anything. Just stroke the ball directly at the cup. Few people believe this, but those who do—and possess a sound stroke—will run the table.

All right, now we are—you and I—on the 1st tee, gazing out over a monotonous stretch of flattish fairway, a good hundred yards wide in the tee-shot landing area because it encompasses both the 1st and 18th holes. There is little to arrest the eye, even less to please it. The scorecard shows 6,566 yards, par 72; but what I call the "tourist tees" make it some

Opposite: St. Andrews Old Course, 18th. Previous spread: 4th.

250 yards less, as a rule. This opener, all of 350 yards, can be very difficult, because the Swilcan Burn actually defines the front of the green. With the wind at our back and the cup down front, our 9-iron will finish so far past the hole that three-putting becomes a clear danger. If, however, the wind is in our face, the playing value of the hole is rather like 400 yards, and it is the stream that becomes a clear danger.

With the 2nd hole, we find ourselves abroad in a sea of heaving turf and playing to the first of the seven double greens, this one also containing the cup for the 16th. The ground from here on will be undulating, everlastingly in motion, triggering awkward lies and stances. And though the flag will generally be in sight, there is nothing to serve as a background for it. Often there is a shimmering, miragelike quality to what our eye takes in, with the green itself maddeningly ill-defined.

There is a similarity to most of the par 4s going out—2, 3, 4, 6, 7—that makes it difficult to tell one from another. All head in much the same direction, and all present blind or semiblind forced-carry drives over rough or broken ground. The inbound half, on the other hand, is remarkably diverse. It is also one of the very best nines in the world. At least five holes are great.

From an elevated tee, the 170-yard 11th—the shortest hole on the course—plays squarely across the 7th fairway to a mildly elevated green backdropped by the Eden estuary. In the landmark book *The 500 World's Greatest Golf Holes*, by George Peper and the editors of *Golf Magazine*, the 11th is singled out as one of the world's hundred greatest holes. Hill Bunker, nearly 10 feet deep, patrols the left side of the green. (All 112 Old Course bunkers have names, some with an ominous ring: Coffin, Grave, Hell.) Strath Bunker, a mere seven feet deep but decidedly less roomy, eats into the right front of the green. There is considerable space between the two, and we ought to be able to steer clear of both. Aye, there's the rub: *steering*, instead of swinging full out with confidence. Moreover, because the green tilts steeply down from back to front, putting from well above the hole is a test. Wrote Alister MacKenzie in *The Spirit of St. Andrews:* "The eleventh hole at St. Andrews requires a greater variety of shots under different conditions of wind and changes in position of the flag than any other short hole. It also produces more interest, excitement, and thrills than any other hole, and for these reasons I consider it the greatest of all short holes." High praise indeed from the man who had already created the imperishable "trans-Pacific" 16th at Cypress Point.

Step off the back of the 11th green now onto the 12th tee. Is this, in the world of golf, the one place to be above all others? Gaze out over the broad Eden estuary as it stretches away to the North Sea. Face left and, beyond the flags for 11 and 7, lie the New Course and the Jubilee, both covered with golfers, and beyond these two eighteens are the white-capped waters of St. Andrews Bay, tumbling onto the West Sands. Immediately to your right is the Eden Course, and next to it, the Strathtyrum. More golfers. What an immense playing field it all is—links, links, links, gray green and undulating, studded with low dunes and gorse and heather and fearsome sandpits, not beautiful in the conventional sense, perhaps, its ineluctable charm the product of its naturalness. And now look dead ahead, down the 12th fairway and beyond the red flag. In the far distance lies the beloved old town itself, above the rocks and the sea on a gentle bluff, its low, gray silhouette punctuated by a handful of church spires. As we play our way home, each stroke draws us closer to it.

As for the 12th hole itself, 316 yards long, it was here in the 2000 Open that Tiger Woods unveiled a new concept in course management. Leading by 4 or 5 strokes as he came to this hole in the final round, he

elected to take the trouble—the gorse and sand short of the green—out of play by the simple expedient of firing his tee shot *over* the green. The little pitch back could hardly produce more than a 4.

At the great 400-yard 13th, the drive must be kept right of the three Coffins bunkers; the blind second shot, anything from an 8-iron to a 3-metal, depending on the wind, must clear a low ridge first and then a nightmarish tangle of broken ground, bunkers, and deep rough.

This is followed by the even greater 14th, for me the finest par 5 on the planet. Littered with 15 bunkers and bordered tight on the right by a low stone boundary wall separating the Old Course from the Eden, this 523-yarder strikes us at first as classically penal. In fact, it is classically strategic. There are three routes to the green: the conservative path, left down the 5th fairway; straightaway, for a chance of getting nearly home in two if we can carry Hell Bunker; and right, taking the sand out of play but flirting with the boundary. In the 1995 Open, Jack Nicklaus found cavernous Hell Bunker with his second shot and struggled ingloriously to

Opposite, top: St. Andrews Old Course, 11th; bottom: 12th. Below, the 4th and 14th greens.

Above: St. Andrews Old
Course, 16th. Opposite: 17th.

a 10. Over the months that followed, visitor after visitor came to the 14th bent on "beating Jack Nicklaus." I played with a few of these giant-killers. I recall one fellow who, after finally managing to extricate himself from Hell, reached the green in 8 and holed a 14-footer for 9. His joy knew no bounds. This hole was named one of the 500 *World's Greatest*.

The 16th, 351 yards, is also great and also hostile. A tight cluster of three bunkers called the Principal's Nose awaits in the left center of the fairway, 200 yards out. The right side of the hole is bordered by an out-of-bounds fence 29 yards from the triune hazard of the Nose. The timorous tee shot will be kept left of it, but the approach shot will then be imperiled by Wig Bunker, which knifes into the left front of the low-plateau green. Aiming right of Wig brings into play the boundary fence, which lurks only a few feet from the right edge of the putting surface. Of course, a strong and straight drive over the Principal's Nose sets up an easy short iron to an open green. The 16th is a model of risk/reward golf.

The 17th is the hardest par 4 in major championship golf. Called the Road Hole and measuring 461 yards, it was chosen as one of the top

18 in the 500 *World's Greatest*. The blind drive must wing its way over the addition to the Old Course Hotel, which simulates the train shed that for decades stood there in the crook of the right-hand dogleg, squarely on the line of flight. The rectangular green, situated diagonally across the second shot and built on a plateau three or four feet above the fairway, is backed at the right and the rear first by a gravel pathway, then by a paved road, and finally by a stone wall, all of them in play. There is no free drop here. A devouring and claustrophobic sandpit, the merciless Road Bunker invades the left side of the putting surface. In short, this hole is an instrument of torture. In 1984 Tom Watson finished second in the Open, 2 strokes behind Seve Ballesteros, having played the hole 5-6-4-5.

The 18th, by contrast, is altogether congenial—354 yards, the broadest of fairways, an immense single green, not a bunker to be found. We drive well left of center, aiming for the red-and-gold clock on the Royal & Ancient clubhouse and giving a wide berth to the out-of-bounds on the right. Determined not to come up short in the Valley of Sin, we now play the approach too boldly and finish 35 feet past the cup. Leaning over the railing behind the green are spectators—3, 7, 10, 20—regardless of the time of day (I once completed a round in late June in the dark, at eleven o'clock, and was warmly applauded for my intrepid two-putting). Minimally downhill, this 35-foot lag is somehow not disturbing. Surely if we lay our hands softly on the grip and put an unhurried stroke on the ball, it must feed its way down and expire somewhere within the haven of a two-foot circle. And so it does. We tap in for a 4, retrieve the ball—and slowly exhale.

On a hole that has witnessed more than its share of Open history, the dramatic victory of Jack Nicklaus in 1970 remains vivid in memory. Doug Sanders, he of the peacock wardrobe and the truncated backswing, missed a three-footer for the title on the 72nd hole to give Nicklaus new life. In the 18-hole playoff the next day, Nicklaus clung to a 1-stroke lead as they came to the home hole. Hitting first, Sanders drove to within 25 yards of the green. Now the thirty-year-old Ohioan, after shedding his sweater in an unconscious gesture that suggested it was high time he took off the wraps, launched a colossal drive (Have we forgotten how truly long he was, pregraphite, pretitanium, and pre-rocket-balls?) that skimmed through the Valley of Sin, just missed the flagstick as it raced across the green, and finally stopped on the overgrown bank behind the putting surface, some 375 yards from where it had begun its journey. Sanders ran his chip to within four feet of the cup for a likely birdie. Nicklaus's pitch from the heavy grass pulled up seven feet short of the hole.

Ten years later I would ask Jack whether, when the ball left his putter blade, he thought he had holed the seven-footer.

"Yes," he replied. "Of course, that putt breaks a little left to right and the ball did go into the right center of the hole. But I knew I'd stroked it well." He paused, then added with a smile, "As a matter of fact, it came closer to missing than I thought it was going to."

From time to time I am asked how a visitor gets to play the Old Course. There are five ways. First, you can reserve a tee time by contacting the Links Trust long in advance. Second, you can book a package with any of several St. Andrews hotels or international tour operators that are regularly allocated Old Course tee times. Third, sign up for the Old Course Experience, a costly investment that covers a round on the Old, a round on one of the other courses, a caddie, a five-star hotel, and fine meals. Fourth, enter the ballot, no later than 2:00 P.M. the day before you wish to play, and hope your name is drawn. And finally, speaking of luck, you can try yours the same way I do, as a standby. Simply give the starter your name—first come, first served. Though all tee times are taken, some will be the property of twosomes or threesomes, thus creating an opportunity for a standby or two. An average of twenty to twenty-five are put out daily. The starter can be counted on to be courteous and helpful.

Over the years I've played the Old Course with more than two hundred and fifty people. All kinds of people: Flora, a ninety-six-pound middle-aged Filipino opera singer, who was unable to break 150 but relished every stroke she played. . . . Brian, in his early fifties and one of the two or three best one-armed golfers in the British Isles (left arm off at the shoulder), who drives the ball 230 yards and who finished that day with 81 (38–43: fierce headwind on the second nine). . . . Lars, a twenty-year-old Swede who fired a 2-under-par 70 and was working as a dishwasher in one of the St. Andrews University dorms while he went on honing his game "for as long as it takes." . . . Gary, a thirty-four-year-old who owned two stalls (games of chance, two pounds to play) on the seaside promenade down in Blackpool, England, minutes from Royal Lytham & St. Annes. . . . Bill, a husky retired U.S. Navy pilot who flew six hundred missions in Vietnam, who plays golf daily, and who said, "If I ever find that I can't drive the ball two hundred eighty yards anymore, I'll give up the game" . . . Steve and Michael, a life insurance salesman and his fifteen-year-old son, from San Luis Obispo, California, who insisted that I accompany them to the Quarto bookshop, just around the corner from the 18th green, so they could buy a copy of my Scotland book and have me inscribe it.

I don't think you could meet such a diversity of golfers on any other course in the world. But then, the Old Course is unlike any other course in the world. It is sui generis, a law unto itself. It stands alone, the shrine of shrines. Several years ago in a game at Pine Valley, I said to Alan MacGregor, manager of the St. Andrews Links Trust, as we stood on the hilltop 18th tee, "I hope you agree that Pine Valley is the greatest course in the world."

He hesitated, then replied, "I agree that Pine Valley is the *best* course in the world, but the Old Course is the *greatest*."

OTHER ST. ANDREWS LINKS TRUST COURSES

There are five more links courses at St. Andrews. Old Tom Morris designed and built the **New Course** in 1895. Enjoying much the same undulating linksland as the Old, which is right beside it, it measures 6,362 yards from the regular markers; par is 71. Three holes show the New at its best: the par-5 8th, where a narrow gap between two high sand hills defines the approach to a hidden green; the 225-yard 9th, a rising shot along the Eden estuary to a punch bowl green; and the great par-4 10th, 464 yards, played from an elevated tee to a blind and sloping fairway, the exacting second shot

Opposite: St. Andrews Old Course, 18th.

Above, left: St. Andrews
New Course, 10th; right:
St. Andrews Eden Course,
8th. Opposite: St. Andrews
Duke's Course, 15th.

along a dune-framed valley to a green backed by low sand hills. The New appears regularly on lists of the top hundred courses in the British Isles.

On the seaward side of the New—and even more testing—is the **Jubilee**, which opened in 1897. The holes today are largely the work of Donald Steel, who has imbued this eighteen with character and variety by skillfully employing two parallel spines of sand hills. Par is 72 on this 6, 424-yard layout.

The **Eden** was a collaboration in 1913 by two of the very greatest figures in golf course architecture, Harry Colt and Alister MacKenzie. Despite many changes over the years, some top-notch Colt-MacKenzie holes remain, including two short par 4s that play right beside the estuary to plateau greens perched teasingly above it. The Eden measures 6,200 yards against a par of 70.

The **Strathtyrum Course**, which opened in 1993 (5,100 yards, par 69), was designed by Steel expressly for high handicappers. Fairways are wide, bunkering is light. Adjacent to the Strathtyrum is a little nine-hole layout called **Balgove** (1,530 yards, par 30), an ideal spot for youngsters to get their first taste of the game.

An important addition to the St. Andrews Links lineup is a-budding. The course is being built on high ground along the coast between Kinkell Braes and St. Andrews Bay Golf Resort & Spa. Scottish-born David McLay Kidd, architect of Bandon Dunes and suburban London's Queenwood course, designed the new eighteen, which is expected to open in 2008. Early reports on the complete routing plan and the handful of holes already fashioned strongly suggest that this course will take its place among the very best in Scotland.

THE DUKE'S COURSE

Herb Kohler (bathroom fixtures, Whistling Straits, and much more) rather recently acquired the Old Course Hotel and with it the Duke's Course, which was laid out by Peter Thomson in 1994. Mr. Kohler promptly ordered a revamping of the Australian's layout. The net of it is seven extensively redesigned holes, a number of remodeled tees, and a new drainage system. The "new" Duke's is excellent. Time will tell whether it is better than the "old" Duke's.

In 1910 Bernard Darwin, grandson of the great naturalist Charles Darwin, wrote, "I once met, staying in a hotel at St. Andrews, a gentleman who did not play golf. That is in itself remarkable, but more remarkable still, he joined so unobtrusively in the perpetual golfing conversation that his black secret was never discovered."

Yes, there is in St. Andrews life apart from golf. The compact and level "ault grey toon," a place of exceptional richness and antiquity, is ideal for walking. Of the three principal streets—North, Market, South—it is South Street that most fully embodies the ancient heritage of St. Andrews. Let's enter it through the West Port, carved out of a still-intact section of the fourteenth-century wall. We now stroll up the spacious cobbled thoroughfare. Landmarks dot the way: the roofless remains of Blackfriars' Chapel (1525); Madras College, a coed preparatory school founded in 1832; the Town Hall; Holy Trinity Church, dating from 1410.

A bit of a detour now for the Lade Braes Walk, roughly a mile and a half long. Much of it follows the embowered Kinness Burn, where several sylvan scenes (Law Mill provides one of them) are straight out of Constable.

The final leg leads down a narrow lane of gardens belonging to houses of all shapes and sizes and ages that may be short on grace but are long on personality. Where must the Lade Braes walk end? Why, back at South Street, practically next door to Blackfriars' Chapel.

A block or two farther along, we enter the lovely old quadrangle of St. Mary's College, dominated by a mighty oak tree. The first student matriculated in 1522; upstairs, a room from that period is preserved as it was.

In the last block of South Street is a house where Mary Queen of Scots is believed to have resided for a time in 1564 and where Charles II certainly did in 1650. Quite nearby is the Pends, a harmonious arched stone gateway leading to the cathedral precincts. Legend has it that the Pends will collapse when the wisest man in Christendom walks through the archway. The Pends still stands.

Regrettably, the same cannot be said of the cathedral, which is largely in ruins. But what evocative ruins they are, here on a splendid promontory above the sea. What brought the once-exalted house of God so low was the Protestant Reformation, with mobs sweeping

down South Street to this seat of popery, there to sack and smash and loot. For years, local stonemasons found the cathedral to be a convenient quarry; many of the best houses in St. Andrews incorporate fragments of the noble church.

An unusual assortment of monuments and tombstones lures us to the graveyard. Old Tom Morris is buried here. Next to him is Young Tom, also a four-time Open champion, who died heartbroken, at the age of twenty-four, three months after his wife succumbed in childbirth, as did the son, their first offspring.

Just east of the cathedral, on The Scores, is the castle, begun in 1200 and long the seat of the Archbishop of St. Andrews. Guarded by cliffs and the sea, this haunting ruin was the setting for bloody drama on more than one occasion as the Reformation engulfed Scotland.

Over on North Street, a block away, are the Crawford Centre for the Arts, St. Salvator's Church, and Younger Graduation Hall, site of one of the most poignant moments in the history of St. Andrews. When Bob Jones came back in 1958 as nonplaying captain of the United

From left: the practice tee; Market Street; Union Street sign (top) and Old Cathedral (bottom); Old Cathedral sign. Opposite: the Old Cathedral.

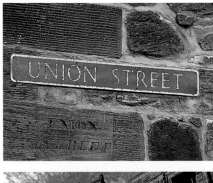

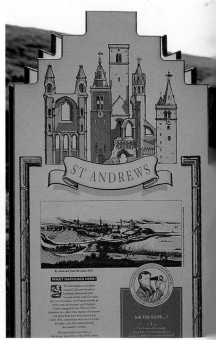

States squad in the inaugural World Amateur Team Championship, the town fathers took the opportunity to make him a freeman of the Burgh of St. Andrews. Only Jones had won both the Open (1927) and the Amateur (1930) on the Old Course, an achievement unlikely to be equaled. And his fineness of character and gentlemanly demeanor had registered as powerfully upon St. Andrews as his flair for playing links golf. Now crippled by a rare spinal disease, he needed a golf cart to get around.

More than two thousand people crammed Younger Hall that evening. After the provost spoke of the abiding friendship between Jones and the townspeople, Bob edged his way painstakingly along a supporting table to the lectern. Without benefit of script or notes, he recounted the high and low points of the championships in which he had competed on the Old Course. "I could take out of my life everything except my experiences at St. Andrews," he said, "and I would still have had a rich and full life." He concluded by speaking of friendship: "When you have made me aware on many occasions that you have a kindly feeling toward me, and when you have honored me by every means at your command, then when I call you my friends I am at once affirming my high regard and affection for you and my trust in the sincerity of your expression. And so, my fellow citizens of St. Andrews, it is with this appreciation of the full measure of the word that I salute you as my friends."

As he guided his "electric buggy" down the center aisle, the entire gathering rose and broke into an unutterably moving rendition of the old Scottish song "Will Ye No' Come Back Again?" As it happened, he never would.

My wife and I customarily stroll The Scores (the hotel takes its name from the street) after dinner, as you might a boardwalk. The sea is close at hand. We pass the bandstand and Martyrs' Monument, then a number of appealing hundred-year-old residences, several small hotels, and university buildings, including St. Salvator's. Sometimes we sit on a bench beneath the trees, gazing at the ruins of the castle. Other times we walk a block farther, to a spot that commands not only the sea but the cathedral and its graveyard, with the monument to Young Tom Morris in full view. And then it is time to retrace our steps, back along The Scores.

I remember the November evening many years ago when, on the return leg of our walk, we discovered a way into the grounds of St. Salvator's from The Scores. Turn down Butts Wynd, a narrow lane linking The Scores with North Street, and your venturesomeness will be rewarded by finding a gateway in the wall surrounding the college. That night, for the first time, we passed through it into the beautiful quadrangle. Shadows and silence, the great collegiate church mantled in darkness, its cloistering scarcely discernible, and, on the far side of that perfect lawn now dampened with dew, a light or two in the Jacobean facade of Lower College Hall. Ancient universities (this one founded in 1412), beguiling by day, can be even more bewitching by night. No student stirred as we stood peering up at the church spire, its pinnacle soaring above North Street and lost in the night, before we retreated through the gateway in the wall and down Butts Wynd to The Scores.

Along the seaward side of The Scores now, if it is a clear night, with stars thickly sewn in the heavens and perhaps the moon glinting off the gentle swells of the North Sea, the lights on the Angus coast—Carnoustie, even Arbroath—will glow softly golden far across the water. But if there should be a mist, why then, we are content with the shushing of the surf on the rocks at the base of the bluff. It is sweet indeed.

Fife has a number of nongolf attractions a short drive from St. Andrews. The royal burgh of Falkland revolves around Falkland Palace, begun in the fifteenth century as a hunting lodge for the Stuarts. Flemish tapestries, carved oak ceilings, and stained-glass windows all lend a regal look to the great house. And in the exquisite garden is a royal tennis court that dates from 1539. Court tennis is an eye-opening combination of squash and tennis. In the village are two good eating spots, The Covenanter Hotel, on the square, and, just off the square, the Stag Inn—dim, snug, and with old wooden booths.

Some twenty minutes northeast of Falkland, in pretty Ceres, is the Fife Folk Museum: costumes, tools, and utensils from the farms, homes, and workshops of bygone days. Also in Ceres is an unusual shop that specializes in linens and antique children's clothes, and no dis-

Opposite: the Old Cathedral. This page: views of Falkland Palace and its gardens, except the monument to Young Tom Morris (top left) and the inside walls of Old Cathedral (top right).

tance outside the village is Hill of Tarvit Mansionhouse, an imposing Edwardian manor that showcases the late Frederick Sharp's collection of Flemish tapestries, Chinese porcelains and bronzes, French and Regency furniture, and European paintings. The gardens are still carefully maintained, but gone is the nine-hole golf course that Sharp built for himself and his friends and made available, free of charge, to the residents of Ceres.

DINING

Eating in St. Andrews can be a town or country pleasure.

- Leading the town restaurants is the **Road Hole Grill**, on the top floor of the Old Course Hotel. The dishes, beautifully prepared and presented, incline to be sophisticated, and the wine list and service in this stylish milieu are equally outstanding.

- Not to be overlooked is the dining room in the **Links Clubhouse**, where the setting sparkles, the menu is imaginative, and the view over the links is irresistible.

- In the heart of town is the **Vine Leaf**, with eclectic decor and an equally eclectic menu.

- The **Balaka Bangladeshi** is consistently ranked among the best of the United Kingdom's eighty-five hundred Bangladeshi, Indian, and Pakastani restaurants by the *Good Curry Restaurant Guide*.

- Another good ethnic restaurant, this one Thai, is **Nahm-Jim**, on Crails Lane.

- Just beyond the bandstand on The Scores and hanging over the sea is the smartly contemporary **Seafood Restaurant**.

- For a pub lunch or a nightcap, duck into the old and atmospheric **Jigger Inn**, beside the Road Hole; or the lively **Dunvegan Hotel**, on Pilmour Place, with its American proprietors and its first-rate cheeseburgers; or the **St. Andrews Golf Hotel**, on The Scores, where, if the university is in session, college kids throng the rathskeller nightly.

In the countryside ringing St. Andrews is a quartet of superior restaurants:

- The **Grange Inn** (beam ceilings, log fires), on a hillside immediately south of town and with enchanting views of it, used to be renowned for its soups. Now, just about everything on the menu turns out to be delicious.

Clockwise from top: Myres Castle; Hill of Tarvit interior; a view of St. Andrews; exterior of Hill of Tarvit.

- Perhaps 15 minutes northwest of town is **Craigsan-quhar House**, whose dining room provides a long, captivating view over the fertile fields of Fife.
- About ten minutes southwest of town is the **Inn at Lathone's**, where the cooking bows toward France and the dining room has a warm informality that inclines us to linger over the wine.
- Not five minutes from Lathone's is the **Peat Inn**, our favorite place to eat in Scotland. The principal dining room in this old whitewashed stone farmhouse looks over a simple garden to uncultivated fields. The French-influenced menu is chock-full of exceptional choices: julienne of pigeon breast on a confit of spiced pork, saddle of venison with a wild mushroom and truffle crust in a red wine sauce, *feuilleté* of white chocolate ice cream with a dark chocolate sauce. The impressive wine list even contains some attractive vintages for less than fifty dollars. The Peat Inn, it might be noted, is *in* Peat Inn.

LODGING

Since St. Andrews is, as much as anything, a seaside resort, it offers a variety of places to stay. You can find a room in a university dorm (often with bath) or in one of the countless B&Bs, a number of them on Murray Place.

- **Waldon House**, smack on the 18th hole of the Old Course, is a B&B owned and operated by the R&A. When any of the eight rooms is not occupied by a club member or his guest, that room is generally made available to the public.
- In the countryside outside the village of Auchter-muchty (thirty minutes from St. Andrews) is **Myres Castle**, which dates from the sixteenth century. A private and luxurious house, it is rented exclusively to parties ranging from six to eighteen; minimum stay, two nights. The nine bedrooms in this period paradise, each with its own bath, are individually appointed. The cooking is superb.
- The five-star **Old Course Hotel & Spa** is all that a great hotel should be: stylish, luxurious, supremely comfortable; world-class amenities, cuisine, and views; an up-to-date spa with a small but pleasant pool; faultless service. Very recently refurbished by

new owner Herb Kohler, it is one of the half dozen best hotels in Scotland, and *mirabile dictu*, it may even be able to get you on the Old Course!
- A couple of miles out of town on the Strathkinness Low Road is **Rufflets**, an inviting country-house hotel. Accommodations are bright and cheerful, cooking is creative, and the topiary garden, beside a stream, is idyllic. Rufflets was for years the choice of Jack and Barbara Nicklaus.
- Another legendary golfer's favorite is **Rusacks Hotel**, where Bob Jones stayed. Overlooking the first and

last holes of the Old Course, it is casual and hospitable, with good food and unforgettable views.
- The **Scores Hotel**, where we first stayed in 1971, is a traditional haven for golfers, sitting on a rise above the R&A clubhouse. Comfortable accommodations, worthy cooking, and a kindly welcome are the chief reasons why travelers return to it regularly, not to mention the stunning views of the sea and the West Sands from the front rooms and the thirty-eight-second walk to the 1st tee of the Old Course from the front door.

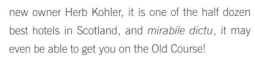

Clockwise from top left: Jigger Inn; Grange Inn; Rusacks Hotel; Royal & Ancient Golf Club; Old Course Hotel.

ST. ANDREWS BAY

In 1998 American pharmaceutical magnate Donald Panoz (his Elan Corporation devised the nicotine patch) flew in from Atlanta. For all of five minutes, he surveyed the potential site for a golf resort on the outskirts of St. Andrews. Then he said simply, with a smile, "This'll do me."

It's no wonder the decision on the 520-acre tract was so easy. In addition to sea frontage of more than a mile, this property, which varies between twenty and eighty feet above the rocky strand, offers mesmerizing views across the bay to the medieval quarter of St. Andrews.

At the heart of the St. Andrews Bay Golf Resort & Spa are a 209-room hotel and two outstanding eighteens, the Torrance Course and the Devlin Course. Sam Torrance, captain of the 2002 European Ryder Cup team and himself an eight-time Ryder Cupper, was assisted on his design by Atlantan Denis Griffiths and by the late Gene Sarazen, who, at age ninety-six, visited the site and drafted some key recommendations.

ON THE TORRANCE COURSE

The Torrance is an aesthetic delight—sea views from every hole, St. Andrews views from many holes—and a challenge. It can play as long as 7,020 yards, as short as 5,380; par is 72. The overall elevation change is about 40 feet. There are numerous opportunities to play links-style running shots. Stone walls, golden fescues dotted with wildflowers, and winding burns are all part of the game here. Trees are not.

The course is studded with holes that combine charm with test. At the 167-yard 11th, our eyes first spot the flagstick and then, on the same line but on the far side of the bay, take in ancient St. Andrews—the town wall, St. Rule's Tower, the spire of St. Salvator's, the cathedral and its graveyard—all of it perfectly framed in the distance. Golfers have never before been blessed with this vista. It is incomparable and it is unforgettable.

The penultimate hole, one of the cliff-toppers skirting the sea, is also marvelous. On this 427-yarder the prevailing wind is into us and left to right, blithely tossing the frail drive over the cliff and down into the sea, where basking seals bark mockingly.

ON THE DEVLIN COURSE

Bruce Devlin, who has played a principal role in the design or remodeling of more than one hundred fifty courses worldwide, was given more land and more sea frontage than Torrance, to say nothing of ground with greater elevation change. This acreage is also richer topographically, with more features, including Kittock's Den, a vast and deep hollow with trees and scrub and the promise of several adventuresome golf holes. Two sizable ponds have been introduced in this par-72 layout. Championship markers are set at 7,100 yards, daily tees at 6,200.

Opposite: St. Andrews Bay, 17th. Above: 10th.

Following a pleasant 512-yard opener, we face a short par 4 and a short par 5, both long on peril thanks to those two ponds. But having sufficiently unnerved us, Devlin and his associate, Denis Griffiths, now back off, all the way: no more artificial water hazards.

The 6th is nothing less than a great two-shotter. From the back tees, it measures 467 yards; for mere mortals, 410. Kittock's Den rears its intimidating head here for the first time. A proper drive leaves us on a fairway plateau short of a steep descent into the wicked scrubby hollow. There is no mystery to the second shot, a forced carry of 180–190 yards over this hazard to the safety of the green on the opposite hill. Thin the shot or pull it or push it or pop it up, and the result will be calamitous.

It is at the 361-yard 9th that we reach the sea for the first time, playing along it and high above it, much of the hole downhill. The 330-yard 10th and the 13th, 510 yards, head inland to climb the same steep hill, but the 11th and 12th find us back at the sea, their greens at the cliff's edge. This routing plan is a jewel, not simply unpredictable but also taking full advantage of every natural feature here.

Kittock's Den is much in play at the 14th, 16th, and 17th. The 403-yard 17th is the single best—and most thrilling—hole at St. Andrews Bay. The green cannot be seen from the tee. A drive clearing the bunkers on the right brings us to the crest of the hill. Far below, sitting defiantly on an old Roman fort with nothing but the slate-blue North Sea behind it and

Time now to head to the thoughtfully appointed clubhouse. The enthralling views take in St. Andrews to the west; the Angus coast to the north; the Torrance Course to the south; and the Devlin to the east. The **St. Andrews Bay Hotel** has an exterior design that leans vaguely toward France and an overall feeling that may be more Scottsdale than Scotland. All 209 guest rooms overlook golf holes; most have sea views and/or views of St. Andrews. The spa has a gym, a heated indoor swimming pool, Jacuzzi, whirlpool, sauna and steam room, plus a wide range of body and beauty therapies. The resort offers five places to eat, the dining room in the clubhouse and four restaurants in the hotel:

- The informal **Atrium** is the centerpiece of an immense four-story-high enclosure of space guaranteed to stop you dead in your tracks at the top of a sweeping divided staircase. The cooking, bistro style, is good.
- Overlooking the atrium, and boasting a large fireplace, is **Kittocks Den**, which serves drinks and snacks throughout the day.
- **Esperante**, the fine-dining restaurant, is a stylish and intimate room, with the emphasis on Mediterranean-type dishes.
- **The Squire**, Scottish dining with a contemporary flair.

little but sand in front of it, is the green. Threatening on the right the length of this heroic second shot is the Den. All that is required of us here is a lifetime swing. If we should somehow manage to unfurl just that, gain the green, and get down in two putts, the result will be euphoria.

The 18th is a rare occurrence on a championship-level course, a par 3 to conclude the round. This one tiptoes along on the brink—187 yards from all the way back, 147 from the daily tees—scarily close to the cliff edge from tee to green, some 75 feet above the shore. The shot hit even minimally out to the right is out to sea. To the very end, Devlin and Griffiths have provided shot values of a very high order and just about the right degree of pressure on the swing.

KINGSBARNS

Just down the coast road from St. Andrews and about ten minutes beyond St. Andrews Bay lies the Kingsbarns Golf Links. It was designed and built by two Californians, Kyle Phillips and Mark Parsinen. What they accomplished here is pure magic. They took 190 acres of what had been pasture and crop lands (wheat, beets, corn) along the sea and created, out of whole cloth, a magnificent and sublimely natural-looking links course. This was legerdemain on the grandest scale, with dunes of various shapes and sizes, crumpled fairways, a plethora of humps, hillocks, and hollows, cunning little rough-cloaked mesas and promontories, and spirited greens that are a clear by-product of the immediately surrounding terrain. But this links is entirely manufactured. Nature had essentially no hand in it, except to provide the entrancing seaside setting with the surf surging against the rocky foreshore. Yet even the most experienced observer would swear that it is authentic, its contours surely the result of the receding seas and the persistent winds over tens of thousands of years.

Not so. It was excavators, dumpers, bulldozers, and backhoes.

In late July 1998, two years before the course was completed, I visited the site, touring it with Mark Parsinen in his mud-caked black Range Rover. Solidly built and then in his early fifties, he struck me as the kind of man who would not hesitate to dig in—*literally*—to get the job done.

"I was studying at the London School of Economics in 1969," he said, "and every chance I got I'd head up to St. Andrews and Carnoustie or to Muirfield or Troon or Dornoch. During the eighties and nineties I made some money in the computer business, but I knew this would never be as satisfying as building golf courses. So I teamed up with Kyle Phillips—he'd been designing courses all over the world with Robert Trent Jones Junior—and along came the chance for us to do Kingsbarns: not only in Scotland and smack beside the sea, but practically on the doorstep of St. Andrews.

"We jumped at it. I realized that if we were going to create a links at Kingsbarns—you know, there was a nine-hole course here for over a hundred years, but they had to give it up when the war broke out in 1939—anyway, I figured I better learn a lot more about links courses than I knew from just playing them.

"I read Robert Price's book *Scotland's Golf Courses,* which concentrates on how the natural landforms themselves have played such a critical role in the development of the courses, and then I hired Dr. Price to consult on Kingsbarns. He and I walked the Old Course, looking closely at the little ridges there, then over to the Jubilee, where you have much bigger dunes. The two of us would get down on the ground to examine just why it is that things look the way they look."

Mark Parsinen and I bumped along over the embryonic layout that day, often high above the strand, from one end of the mile-and-a-half-long sea frontage to the other. He talked animatedly while he drove (also animatedly). Again and again he stopped so we could jump out and he could explain the particular hole. He made the point that every hole views the sea and that six holes play along it. His enthusiasm was contagious.

"After I got Dr. Price on board," he continued, "I went back to a number of those wonderful links I'd been playing, in Ireland as well as Scotland. I was examining their dune systems—they're not all the same, by any means—and their green sites and green complexes. I even sent our two shapers over to Troon and Turnberry and up to Cruden Bay to see firsthand what I was talking about.

"And then, to make sure we would end up with real links turf—the right grasses, the fescues, the bents, in the right combinations, growing in the right soil—I retained Walter Wood, who had just retired as greens superintendent at St. Andrews, to consult with me on an ongoing basis. We spent fifty thousand pounds on soil analyses to make certain we could produce consistent soil conditions for sand-based fairways throughout the links."

ON THE COURSE

Kingsbarns, which opened in 2000, can be played as long as 7,120 yards, as short as 5,140. Because it is quick-draining, in season the fairways are firm and fast. The game on the ground is at least as important as the game in the air. Run of ball was a major consideration in the design; angles of play would be strong elements in the course's defense against the attack of an accomplished golfer.

Opposite: Kingsbarns, 15th.

game here enormously—they are marvelous fun—and distinguish it markedly from dart-throwing parkland golf.

Strategy is at the core of the design, strategy clearly based on the risk/reward principle. So, if we adopt the more courageous line off the tee, a well-struck drive will earn the easier approach to the green. Timid tee shots often leave second shots over bunkers or rough or dunes or swales.

On a course where no hole is less than very good, there may be eight that are great, four on each side. Going out, the four are consecutive—4, 5, 6, and 7—and all two-shotters, yet they could scarcely be less alike.

At the 390-yard 4th, a drive carrying some 210 yards over a deep bunker is the only way to get into position for a straightforward iron to an exposed, windswept green open across the front. On the next hole, 20 yards shorter, with the green hidden away to the right in a dell of dunes, a clear shot into it will be merited only by a drive that is lined farther left than we can comfortably envision.

The 6th is spellbinding. The tee on this 318-yarder, well up the side of an imposing sand hill, discloses a majestic panorama of golf holes rippling along far below, waves cascading onto the foreshore, and, miles away down the coast, the clubhouse at Crail perched on its promontory. Drive straight at the flag and you are left with a blind short pitch to a green ringed by low dunes and rough and abrupt little falloffs. But there is another route. Drive well out to the right, up onto a raised and generous plateau of fairway. Gazing down from here, you enjoy not only a good view of the putting surface but also an approach angle for this very short falling pitch that enables greenside contours to feed the ball neatly toward the flagstick.

The 7th, on the other hand, is a model of decorum. It is muscular, 436 yards long, uphill, with emphatic right-to-left contours all the way. Two aggressive hits, both held determinedly to starboard, will be the ticket.

On the second nine the great holes are 12, 15, 17, and 18. Measuring 566 yards from the white markers, the 12th sails along spectacularly beside the sea all the way, high above it from the hilltop tee, then plunges to a broad and tumbling fairway, now curves left to begin a moderate ascent to the astounding green set on the diagonal and itself continues the ascent, all 72 yards of it! The difference in extreme cup positions, right front as opposed to left rear, will be at least five clubs. The word *exhilaration* does not do this hole justice.

The 185-yard 15th is more of this tremendous stuff. The target is sited on a spit of land jutting into the sea to our right. If the wind is into us, the playing value from the elevated tee of this forced carry over surf-

In addition to the pleasure of runups from as far out as 100 yards off the green, here at Kingsbarns we relish the thrill of a 3-metal shot skimming up a slope to reach a putting surface that may be as much as 235 yards away. The course plays shorter than the card suggests, but the ball is inclined to be less obedient than we might wish.

Bunkering is not heavy—some eighty sand hazards all told. But these pits, most with steep revetted faces, are frequently deep, and because of crafty fairway contouring, they tend to gather a ball that had seemed to be skating safely clear of their clutches. The greens, large enough to be hittable targets in a robust wind, are splendid, though perhaps, on occasion, a little too festive. Even a player with a solid short game may find himself three-putting four or five times and failing two or three more times to get up and down from just off the green. That's a lot of strokes to surrender. Still, these slopes and curls and angles enrich the

Above: Kingsbarns, 6th.
Opposite: 8th.

spattered rocks can easily be 200 yards. Is there any hole at Kingsbarns where the embrace of the sea is more powerfully felt?

Like the 7th, the 17th is brawny, 432 yards. The green sits far above the fairway. Only the sloping false front is visible, to remind us that a ball landing here will retreat well down the hill. There may be no more rewarding full-blooded shot on the course than the one that gains this green.

The home hole offers little in the way of refuge. It is 414 yards long, with concealed bunkers down the left on this blind drive. Then, for the last swing of the round, comes a win-or-woe second shot that must traverse a deep valley with a trickle of burn at the bottom to devour the ball that fails by feet to reach the elevated bilevel green. It is a rousing finish.

Kingsbarns is inordinately rich, complex, full of feature and of shot-making options. This is one of the two best courses (Loch Lomond is the other one) to open in Scotland since Turnberry was rebuilt after the Second World War. From start to finish, it is a triumph of study and creativity, of artistry and daring and challenge and beauty, and, yes, of money over nature. It is links golf of the highest order, deserved to be ranked among the top fifteen courses in the British Isles and among the top fifty in the world. Could this breathtaking faux links be the single most extraordinary achievement in the history of golf-course construction? Or should it be viewed as one of a triumvirate, the other two in this rarefied air being Pete Dye's Whistling Straits and Tom Fazio's Shadow Creek?

Opposite: Kingsbarns, 12th.
Above: 17th.

CRAIL

Not ten minutes farther along the coast road from Kingsbarns is the seventh-oldest golf club in the world, the Crail Golfing Society, founded in 1786. Initially, the society played on the narrow strip of linksland at Sauchope, at the northeast end of town. Sandy Herd, who won the 1902 Open Championship and had worked for several years as a plasterer in Crail, attributed his straight driving to the tightness of the eight holes at Sauchope.

In the late 1850s the society began to play much of its golf on the Balcomie Links, generally regarded as the windiest spot in the East Neuk of Scotland. Crail golfers made a lasting contribution to the art of greenkeeping in 1874, when its committee agreed that "iron cases be got for the eight holes on the links to prevent the holes from being destroyed." There exists no earlier record at any course of the insertion of metal cups into the holes.

It was Old Tom Morris who laid out a proper nine-hole course at Balcomie, in 1895. Four years later he added a second nine. Though there have been some changes over time, the Balcomie eighteen today is largely the one laid out more than a century ago. Golfers come from all over the world to play Balcomie—it is almost a point of pilgrimage—for several reasons: its age, its quirky charms, and its attribution to Old Tom alone.

Over the years, I have come to prize a friendship with Crail's head professional, Graeme Lennie. With his many duties—giving lessons, selling equipment, collecting green fees, and administering the game on two eighteens—he plays very little golf. So whenever I've been in St. Andrews for an extended stay, I have insisted that he accompany me to Carnoustie or Royal Aberdeen, to Murcar or Cruden Bay or Peterhead. And at one or another of our stops, I can count on him to say, with wry resignation, "If you didn't come to Scotland, I'd never get to play."

Graeme is a member of the James Braid Society and the British Golf Collectors' Society. The Scottish PGA honored him by naming him its captain for 2003 and 2004. The post is largely ceremonial, but a professional is not elected to it unless he has earned the respect and regard of his peers. I recall how pleased he was when, scheduled to preside for the first time over an assembly of the membership, in

Glasgow, he called British PGA headquarters, at the Belfry, to ask whether it might be possible to display the Ryder Cup at this meeting. The small gold trophy was delivered to him by courier.

ON THE BALCOMIE COURSE

Total yardage on the Balcomie Links is 5,922, against a par of 69. Two of the six par 4s on the outbound nine measure 459 and 442 yards; the other four range from 306 to 349. The second nine is a crazy quilt of golf holes—two par 5s (back to back and side by side), three par 4s, and four par 3s (two of them over 200 yards). You never know what to expect next.

On the 1st tee, where the drop to the fairway may well measure 100 feet, we get a feel for the entire course because so much of it is spread out below us. What we observe from our hilltop is a vast and well-nigh treeless meadow sweeping down, in vaguely terraced formation, to the sea. There seems to be minimal separation between holes and little definition to them. It all appears to run together.

Balcomie's appeal lies principally in the surprising diversity of shots called for, many of them requiring skill at the ground game and virtually every one of them executed within sight of the sea. The very walk over the rolling, sometimes hilly, terrain is a treat, so enthralling are the views. Simply to be out on Balcomie is cause for rejoicing. As a long-ago member, Professor Dow, never tired of saying, "One half hour of the air at Balcomie is worth more than all the medicines in Jimmy Smith's [apothecary] shop."

But, you insist, that is hardly enough. Wherein lies the test, the challenge? Largely in a single circumstance: the wind. No hole is sheltered from it. On a course where conventional hazards—bunkers, burns, boundaries—rarely vex us, the wind harasses us relentlessly.

The 2nd hole (a grand uphill par 5, its small green full of slippery slopes), the 3rd (a blind 184-yarder with a long, narrow green), the 4th and the 5th—all play along and above the sea, with the tee shots on 4 and 5 daring us to bite off large chunks of these perilous right-turn doglegs, disaster waiting on the wave-washed rocks below. At 459 yards, the par-4 5th, with the sea menacing both of our all-out swings, is a genuinely heroic hole and,

Opposite: Crail Balcomie, 1st.

in fact, the strongest test on the course. Now little more than a dozen years old, it was impudently saluted by a member the day it opened for play: He holed his second shot!

The next eight holes, though not seaside, are nonetheless peppery, and the final hole in this inside stretch is a particular favorite of mine. A 219-yarder, the 13th plays forcefully uphill over a rocky escarpment smothered in long rough grasses. The climb itself looks daunting, and into the wind, as seems often the case, the shot to the blind green is fearsome.

And now that we have played straight up, we turn our back on the nearby clubhouse and, from the 14th tee, play straight down, 150 yards, to a green far below ringed by six bunkers. The world of Balcomie lies all around us, links and sand and sea importuning us to pause and drink it all in.

The par-4 15th, 265 basically level yards, is a bona fide birdie hole, if only we can time our driver swing between the waves crashing on the shore, perhaps a dozen paces away. Sixteen, up a steep hill, calls for a very soundly struck iron—the measured 163 yards plays at least 175. The 462-yard 17th, often downwind from its hilltop tee, is the number-two

Left: Crail Balcomie, 15th.
Above: 16th.

stroke hole and a stiff par 4 (or certainly *used* to be). And the 18th, though hospitably open across the green's broad front, is, at 203 yards, tough to par when par is what we must have to rescue the match.

So much for the morning round. It was nonstop fun, where the sea was always in sight, the target was generally within reach, and the penalty for failure was rarely stringent. We may even have played to our handicap.

Time for a sandwich and a beverage now in this brilliantly sited clubhouse atop an old quarry on the property's highest point. The rambling stone structure, with its abundance of glass, was obviously built with the view in mind. And what a view it is! On a day that is truly crystalline, we can take in from this pinnacle (we may have to step outside to appreciate some of the noble panorama) more than a hundred miles of coastline, from Montrose in the north, then south across the Firth of Forth and down the East Lothian coast past Dunbar to St. Abb's Head, near Berwick-upon-Tweed (and just a few miles from the English border). You may want to pull out a map and see what it is I'm trying to convey here—I know that my words are inadequate.

ON THE CRAIGHEAD COURSE

If the Balcomie Links is true holiday golf, its sister course, Craighead, next door, is true championship golf. It came along a hundred years later (the Crail Golfing Society does not incline to rush into these things) and it is the work of America's Gilbert Hanse. Among his most highly regarded courses are Applebrook and French Creek, outside Philadelphia; Rustic Canyon, Los Angeles; and the Boston Golf Club.

In order to produce a genuinely natural course, Hanse moved little earth, accepting the gently sloping terrain much as he found it. The eighteen is laid out high above the sea and, for the most part, at a bit of a remove from it, as is the case with Muirfield. Indeed, the similarity in appearance to the great East Lothian course is unmistakable, with the fairways here also framed by thigh-high golden-beige native fescues, which look like wheat waving in the wind. Craighead's fairways, however, are very broad, averaging a good 60 yards across. Still, in a 30 to 40 (to 50) mile-per-hour wind, a ball with even a scintilla of sidespin can sail alarmingly wide of the mark.

If the wind and rough are deterrents to low scoring here, so are the green complexes. Admittedly, most putting surfaces are open across the front, so there is plenty of room to play the ball along the ground. But a number of greens incline to shed the approach shot, to shrug it off. In fact,

half a dozen of them—the 2nd, 7th, 9th, 12th, 15th, and 17th—are among the least receptive greens you will ever play to. And when you miss these targets, be prepared to recover from the base of a steep little falloff or from the bottom of a deep revetted bunker with a sheer front wall.

This layout—it has a par of 71 and can be tackled at 5,400, 6,250, or 6,725 yards—is studded with outstanding holes, particularly the final five. The 414-yard 14th walks a tightrope along the clifftop from tee to green, with the sea far below on our left. It may be the most dramatic hole on the course.

Gil Hanse said to me, "This green, which is tilted from right to left, is a reflection of the slope that was here. The hole is a natural, and I left it as I found it."

At 516 yards from the regular markers (554 from the back) and dog-legging smartly right, the 15th plays from a tee quite near the cliff edge to a landing area corseted by sand and with a tiny pot bunker in the center of the fairway. The uphill second shot calls for a decision: Either lay up short of Danes Dyke, leaving a semiblind third shot to the world's knobbiest green, or clear the ancient stone wall (shades of North Berwick) with a

Opposite: Crail Craighead, 9th. Above: 17th.

Crail Craighead, 18th.

fairway metal and now enjoy the luxury of a 70-yard pitch. Terrific stuff, whatever you elect to do.

From a platform tee the 16th, 373 yards and bending left, recrosses Danes Dyke to a fairway with a massive bunker complex in the crook of the dogleg. The smallish green is crowned; it is also guarded at the left by four deep pits.

On the last par 3 (17, 175 yards), a pair of large and deep and fanciful bunkers pinch the entrance to the green. The only way on is up and on. And when we get there, the rollercoaster green makes putting perilous. This is a great—and memorable—one-shotter.

At 425 yards, the home hole calls for solid hitting, not to mention real control if we are to avoid the cluster of bunkers on the right eating into the tee-shot landing area and then, on the long second shot, skate through the Valley of Sin (a bow to the Old Course) immediately short of the green.

After taking a good look at Craighead, Peter Thomson volunteered that it could serve well for final qualifying in the Open Championship.

Crail Golfing Society annually hosts a tournament that is a test not only of skill but of endurance. The competition, which dates to 1895, is called the Ranken-Todd Bowl, the bowl itself a huge ribbed silver vessel that looks to be worth the crown jewels. Eight or nine local golf clubs, including St. Andrews, Leven, Lundin, and Elie, are invited to send a four-man team. Each team plays only two balls, both balls counting in this alternate-stroke arrangement. A qualifying round is held in the morning to eliminate all but four clubs. The semifinals are held in the afternoon, and in the evening the 18-hole final is contested. Though the world is full of 54-hole invitational tournaments, this may be the only one that is settled in a single day.

The East Neuk fishing villages of Crail, Anstruther, Pittenweem, St. Monance, Elie, and Lower Largo are picturesque without being precious, some more workaday than others. All reward even the most casual sightseeing. But if you had to settle on just one as the most appealing example of the genre, it would probably be Crail. Here we find a spacious and well-proportioned town square, called Marketgate (poke your head into the Jerdan Gallery and enjoy the paintings in the house and the sculpture in the garden); the Collegiate Church of St. Mary, parts reaching back to the twelfth century; the Tolbooth, dating to the 16th century and formerly containing the council chamber, courtroom, and prison cells; the seventeenth- and eighteenth-century stone cottages, with their crow-stepped gables and red tile roofs; and the narrow, cobbled lanes spilling down to the protected harbor.

Crail has a couple of small hotels that might catch your fancy. Closest to the golf courses is the **Balcomie Links Hotel**: several rooms with distant sea views; nonsmoking dining room; live music in the lounge bar at weekends. On a bluff above the sea is the **Marine Hotel**, within a five-minute walk of the harbor: smallish but spiffy rooms, most of them with beautiful views over the Firth of Forth; al fresco dining in the garden.

Views of Crail.

Less than twenty minutes driving west on the coast road from Crail brings us to the seaside town of Elie and to The Golf House Club, Elie. You may wonder about the origin of this unusual name.

The original golf club in these parts, and the one that first used this linksland, was the Earlesferry & Elie Golf Club, founded in 1858 (Elie and Earlesferry were adjacent villages). The club did not own the links; it just had the right to play there. Nor did the club have a clubhouse. It used the Golfers' Tavern for most meetings. In 1875 a second and a third club were formed, also with the right to use this same links. The membership of the second club may have been a shade tonier than that of the Earlesferry & Elie club and of the other new club, the Thistle. In any event, this second club, at its inaugural meeting, vowed to erect a clubhouse. It was this decision that gave the club its peculiar name: The Golf House Club, Elie. Which is to say, the club that had a golf house, as distinguished from the two clubs that did not. The Earlesferry & Elie Golf Club disbanded in 1912.

Elie's women golfers have their own organization, the Elie & Earlesferry Ladies Golf Club, founded in 1884. Over the next forty years the ladies applied again and again for permission to occupy some modest space in what was viewed as the men's clubhouse. Again and again they were rejected. Then, in 1927, an outrageous incident occurred. A deputation of three ladies, including the club secretary, was invited to The Golf House Club to discuss the possibility of using a room in the clubhouse. However, on arriving they were advised that ladies were forbidden to enter by the front door and that, unfortunately, the steward had gone out, locking the back door. The only way to get in, it was suggested, was to climb through a window. This proved relatively easy for two of the ladies but intimidating for the secretary, who was elderly and of ample girth. Finally, that good woman also made her way in, amid a flurry of petticoats. The personal indignity she suffered so shocked both organizations that the Ladies Club was granted space in the clubhouse at last.

Ironically, the clubhouse today has something of a feminine aspect, at least on the exterior. There is a lightness about it, and a fanci-

ful nature, a sunny holiday spirit. My good friend Alec Beveridge, a long-time member of The Golf House Club, calls the clubhouse "couthie," a Scottish word that suggests niceness, in this case a hospitable niceness that inspires affection and hymns the joy of the game.

The clubhouse is one thing, the starter's hut quite another. This shack is one of golf's great curios. Mounted within it and jutting boldly up out of it through the roof is a submarine periscope. Dubbed Excalibur, it was presented to the club forty years ago. It enables the starter to see over the hill that rises precipitously in front of the first tee, in this way making certain that the players who have disappeared beyond the crest are now out of range.

From time to time over the years, the starter has had considerable authority with respect to the order of play. So if one wished to tee off at 9:00 A.M., it was well to be in the starter's good graces. According to a

Opposite: Elie, 13th.
Above: The clubhouse and starter's hut, with periscope.

favorite club story, a visitor arriving for a week's holiday slipped the starter a banknote to assure a favorable tee time throughout his stay. For several days he got just what he wanted. Then, abruptly, he found himself with an eleven o'clock starting time. When he asked the starter for an explanation, what he got was a laconic, "Yer money's run oot!"

ON THE COURSE

The course we play today was laid out by Old Tom Morris in 1895 (the same year he laid out the first nine at Crail), with revisions by James Braid in the 1920s. Braid, who would win the Open Championship five times, was born and raised in Elie and learned to play the game here.

The course measures 6,273 yards against a par of 70. There are no par 5s and only two par 3s. On the face of it, Elie ought to be a bore. It emphatically is not. Its 16 two-shotters range from 252 to 466 yards, they run to every point of the compass, the wind is frustratingly fickle, and blind shots pop up with bewildering frequency. What's more, the greens are full of fun, the bunkers are full of woe, and the topography overall is remarkably varied.

Elie's opener is a bear: 420 yards long, a blind drive, a low stone boundary wall along the right, and bunkers on both sides of the green. And if the 1st is a likely bogey, the uphill 2nd, only 284 yards, is a possible birdie. The green here affords one of golf's memorably lovely moments. It is the highest point on the links, and from it we look down on the rooftops of the town in the foreground and, beyond them, to the Firth of Forth itself: The Isle of May, Berwick Law, and Bass Rock all vie for our attention in the distance. The East Lothian coast—Muirfield, Gullane, North Berwick—stands out in bold relief across the water, and backdropping it is the shadowy outline of the Lammermuir Hills. The distance across the sea to Muirfield is only ten miles, but it's the best part of two hours by car.

Below: Elie, 10th. Opposite, left: 2nd; right: 3rd.

Only on the 1st and 18th is the sea out of sight. On holes such as the 4th and 5th, we catch glimpses of it down lanes or between houses, a patch of frothy blue bobbing up here and there if we look left as we walk down the fairway. At the 5th, 365 yards, our drive comes to rest in a patch of tumbling fairway that reminds us not of the seas receding to those thousands of years ago but rather of coal miners retreating to those hundred and fifty years ago. And at the 316-yard 6th, with its downhill pitch to a green running away, we command the full sweep of West Bay 'round to Kincraig Point and its extraordinary rock formation called "Daniel Preaching to the Lion."

Out at the far end of the links there is a cluster of four holes that is characteristically Elie, the first two cunning and old-fashioned, the other two classic and rigorous. At the very short par-4 10th, our tee shot sometimes scales a steep hill and races down an even steeper one, perhaps to finish on the sloping green above the beach. Here the seabirds strut on the rocks, and holiday makers build castles on the sand.

Only the flag is visible on Sea Hole, the level 125-yard 11th, where the sea wall is scant steps from the green's left edge. In days long gone

caddies who were stationed in the rocks beside the green would fabricate a hole-in-one here in the hope of pocketing a bigger tip. When a shot would finish quite close to the cup but out of the player's sight, three of the four boys would leap up, cheering and gesticulating, while the smallest one would steal onto the green and pop the ball into the hole.

The 466-yard 12th clings to the curving shoreline, with MacDuff's Cave barely discernible in a distant cliff. From the scrap of tee just above the strand, only the strong and brave will cut off enough of the beach to get home in two. This is a risk/reward hole, and a great one.

The 13th is also great. Braid once called it "the finest hole in all the country." Its measured length, 386 yards, is not disheartening, but the second shot, often into a left-to-right wind off the bay, tends uphill to an angled shelflike green that is 190 feet wide! A deep swale captures even the slightly underhit approach. Immediately behind the putting surface is a steep bank, which used to be counted on for a kindly roll if we had overclubbed. (In the 1973 British Senior Professional Championship, Roberto de Vicenzo deliberately overclubbed here in the final round and

and a mutual friend were awaiting our turn to begin the round. Immediately ahead of us was a couple in their early fifties who sounded Swedish to me. He sent his drive over the blockading hill. She did not follow suit. Demonstrating one of the most unconventional swings I've ever seen, she lurched back on the takeaway so far off the ball that for an instant I thought I was in danger of being brained, then lunged violently forward to stab the turf with the driver head and bounce it neatly over the ball, which stayed steadfast on the wooden peg. Assuming her stance again, she proceeded to repeat the swing, this time, however, cleanly fanning the ball without touching the ground. On her third attempt she fanned once more. Her fourth swing propelled the ball vigorously along the ground and markedly to the right, skipping between the starter's hut and the clubhouse. Trolley now in tow, she briskly set out after her version of a successful drive. Seconds later the starter emerged from his headquarters and approached us, displaying a trace of a smile. He summarized her performance as "one divot, two fresh airs, and a lucky hit," adding, "That woman will bear keeping an eye on." He promptly retreated to his hut and glued his eye to the periscope.

NEARBY COURSES

Midway between Crail and Elie lies Anstruther, an old fishing port. The **Anstruther Golf Club**'s course—nine holes, 2,000 yards long, par 31—contains one of the most thrilling, challenging, and eccentric par 3s on the globe. The 5th, called Rockies, is 236 yards long. Paralleling the shoreline (the sea is on our left), it plays downhill from a clifftop tee to a hidden green tucked around to the right, behind a small outcropping of rock. The shot is blind, and for most people the hole, generally played into or across the prevailing wind, is actually a dogleg. The net of it all is a blind dogleg par 3. A local who is not a member at Anstruther confided to me that in July 2000, when the Open was held at St. Andrews, a very great young golfer from America, not yet twenty-five, clattered in on a helicopter to examine this remarkable hole, did so, shook his head in disbelief, climbed back into the helicopter, and clattered away.

Just outside Colinsburgh and not ten minutes from Elie is a parkland eighteen called **Charleton**, now a dozen years old. It ranges from rolling to hilly, the pastoral views are gorgeous, and since there are no hazards, a stiff breeze is needed to make it testing. The lively green complexes lend character to a course whose green fees are appropriately low.

wound up with a tap-in birdie that led to victory.) Today, however, that bank in back is no longer shaved, and the ball that runs up it stays up it, presenting a vexing little pitch down the slope. The 13th was selected for the book *The 500 World's Greatest Golf Holes.*

To the surprise of absolutely no one, the final five holes are all par 4s, three of them well over 400 yards. Chances of making up strokes as we head for the "golf house" are not good unless we can birdie the 359-yard 18th, which in 1935 witnessed an astonishing double bogey: In it were 4 penalty strokes. A saddler named Ken Foster followed a good drive by firing his 135-yard second shot dead left through a clubhouse window. He dropped another ball and, now playing 4, flew it through the same window. He then dropped a third ball and holed it for 6.

Elie seems never to be short on anecdotes. Perhaps the goings-on that I witnessed in 2003 might be added to the stock. My elder son and I

Mellow and traditional Elie, with its charming seventeenth-century parish church, provides the best bathing in the East Neuk, not to mention windsurfing, sailing, and canoeing. All of five minutes away is Kilconquhar, a picture-postcard village on the shores of Kilconquhar Loch. Kellie Castle, three miles northwest of nearby Pittenweem (Lumsden Antiques, at the harbor, offers some choice pieces at reasonable prices) is a tower house—more fortress than mansion—dating to the fourteenth century and affording pretty views across farmland and woodland to the Firth of Forth. Also well worth visiting is the Scottish Fisheries Museum, in Anstruther, which illustrates with real boats as well as models many aspects of sea fishing and life in early fishing communities.

You might want to keep in mind two eating places in Anstruther:

- The **Dreel Tavern** is good for a pub-food lunch: beam ceilings, fireplaces, dark paneling, and, when the day is fine, dining in a simple garden above the Dreel Burn, a stream that runs through the heart of town.
- For dinner, the standout choice is **The Cellar**, hidden on a back street near the children's amusement pier and possessing an intimate, romantic ambience (log fire, beam ceiling, natural stone walls, candlelight). The cooking is superlative. After a hot quiche of smoked sea trout and lobster, try the roast monkfish and scallops flavored with herb and garlic butter and served with a sweet pepper risotto. The Cellar gets a pile of votes as Scotland's best seafood restaurant.

Clockwise from top: the gardens at Kellie Castle; the castle; the village of Anstruther; church in Kilconquhar.

LUNDIN AND LEVEN

The Lundin Golf Club and the Leven Golfing Society, two more of the old East Neuk clubs with authentic seaside links, were once coupled, bound together by their golf holes. But perhaps the explanation can wait a bit, till we arrive at the point on the courses where this is more easily understood.

It was about thirty years ago that I first visited the Lundin Golf Club, in Lundin Links, about fifteen minutes west of Elie. In the monastic changing room that day, I overheard a conversation between two quite elderly members. One was remembering a match in which "Jimmie whipped Sandy," on the 17th, by playing a miracle 4-iron from a bunker "to within six feet of the cup for his birdie, turning what had looked like a certain loss into a certain win."

Shortly afterward, in the lounge, as I was chatting with the secretary, the storyteller came up to us. His name was Fred Horne and, eighty-six years of age and a member since 1910, he was the club's oldest active member. I said I'd heard him talking about a match at Elie and couldn't help but wonder about the identity of the two players.

"Braid it was," he said, "Jimmie Braid. Braid and Sandy Herd. Over at Elie."

"You knew Braid?" I asked.

"Indeed I knew him," the old man answered. "There was a time when I would have a game with him once a year over at Elie. But of course he's been gone for some years now." Braid died in 1950.

ON THE LUNDIN COURSE

The start at Lundin is exhilarating: This 424-yarder is hard by the sea, the tee perched atop a ridge of sand hills, the beach itself some 40 feet below us on our left. We should swing freely, because the landing area, shared with the 18th fairway, is a very broad and inviting one and because a long drive will be useful when it comes to tackling the second shot, a rising one back up to the great dune ridge, where a large, lightly bunkered green awaits. This is one of the best opening holes in my experience, to be spoken of in the same breath as the 1st at Machrihanish, at Aronimink, and at Sand Hills.

The next three holes carry us farther west along the coast, the 2nd and 3rd a pair of beguiling short two-shotters played from high in the dunes down to fairways with sand on the right and greens with deep bunkers in front. A mighty 452-yard par 4, the 4th ripples determinedly straight along above the sea on a broad plateau for about 425 yards, at which point a sliver of burn crosses the fairway at the bottom of a steep and narrow dip. A crisp 5-metal may clear this implacable hazard. Or is a 3-metal called for? Or should we lay up and accept a bogey? This is a true death-or-glory hole, the only one on the course. A great second shot will produce an opportunity for a 3, and an almost great second shot will produce the likelihood of a 6.

Opposite: Lundin, 5th.
Above: 2nd.

Whatever the outcome of the altogether splendid 4th, we have come to a dead end on our trek down the coast from the clubhouse. We have reached Mile Dyke, a low stone wall. On the other side of it are golf holes like the four we've just played, stretching away beside the shore for what must surely be a mile. However, they don't belong to the Lundin Golf Club, though Lundin once co-owned them. Now they are the property of the Leven Golfing Society.

Here is how this happened. When the Lundin club was founded, in 1868, it shared an 18-hole layout with Leven. The course was two fair-

ways wide and nine holes long, fitting nicely between the sea and the railroad on ideal linksland, undulating and sand based.

Often in Scotland two (or three or four) golf clubs will play over the same course, especially if it's a municipal facility, as in the case of St. Andrews and Carnoustie. What was unusual—in fact, highly unusual—about this case was that Leven's clubhouse was at the west end of the links and Lundin's at the east end. Play began at *both* clubhouses, about two miles apart, with the golfers aiming to reach the halfway mark at the *other* clubhouse. Imagine the potential for confusion and crowding at the turns,

Above: Lundin, 14th.
Opposite: 18th.

not to mention the complexity of allotting starting times on an equitable basis, especially as the game became more and more popular. By 1907 Lundin had almost four hundred members and Leven almost a thousand.

In 1908 the two clubs agreed to cut the course in half. Each took the nine holes on its side of Mile Dyke, and never again would the twain meet. To come up with nine more holes, each club spilled over onto the inland side of the railway. Lundin seized the opportunity to call in Braid and have him lay out new holes and incorporate them into the eighteen we play today.

The same burn that gave us pause on Lundin's terrific 4th now bedevils us on its 140-yard 5th, corkscrewing across our path on a right-to-left diagonal and joining forces with bent-clad sand hills and clustering bunkers to demand a good short iron here. En route to the 6th tee, we cross the abandoned railway line—the trains and tracks are gone nearly fifty years—to play the nine "new holes," which were routed over what might be called a cross between links and parkland in both turf and topography. Following three solid par 4s, the nine ends with a gently rolling 555-yarder into the prevailing wind. It is a legitimate three-shotter.

Two difficult par 4s—the 10th finds a heavily bunkered green set in a natural dell shaped by sand hills, and the straightaway 466-yard 11th is simply very long—bring us to the sharply uphill par-3 12th. The green here, as well as the entire par-5 13th and the tee of the 175-yard 14th, is laid out on a broad plateau that provides panoramic views of the links far below and of the Firth of Forth to East Lothian. It is all of a heart-stopping grandeur.

Once we've returned to the less heady but more satisfying golfing country at sea level, with its tossing, tumbling terrain, we commence the march for the clubhouse, first with a long two-shotter for the 418-yard 15th to a blind green secluded in a hollow. Then it's two shortish par 4s that contain blind shots and a pitch over a burn—plenty of surprise and suspense on the double-trouble 16th. Finally, the uncompromising home hole: Its length alone—442 yards—is daunting. The landing area for the drive is generous (shared with the 1st fairway), but the long, narrow green is sited in a kind of saddle between the sea on the right and a boundary road on the left. To get home in two we must propel the ball more than 200 yards with little deviation from string straight.

Lundin is a thoroughgoing delight. It is full of character and charm, of variety and test, and of holes with strong shot values. What it is not full of is serenity. This is one of the most spirited courses in the land. There is a lot going on in these 6,377 yards (par 71). Six different factors—the breeze, bunkers (120 of them), burns, bents, boundaries (on 16 holes!), and the "blinds" (6 drives, 4 shots to the green)—contribute to the challenge. All of which helps to explain why this rather short course has hosted the Scottish Professional Championship, the British Seniors, the World Senior Professional Championship, the Scottish Amateur Stroke Play Championship, the East of Scotland Amateur, and final qualifying for the Open Championship. It is also the venue every summer for the Scottish Police Golf Association Championship.

My most recent visit to the club found me playing on an early evening when this competition was being held. My companion was Malcolm Campbell, longtime Lundin member and author of the informative and immensely readable *Scottish Golf Book,* to say nothing of nine or ten other works on the game. We could not ignore a temporary sign, black type on a yellow board, prominently displayed at the 1st tee: PLEASE REPORT ANY SUSPICION OF SLOW PLAY. OFFENDERS ARE LIABLE TO PENALTY OR DISQUALIFICATION.

ON THE LEVEN COURSE

Leven may well be next door, in a manner of speaking, but we do not simply walk over and hit off. In truth, reaching the 1st tee from Lundin requires a drive along the coast road for a couple of miles.

Dating back to 1820, Leven is the twelfth oldest golf club in the world. The clubhouse itself, a three-story redbrick building more than 110 years old, is stately, with high-ceilinged rooms that, though not luxuriously furnished, are attractive. Tom Anderson—small, animated, in his early sixties, an officer of the society—showed me around on my first visit. "Purpose built to be just what it is," Tom said, "a clubhouse for golfers. Only one or two others—the R&A, of course—are older than it and in continuous use as a clubhouse right down till today."

Leven has an impressive collection of trophies: silver cups, gold and silver medals, and the like. One of them, a handsome gold medal, was first competed for in 1870. Tom said, "That's the prize for the oldest open amateur tournament in the world. In the beginning it was restricted to players from local golf clubs. But today they come to Leven from all over the country to play for it. The tournament actually goes back fifteen years before the Amateur Championship itself."

In a wall of the billiards room, which is on the second floor, Tom raised a small panel that revealed a dumbwaiter. "No need to run up and down the stairs to get a pint," he said, with a smile. "A man can concentrate on the snooker." Downstairs, a sign on the bar caught my eye:

NOTICE

THE SUGGESTION BOOK WILL NOW BE KEPT
BEHIND THE BAR AND AVAILABLE THEREFORE
FROM THE STAFF, WHO HAVE BEEN INSTRUCTED
NOT TO RELEASE THE BOOK TO MEMBERS WHO
HAVE BEEN DRINKING EXCESSIVELY.

JOHN BENNETT, SECRETARY

Suggestions in the years that followed may not have been quite so stimulating as those that preceded Mr. Bennett's term.

The links we play today at Leven is to some degree the work of Old Tom Morris, but it is not easy to say precisely where his fine hand can be seen. In any event, as we stand on the 1st tee, the outlook is not appealing. Oh, the Firth of Forth is there, but blocking it from sight are several low, scruffy structures. Regrettably, nothing conceals the trailer park and a nearby jumble of nondescript buildings. A couple of low dune ridges signal the authentic linksland, but there is nothing akin to the restive topography on the adjacent links of the Lundin club. A well-nigh featureless tract awaits, gray green, austere, an occasional yellow or red flag contributing the only touch of color. But then, the Old Course itself is scarcely a visual feast at the outset. Perhaps, I thought, there is more here than meets the eye. From the medal tees, the course measures 6,435 yards against a par of 71. The visitors' tees add up to just over 6,000 yards.

The first four holes roll straight along, parallel to the sea, one after another like railroad cars. All are two-shotters, two of them, the 1st and 4th, long at 413 and 449 yards, respectively. The 381-yard 2nd may be the finest of the quartet. We can play safely right to an expansive fairway in a dune-framed valley, from which, however, there is no view of the green; or, with our drive, we can risk a long, forced carry over two bunkers in the face of a modest slope in order to gain a plateau of fairway on the left from which the entire green complex is visible. A classic risk/reward option.

Following the stoutly bunkered 158-yard 5th comes the longest hole on the course, 567 yards, with a boundary to unsettle the fader much of the way and plenty of sand at the green. Eight bunkers encase

Below: Leven, 7th.
Opposite: 10th.

Leven, 18th.

the relatively small green on the 184-yard 7th, and on the 8th, a 348-yarder, back comes that boundary on the right to beleaguer us.

I had a very odd experience on the 173-yard 9th, where the green, just over a rise, cannot be seen, though the flag can be. The hole was playing into the wind. I flared a 4-metal wildly right and out of sight over the rise. I hit a provisional—perfectly, in the literal sense of the word. My search for the first ball proved unsuccessful. The second ball, on the other hand, lay snugly at the bottom of the cup. This marked the only time I ever holed out from the tee but had to write 3 on the card.

The more I played Leven, the more admiration I had for its character and complexity. Gorse, heather, and the long bent grasses that cloak the ridges must be avoided. The rumpled fairways sometimes trigger awkward stances and lies; bunkers are often deep; blind shots surface with some frequency—on the 10th, for instance, both drive and second

shot. But there is nothing contrived about this. It's simply a reflection of the natural flow of this ancient linksland, untouched by a bulldozer.

Par on the second nine is 37, and the last four holes are hard. Well, at least three of them are: the 188-yard 15th, with its creatively contoured and inhospitable green; the 386-yard 16th, rising and into the prevailing breeze to finish within steps of the Leven Bowling Club's green; and the 414-yard 17th. The par-4 18th cannot be classified as hard: It is a killer, 457 yards long, more often than not into the wind. Those are the minor considerations. The major consideration is the broad Scoonie Burn, which crosses the hole just short of the green and then slinks beside its right edge. Even the powerful player is often confronted with a true go/no-go dilemma. In all of Scotland there may be no more lethal a finishing hole. When St. Andrews hosts the Open Championship, qualifying is sometimes conducted on the worthy links of Leven.

Five minutes from Lundin Golf Club and smack on the quay in Lower Largo is the **Crusoe Hotel**, so named because this village is the birthplace of Alexander Selkirk, the castaway sailor whose adventures were immortalized by Daniel Defoe in his novel *Robinson Crusoe*. All guest rooms, which are comfortable but not necessarily spacious, enjoy captivating harbor or sea views. The public rooms—fieldstone walls, fireplaces—are cozy.

Quite nearby, on the Leven Road, is the three-star **Lundin Links Hotel**, a mock-Tudor structure with attractive public spaces and guest rooms. Several accommodations afford striking views over the rooftops of the village and across the Firth of Forth to the East Lothian coast. The particularly spacious room with the canopied four-poster bed and the grand sea view—ah, we could gratefully settle into it for a week! The cooking at both hotels is generally reliable.

Views near Largo, and the Lundin Links Hotel.

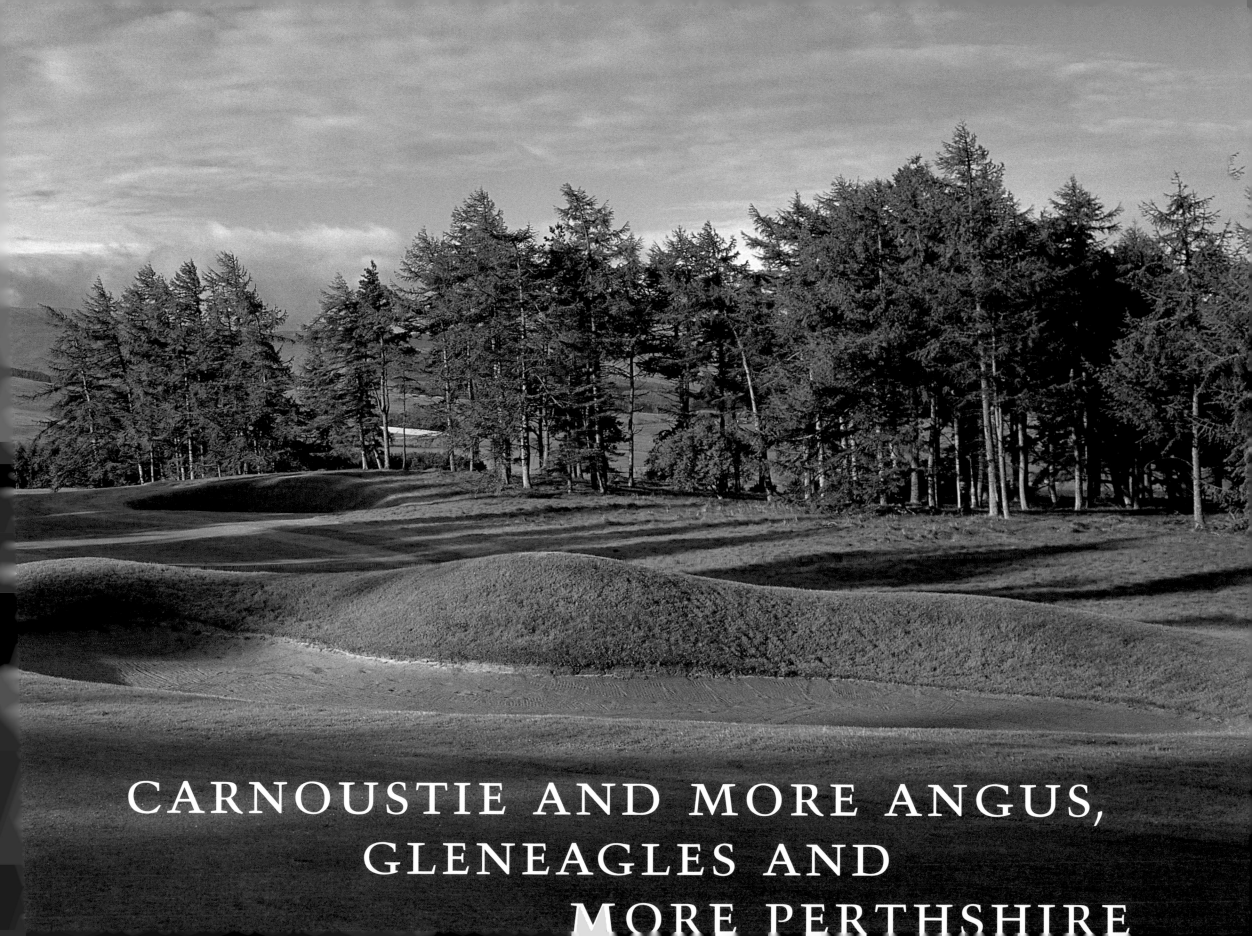

CARNOUSTIE AND MORE ANGUS,
GLENEAGLES AND
MORE PERTHSHIRE

CARNOUSTIE

For very nearly thirty years, I had not been a fan of Carnoustie. "The terrain is flat, bleak, and uninviting," I wrote in *Golf Magazine.* "There are half a dozen mediocre to weak holes, and only two great ones." Another example: "If the finale [17 and 18] is mighty, it serves to point up the prosaic nature of too much that has gone before. This historic links simply sits there, flat, severe, dour."

Not everyone agreed. A number of years ago Jack Nicklaus said to me, "When I first went to Carnoustie in 1967 to play a television match with Arnold [Palmer] and Gary [Player], I thought Carnoustie was the worst golf course I'd ever seen. And by the time I'd finished the Open in 1968, I thought it was the hardest golf course I'd ever seen, but a darn good course, and I really had great respect for it. And the last time I went back, in 1975, I had even greater respect for it. Now Carnoustie is one of my favorites."

Did the great man's thoughtful reevaluation prompt me to back off? No. Carnoustie, with the brown silos of a malting plant looking sternly down on it, was for me ordinary and cheerless. I found it reassuring that the R&A had quietly dropped it from the Open Championship rota.

Serious efforts here to fashion golf holes as we know them began with Allan Robertson's laying out a ten-hole course in 1850. Over the next eighty years Old Tom Morris, Willie Park Jr., and James Braid all took a hand in either adding to or remodeling what is now known as the Championship Course.

A little over a hundred years ago, Carnoustie—the town, then, as now, a drab huddle of one-story gray stucco cottages—served in a very real sense as a fountainhead for American golf. Some three hundred of the young men of this Tayside town emigrated to the United States to earn their living as golf professionals, staffing the pro shops, making clubs, giving lessons, and competing in tournaments. Among them were the three Smith brothers (Willie and Alex both won the U.S. Open) and Bobby Jones's swing model, Stewart Maiden. Wrote Jones: "The biggest piece of golfing luck I ever had was when the Atlantic Athletic Club got Stewart Maiden for its professional. . . . Stewart never gave me any lessons. I just followed him around the course and watched him. I imitated his style, like a monkey, I suppose."

It was in 1931 that Tommy Armour, the Edinburgh expatriate who had won the 1927 U.S. Open and the 1930 PGA, captured the first Open Championship held at Carnoustie. Here, six years later, Henry Cotton carried off the second of his three Opens, turning back a powerhouse field that included the entire American Ryder Cup team (Nelson, Snead, Sarazen, Guldahl, et al.).

The British Open came back to Carnoustie in 1953. This marked the only time Ben Hogan competed in the most important of all championships. He won by 4 strokes, improving his score with each round: 73, 71, 70, 68. In a piece he wrote (with Gene Gregston) for the *Saturday Evening Post,* Hogan covered the championship in detail, including the qualifying round and his caddie:

When I walked up to the first tee at Burnside for my first qualifying round and my first official shot in a British Open, I didn't see anyone in charge, no one announcing players as we do in America [Hogan had earlier that year won the Masters and the U.S. Open]. There was a little house off to the side and a woman sitting in it by herself. The twosome in front had teed off and hit their second shots; still no one . . . said anything to me about teeing off. So when I thought it was about time, I walked onto the tee and put my ball down. Some people shook their heads negatively.

While I was waiting for some word, a train came up the tracks that run alongside the first fairway. The engineer gave me three short blasts on his whistle, stopped the train and waved. I didn't shoo him away, as the news stories reported. I merely waved back to him. Then I heard this horn go "beep-beep." The woman in the little house had blown the horn, and that was the signal to tee off. All the people lining the fairway on both sides nodded their heads, indicating it was now all right for me to drive. Valerie [Mrs. Hogan] said later that she could see I was about to burst with laughter, and I was. It was all new and funny to me, but, I guess, perfectly normal to them.

On that first qualifying round I also learned that my caddie, Timmy, is a very nervous fellow. He was a good caddie. He treated my clubs as if they were the crown jewels and . . . he took my shoes home with him every night to polish them. But when things got tight on the course . . . the more nervous he became the more he would talk. Each time, I'd stop and quiet him. Many times when I'd have a long putt he'd hold his head down between his arms and wouldn't look, indicating his lack of confidence in my putting. . . .

I carried some candy fruit drops in my bag and ate them frequently for energy. At the start I gave Timmy a share of this candy, but in two rounds he ate all of his and mine too. Finally, after two or three warnings, he was convinced he'd better leave my candy alone.

Below: Carnoustie, 2nd.
Opposite: 3rd.

When the Open returned to Carnoustie, in 1968, Gary Player won. The decisive stroke was a 4-wood over the Spectacles bunkers to the concealed green on the par-5 14th, the ball finishing less than three feet from the hole for an eagle. In 1975 Tom Watson captured the first of his five British Opens when he downed Australia's Jack Newton here in an 18-hole playoff with a 2-iron over the Barry Burn to the home green for a regulation 4.

Ten years went by, then fifteen, and one heard little or no mention of the Open returning to Carnoustie. The shortcomings of the links were not lost on many observers. Once past the 3rd hole, play was on a vast, flattish, and monotonously pedestrian landscape. Holes were often neither arresting nor inviting. There was too much of a dull slog.

And when it came to accommodations and dining for today's traveling golfer—not to mention the thousands of spectators that an Open would attract—the little town's facilities were inadequate. Nonetheless, a number of stalwart locals felt that the situation was not irreparable. First of all, the course had to be improved, markedly. The task got under way in 1992. Second, a hotel of size and substance would have to be built. In 1994 the R&A announced that the Open would return to Carnoustie in 1999, and in 1997 ground was broken for a hotel on the site, squarely behind the 1st tee and the 18th green.

It was in midsummer of 1998, exactly eleven months before the scheduled Open, that, for the first time in ten years, I got back to what was my least favorite Open Championship course. I was bowled over. The new Carnoustie was a revelation. This was Carnoustie reborn—and without any alteration to the routing plan. The holes would go where they had always gone, never more than two consecutive holes heading in the same direction, so that the judgment of wind and distance would still be a consistently provocative business.

In this sweeping makeover, no hole was left untouched. Five greens were totally rebuilt and recontoured, including the 11th, which was moved in the bargain, and the 3rd, which was extended forward to the very edge of Jockeys' Burn in order to imperil the short approach shot. Certain greens were intriguingly angled to the line of flight of the incoming shot. Two new championship tees were built, and some of the regular tees were raised and realigned. Bunkers were filled in on 6 holes; new bunkers were installed on 10 holes; several greenside bunkers were enlarged; and every one of these 118 pits—sod-faced, they range from penal to lethal—was fully reconditioned. As for fairways, they are no longer straight strips. Their widths and perimeters were redefined, so that now they swing a little, narrowing here, expanding there. Complementing all these improvements was new turf, a combination of bent grasses (greens and tees) and creeping fescues (fairways) that makes the entire playing surface the equal of the best in Scotland. Fairway lies are superb; greens are true and beautifully paced. A sow's ear had metamorphosed into a silk purse. This eighteen is the ultimate golfing challenge.

ON THE CHAMPIONSHIP COURSE

Carnoustie puts more pressure on the swing than any course in the British Isles. No hole is a breather. In truth, no shot is a breather. This is the most confrontational golf course we will ever play. Each time we take club in hand, from our drive on the 1st (gorse and boundary left; sand, mounds, and rough right) to our shot to the green on 18 (the broad Barry Burn just short of it, sand right and left of it) there is the threat of danger, tangible, looming. Most hazards are located to punish the shot that is just slightly off the mark. This combination of bunkers (every full shot, without exception, is menaced by sand), boundaries, gorse, thick rough, mounds, and water is relentlessly inimical. Water at the Barry Burn, Jockeys' Burn, and two or three unnamed wet ditches awaits the misguided stroke on 10 holes. Does water menace the shot at Carnoustie as often as on all the other Open Championship courses put together? Club players with handicaps of 2 or 3 tackle Carnoustie in a lively breeze, say, 15 miles per hour, and, their swing in tatters, do not break 85. (How eagerly they retreat to St. Andrews and the comfort of the Old Course!)

Whether we play from 6,100, 6,400, or 6,700 yards, par is 70. The course measured almost 7,400 yards for the 1999 Open; par was 71. There seem to me to be eight incontestably great holes, three going out, five coming in. Following the 380-yard opener, with the rising fairway dropping off to a sunken green in a dell, we face the great 2nd, 395 yards, where the notorious Braid's Bunker, in the center of the tee-shot landing area, stares us down and a channel of fairway (mounds, sand, rough) leads to a 55-yard-deep, narrow, bilevel green corseted by low dunes. The 3rd hole, only 306 yards, is one of the best short two-shotters in my experience: mildly elevated tee (the high point of a course that has otherwise nothing to speak of in the way of ups and downs), rough-clad slope on the right, sand and mounds on the left, Jockeys' Burn running ominously and immediately in front of an irrepressible putting surface with bunkers eating into it on both sides. A wonderful chance at 3 or 6.

The 4th and 5th are solid two-shotters, both curving smoothly right, and the 6th, a 490-yard par 5 from the regular markers, 570 from the tips, is straight almost all the way and is played into the prevailing wind, with the green tucked a smidge right. George Peper and his *Golf Magazine* colleagues chose it not simply as one of the five hundred greatest holes for their book but as one of the very greatest of the great, one of the top eighteen. Short on natural features, it is flat. Skirting the hole its entire length on the left is a boundary fence. In the center of the driving area is a pair of fearsome bunkers, one behind the other. We have three options from the tee: Carry the central bunkers, a very big hit; tack warily out to the right, aiming to avoid a bunker and rough there; challenge the out-of-bounds on the left with the intention of slotting our drive into the 28-yard-wide landing area between the fence and the two bunkers. Ben Hogan owned this third—and most daring—option. In both rounds on the final day of the 1953 Open, he cracked his drive down the fence

line, his customary soft fade drifting the ball perfectly back into the harbor of the fairway, left of the pair of pits. Then, morning and afternoon, he flighted a perfect 4-wood to the green for two-putt birdies.

Jack Nicklaus did not have Hogan's mastery of this hole. "Do you remember," I once asked Nicklaus, "hitting your drive out-of-bounds on the sixth at Carnoustie in the last round of the 1968 Open?"

"Oh, yes," he said, "sure. That shot cost me the tournament. I had a driver with the softest shaft I've ever used. It was an old TTW shaft. The wind was probably the easiest I've ever played it on that hole, because you could get by that right-hand bunker with a good tee shot, so I thought I'd just go ahead and set it out on the right side and turn it by the bunker—and I hooked it out-of-bounds."

The drive on 6 is only part of the story, albeit the most dramatic part. Nudging the right edge of the fairway about 200 yards beyond the two fairway bunkers is Jockeys' Burn. The space between it and the boundary fence is all of 25 yards. As for the green, it is wide but shallow, oblique to the line of play, and defended by five pits. The entire adventure, from tee to cup, has about the same feeling as tiptoeing through a minefield.

Now that the 456-yard 14th, the Spectacles, has been designated a par 4, it strikes me as a truly great one, with a strong forced carry over gorse from the tee to a blind fairway pinched by sand precisely where the hole turns left, then a long and thrilling play over the Spectacles bunkers in the sand hill to the hidden green. The test inherent in this second shot may be the one moment in the entire round that brings a smile to our lips—a wry smile.

Above: Carnoustie, 6th.
Opposite, left: 14th;
right: 15th.

The 15th, 425 yards long, bends left along a hog's-back fairway, crumpled and tumbling, gorse on the left, sand and low dunes on the right, the flagstick (but not the putting surface) visible on the second shot, the green complex full of mounds, sand, slopes, and unpredictable caroms. A perfect hole—better yet, a perfect links course hole. Please take my word for it.

It is hard to make a 3 on the 223-yard 16th (250 yards from the back), played into the prevailing wind. The three bunkers right and short of the green are now of the gathering type and surely attract a lot of customers. The two bunkers short and left are less possessive. The long, narrow green, only a couple of feet above the fairway on its cunning plateau, inclines to shun the ball, thus putting to good use the little falloffs all around. It is a great hole, as witness its selection for the *World's* 500 book, and it is probably an original hole as well.

The 17th is also unique, and it was named one of the top hundred in the 500 volume. Measuring 390 yards (459 from the tips), it takes its name, Island, from the path of Barry Burn, which snakes back and forth across the hole, isolating sections of the fairway and demanding that we traverse this serpentine hazard not once, not twice, but three times.

The 18th, 428 yards long and chosen by Chris Millard for his book *Golf's 100 Toughest Holes*, heads in the opposite direction. Once again that sinuous stream is the riveting element. We must cross it twice, from the tee and then to gain the green, but the second shot here, with the 20-foot-wide waterway no more than a dozen paces short of the green, has always struck me as harder than either shot on 17.

It is impossible to play the last hole at Carnoustie without remembering the 1999 Open and the French farce—or was it *Les Miserables*?—that was enacted when Jean Van de Velde, needing only a double bogey to claim the claret jug, sloshed around in the burn to the tune of 7 and then bowed, along with Justin Leonard, to Paul Lawrie in the four-hole playoff that followed. But the tragicomedy aside, what kind of golf course

was it that flayed this mighty field? In truth, a largely unplayable one made up of dense knee-high rough, unconscionably narrow fairways (a couple of which were, in places, only 12 yards wide), and hard, fast greens, all of which contrived to render helpless the best players in the world. Six-over-par 290 tied for first, the highest leading score in relation to par at a major championship in twenty-five years.

Green superintendent John Philp, the hero of Carnoustie's astonishing restoration, was now the villain of the piece. Many thought he would be—should be—fired. Many thought the Open would never—should never—return to Carnoustie. All were wrong. Philp kept his job. (You've got to love the man who, in the face of the torrent of whining by the professionals, said, "Look, they've got titanium and psychologists. All I've got is nature.") And early in 2004 the R&A announced that Carnoustie would host the Open for the seventh time, in 2007. Expect this championship to be a rigorous but fair examination. And count on this noble muni to reveal itself as one of the very greatest major champi-

Opposite: Carnoustie, 16th.
Above: Carnoustie Burnside, 14th.

give pause. The ground ranges from undulating to hummocky; bounces can be capricious and short pitches tough to control. Two holes are great: the 228-yard 14th, with dunes right and left and a deep swale in front of a green that is surprisingly angled to the line of flight of the shot; and the 473-yard par-4 17th, longer than the celebrated 17th on the Championship Course and also haunted by the Barry Burn.

The third of these municipal layouts is the **Buddon Links**, which was originally a short, artificial, uninspired business. A recent remodeling has considerably improved it.

NEARBY COURSES

Some six miles north on the coast road is the **Arbroath Links**, laid out over undulating linksland and measuring 6,185 yards from all the way back (par 70). Arbroath boasts half a dozen downright delightful holes, their charms generally stemming from greens adroitly sited on knobs or in dells, and ten holes where burns endanger the shot.

No more than a mile or two south of Carnoustie, in Barry, is the **Panmure Golf Club**, which has six excruciatingly dull holes, the first three and the last three. The middle twelve, however, are top-notch. Full of diversity and character, they meander along over low ridges of sand hills. Prior to his triumph up the road in 1953, Hogan did much of his practicing here. He singled out the 6th hole—387 yards, landing area for the tee shot blind and sloping right while the hole itself bends left and drifts uphill—for praise, saying that it could be put on any course and be outstanding.

Next door is the **Monifieth Golf Links**, with its two municipal eighteens. The secondary course, **Ashludie**, measures only 5,123 yards, par 68. The main course, 6,459 yards from the regular tees against a par of 71, is a no-nonsense layout. We get what we hit, and the number of long par 4s sees to it that we are often called to hit full out. The course is a hybrid. With its undulating fairways, modest sand hills, and greens sometimes nestled in dells, it feels like seaside golf. But because of the abundance of mature trees, it looks like parkland golf.

About twenty minutes from Monifieth, on the outskirts of Dundee, lies the **Downfield Golf Club**, with its classic and lovely parkland eighteen by James Braid. The terrain is rolling, a burn cuts through half the holes, the turf is superbly conditioned, and mature trees, both evergreen and deciduous, frame a number of fairways. Testament to its quality is the fact that Downfield hosted final qualifying for the 1999 Open.

onship tests in the world (are Whistling Straits and Bethpage Black its equals?), a course that can stand up defiantly under the assault of the game's finest players, the most forbidding links of all.

OTHER CARNOUSTIE COURSES

Downfield, 11th.

James Braid, who has left his mark on the Championship Course, gets sole credit for the second of the town's three eighteens, the **Burnside**. It is a jewel. Par is just 68 on this textbook links course: dunes, gorse, heather, tussocky rough grasses, a few blind shots, and, as is the case next door, bunkers with near-vertical "bricklayer" faces and streams to

Carnoustie itself is scarcely the place for sightseeing, but Arbroath, Dundee, and Barry all have something that's worth a stop. Arbroath Abbey, in the center of town, is a ruin but a strikingly beautiful one of red sandstone that dates to the twelfth century. On the Dundee waterfront is the *Discovery,* the triple-masted square rigger that was built here and in which Robert Falcon Scott sailed to Antarctica in 1901. And at the Barry Mill, a working mill nearly two hundred years old, we relish the splash of the waterwheel and the sound and smell of real corn being ground.

The **Carnoustie Golf Course Hotel & Resort**, a four-star facility at the Championship Course, has seventy-three double rooms and thirteen suites. Accommodations, some with balconies, have attractive views over the links or the Tay estuary. Both the dining room and the bar/lounge area (informal fare here) can be relied on for good food. The hotel has a number of daily starting times on the great course that are reserved for its guests.

About a mile from the links is **Carlogie House**, a long-established and hospitable sixteen-room hotel on pretty, secluded grounds. Public rooms are inviting and comfortable, but the guest rooms, which are quite spruce and afford pleasant views over the gardens and

farmland, are short on charm and space. The cooking has a large local following.

Five Gables House is a simple, homey B&B (all rooms with private bath) perched in its own terraced gardens above the Arbroath eighteen that offers lovely sea views over the links from the lounge and the dining area. It can accommodate eleven people; rooms are small. On the main road leading into Arbroath from Carnoustie—and directly across from the pitch-and-putt course—is an atmospheric old whitewashed pub called **Tuttie's Neuk**, which is very agreeable for a drink and basic pub food.

Clockwise from above: the ship *Discovery*; on the ship; the sea at Arbroath; and two scenes near the Angus Folk Museum.

MONTROSE

A mericans don't bother much with Montrose. Yet in this town of ten thousand, about thirty minutes north on the coast from Carnoustie, a truly ancient links can be found. Part of the Medal Course that we play today actually hosted golfers in 1550, as the diary of Montrose's James Melville, born in 1556, makes clear. Melville tells us that he was taught from the age of six "to use the glubb for goff." Montrose thus takes its place with Leith (Edinburgh) and St. Andrews among the very earliest incubators of the game. And by the middle of the nineteenth century, Montrose was distinguished by the sheer number of its golf holes, twenty-five, probably more than any other single course has ever had.

There are two 18-hole municipal courses at Montrose today: the Broomfield, only 4,800 yards long, and the Medal, 6,451 yards at its longest, 6,231 from the regular markers, par 71. Both eighteens owe much to the hand of Willie Park Jr., in 1903, but Old Tom Morris had provided a number of revisions to the Medal Course twenty years earlier. In the 1960s and 1970s, Montrose hosted the Scottish Professional Championship twice and the Scottish Amateur once. But it's just not long enough anymore.

ON THE MEDAL COURSE

Though a genuine pleasure to play, the Medal Course is not a great links; in truth, it may not offer even one inarguably great hole. There are three or four quite ordinary holes, the bunkering is comparatively light, fairways are generous, and strategic considerations are minimal. Still, this is classic seaside golf, a combination of imposing sand hills, often violently rumpled fairways, gorse, heather, and long rough grasses. Again and again, shots to the green are played along the ground rather than through the air. There is a lot of pure shot-making fun to be had at Montrose.

The first nine is the more appealing of the two. This is signaled at the start as we head uphill into the grand duneland on a delightful 390-yarder. At the sand-free 2nd hole, also 390 yards, the drive calls for a stiff forced carry over wildly broken ground, and at the 152-yard 3rd the shot must carry an overgrown hollow to gain a plateau green that is much wider than it is deep. This is stirring stuff, as indeed are the next five

holes, in the very heart of the dunes, with the 6th, a par 5 of 468 yards, perhaps the favorite among them. The tee here is a tiny platform at the peak of the huge sand hills, with the beach of tawny sand far below on the one hand, the fairway far below on the other.

The 8th, with another lovely falling tee shot, leads us out of this magical golfing country into more open terrain that has little in the way of elevation change.

Paradoxically, the less dramatic second nine is more difficult to score on. Three of the two-shotters are over 400 yards, and one of the par 3s is well over 200 yards. The first time I visited Montrose, I was invited

Opposite: Montrose, 2nd.
Above: 3rd.

on the 14th, a 407-yarder, to join two young men, Martin and Ian Smith, playing just ahead of me. They pointed out that the pair of golfers in front of us were also Smiths, their father and brother. Why, you might wonder, weren't the four playing together? Because the round would be too slow, close to an hour longer than any of them would tolerate.

The four Smiths lived in Oxford. Two of them were studying at the university, and three of them were musicians: a pianist, a violinist, and a trumpeter. They came to Montrose every summer for a golfing holiday. My two companions, who knew the course well, were helpful guides, warning of dangers, explaining subtleties. I earned a "Well done indeed" when I dropped a sliding five-footer for 3 on the 226-yard 16th, with its devilishly contoured green. I also earned a sympathetic "Unlucky" when I just missed from five feet on the 410-yard 17th. The course's best hole,

it curves mildly, gorse on both sides, and only a perfect approach will find the elevated shelflike green carved out of a dune at the left.

They called my attention to a half-timbered house on the periphery of the course, saying that it had been the holiday home of the head of the Secret Service (is it possible, John le Carré, that great deceptions and great treacheries were concocted here?). A widower during the last years of his life, the UK's number-one plotter stayed here with a woman he did not marry, who inherited the property when he died.

I was agog at these revelations. "If you don't mind my asking," I said, "how do you know about this?"

"The piano," Ian replied. "The lady has a concert grand piano in the drawing room, and she likes to stage recitals there. Somehow she learned about our musical bent."

ground, and the long views of the Angus countryside are gorgeous. Edzell measures 6,050 yards from the regular markers, 6,350 from the medal tees; par is 71. There is quite enough sand, including five old-fashioned cross bunkers. Among the better holes, on a course that is solid and testing but rarely if ever exhilarating, are the 2nd, 436 yards and into the prevailing wind, slightly rising at first, then downhill, a boundary close on the right all the way, the shot to the green blind, with bunkers right and left; the 342-yard 8th, swinging right, the approach shot falling to a two-tier green; and the quirky 16th, only 302 yards, cross bunkers short of the sharply elevated plateau green.

Back to the coast and north now, the drive is about thirty minutes to **Stonehaven**, where a first-rate seafood restaurant called **The Tollbooth** sits smack on the harbor and the golf course sits on considerably higher ground. It has been dismissed more than once as "clifftops and railroads." You must come here expecting the unconventional, even the bizarre.

Let me set down some hard facts to guide—or deter—you. Total yardage from all the way back is 5,103. Par is 66. This eighteen is laid out on all of sixty-two acres. There are seven par 3s. The 4th, 5th, and 16th are crisscross holes, but it is the 5th that takes the palm. Here the drive from a hilltop tee sails straight toward the sea and, along the way, *directly over both the 16th and 4th fairways.* The Dundee/Aberdeen railway line features two-car "sprinters" (the locals' term) that race through the middle of the golf course in the middle of your backswing, seemingly five or six times during the round. The holes are laid out in three separate sectors: on the high meadow beyond the tracks, in the narrow neck beyond the railway viaduct, and the majority on the steeply sloping headlands high above the sea. Three of the seven or eight blind shots occur on par 3 holes. Bunkering is light. The greens, which incline to be small, are true, nicely paced, and easy to read. A handful of them are set uncomfortably close to the cliff's edge. The same can be said of four tees on the first nine—at 2, 6, 7, and 8—which are all but cantilevered vertiginously out over the wave-washed rocks far below.

For pure theater, the isolated tee on the 203-yard 2nd rivals the fabled launching pad on the 9th at Turnberry's Ailsa. So totally exposed and so precariously sited is it that I would think twice before going out there in the 30- to 40-mile-an-hour winds that often buffet Stonehaven. And as for that blind 203-yard shot itself, first it has to clear the abyss formed by a cleft in the cliffs, and then it has to carry a humpy ridge in order to gain a wide plateau green bunkered left and right. Inarguably an original golf hole.

"So we've been to the house a number of times and grown quite friendly with her," Martin concluded the explanation.

I never did think to ask whether the Secret Service head was a golfer.

One Montrose golfer, Alex H. Findlay, made a name for himself in America as a course architect (The Breakers, Llanerch, and Basking Ridge, among many others). But his proposal in 1926 to lay out a six-hole course for Pope Pius XI in the Vatican Gardens was rejected. "This was," he would say with a smile, "the only thing I ever failed in."

NEARBY COURSES

Some twenty minutes from Montrose on a northeasterly heading is the pleasant inland village of Edzell and, not far from its center, the equally pleasant eighteen of the **Edzell Golf Club**, dating to 1895. The 1933 revisions of James Braid and the vigorous tree planting to follow give the course its look and quality today. The holes are routed over gently rolling

Stonehaven, 17th.

You will want to have lunch or at least a beverage in the quaintly charming old **Stonehaven** clubhouse, which rambles along the hillside and commands the sea. I remember buying a club necktie, green and white regimental stripes, on my first visit. Though not normally given to such extravagance, I thought it might be useful later to prove that the eighteen at Stonehaven had indeed been real, that I had not dreamed it.

The town of Montrose presents rather too much soot-stained granite to be considered attractive. Nevertheless, the broad High Street has several dignified buildings, among them the Old Church (circa 1832), with its pinnacled square tower and graceful steeple, and the Old Town Hall (1763). Immediately outside town is the Montrose Basin Wildlife Centre, a rich feeding ground for thousands of resident and migratory birds. Unusual displays show how a tidal basin works. Overlooking the basin is the House of Dun, a Georgian residence designed in 1730 by William Adam and featuring superb carved plasterwork. A miniature theater and a Victorian walled garden are charming elements. The **Park Hotel**, in a pretty little park two blocks off the High Street, has a congenial atmosphere. Guest rooms are comfortable, and the cooking in both the brasserie and the dining room will do nicely.

Clockwise from top left: on the boardwalk in Montrose; Dunnottar Castle; Edzell Castle's gardens; the entrance arch to Edzell; Stonehaven. In the center: rapeseed field near Montrose.

BLAIRGOWRIE

ome fifteen miles northwest of Dundee, which would put it about twenty-five miles from Carnoustie, lies the Blairgowrie Golf Club, where the game was first played in 1889. The Dowager Marchioness of Lansdowne leased the land to the club for twenty-five pounds a year, stipulating that this charge would be reviewed after ten years. And so it was, with the result that the annual rent was reduced to twenty pounds!

There are three courses here, the Rosemount and the Lansdowne, both full-length eighteens, and the Wee Course, a par-32 nine. It is the Rosemount, the eldest of the three, that lures visitors.

The course has a remarkable pedigree. Old Tom Morris provided the layout of the earliest holes in 1889. Alister MacKenzie revised the Morris nine and added a second nine in 1923. Then it was Braid's turn, in the early 1930s. He extensively reworked MacKenzie's layout, even siting new tees and greens. Although this is a good course, sometimes very good, it is not great, though many have called it so.

ON THE ROSEMOUNT COURSE

Perhaps those who praise the course immoderately have been overawed by the setting, for this is an extraordinarily beautiful place, reminiscent, in fact, of the heathland courses in Berkshire and Surrey (e.g., Sunningdale, Swinley Forest, The Berkshire) outside London. Each hole on this gently rolling Perthshire tract is played in near total isolation; we stroll along lovely avenues of pine and larch and silver birch, with heather often serving as ground cover in the rough. The tranquillity is exquisite. The springy moorland turf, on a sand-and-gravel base that assures quick draining and a free run on the ball, is a delight to walk on and to hit from. And because the holes are framed by mature trees, the effect of wind on our shots is markedly lessened. Scotland actually has very few courses that look and feel and play like Rosemount.

The holes are nicely varied, and the routing of them is imaginative. Hole after hole strikes off in a fresh direction. And since the fairways are surprisingly broad—75 to 85 yards in the landing areas most times—we

swing away with impunity. The shots to the generous and often passive greens, however, are consistently testing, in large part because of the adroit bunkering that is the legacy of two masters of the art, MacKenzie and Braid.

Rosemount measures just under 6,600 yards from the medal tees (par 72), 6,240 from the regular markers (par 70). The opening three holes and the closing three are Rosemount at its best. The round begins with a strong par 4 rather before we are up to it, a 429-yarder that falls ever so slightly as it curves smoothly left through the trees to a green with a lone bunker, at the left front. Next comes one of the short two-shotters, a straightaway 321-yarder with a raised and heavily bunkered green, where we could pick up a birdie to offset that likely bogey on the 1st. Let us hope

Opposite: Blairgowrie
Rosemount Course, 16th.
Above: 1st.

so, anyway, because the 206-yard 3rd, its pear-shaped green pinched at the front by sand right and left, calls for something akin to a perfect swing.

Now, skipping over a dozen attractive holes that include a couple of short par 5s where 4 is highly possible, we face the challenge of the last three holes. The altogether excellent 16th is a 435-yarder that begins with a drive over a corner of Black Loch. The fairway narrows (but only by Rosemount standards) in the tee-shot landing area, then bends quietly left. The long second shot must take into account a boundary fence skirting the fairway tight on the left all the way and a green guarded on the right by high mounding, on the left by trees, and on both sides by sand. We need to hit full out, but we find ourselves swinging defensively.

The falling 17th, 165 yards long and one of the 500 *World's Greatest*, traverses a valley to an immense bilevel green. Hitting the green is not the problem; hitting the sector that contains the cup is. Failure to do so is inevitably followed by three-putting (or worse).

The 382-yard 18th is a sparkling finisher. As the hole curves right, 200 yards from the tee, the fairway dips sharply and trees on the inside of the dogleg force the prudent drive out to the left. The two-tier green is forcefully defended by bunkers front left and front right.

Thirty years ago, when it was not thought necessary for courses to measure 7,450 yards in order to host a professional tournament, Rosemount was the venue for the 1977 Martini International, won by Greg Norman. This marked the first European Tour victory for the twenty-two-year-old Australian, whose 277 total included a course-record 66.

ON THE LANSDOWNE AND WEE COURSES

It was in 1979 that a second course, called Lansdowne, opened. Designed by Peter Alliss and Dave Thomas and measuring 6,437 yards from the daily markers, it roams through the same woodlands and over the same heathery expanses as Rosemount. But it lacks the shot values of that eighteen, inclining often enough to be both dull and easy.

The Wee Course, on the other hand, is a joy. Braid laid it out in the 1930s. Its length is just 2,327 yards; there are four par 3s and five par 4s. Indicative of the course's challenging nature is the 335-yard 2nd. It doglegs moderately right and drifts downhill in the driving area to leave a pitch that must be landed short of the green and beyond the bunkers well out front, but the shot must come in under two towering firs, one right and one left, whose limbs all but touch as they spread across the line of play before the green. Gaining this green in regulation calls for skillful shot-making.

Be sure to have lunch in the handsome white pebbledash clubhouse, with its large bow windows. If you eat upstairs, in the main dining room, your meal will be accompanied by beguiling views over the start and finish of the Rosemount Course.

NEARBY COURSES

Less than fifteen minutes from Blairgowrie, on a northeasterly heading, lies the **Alyth Golf Club**, founded in 1894. The course, which reflects Braid's extensive remodeling efforts in 1934, measures 6,000 yards from the regular markers, 6,200 from the medal tees. Against the backdrop of pastoral Perthshire—rolling farmland and woodland, grazing cattle and sheep, heather-clad hills—some holes are routed over open ground, others along beautiful allées of evergreen and silver birch. Five or six holes are very good. The 329-yard 5th, for instance, teases us on the tee with a burn we may be unable to carry and then completes the challenge with an angled and elevated plateau green. But the flair inherent in this hole surfaces all too infrequently.

Opposite: Blairgowrie
Rosemount Course, 17th.
Above: 18th.

At **Kirriemuir**, about twenty minutes farther northeast along the road (the A926), the countryside continues to enchant, croplands alternating with pasture around the perimeter of the course, the Grampian Mountains dominating the long vistas, the course itself gloriously sited above the great vale of Strathmore. An extremely short course (5,553 yards, par 68), it is saved by Braid's irresistible second nine, with its rolling terrain, plateau greens, and sentinel trees. The round concludes with two superb holes. The 17th is a falling 200-yarder called Braid's Gem, where the green, defended by sand and trees, is angled to the line of play. As for the home hole, it is a potent uphill 400-yarder with a deep hidden swale short of the green. At the bottom of this hollow is a voracious sandpit.

Less than twenty minutes southeast of Kirriemuir is the **Forfar Golf Club** eighteen (5,800–6,050 yards, par 69), another inland course properly attributed to Braid. The very ground intrigues us. Though we are a dozen miles from the sea, the fairways are wrinkled, rippling, little short of being a washboard. (How to account for this linkslike feature? "Rig and furrow" cultivation of flax here 150 years ago.) Most holes, though framed by evergreens, are not corseted by them. There is room to open our shoulders. The generous putting surfaces are among the finest and most beautifully contoured in Scotland. In truth, the greens and bunkers are Braid at his best.

Letham Grange Golf Course, in Colliston, a fifteen-minute drive essentially due east of Forfar, hosted the 1994 Scottish Amateur. It measures 6,954 yards from the championship tees, 6,348 from the regular markers. Par is 73. This is big "swing away" golf, with wide fairways, light bunkering, forgiving rough. There is considerable water—ponds on four holes, streams on six others. The topography ranges from rolling to hilly. The first six holes are routed over open terrain, the next four are carved out of the woods, and the last eight reprise the spacious theme. At least half a dozen holes are excellent, including several that are not easily forgotten. The 166-yard 8th, for instance, is framed by tall pines, and a pretty lagoon extends from tee to green. The obvious inspiration for the hole is Augusta National's 16th. The 14th, on the other hand, may be an original. A 480-yard par 5, it edges left as it climbs on a narrow shelf of fairway to a matching shelf of green carved out of a right-hand hill. The muscular hitter senses a chance to get home in two, but a pulled or hooked second shot will miss the shelf and tumble down into the trees. It is a lesson in how a birdie 4 becomes a double bogey 7.

In addition to the agreeable golf, there is another good reason to visit Kirriemuir. It was in this village that James M. Barrie was born and in its hilltop cemetery that he is buried. The creator of *Peter Pan,* not to mention *The Little Minister, Quality Street,* and other plays and novels, was born in "The Tenements," 9 Brechin Road, a small whitewashed stone cottage that today is a museum. It evokes in vivid detail the circumstances in which a linen weaver, Barrie's father, and his large family (the author was one of ten children, and "box beds" were the only answer) lived in Victorian times.

Kinloch House Hotel, set strikingly in 25 acres on a gentle hillside in neighboring Dunkeld, with views to the Sidlaw Hills, is within five minutes' drive of Blairgowrie. The public spaces (antiques, log fires, oriental rugs, oak paneling) and the guest rooms in this graceful country house built in 1840 are enormously appealing, and the cooking is outstanding. A welcome amenity here is the fitness center with indoor swimming pool.

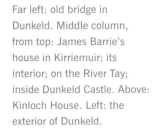

Far left: old bridge in Dunkeld. Middle column, from top: James Barrie's house in Kirriemuir; its interior; on the River Tay; inside Dunkeld Castle. Above: Kinloch House. Left: the exterior of Dunkeld.

GLENEAGLES

<img block A>t this moment I find myself recalling a piece by Henry Longhurst, golf columnist for the *Sunday Times* long before Americans came to know him as a commentator on televised tournaments. Unfortunately, I'm unable to put my hands on the essay. But I do remember how it began. He wrote of leaving his London office at the end of the working day and of "the anticipatory dinner" at his town club, followed by the cab ride to King's Cross Station, there to fall quickly asleep in his compartment on the night train, secure in the knowledge that when he awakened early the next morning, it would be at one of his very favorite places in all of golf, Gleneagles.

There are about 120 outstanding golf resorts in the world, somewhat fewer that can be termed full-facilities golf-centered resorts. At the top of the list, we instinctively place three at the sea, Casa de Campo, The Cloister, and Turnberry; and three in the mountains, the Greenbrier, the Homestead, and Gleneagles. Judge them for setting, accommodations, cuisine, breadth of activities, service, amenities, and, most important, golf.

On the doorstep of the Highlands, Gleneagles possesses a setting of flabbergasting beauty—at the head of glorious Glen Devon, with forty-mile vistas to the Ochil Hills in the east and south and to the heather-tinged foothills of the Grampian Mountains in the north and west. The openness, the vastness, the grandeur, the shifting patterns of light and shadow on the distant multihued slopes—the forest green of stately firs and pines, the golden beige of hay fields, the gray green of meadows—this is the Scotland of your dreams. And it is there, all of it, with every shot you play on the three superlative eighteens.

The King's and Queen's courses, which opened in 1919, are the work of James Braid and his associate Colonel C. K. Hutchison. Routed dazzlingly over a stretch of wild Perthshire moorland, this collection of thirty-six golf holes, so many of them genuinely arresting, has been painted with bold brushstrokes on a canvas of hills and valleys, ridges and plateaus. Noble hardwoods and equally noble evergreens, bracken and broom and heather and gorse, all contribute to the playability and aesthetic delight of this monumental golf experience.

ON THE KING'S COURSE

Hotel guests will play the King's at 6,471 yards (par 70) or 6,125 yards (par 68). The architects employed the natural folds of the land to give many holes a nice sense not of seclusion or isolation but, if you will, of separateness, which contributes to their individuality. There are a number of elevated tees and some stern forced carries. This is big golf: half a dozen two-shotters ranging from 405 to 466 yards, broad fairways, sprawling greens, deep bunkers (all told, 110 pits), bold elevation changes. There is a magnificence to this eighteen that is exhilarating.

Among the most challenging holes are a couple of par 3s. The 161-yard 5th, called Het Girdle ("hot griddle," or "skillet"), presents one of the great and thrilling knob-to-knob shots. Come up short of this windswept table-top green by so much as three feet and you court calamity in the sandpits far below. No such drama greets us on the 11th, a 221-yarder uphill and over scrub to a closely bunkered green. Most days, anything less than a perfectly struck driver is a losing proposition. The 2nd at Shinnecock Hills is its twin, even to the yardage.

Of the many strong par 4s, two are especially memorable. The 3rd, measuring 374 yards and playing not less than 415, is a good example of holes prebulldozer. It climbs steeply up a fairway full of humps and hollows, the long, blind second shot having to surmount a high ridge far above in order to find a green concealed in yet another hollow. As for the 13th, called Braid's Brawest (*braw* being Scots for "splendid"), it is a 448-yard rollercoaster. A ridge containing a pair of fearsome bunkers blockades all but the stoutest drive; the dispiritingly long second, over a great dip in the early going, must then carry a cross bunker and avoid at the left a steep heather-covered slope and more sand. In all of Scotland there may be no more magnificent two-shotter.

Over the years a number of important competitions have been played on the King's, including the Curtis Cup, the British Ladies', the Dunlop International, the 1977 Skol Lager (Nick Faldo's first victory as a professional), and the Scottish Open half a dozen times in the 1980s and 1990s. In the 1992 Scottish Open, Colin Montgomerie shot 65 on the last day for what

Opposite: Gleneagles King's Course, 1st.

appeared certain to be the win. Not so. The young Australian Peter O'Malley played the final five holes 7 under par—2-3-2-3-3, two eagles and three birdies—for a round of 62, enabling him to beat Montgomerie by 2 strokes. It was surely the gaudiest finish ever in professional golf.

ON THE QUEEN'S COURSE

If the Queen's Course has never witnessed anything like O'Malley's victory, there is still so much golf of a very high standard here that we actually forget the wonders next door. A glance at the scorecard is deceptively encouraging: 5,965 yards, par 68. But a closer look reveals that seven of the dozen two-shotters range from 409 to 437 yards. Two examples are the 9th and 10th, reverse images of each other. The 419-yard 9th climbs steadily from tee to green—playing value a good 460—and bends emphatically right, with the green tucked up and away behind a right-hand slope. The 421-yard 10th—playing value more like 390—falls and bends sharply, but from right to left. This green is also tucked away, below and left, around a corner and beyond a high left-hand shoulder of ground, cloistered in its dell and concealed almost till the very moment you step onto it. An original golf hole—and a beauty.

The last five holes are as rich and rewarding as all that go before them. At 215 yards, and rising gently to a two-tier green with a five-foot difference in levels, not to mention bunkering and a steep falloff on the right down to

Opposite: Gleneagles King's Course, 13th.

water, the 14th is a truly great one-shotter, perhaps the best par 3 at Gleneagles. The 15th, a mere 252 yards, is one of those bewitchingly driveable par 4s that finds the player coming out of his shoes and maybe going into the trees. And the 378-yard 16th is a straightaway two-shotter from a slightly elevated tee, the green sloping away from front to back and left to right.

The 204-yard 17th is fiendish. The tee is high, the green is narrow and deep (200 feet deep!) and pitches sharply to the right. We would like to bail out left, but three small bunkers lurk there. Still, the shot from

any of them is playable. This is not the case from the mine shaft disguised as a sand bunker below the right side of the green. It is some 12 feet deep and brags of a nearly vertical face. My strongest swing and most precise contact with a sand wedge finds the ball failing to scale the heights by about a foot, then tumbling down this sheer bank to come to rest within a club's length of where I am standing.

The last hole, Queen's Hame, measures 412 yards, but, from the top of a high hill and with the prevailing wind at our back, plays more like

Opposite: Gleneagles Queen's Course, 9th. Above: 10th.

375. The forced carry from the tee over wetlands and gorse is well within our capacity, and the vast green is hospitably open across the front.

The ideal day of inland golf in Scotland? Surely it must be the morning round on the King's, lunch in the Dormy House, and the afternoon round on the Queen's.

ON THE PGA CENTENARY COURSE

Or we could choose the third course in the triumvirate for one of the games. It, too, is a winner. Jack Nicklaus was responsible for the design. My wife, Harriet, and I were on hand for the grand opening, in May 1993. Among the celebrities were Jack and Barbara Nicklaus, Her Royal Highness Princess Anne, Sean Connery, His Royal Highness Prince Andrew the Duke of York, Gene Hackman, His Royal Highness Prince Abdul Hakeem of Brunei (a legitimate 3-handicap), Chris de Burgh (his song "The Lady in Red," no longer high on the charts, is still dear to our hearts), the Duke of Roxburghe (a 9-handicap, given of an

Opposite: Gleneagles Queen's Course, 18th. Above: 14th.

evening and while still in dinner jacket to hitting golf balls over the roof of his ancestral home, Floors Castle), Cheryl Ladd (it is now twenty-nine years since she appeared in *Charlie's Angels*), and Jackie Stewart (the storied racing champion, who has a vested interest in Gleneagles). During the weekend I made a few notes.

Sean Connery, resplendent in tartan kilt and dinner jacket, said grace at the banquet Saturday evening. Reverently he intoned:

We thank Thee for these gifts divine,
For turning water into wine;
Protect us from these foolish men
Who wish to turn it back again.

Cheryl Ladd demonstrated her takeaway for Jack Nicklaus at the bar Friday evening while both were waiting for drinks to be mixed. She appeared to have her hands in the right position at the top of the backswing, but it was not easy for Jack to tell whether the imaginary club was pointing down the line. He did smile agreeably, but he did not nod approvingly.

The Prince of Brunei was the hero of the charity auction. His was the winning bid (a whopping $49,000) on the caricatures of the feature foursome—Nicklaus, Prince Andrew, Connery, Stewart. Then, obviously operating on the principle of noblesse oblige, he promptly bestowed the drawings on Princess Anne so that she might sell them at auction in the future for her favorite charity. Prince Abdul Hakeem's uncle the sultan was widely believed at that time to be the richest man in the world.

Above: Gleneagles PGA
Centenary Course, 1st.
Opposite: 2nd.

It was on Saturday at the Moët & Chandon tent near the 18th green (champagne and smoked salmon were served there all day) that my wife and I hobnobbed with royalty. As we approached the tent door, a middle-aged woman in raincoat, wellies, and kerchief stood off to the side, gathering herself after the walk through the cold, light rain. Harriet preceded me but hesitated momentarily, not certain which way the door opened. The woman now stepped in ahead of me, and I heard her murmur something. The door swung open, and as I reached out to hold it, I recognized the woman between me and my wife as Her Royal Highness Princess Anne. Inside the tent now, I said excitedly to Harriet as we headed toward a table, "That was Princess Anne. I heard her speak to you as you went to open the door. What did she say?"

"She said, 'Pull.'"

The PGA Centenary Course, as the Nicklaus eighteen is called, rolls consistently. There is water but not in excess. Three of the par 5s present the big hitter with that classic risk/reward situation: Go for the green on your second shot, but chance a dunking if you do.

From the championship markers, the course measures nearly 7,100 yards. I suspect that when it serves as the venue for the 2014 Ryder Cup, it will be at least 250 yards longer. Most visitors elect the white markers, at 6,550 yards.

The 1st (394 yards) and 2nd (501 yards) move gently downhill to shelf greens, both holes aiming squarely at breathtaking Glen Devon. They are utterly captivating, and neither is beyond our capacity. The next

up a short pitch for a birdie. The 17th, 179 yards, is a falling shot—and an inviting one—to an angled green that is open across the front. And the wiggling home hole, 484 yards, is an uphill double dogleg (maybe triple) par 5 that at no point intimidates us and again is a birdie chance. It's as though Jack Nicklaus were bent on having us walk off his course in a sunny frame of mind.

How does the PGA Centenary stack up against the two "royal" all-world jewels here that have been thrilling golfers for nearly ninety years? As far as test goes, the three are on essentially the same serious level. But perhaps the King's and the Queen's have a bit of an edge when it comes to sparkle and originality—to brio, if you will. Our instinct is to cherish them. And it is a sound instinct, for we shall not see their like again.

AUCHTERARDER

When playing the 15th on the PGA Centenary, you may notice a neighboring golf hole that does not belong to the Nicklaus eighteen. In fact, it is the 6th at the Auchterarder Golf Club, where the game has held sway since 1892. Peter Alliss, Lee Trevino, and Ben Crenshaw are honorary members at this very inviting club. This is a short course—5,800 yards, par 69—with spunk. Though it can in no sense be discussed in the same breath with its neighbors, there are some first-rate holes, the moorland turf is crisp and springy, and the views down Glen Devon are awe-inspiring.

The merits of the course can best be appreciated in the final five holes, which are like no closing cluster I've ever encountered: a par 4, a par 5, and three par 3s. The 214-yard 14th is blind, the high face of a cross bunker hiding a long, narrow green in a little dell. At the very good 15th, 513 yards long and uphill off the tee, a deep dip immediately in front of the green complicates the pitch shot, particularly with the cup cut toward the front of the green. The 16th—great by any standard—is 219 yards long and plays into the prevailing breeze. Gazing down Glen Devon, we play from a knob of a tee across a rough valley to a green that is slightly narrower than instinct tells us it should be and bunkered on both flanks. To hit this green, a string-straight shot, often with a driver, is called for. The 445-yard 17th requires two first-class shots, a drive that carries a vast swale in the fairway and a long second soaring downhill to a big green that is open across the front. The round concludes with a par 3 that measures 188 yards, but, uphill and generally into a left-to-right wind, plays at least 210. Sand at the left and a high hedge tight across the back cannot be ignored.

Above: Gleneagles PGA Centenary Course, 4th. Opposite: 16th.

three holes bring us back to earth with a vengeance. On the 390-yard 3rd, from an elevated tee (Nicklaus is a fan of high tees, confident that golfers are grateful for them) our drive plunks into an opposing hillside, at which point the hole bends right, around a cluster of three bunkers in the crook of the dogleg, and continues its climb to a green pinched at the front by sand right and left. If we can hit it 211 yards uphill (240 from the tips) on the straightforward 4th, carrying an immense bunker at the left front of the green, we have a chance for a 3. At the 5th, a 423-yarder, we drive blindly over the rise in a saddle-shape fairway, then thread the long second shot through trees, uneasily conscious of wetlands just short of the green at the right. It is a great hole, a beautiful killer.

The second nine, also par 36, provides that happy mixture of three par 3s, three par 4s, and three par 5s. What may come as a surprise is that the closing holes give us an opportunity to make up some ground. The downhill 16th, 518 yards, dares us to carry a pond on our second shot, thus setting

Remarkably, it is the not the great golf alone that accounts for the preeminence of Gleneagles. The **Gleneagles Hotel** itself, architecturally more akin to a Loire Valley chateau than a Scottish baronial castle, tellingly calls up the past, specifically the halcyon days of Edwardian country-house luxury. Whether in the public spaces or the guest accommodations, we are struck by the stylish Art Deco–inspired appointments—the fabrics, the furniture, the wallpapers, the floor coverings, the paneling, the light fixtures, the paintings, the objets d'art.

Nor does the display of the decorative arts put the cooking in the shade. A total of thirteen restaurants and bars are scattered about the 850 acres:

- The principal dining room is the immense and sumptuous **Strathearn** (fluted pillars, coffered ceilings, garden views, impeccable service), with its extensive à la carte menu.

- On a considerably more intimate scale—can this room with the velvet hangings seat as many as forty-five?—is the **Andrew Fairlie**, with its Michelin star and six-course *menu degustation*.

Time now to turn away from the cuisine in order to look at the diversions offered here as part of the astonishing tapestry that is Gleneagles. The royal and ancient game certainly gets its due—and rather more—with the three eighteens, to which can be added the Wee Course (nine short holes that provide plenty of fun for family foursomes) and the nine-hole pitch-and-putt course. Also on hand are tennis and squash courts, croquet lawns, a jogging track, a billiards parlor, and a spa (two swimming pools, gymnasium, solarium, sauna, hot tubs, Turkish steam baths, massage and beauty treatment quarters). And there is more:

- At the Jackie Stewart Shooting School, clay pigeons are launched over the heath to simulate the flights of ten different game birds (woodcock, pheasant, partridge, et al). A rustic lodge with an open-hearth fireplace is here on the moors so that marksmen will not have to rough it.

- The Mark Philips Equestrian Centre has three arenas, two of them enclosed and air-conditioned; more than thirty horses available for guests; and numerous activities ranging from dressage to polo.

- For those who have dreamed of tooling across the moors in a Land Rover, the Gleneagles Off-Road Driving School is at the ready.

- For anglers, Gleneagles maintains five beats on the River Tay (salmon and sea trout). Brown trout can be caught in local lochs. Count on the hotel's gillies to know where the fish are biting.

- The British School of Falconry at Gleneagles is an aristocratic experience with a choice. Enjoy it either on horseback (it's called Hawks and Horses) or on foot. Eight Harris hawks are housed here, and two instructors are on hand every day.

Gleneagles has everything you would expect in a great full-facilities golf resort (maybe even a few things you might not expect) and all of it in a setting of surpassing natural beauty. One final point: By most contemporary standards, Gleneagles is not a big hotel. There are 286 accommodations, including 18 suites. The madding crowd is absent. So is the attendant hassle. This is a tranquil place, all the more remarkable when you consider the abundance of diversion. At the time it opened, nearly ninety years ago, the British press saluted Gleneagles as the "palace in the glens" and the "playground of the gods." Both characterizations were fitting then, and they are apt today. Some widely traveled golfers have been tempted to trot out a Scottish phrase: *"heich abune the heick"*—"better than the best." The only way to check the validity of this appraisal is to go there and see for yourself.

The Gleneagles Hotel is not the only place to stay if you want to play its courses. Five minutes from the great resort sits the **Auchterarder House Hotel**.

Below: Gleneagles Hotel.
Right, top: the Andrew Fairlie;
bottom: a guest room.

Dating to 1832 and built on seventeen acres in the Jacobean style, it somehow manages to be stately yet welcoming, grand yet intimate. The explanation lies in the numerous fireplaces, the beautiful old paintings and oriental rugs, and the antique oak paneling. We've stayed in the spacious Maxwell Room, which has a tile-faced Victorian fireplace and captivating views over the hotel gardens to the Grampian Mountains. The cuisine is ambitious, and successfully so.

The unexceptional village of Auchterarder has several antiques shops and the Glenruthven Weaving Mill, which was the last business in Scotland to convert from steam to modern power. Weaving is demonstrated, and a shop sells locally woven products. Not ten minutes north of the village are the Strathallan Aircraft Museum (aircraft and allied equipment dating to 1930) and, rather in an opposite mode, Tullibardine Chapel, a rural fifteenth-century chapel complete and unaltered.

PERTH

One of the rewarding aspects of driving to Auchterarder from Dundee (or from Blairgowrie, Kirriemuir, or Alyth) is that Perth is squarely on your route. You will not want to bypass this city of about forty-five thousand inhabitants, which is spread pleasantly along both banks of the River Tay. Once the capital of Scotland, it is a dignified and prosperous place. Visit fifteenth-century Balhousie Castle, with its Museum of the Black Watch Regiment; St. Ninian's Cathedral, a handsome nineteenth-century Anglican church; and the Fair Maid's House, where a medieval wall may be seen and a gallery with exhibitions by Scottish artists is open daily, as is a shop selling high quality Scottish craftwork and knitwear. Speaking of commerce, there is a section in the center of town, marked by hanging flower baskets and a total absence of cars, where shopping—or window shopping—in a variety of stores, some old, some new, is most enjoyable.

Mere moments outside Perth is one of Scotland's fabled castles, Glamis. Dating to the fourteenth century and used by Shakespeare as the setting for *Macbeth,* it has turrets and battlemented parapets looking down on a late-nineteenth-century English formal garden and an Italian garden, opulent rooms with a wide range of furniture, porcelains, paintings, and tapestries, and the Grampian Mountains as its backcloth. Glamis was the childhood home of the late Queen Mother and the birthplace of the late Princess Margaret.

Far left: Doune Castle. Middle column, top: the gardens; bottom: grounds of Glamis Castle. Above: Glamis Castle. Left: Scone Palace in Perth.

ABERDEENSHIRE AND NAIRN,
THE HIGHLANDS AND DORNOCH

ROYAL ABERDEEN

I t has taken decades, but American golfers are at last finding their way to Aberdeenshire and its handful of outstanding links courses. Royal Aberdeen itself is the jewel in the crown. Here we find that rarest of combinations: a great and historic club and a great and historic links.

Royal Aberdeen is the sixth-oldest golf club in the world (Royal Blackheath, Royal Burgess, the Honourable Company of Edinburgh Golfers, at Muirfield, the Royal & Ancient, and the Bruntsfield Links Golfing Society are its predecessors). It traces its origin directly to the Society of Golfers at Aberdeen, which was formed in 1780 (and in 1783 introduced the five-minute limit on searching for a lost ball), became the Aberdeen Golf Club in 1815 (annual dues, five shillings), and in 1903, by grace of King Edward VII, was named Royal Aberdeen Golf Club.

During its first hundred years, the club played on common ground within the city. When that links became overcrowded, a lease was negotiated in 1887 on land just north of the estuary of the River Don, at Balgownie, as the links of Royal Aberdeen is sometimes known. Robert and Archie Simpson (Carnoustie brothers, Archie was at one time Royal Aberdeen's professional), Willie Park Sr., and English-born Tom Simpson all took their turn in shaping the superlative golf holes we play today.

ON THE COURSE

The very location of the teeing ground on the 1st hole can prompt jitters, for that swatch of turf happens to be tucked neatly between two large bay windows of the clubhouse's principal rooms, where fellow golfers will be on the lookout for our nervous first swing. Nonetheless, the fairway that awaits below is a generous one, the sea that lies beyond is shimmering, and the prospect of a grand day on the links will never be brighter. So we swing away on this 410-yarder and, avoiding the three bunkers at the landing area, put ourselves in position to reach the green, which, boldly undulating, sits on a rise just beyond a deep, hidden dip and is silhouetted against the sky and the sea. Can the course live up to such an overture?

The answer is promptly forthcoming. Beginning high above the beach on a lonely perch in the sand hills that is the tee of the 530-yard

2nd, the next eight holes weave their way naturally and hauntingly through a landscape of towering dunes and over pure links terrain that ranges from rippling to tumbling to billowing. All the elements are present: gorse, heather, long bents (sometimes dotted with bluebells), tightly textured turf to accommodate the game on the ground, punitive sandpits, an occasional burn, an occasional blind shot, an occasional mischievous bounce, tees atop dunes, greens in hollows, greens on plateaus, forced carries over forbidding country, and ribbons of fairway tracing their cloistered paths along dune-framed valleys.

Opposite: Royal Aberdeen, 2nd. Above: 3rd. Previous spread: Skibo Castle, 11th.

We play this first nine at Balgownie in seclusion. We also play it in awe and something close to rapture. Every hole is an unalloyed delight. The two one-shotters—the splendid 223-yard 3rd, from a top-of-the-world tee to a green far below in a natural amphitheater, and the 147-yard 8th, essentially level, the green ringed by low dunes and ten bunkers— are not easily forgotten. Nor are the two longest par 4s, which are among Scotland's best holes. On the 4th, 423 yards, the drive is launched from another of those lofty tees, with the long second shot menaced by hummocks and dips, not to mention sand at the front, left, and right of the deep, narrow green. As for the finale of this nonpareil nine, it is altogether magnificent. The tee shot on the 453-yard 9th is also fired from on high, this time down over a diagonal ridge of deep rough to an angled fairway well below that turns right. The long second—surely a fairway metal—must climb a goodly hill to gain the well-bunkered, bilevel green. From the medal tees, the outbound nine measures 3,372 yards against a par of 36.

The inbound half, only 3,060 yards but played into the prevailing wind, is routed over less thrilling terrain. The majestic dunes are gone now and with them some of the magic. But the test remains, and the last three holes are especially fine. Gorse and sand on both sides threaten the drive on the 392-yard 16th; sand alone, in five bunkers, patrols the green. Half a dozen pits defend the slightly elevated two-tier green on the 180-yard 17th.

As for the 434-yard 18th, it is one of the outstanding finishing holes in the land (its equals are at Leven, Carnoustie, Muirfield, Loch Lomond, Lossiemouth, Skibo Castle, and Kingsbarns). The platform tee enables us to assess the dangers: Sand awaits the wayward drive, as do gorse and the omnipresent thick rough grasses; a sound drive will stop in a dip. A plateau green now awaits some 200 yards away on the far side of a steep swale. Into the prevailing wind, even a well-struck shot is not likely to chase up the face of this bank. There is a much better chance that it will retreat into one of the gathering bunkers at the bottom. A splendid hole and a fitting climax to

a great links, one of the top ten courses in Scotland and the site in 2005 of Tom Watson's second victory in the Senior British Open.

Plan to have a sandwich-and-beverage lunch in the clubhouse's many-windowed lounge, with its views of the starting and finishing holes and the sea. The atmosphere is not stiff, and you will quickly sense the antiquity and distinction of this club. There are old silver and paneling, old pictures and books. Women visitors are welcome in this room, notwithstanding the presence of the charming little black-and-white clubhouse of the Aberdeen Ladies Golf Club, clearly designed in sympathy with the men's, about 150 yards away. Beside it is the 1st tee of the Silverburn eighteen, which the ladies enjoy immensely and which Donald Steel reworked in 1995 to provide a little more spine.

Above: Royal Aberdeen, 9th.
Opposite: 15th.

MURCAR

Next door—in literal truth, next door—is Murcar Golf Club. Murcar was the only club in Scotland to own a railway, the famous Murcar Buggy, by which members in the early days were transported from the Bridge of Don to the clubhouse for a penny. Its driver, one Jimmy Fiddes, could always be counted on to delay the last run back to the Bridge at night on the promise of a wee dram.

Archie Simpson walked over from his golf shop at Balgownie to lay out the Murcar holes. The 1930s saw a number of revisions by James Braid and his constructor, John Stutt. Together, the three men produced a first-rate eighteen and a very useful relief nine of 2,850 yards.

The terrain here slopes from the high ground, where the clubhouse is situated, to the shore in a terraced fashion, with the result that virtually every point of the course provides views over the water. There is much to engage the eye: south past Aberdeen's busy harbor to the Girdleness Lighthouse, east over the open sea and beyond the oil-drilling rigs to the horizon, and north to the farmlands and coastline at Cruden Bay and Peterhead. But vistas, for all their charm, are not so important as the golfing ground itself. Murcar's is excellent: tall sand hills, springy fairways that range from undulating to violently tumbling, dramatic elevation changes, gorse, heather, long and thick marram grass, and three burns crossing the links and adding substantively to the round's challenge and diversity.

Opposite: Royal Aberdeen, 17th.

The course measures 5,800 yards from the regular markers (par 69), 6,240 yards from the medal tees (par 71). The first couple of holes are unexceptional, but the 3rd, 401 yards, dives off a shelf of fairway into a long gully with a green set in a punch bowl at the far end. Overlooking this green is the elevated 10th tee at Royal Aberdeen. More than once over the years, newcomers to Murcar have been known to putt out on the 3rd hole, climb the hill to the adjacent teeing ground, and hit away, blissfully ignorant of the fact that they were now playing Balgownie.

Even when we do head in the right direction and reach Murcar's 4th tee, in the sand hills above the beach, we are amused to learn that this patch of land belongs to Royal Aberdeen and is on a sort of permanent loan to its good neighbor. In any event, here begins a run of six terrific holes. Again and again we are driving from tees high in the dunes, down into hummocky valleys, then shooting uphill to a green that is good-size,

sometimes framed by low dunes, at other times exposed, and always lightly defended by sand. One hole in this skein is unforgettable. Its name is Serpentine; Tom Doak has called it "all world," and it is 423 yards long. Launched from a hilltop tee, our drive must carry two branches of the stream that gives the hole its name. The second one crosses the fairway in the valley far below at about 190 yards. The sliced tee shot vanishes into a ravine, the hook into heavy rough. A straight and sound strike, however, sets up the opportunity to execute a full-blooded second, possibly a 5-metal, up a rising dune-framed channel to a green, bunkered right and left, at the crest of the hill. This is seaside golf at its most natural—and at its best.

The second nine at Murcar, as at Balgownie, finds us turning away from the coastal sand hills into less adventurous terrain. But the holes still sparkle, and getting our figures continues to be a task, albeit an agreeable one.

The **Marcliffe at Pitfodels** is widely viewed as the finest hotel in the Aberdeen area. A member of Small Luxury Hotels of the World, the Marcliffe is extremely comfortable, furnished partly with period pieces, and characterized by highly personalized service. There are two dining options: the informal and cheery **Conservatory** and the dressier and intimate **Invery Room**. In both cases the menu is imaginative and the cooking quite good.

Meldrum House, some twenty-five minutes west of Aberdeen, is a rambling stone manor that dates to the thirteenth century. It is filled with antiques, objets d'art, and ancestral portraits. The spacious and charming guest rooms, recently refurbished, provide lovely views over the countryside and/or the golf course. Dining is a matter of superior cuisine in a beautiful room in which you may find yourself at a fireside table. (As for the golf course, it is nine years old. Routed through wood-

lands and over meadows, it has water on eight holes, nicely contoured greens, and, on the second nine, pronounced elevation changes and panoramic views.)

Among the attractions of Aberdeen itself are the harbor, St. Andrew's Cathedral (interior with white walls and pillars in sharp contrast to the bright coloring of the coats of arms on the ceiling), and Provost Skene's House (450 years old and containing several carefully re-created period rooms). A half-hour's drive into the country will bring you to Castle Fraser and Crathes Castle, both sixteenth century and in excellent condition. The gardens at Crathes are particularly prized.

Another hour west and you reach Balmoral Castle. When the royal family is not in residence—and they are rarely there for more than four or five weeks, in summer—the public is welcome to visit and gain insight into 150 years of royal living in Deeside.

From left: downtown Aberdeen; Bridge o'Balgownie; Corgarff Castle.

CRUDEN BAY

Up the coast, some sixteen miles north of Royal Aberdeen, is Cruden Bay, one of the dozen courses in Scotland that should on no account be missed. Nor is it necessary to play so much as a stroke to confirm this imperative. You have merely to park your car on the heights beside the clubhouse and look down. Below, in all its turbulent splendor, lies one of the most awe-inspiring stretches of linksland ever dedicated to the game. Against a backdrop of North Sea whitecaps stretching away to the horizon, the sand hills rise as high as sixty feet, their shaggy slopes covered with long and throttling golden grasses. For sheer majesty of setting, no Scottish course surpasses Cruden Bay, and only two or three might claim to equal it.

The original holes were laid out by Old Tom Morris in 1899 as the main attraction of an elite resort hotel. However, the course today, while retaining much of Old Tom's basic routing and a number of his green sites, is largely the work of Tom Simpson, in conjunction with Herbert Fowler, in 1926. An English barrister turned golf architect, Simpson was rich, eccentric, dashing. He traveled from course to course in a chauffeur-driven silver Rolls-Royce, emerging from its cosseting interior to tramp the particular tract wearing an embroidered cloak and beret and carrying either a shooting stick or a riding crop. It is said that he hired Philip Mackenzie Ross (Turnberry, Portugal's Estoril, et al.) as his construction boss because Ross showed him how to mount a license plate most becomingly on the Rolls-Royce. Simpson and Fowler were also responsible for the superb St. Olaf Course, a relief nine of 2,550 yards, par 32, laid out over the same marvelous linksland as the principal eighteen.

Though the hotel fell victim to the Great Depression and the Second World War and was razed in 1952, the great course itself survived when an Aberdeen stockbroker, a Cruden Bay hotelier, and a Peterhead solicitor teamed up to buy it. The solicitor, John A. S. Glennie, went on to found the Cruden Bay Golf Club and become its first captain. One of the outstanding amateurs in northeastern Scotland between 1920 and 1960, the brilliantly analytical Glennie was the man who put Scotland's handicap system on a realistic, workable basis. He loved the game as few men do and understood it as do even fewer. My wife and I came to know John and his wife, Edda, who served as ladies' captain for several years, visiting them at both their house in Peterhead and their tiny, picture-windowed chalet above the 1st hole at Cruden Bay, where they lived from June through September. "It's a prefab," John told us. "It cost four hundred and ninety-five pounds back in 1965 and it was put up in a day. We've been using it now for twenty years. If my mathematics is correct, that comes to about twenty-five pounds a year—not at all bad for a long summer holiday."

John Glennie had a rich fund of golf stories at his fingertips, some of them about famous figures in the game. At Mougins, in the south of France, he played a round one winter with Henry Cotton, whom he had known for some time. He asked Cotton what kind of match they might make.

"We'll play even," Cotton said.

"Even it is, then," John replied, "despite the fact that you've won three Opens and I haven't struck a ball in four months."

John continued, "Cotton and I were playing what you call a nassau. Going out he beat me one down, but I had him by a hole on the inward half as we came to the eighteenth. Then he hooked his tee shot out-of-bounds and that was the match. As a matter of fact, he never did play the hole. He simply walked straight to the clubhouse."

Glennie was instrumental in bringing in as head professional, first, Eric Brown, then Harry Bannerman, to Cruden Bay. Brown ran the shop at Cruden Bay from 1963 to 1968, having made his reputation in a series of Ryder Cup Matches in the 1950s, when he won all his singles (then 36-hole contests), in turn downing Lloyd Mangrum, Jerry Barber, Tommy Bolt, and Cary Middlecoff. The Bolt match was downright hostile. The two players refused to shake hands at the conclusion, Brown taunting his vanquished foe: "You knew when the games were drawn that you never had an earthly hope of beating me." In the locker room afterward, Bolt is said to have broken a wedge in half, and he elected not to appear at the presentation ceremony.

Harry Bannerman took the Cruden Bay job in 1976, five years after his only Ryder Cup appearance, at Old Warson Country Club, in suburban

Opposite: Cruden Bay, 4th.

graciously consented when John Glennie asked him to join me for a round. I was familiar with the course, having played it three or four times since my first visit, in 1978. We both carried light bags, though we could have chosen to pull a trolley.

Of average height and a little on the heavy side, Harry smoked a cigar that day with me, just as he had fifteen years earlier in the Ryder Cup. He had those powerful forearms that almost all world-class players seem to be endowed with, and he drilled his drives—no float whatsoever to them—some 275 yards. That put him 60 yards in front of me. Rarely missing a fairway, he hit fourteen greens in regulation.

ON THE COURSE

The course was quite short for Harry (and just about right for me) at 6,370 yards, par 70. The first three holes are spirited par 4s (my companion drove the green on the blind 286-yard 3rd for a two-putt birdie), but they scarcely prepare you for what comes next: four consecutive *great* holes.

The 193-yard 4th is one of Tom Simpson's finest par 3s, as well as a selection for *The 500 World's Greatest Golf Holes*. It plays straight toward the sea (and often straight into the wind) from an elevated tee carved out of one sand hill across a deep, grassy hollow to an elevated green carved out of the facing sand hill. A bunker at the left front in the slope and a steep falloff on the right dictate the need for a well-nigh perfect stroke. The harbor of the old fishing village is visible in the distance.

The 453-yard 5th is doubly demanding. First comes a blind drive from high and deep in the dunes, sighting on the wispy top of some vague hillock. This is followed by a full-blooded metal along the valley floor to a large but ill-defined green (how far short of the putting surface *are* those two bunkers?) in a charming dell. The cloistered quality of many holes, and with it the feeling that we have the course to ourselves, is created by the massive dunes.

The 524-yard 6th, appropriately named Bluidy Burn, is a dogleg left. Once again the tee is well up in the sand hills, but this time the green, feverishly undulating, is tucked away beyond a dune and protected from the birdie seeker's aggressive second shot by a hidden little burn some 60 yards in front. Even Harry prudently chose to lay up.

As for the final hole in this extraordinary quartet, the 7th, 390 yards, commences from yet another beautifully sited tee high in the sand hills. If we somehow find the fairway with our blind drive, we make a 90-degree left turn and face uphill, where the flag beckons from beyond two

St. Louis. The United States won, 18½ to 13½. The twenty-nine-year-old Bannerman teamed with Bernard Gallacher in the foursomes on the afternoon of the first day to turn back Billy Casper and Miller Barber, 2 and 1. The next morning Bannerman and Peter Townsend bowed, 2 and 1, to Jack Nicklaus and Gene Littler in a four-ball match; then, despite a 6-under-par 65 in the afternoon, they lost a heartbreaker to Nicklaus and Palmer when Nicklaus holed a 16-footer on the home green for a birdie. On the final day (singles in both morning and afternoon), the cigar-smoking Bannerman halved with Palmer in the morning (the Scot was 2 up after 12) and beat Gardner Dickinson, 2 and 1, in the afternoon. Dickinson had never before lost in Ryder Cup competition, having won either solo or in partnership nine times.

The future looked highly promising for Bannerman, but a bad back cut short his competitive career, and a series of club jobs followed. On a gloomy but dry and relatively calm mid-November day in 1986, he

Above: Cruden Bay, 5th.
Opposite: 6th.

dunes that stand sentinel at the narrow green like the Pillars of Hercules. Four great and unforgettable holes in succession—par 3, 4, 5, 4.

Then comes the 258-yard par-4 8th, which Tom Simpson called an "outstanding jewel of a hole, mischievous, subtle, and provocative, the element of luck with the tee shot being very high." The hole is set in a confluence of sand hills, a confined territory of hilly, broken ground. The slightly elevated green, a roughly triangular upthrust sloping away sharply on the sides, confounds us; the little pitch calls for uncommon deftness. It is easier to make 5 than 3. John Glennie once holed a 1-iron here. Both of us had to accept frustrating 4s.

Well, I *think* he felt frustrated, but I can't swear to it. I could not tell from his demeanor whether he was making a birdie or a bogey. He was comfortable to be with, but quiet. He volunteered nothing. I commented that his match with Palmer at Old Warson must have been tense.

"Aye," he said, "it was that. I had him, going to the last hole. But I let him off the hook when I missed the green with my five-iron and couldn't get up and in from the heavy grass. The golf was good, but a handshake turned out to be all there was in the match."

The second nine begins at the highest point of the course. The panorama of links, rocks, sea, beach, and ruined Slains Castle is heart-

Below: Cruden Bay, 7th.
Opposite: 17th.

SCOTLAND

stopping. Ireland's Bram Stoker, of *Dracula* fame—there is no evidence that he played golf, but he came here year after year on summer holiday and regularly roamed the links—was standing on the 10th tee when he envisioned the bay, with its great promontories jutting into the North Sea itself, as the jaws of a wicked monster luring ships to destruction on the rocks.

The next three holes are good but not particularly memorable. Fourteen, 15, and 16, however, are quintessential Cruden Bay, the first two playing from tees above the beach into a very narrow neck of land squeezed by a towering gorse-clad hillside on the left and the dunes that shield the course from the sea on the right. The blind approach shot on the 372-yard 14th disappears over a direction marker into a hollow, where the long green, suggestive of a sunken garden, gathers the ball. The one-shotter 15th borders on the bizarre. On this 239-yarder we stand on an elevated tee and gaze over broken ground down a dune-framed chute. Nothing beckons. Both green and flagstick are hidden. We take it on faith that they await. As it happens, the green falls away toward the back and the well-struck shot creeps inexorably over it into the short rough. But at least you don't have to watch this take place.

The next hole, hillside to hillside and also a par 3, seems almost conventional. *Almost*. The green and its protective bunkers are concealed, but, thankfully, the flagstick is in sight.

The round concludes with a pair of exacting two-shotters. On the 428-yard 17th there is a curious mound—a sugarloaf, really—perhaps 12 feet high and rearing up in the middle of the fairway about where a solid drive finishes. Some believe that it was a burial mound for Danish invaders, who were finally driven out of Scotland when they were defeated right here on the linksland of Cruden Bay almost exactly a thousand years ago, in 1011.

The home hole, 416 yards, presents a broad fairway on two levels, boundary on the left, a burn to snare the cut shot, undulating ground ending in a diagonal ridge just short of the spacious green. We made pars, mine with a chip and a putt, Harry's when a 12-footer for birdie slipped by on the low side. He had struck the ball well but had putted indifferently. I had struck the ball as well as I know how and had putted the ball better than I know how. We had not kept a card, but I was able to account for our strokes. We each shot 73. This parity would have been of no interest to him.

We climbed the very steep slope to the modest clubhouse, since replaced by an impressive edifice with enthralling views over the links to

Peterhead, 17th.

the sea. For me, it had been one of the half-dozen rounds of a lifetime. For Harry Bannerman, it had been a way to oblige John Glennie, the man who had given him this decent job. There seemed to me to be a hint of melancholy about the Ryder Cupper, or was it simply seriousness? He left Cruden Bay a couple of months later, and I never saw him again.

I recall reading some time ago that Pete Dye had singled out five courses as his particular favorites, making no claim that they were the greatest or the toughest, just that they were the five he liked most of all: Pinehurst No. 2, Pine Valley, Portrush, Camargo (a Cincinnati course laid out by Seth Raynor), and Cruden Bay. The bedrock appeal of this Aberdeenshire links is obvious. What a wonderful time we have playing on this glorious ground, over which are routed truly natural holes—some great, some unique, some nonconformist, all invariably fun. This is links golf to dote on.

PETERHEAD

Five miles north of Cruden Bay lies prosperous (North Sea oil) Peterhead. The Peterhead Golf Club, founded in 1841, has 27 holes. Measuring not quite 6,200 yards (par 70), the principal eighteen is largely a testament to Braid. The first three holes may possess an inland feeling, but beginning with the 4th the course takes on a true seaside character. We now find ourselves in golfing country of knobby greens whipped by the wind, secluded holes framed by tall sand hills, and heaving fairways corseted by tussocky grasses. The sea pops into view every time we climb up to a tee, and if Peterhead is not filled with great holes—although the one-shotter 6th and the 460-yard par-4 15th certainly are great—it is filled with good golf. You will not regret time spent here.

In Newburgh, about twenty minutes south of Cruden Bay, is the well-regarded **Udny Arms**, a homey old inn where some of the rooms can be cramped but the cooking is outstanding. In Cruden Bay itself, the **Red House Hotel** is one favorite of golfers: small, simple, comfortable, quiet, the front bedrooms and the dining room looking directly out over the links to the sea.

Very nearly in the lee of the 4th tee is the **Kilmarnock Arms**, where Bram Stoker used to hole up. Harriet and I still smile at the memory of a short walk we took along the Water of Cruden after dinner in the Kilmarnock Arms nearly thirty years ago. Spanning the stream and leading to the bathing beach, a narrow wooden suspension bridge creaked in the wind, its coat of white paint rendering it eerily ghostlike in the moonlight. Few lights were on in the small, severe cottages—the fisher cottages, they are called—which are built hard against one another and against the sidewalk. Nor was anyone abroad on the darkened street. No boats were tethered in the snug, stone-walled harbor, but a few ill-used fishing smacks were pulled up onto the grass-overgrown quay. The wind, less powerful than during the round that afternoon, was still fresh, and as we approached the high seawall, a wave crashed against it and sent Masefield's "blown spume and flung spray" right over that sturdy barrier and down upon us. We laughed like children in a sun shower and headed back to the haven of the inn.

In the immediate environs of Cruden Bay are the roofless remains of Slains Castle, dating to 1597 and dramatically clinging to the cliff's edge, dizzyingly high above the roiling seas. Quite nearby are the Bullers of Buchan, a natural feature that finds a path tiptoeing along the rim of a sheer two-hundred-foot rock chasm, probably once a vast cave whose roof has collapsed. This is especially compelling in powerful winds, when the waves boil in through the natural stone archway.

The Maritime Heritage Museum, in Peterhead, presents the seafaring past of the people here (building wooden boats, hunting the whale, et cetera) and does so with audio-visual programs, computer touch screens, and hands-on displays. On Kinnaird Head, in Fraserburgh, is Scotland's Lighthouse Museum. Containing a collection of lighthouse artifacts from all over the land, it stands in the very shadow of Kinnaird Head Lighthouse. A museum visit includes a guided tour to the top of the lighthouse. The Lighthouse Tearoom, with its marvelous views, is ideal for lunch.

Just off the A947, some eight miles southwest of Turiff, stands Fyvie Castle. Dating back more than seven hundred years, it boasts an exceptional circular staircase (ascending through five floors), tapestries, arms, armor, paintings (Gainsborough, Raeburn, and Romney, among others), a picturesque lake, a 1903 racquet court, and a bowling alley. A shop sells mementos of your visit to what is one of the stateliest castellated mansions in Scotland.

Top: shoreline at Cruden Bay.
Above: the Udny Arms. Left:
the Bullers of Buchan.

BOAT OF GARTEN AND GRANTOWN-ON-SPEY

In the northwestern corner of the vast Cairngorms National Park, about a two-hour drive from Cruden Bay, are two of the most beautiful courses in the Highlands. Both go back more than a hundred years.

The River Spey runs through the village of Boat of Garten, where a six-hole course opened in 1898. Three holes had been added by 1910, and the course remained a nine-holer until 1930, when Braid laid out a second nine and revised the first nine.

The setting for the golf holes is exquisite, on the edge of the Abernethy Forest. Almost without exception, the fairways are tree framed but not claustrophobically so. The silver of birch, the deep green of pine, and the royal purple of heather combine to delight us at every turn. Deer are often to be spotted in the thickets, and the osprey wings overhead on occasion. In the distance are the peaks of the Cairngorms, snow-capped for nine months of the year.

ON THE BOAT OF GARTEN COURSE

Curiously, the terrain we trod is linkslike: undulating, rumpled. Perhaps we can attribute it to glaciers. In any event, this extraordinary topography gives the Boat, as it is generally called, considerable character. And when coupled with the hills themselves, the result is a veritable dipsy doodle of a layout, with uphill lies, downhill lies, hanging lies, awkward stances, and the occasional blind shot and attendant bell ringing (the "all clear" sound).

The course measures 5,876 yards from the back tees; par is 70. Among the more memorable holes are the 189-yard opener, which, with a boundary tight on the right, drifts downhill, the shot all but funneled into sand at the left front; and the 437-yard closer (the best and toughest hole on the course) bending right, the long second shot uphill to a plateau green.

The course has an amusing distraction, the bordering railway line. Several times during the round, the Strathspey Steam Railway train (featured in *Monarch of the Glen* on PBS) may hoot and chug along beside us.

ON THE GRANTOWN-ON-SPEY COURSE

Ten minutes up the road from Boat of Garten is Grantown-on-Spey, another place that owes its name to the fetching river. Just a block or two off the wide and decorous tree-lined main street is the Grantown-on-Spey Golf Club, founded in 1890. It is little changed since 1910, when Musselburgh's Willie Park Sr., four-time Open champion, extended the course to 18 holes.

This is another very short course—5, 710 yards, par 70. Half a dozen par 4s are under 300 yards; birdie opportunities abound. Bunkering is

Opposite: Boat of Garten, 17th. Above: 18th.

Grantown-on-Spey, 12th.

generally light, and the cross bunkers on 2, 3, and 5 give the course an endearingly old-fashioned feel. Water in the form of burns pops up on five holes, and out-of-bounds threatens frequently.

Holes 7 through 12, routed through moderately hilly woodland, provide the most interest. Bunkers seal off the front of the green on the excellent 380-yard downhill 7th; the 161-yard 8th, steeply uphill, has a playing value of 175 yards; the 11th, measuring 190 yards and playing 210, is another stout uphill shot. And the superb 12th, 413 yards long and the best hole on the course, begins on a mildly elevated tee, then calls for a long second shot, with the heather tight left and right, over a crest to a hidden green.

If Grantown is not quite up to the level of the Boat, it is nevertheless agreeable holiday golf in a beautiful setting backdropped by both the Cairngorm Mountains and the heather-clad Cromdale Hills.

A three-minute walk from the golf club in Boat of Garten is the **Boat Hotel**, a four-star facility whose public spaces, with their highly polished hardwood floors, oriental rugs, and marble fireplaces, have style and warmth. The guest rooms are comfortably traditional, and several of them afford beguiling views over the Victorian railway station to the golf course and the mountains. The hotel's **Capercaillie Restaurant** has a smartly contemporary ambience that is rather in keeping with the cuisine.

Two miles outside the village, on the B970, is a non-golf attraction you may want to take in. The Auchgourish Gardens and Arboretum is full of uncommon and beautiful plants (Himalayan, Chinese, Japanese) as well as rockeries with Alpine flowers and heather beds. Rare white Highland cattle are bred here.

On the northern outskirts of Grantown-on-Spey is Castle Grant, which dates to the fifteenth century and includes eighteenth-century additions by Robert and John Adam. There are a number of Adam rooms with carved plaster decoration in the neoclassical style.

Two moderately priced hotels near Grantown should be mentioned:

- At Dulnain Bridge is **Auchendean Lodge**, built in the Edwardian era. Tastefully furnished, it offers log fires, food with flair, a good wine cellar, and an even better selection of malt whiskies.
- At Ballindalloch is **Delnashaugh Inn**, comfortable and unpretentious. The decor calls up Laura Ashley; the cooking is simple and satisfying.

Ballindalloch is also the location of the Glenfarclas Distillery. After a guided tour, you are invited to enjoy a dram of single-malt whiskey. A number of other distilleries are also within the Cairngorms National Park and make up the famous Whisky Trail. Among those that welcome visitors are Cardhu, Glenlivet, Glenfiddich, Dalwhinnie, and Royal Lochnagar.

Far left: the Spey River. From top: near Loch Ness; the Strathspey Railroad; inside the Boat Hotel.

NAIRN AND MORAY

L

ess than an hour's drive west on the A96 from Elgin brings us to the family seaside resort of Nairn, with its two eighteens: the championship course at the Nairn Golf Club and the Nairn Dunbar layout. The very word *family* reminds me that our first visit to Nairn, thirty-five years ago, was *en famille*—three children and our elder son's high school sweetheart. We had driven up from St. Andrews on Saturday, spending the night at the Huntly Castle Hotel, some forty miles from Nairn. At church the next morning, the pastor announced the banns of marriage for a couple, pointing out that the bride was, of course, known to the entire parish, since she lived here in Huntly. But the groom, from a village in the next valley, was rather an unknown quantity. At first the pastor seemed inclined to provide some details about the young man, particularly concerning his family. Then he threw up his hands, saying, "Well, if I'm not mistaken, none of you know him. But you may take my word for it, he's a fine lad!"

ON THE NAIRN GOLF CLUB COURSE

If there is one course in Scotland that the word *seaside* ought instantly to call up, surely it is the links of the Nairn Golf Club. For here it is entirely possible to slice onto the beach six times in the first seven holes—and, with any luck on the lies, still salvage a couple of pars.

The club was founded in 1887, and it was Royal Aberdeen's Archie Simpson who laid out the course. Old Tom Morris and James Braid each had a hand in revising the Simpson design, with Braid having the last word, in 1926.

The important Scottish championships, professional as well as amateur, have long taken their turns at Nairn, but it was not until 1994 that the British Amateur came here. Five years later, so did the Walker Cup. Great Britain and Ireland, down 7–5 at the end of the first day, surged back in both foursomes and singles, 10–2, on the second day to humble the United States 15–9. Future PGA Tour players who competed were Luke Donald and Paul Casey (for the winning side), Jonathan Byrd, Matt Kuchar, David Gossett, and Bryce Molder.

Visitors are likely to tackle the course at about 6,400 yards; par is 71. This wholly natural links is a lovely walk. The waters of the Moray Firth are always in view, and the dappling effect of sunlight and shadow on the Black Isle, not to mention the beauty of the distant peaks about Strath Conan, makes the round a nonstop aesthetic treat.

The firm and often fast fairways bring even the longest two-shotters within reach. The greens, silken and true, are not difficult to read. On the face of it, we ought to be able to play to our handicap. Then, along about the 6th or the 7th, it becomes clear that we are not getting our figures. Why? For one thing, Nairn is a serious examination in driving. The narrow fairways, undulating, hummocky, and given to the occasional capricious bounce, are hemmed in by heather and gorse. What's more, the approach

Opposite: Nairn, 4th.
Above: 16th.

ON THE NAIRN DUNBAR COURSE

At the opposite (east) end of town is the Nairn Dunbar Golf Club, founded in 1899. Measuring 6,300 yards from the regular markers, this par-72 layout has undulating fairways, gorse, and the occasional elevated tee and plateau green. The first 12 holes are quite satisfying; they provide challenge and a true links feeling. Unfortunately, the next 5 are meadowy and prosaic. Then the vigorous 18th, a short par 5 over heaving ground and with an astonishing rollercoaster green, reminds us all too tellingly of the course's early quality.

ON THE FORTROSE AND ROSEMARKIE COURSE

Forty-five minutes north of Nairn lies the Black Isle's Chanonry Point. Here awaits the short (5,858 yards) but stimulating links of the Fortrose and Rosemarkie Golf Club. Braid—who else?—in the 1930s laid out the golf holes that we play here today. As Malcolm Campbell tells us in *The Scottish Golf Book,* Braid "was able to squeeze 18 holes onto a peninsula that is little more than 500 yards wide at its start and tapers to around 150 yards at the lighthouse end." The wind constantly beleaguers us out on this exposed spit of land, and the sea threatens on 7 holes.

A delightful footnote: Across the water from Fortrose and Rosemarkie lies Fort George. Early in the twentieth century, the club extended honorary membership to the soldiers, among whom was Bandmaster Rickets, who regularly played with his colonel. One day during a round on the links, the bandmaster heard another golfer whistle from an adjacent hole to attract the colonel's attention. Rickets committed the musical notes to memory and later used them in the opening bar of a march he wrote, which he named "Colonel Bogey." It is that same composition that became the jaunty theme music for the Academy Award–winning film *Bridge on the River Kwai,* in which Alec Guiness played the colonel.

CASTLE STUART GOLF LINKS

Nine miles from Nairn and on the Moray Firth, the key figures in the creation of two of Fife's outstanding newer courses, Mark Parsinen (Kingsbarns) and Gil Hanse (Craighead) have teamed up to design and build a new eighteen called Castle Stuart Golf Links. The holes are under construction as this book goes to press, some routed over linksland, others over much higher ground that was formerly cropland. The course will look, feel, and play like a true links, and open in 2008.

shots—to greens that are intriguingly angled or hidden behind dunes (as on the 4th, a wonderful 145-yarder played out to sea) or on troubling plateaus or beyond seemingly innocent little crests—are difficult to judge, even more difficult to hold.

A number of holes are easy to remember, among them the clever 326-yard 8th, where the crowned green wants to shunt off all but the most adeptly struck pitch; the 206-yard 14th, played from on high (the sea view is mesmerizing) down to a green with a deep cleft in it; and the 16th, 417 yards, where a teasing burn just short of the green makes us grateful for the breeze at our back.

But perhaps no hole better typifies the challenge of Nairn than the 337-yard 5th. Here the drive must be fired over the edge of the beach, a pesky Braid bunker awaits in the left side of the fairway precisely where we would choose to land the ball in playing safely away from the water, and the green perches mockingly atop a little plateau. This hole was chosen for inclusion in *The 500 World's Greatest Golf Holes.*

Lunch or a drink in the impressive clubhouse, its broad windows framing glorious views over the Moray Firth to the Black Isle and Cromarty, is not to be missed.

Above: Nairn, 6th.
Opposite: 5th.

MORAY

There are two signs at the 9th tee of the Moray Golf Club's Old Course, in Lossiemouth, an hour east of Nairn. Both get our attention. One, in white letters on a red ground, reads: BEWARE SUDDEN AIRCRAFT NOISE. The other, in red letters on a white ground, reads: BEWARE OF GOLF BALLS FROM THE RIGHT. So, you may wonder, is it worth our life to play this classic links on the Moray Firth, about an hour and a half northeast of Grantown? Nonsense. It's true that the 9th on the Old Course crisscrosses with the 4th on the New Course, calling for alertness and courtesy. And it is equally true that the shrieking jet engines of Jaguar and Tornado fighter bombers from nearby RAF Lossiemouth can terrify the unwary. Please dismiss these distractions. For the game at Lossiemouth is played over rippling and heaving sand-based terrain; and the greens are adroitly sited on low plateaus or in pretty dells or atop teasing ridges; the fairways, burnished in high season (this is one of the driest and sunniest parts of Scotland), play firm and fast, often fiery fast. Old Tom Morris came up from St. Andrews in 1889 to lay out the course, and it is little changed to this day.

ON THE OLD AND NEW COURSES

The regular markers add up to 6,300 yards, with a par of 71. There are 110 bunkers, most of them small. Gorse is plentiful, heather of less concern. Among the outstanding holes are the 3rd, 391 yards, bending right through the gorse and then making a short, steep ascent to a plateau green; the 400-yard 11th, the second shot aimed dead at Covesea Lighthouse, a stream crossing the fairway 50 yards short of the green; the 14th, 398 yards, playing straight toward the sea all the way, the green itself cheek by jowl with the golden beach. Then there is the unforgettable 18th, one of the great finishing holes in Scottish golf: 406 yards long, out-of-bounds down the right, five bunkers along the left, the second shot having to climb over exceedingly restless terrain to reach a deep, narrow green set in a natural amphitheater and defended at the front left by a pair of hellish pits.

As is the case with the Old Course at St. Andrews, Moray's Old Course starts and finishes neatly in town.

It was in 1976 that the New Course, designed by Henry Cotton, opened. Though only 6,000 yards at full stretch, with a par of 69, it has six par 4s over the 400-yard mark. A day at Lossiemouth that begins with a game on the Old, followed by lunch in the sturdy granite clubhouse on the high ground, and then a game on the New is a day to be remembered with affection.

ELGIN

Fifteen minutes inland from Lossiemouth lies the Elgin Golf Club, with its rolling moorland layout and its share of pine, silver birch, and gorse. We are struck at once by the tranquillity of the setting. A couple of rather ordinary short two-shotters notwithstanding, this is a worthy test, nowhere better exemplified than by three par 4s late in the round: the 439-yard 14th, which, uphill all the way, plays more like 480 yards; the downhill 410-yard 16th, both shots blind; and the 18th, 429 yards, the long second shot having to gain an elevated and well-bunkered green below the clubhouse windows.

Opposite: Moray Old Course, 18th. Above: 2nd.

Just across the road from the Moray Golf Club stands the **Stotfield Hotel**, which has been welcoming golfers for the biggest part of a century. Not all rooms are spacious, but some of the larger accommodations enjoy beautiful views over the links and the Moray Firth to the hills of Sutherland. The cooking features the chef's choice of local produce, with the emphasis on fish.

In Elgin, the **Mansion House Hotel**, overlooking the River Lossie, has comfortable guest rooms, good food, and an indoor swimming pool.

Two of the best country-house hotels in Scotland are in the Nairn area. **Culloden House**, a strikingly symmetrical Georgian mansion built in 1788 on forty acres, may be Scotland's single most elegant great house. Every detail of its interior is exquisite, with many one-of-a-kind period pieces, an astounding collection of crystal chandeliers, splendid fabrics at the long windows of the high-ceilinged rooms, and, above all, beautiful Adam fireplaces and ornately carved plasterwork. The guest rooms, unusually spacious, are appointed to the highest standard, some of them with four-poster beds and fireplaces. And from the kitchen comes a parade of marvelous dishes—for example, marinated scallops wrapped in smoked salmon and a phyllo pastry set on a lemon-cream butter; cutlets of Highland lamb topped with black pudding and peaches, and served on a Rosemary jus; white chocolate crème brûlée with passionfruit sorbet.

Boath House, another graceful Georgian mansion, is set on twenty acres of lawns, woodlands, and water. A suspended spiral staircase leads up to the guest rooms, which are surprisingly—and by no means luxuriously—decorated. Dining, solely by candlelight, is a memorable experience. A typical five-course *table d'hôte* dinner: roasted red pepper and plum tomato soup with basil oil; foie gras and chicken liver pâté with an apple and sultana relish; seared medallions of venison on celeriac purée; Howgate brie with an apple and cashew nut salad; and, for dessert, rum *panna cotta* with black currants.

A couple of sister hotels that cater to golfers and to families are within a short walk of the 1st tee at Nairn Golf Club. The **Golf View** has 48 rooms, more than half of them with views of the Moray Firth. Dining in the glass-walled conservatory, which all but hangs over the sea, is a particular pleasure. The castlelike **Newton**, on twenty-one acres of parkland and gardens, provides public rooms and guest accommodations that are smarter

From left: the Golf View Hotel, outside and in-; Culloden House; Inverness.

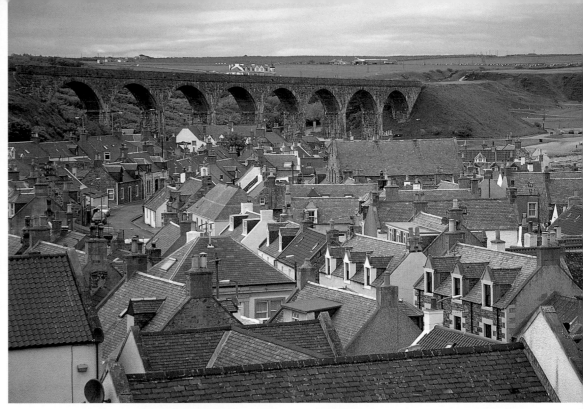

and more luxurious than those of the Golf View. And **Chaplin's Restaurant** here, named for Charlie, who used to bring his family to Nairn for summer holidays, is Manhattan chic in both ambience and menu.

There is plenty to see and do within an hour of Nairn, which itself boasts two extensive beaches, not to mention a seafront promenade (a boardwalk without the boards) and a cozy harbor:

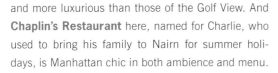

- Inverness, divided by the River Ness (the fabled loch is about twenty miles south of the city), makes for a half-day's pleasant outing.
- Cawdor Castle, scene of Duncan's murder in *Macbeth,* is a medieval fortress with beautiful gardens.
- Seventeenth-century Brodie Castle contains carved plasterwork and French furniture, plus a good collection of paintings (seventeenth-century Dutch, eighteenth-century English, French Impressionists).
- Fort George is the ranking example in Britain of Hanoverian military architecture. A polygon with six bastions, the fort, which once housed twenty-five hundred men, today contains the regimental museum of the Queen's Own Highlanders.
- The area's principal sightseeing attraction is Culloden Battlefield, the site of the last land battle to be fought in Britain (1746), marking the end of Bonnie Prince Charlie's doomed cause.

Top row, from left: Lossiemouth dunes; church in Inverness; the town of Cullen. Middle row: Pluscarden Abbey; Boath House guest room; Boath House. Bottom: Cawdor Castle.

SKIBO CASTLE

As nonmembers of the Carnegie Club at Skibo Castle, you and your companion are welcome to visit this private enclave on seven thousand acres *once* in order to, as it were, test the waters. The per diem tariff for the two of you as this book goes to press is £800 ($1,525), which covers luxurious accommodations in either the castle itself or one of the original lodges; breakfast, luncheon (always at the golf clubhouse), afternoon tea, cocktails, and dinner; all club wines and spirits; as much golf as you can handle (no starting times on the championship-standard links course or the nine-hole parkland course); salmon and trout fishing; canoeing; clay-target shooting and target-pistol shooting; tennis, archery, croquet, and snooker; mountain biking; gymnasium, sauna, and steam rooms; daily falconry display; and swimming in what may well be Britain's oldest indoor pool, a heated marble pool that is the centerpiece of an enchanting glass-roofed pavilion.

A Scot who had emigrated to America when he was thirteen, Andrew Carnegie in 1898—the "Steel King" was now sixty-two and rich beyond the dreams of avarice—bought Skibo, a castle fortress near Dornoch, dating to the twelfth century, that had evolved into a Gothic mansion. He transformed it into a noble rose-tinted baronial castle that would become a haven of peace and tranquillity for him and his wife and their only child Margaret. There are more than two hundred rooms, many of them opulently decorated so that guests such as King Edward VII, Rudyard Kipling, Ignacy Paderewski (the old Bechstein grand piano that he played is in the drawing room for you to play today), Lloyd George, Henry Gladstone, and assorted Rockefellers would feel at home.

In 1899 Carnegie asked John Sutherland, secretary at Dornoch, to lay out nine holes for him and his guests. (Carnegie once said, "Golf is an indispensable adjunct to high civilization," and heaven knows that Skibo was—and is—nothing if not highly civilized.) The Sutherland nine was allowed to go to seed many years ago.

It was in 1990 that Peter de Savary, a visionary English entrepreneur, acquired Skibo for the establishment of the Carnegie Club ("international membership limited by invitation"). He commissioned Donald Steel to

lay out an eighteen. The setting is sublime. The waters of the Dornoch Firth, the River Evelix, and Loch Evelix provide a perfect framework for this contemporary links. The great forests and hills of this corner of the Highlands stretch away as far as the eye can see.

ON THE COURSE

The course can be played as short as 5,540 yards, as long as 6,700; par is 71. A pair of solid two-shotters gets the round under way nicely, the 2nd hole doglegging sharply right, with the shot to the green semiblind. We note that the bunkers are classically links type: generally pot shape and with steep, revetted faces.

At the great 150-yard 3rd, we play from the top of one sand hill across a forbidding rough-clad hollow to the top of another sand hill. There is no margin for error. The same can be said of the 4th (angled,

Opposite: Skibo Castle, 17th.
Above: 4th.

humpy fairway shedding drive into rough or gorse), the 5th (sea on the right awaiting the errant drive and second shot), and the 6th (a 183-yarder in the dunes with a large, deep pit at the left front of the green).

Loch Evelix is put to good use on the par-4 8th and 13th, tempting us on both to save some much needed yardage by carrying a corner of the water. The 545-yard 12th and 550-yard 14th are husky tests, with sand on the 14th menacing all three swings.

The finishing run is top-notch. On the 186-yard 15th, the right side of the green is no more than a short drop from a tidal inlet. On the 16th, 421 yards, the brave drive out to the right, imperiled by a falloff down to the 18th fairway, is rewarded with an open shot to a green set among low dunes. The last two holes are thrillers. On the seductive 280-yard par-4 17th, the green, from a tee set intoxicatingly high above the Firth, is drivable for some—pro-

viding they are willing to flirt with the sea, which is discomfitingly close along the left, and providing they are able to carry the deep bunkers in the heart of the fairway 30 yards short of the green. On the 545-yard 18th, a long forced carry over a corner of the bay is called for to get the ball in play. The fairway then swings vigorously left as it skirts the shore en route to a slightly raised green on a spit of land, with water just left and beyond. A hidden pot bunker greenside at the right will snare the too safe approach. This is a grand finale, where the big basher can again gamble, this time on both shots, in the hope of getting home in 2.

In 1996 Steel laid out a beguiling nine-hole parkland course that can be tackled as either a par-3 layout (the holes range from 145 to 210 yards) or as a mix of par 3s, 4s, and 5s (2,825 yards). This diverting course wends its way over rolling terrain, through copses, and around ponds and marshes.

Skibo Castle, 18th.

Golf at the Carnegie Club, whether on the links or in the park, is a joy. But it is only a part of the Skibo story. The chief attraction here is an elusive lifestyle, at once genteel and luxurious, that has more in common with the Edwardian Age, with 1906, than with 2006. Peter de Savary was at pains to preserve the distinctive quality of Andrew Carnegie's Highland paradise.

Surely the same will be true of de Savary's successor, Ellis Short, of Dallas, the current owner, and Peter Crome, the club's urbane managing director (formerly in charge at St. Andrews's Old Course Hotel and then Hampshire's acclaimed Chewton Glen Country House

on the English Channel). They well realize what is irreplaceable here: the ambience of an Andrew Carnegie house party a hundred years ago. As a result, your sumptuous accommodation may well be the Ospis room, where not only the bedroom (26 feet by 16 feet) has a period fireplace but so does the bathroom (26 feet by 10 feet). And your pink gin during cocktails in the drawing room is served by a white-coated butler who will never again have to be told what you are drinking. And the heavy silk draperies and the oriental rugs and the priceless wall coverings (Spanish tooled leather in one area) and the antique furniture and the gilt-framed oil

paintings that graced this house while the Carnegies occupied it, in many instances, still grace it today. And when, at 8 P.M. sharp, a bagpiper leads the procession melodically from the drawing room into "Mr. Carnegie's Dining Room" (oak paneled, the blaze from the great hearth and the flames from the great candelabra casting a glow upon the massive dark-stained oak furniture) and each regal detail, beginning with that evening's club host at the head of the table leading everyone in a toast "to Andrew," calls up all the latent Anglophilia within you, then you know, irrefutably, that this is *the* place. And the golf, as excellent as it is, seems almost incidental.

ROYAL DORNOCH

Not ten minutes up the road from Skibo Castle lies Royal Dornoch, ranked fifteenth in the world by *Golf Magazine*. Though golf—or some very rudimentary form of it—has been played at Dornoch for nearly four hundred years, the club was not founded till 1877. John Sutherland, who guided its affairs for almost sixty years after being appointed secretary in 1883, played a key role in fashioning many holes. So did Old Tom Morris. Others to lend a hand were five-time Open champion J. H. Taylor; Donald Ross, the club's professional and greenkeeper in the 1890s; George Duncan, principal architect of Stonehaven; and, in contemporary times, Donald Steel.

ON THE CHAMPIONSHIP COURSE

The course measures 6,732 yards from the championship tees, 6,514 from the medal tees, and 6,229 from the regular markers; par is 70. Since neither the par 5s (496 and 506 yards) nor the one-shotters (177, 163, 147, and 166 yards) call for strong hitting, that requirement must be left to the par 4s. In fact, from the regular tees, eight of the twelve extend beyond 400 yards. And in a number of instances the long approach called for is to a plateau green, occasionally crowned and with sharp and shaven falloffs on the sides. Deft little pitches or chips or scuttles with the putter from somewhere off the green are at the heart of good scoring here. No hole is without challenge or charm; many holes possess both.

The round opens with a short and inviting par 4 to get us going in a positive frame of mind, followed by a tough 177-yarder where the modestly raised and tightly bunkered green tends to shed all but the precisely struck shot. One of the arresting moments in golf comes next: After a brief walk on a path through a shoulder-high tract of gorse, we break into the clear. From the high 3rd tee a majestic vista stretches away hole after hole, seemingly limitless, sea and hills and linksland. The world has been left behind, and as we play on, there is this strong sensation of heading toward land's end. The remoteness is total. We feel that we may outrun the district of Sutherland and penetrate to the very wilds of Caithness on this journey over an ancient landscape where so little is owed to the hand of man.

In *The Golf Courses of the British Isles*, Bernard Darwin wrote: "Those who laid out the older links did not . . . think a vast deal about the good or bad length of their holes. They saw a plateau which nature had clearly intended for a green and another plateau at some distance off which had the appearance of a tee, and there was the hole ready made for them. . . . People as a rule took the holes as they found them and were not forever searching for the perfect 'test of golf.'" We are consistently struck by such a wonderful sense of naturalness as we make our way around Royal Dornoch. Everything simply looks as if it has been this way for centuries.

The 3rd (414 yards), 4th (427 yards), and 5th (354 yards) make up a particularly engaging sequence. Two are played from high tees. There is

Opposite: Royal Dornoch, 4th. Above: 5th.

room on all three to let fly on the drive, but, unless our ball finds the right spot in the landing area, the second shot to the plateau green, sited a bit above us, will be very exacting. It is possible on the 3rd and 4th, where the front is open, to chase our long second shot up onto the putting surface. But in the case of the shortish 5th, with its deep green angled to the approach shot and sand blockading the direct access, the only way on is up and on.

Much the same imperative greets us on the 163-yard knob-to-knob 6th, with sand on the left and the right front, a steep falloff on the right, and a stingy target. In sum, a classic hole that was named one of the 500 *World's Greatest.*

Crowned greens, for which Donald Ross is alleged to have developed a penchant at Dornoch and which find their fullest flower on Pinehurst No. 2, are actually not all that common at Dornoch. Pete Dye, who played Pinehurst No. 2 frequently and got to know Ross, says: "The Pinehurst No. 2 greens were rough Bermuda grass, so they kept top-dressing them to make them smoother. That's how the greens became crowned.

Over the years all that sand-based top dressing built up the middle of the green. Everybody thinks Mr. Ross intended to crown the greens, but he didn't. Many times he told me he was going to cut the crowns off. But he died before he could do it. And the world has been copying the crowns he would have cut off had he lived."

The holes coming in are equally fine. Both par 3s are ringed with sand, the beach-side 10th fully exposed to the wind, the 13th somewhat sheltered in the dunes. But it is the celebrated 14th, called Foxy, that is unforgettable. Completely natural—there is not a bunker anywhere in its 445 yards—the hole breaks left in the tee-shot landing area. Then, after proceeding straight ahead for almost 200 yards, it jogs right, the fairway soon to rise abruptly to chest level and to a wide but shallow green. Both changes of direction on what is a double dogleg are prompted by a long, formidable dune jutting in from the right and covered with bushes and rough grasses. This hole is the very definition of "shot values": The drive must be strong and perfectly drawn; the second shot, perhaps a 5-metal,

Above, left: Royal Dornoch, 8th; right: 10th. Opposite: 14th.

ON THE STRUIE COURSE

The championship course is not all the golf to be had at Dornoch. The Struie Course was sweepingly revised in 2002. At nearly 6,300 yards and with newly acquired links terrain for holes 9 through 13, there are good holes here, but we find ourselves wishing for more dash. Perhaps this should be blamed mainly on the absence of elevation change (15 of the 18 holes are dead level) and of feature.

ON THE TAIN COURSE

South on the A9 some ten miles is the royal burgh of Tain and the Tain Golf Club. From the medal tees the course measures 6,207 yards, par is 70. By and large, the undulating fairways on this essentially level tract are spacious, but if we miss them we often find ourselves in dense growths of gorse (lost ball or unplayable lie). Forced carries over heather are also an aspect of the driving. The Tain River makes its bow just short of the green on the 2nd but then is gone until the final three holes. We must carry this broad and sinuous stream twice on the 213-yard 17th and, having done so, also stay clear of it as it edges back toward the right side of the green.

must be high and softly faded. If our long second shot should fail even by inches to gain the table-top green, we are left with a devilishly tricky little pitch or chip—or a rap with a putter for those whose nerves are questionable. In *The 500 World's Greatest Golf Holes,* the 14th has been named one of the top one hundred.

A number of the game's leading players—Tom Watson, Greg Norman, Fred Couples, Nick Faldo, Ben Crenshaw—have made it a point to get to Dornoch. Watson described his three rounds during a twenty-four-hour stay as "the most fun I ever had playing golf." And Crenshaw, in Scotland to compete in the British Open at Muirfield, played a couple of practice rounds there, then seized the opportunity to fly up to Dornoch. When he returned, Keith Mackenzie, then secretary of the R&A, asked him how he enjoyed it. "Let me put it this way," Crenshaw replied. "I nearly didn't come back."

Royal Dornoch, 17th.

CHERISH THE DAY

- Succumb to the spell of **Royal Dornoch**, fifteenth in the world in the 2005 rankings: its compelling golf shots and its heart-stopping scenery.

- Have lunch in the bright and cheery **clubhouse bar**, virtually hanging over the 1st tee.

- Drive twenty-five minutes north on the A9 for the afternoon game at **Brora**, one of Scotland's unheralded yet unforgettable jewels.

- Back in Dornoch, pay homage to **Donald Ross at No. 3 St. Gilbert Street**, the simple row house—still a private residence—where he was born and reared.

- Dine at **Burghfield House**, where the extraordinary cooking has a distinctly Scottish flavor.

- Stay at the **Royal Golf Hotel**, less than 75 yards from the 1st tee at Royal Dornoch.

I can recommend three hotels and one guest house in Dornoch:

- If you stay at the four-star **Royal Golf Hotel**, you will be a mere pitching wedge from the 1st tee. The hotel has style and personality. Bedrooms (several are small) are furnished in a blend of traditional and contemporary. Some overlook the links. Diners can choose between the informal conservatory and the main restaurant. Both provide carefully prepared local game, seafood, beef, and lamb.

- The atmospheric **Dornoch Castle Hotel**, on the town square, also offers thoughtfully appointed guest rooms, some of which have been returned to their original granite walls, dark oak paneling, and high ceilings. Light meals are available in the bar throughout the day; and there is an extensive à la carte menu for dinner.

- On five acres of attractive gardens stands **Burghfield House**, built more than a hundred years ago. Antiques, oil paintings, open fires, and fresh flowers all contribute to the hospitable feel. The guest rooms are comfortable, and the cooking has a distinct Scottish emphasis (for instance, chicken stuffed with haggis in a whiskey and onion sauce).

- On the aristocratic square in the very shadow of the cathedral is a charming B&B called **Trevose Guest House**. All five guest rooms are appealing, as are the gardens ringing the house. Trevose House was an ideal spot for watching the Madonna–Guy Ritchie nuptials unfold. The ceremony itself (by invitation only) took place in the cathedral, which dates to 1225; the reception was held at Skibo Castle, where the happy couple and their friends were lodged. But the square was the place to see the notables, and paparazzi from tabloids all over the world were on hand to record the event for their respective rags. This triggered a windfall for the natives. In order to gain needed vantage points, the photographers and journalists had to buy stepladders locally. When the ceremony was over, these representatives of the Fourth Estate, rushing now to get back to the Inverness airport, abandoned their newly bought ladders. The townspeople, in the best frugal Scots tradition, claimed them and headed smugly back to their homes, certain that this was indeed *the* wedding of the new millennium.

Across the square from the cathedral, beyond the tall shade trees, bulks what remains of the once imposing Castle of the Bishops, a stone tower that is now part of the Castle Hotel. Next door, in the medieval jail, is the crafts center. And just off the square, behind the cathedral, stands the simple row house on St. Gilbert Street, No. 3, where Dornoch's most renowned son, Donald Ross, and his younger brother, Alex, who won the 1907 U.S. Open, were born and reared. Take notice of the three dormer windows in the roof. They were installed when Donald sent money home to his mother in 1900, after his first year in America, money she used to add two bedrooms upstairs under the eaves.

Dornoch Cathedral.

BRORA

BRORA

S urely Dornoch, on the same latitude as Juneau, Alaska, ought to be far enough north to spell the end of the line for even the most venturesome golfer. It ought to be, but it isn't. Less than twenty miles farther up the A9 lies the village of Brora, home of an irresistible links. At only 6,119 yards and with a par of 69, it is unlikely to qualify as a great course. That said, it is packed with shot-making demands over as rewarding an expanse of golfing duneland—every natural contour from moderate wrinkling to fantastic billowing—as any golfer could yearn for. With the land everlastingly in motion, stances and lies can be awkward, and flexibility in setup and swing is called for from time to time.

The club was founded in 1891, and nine basic holes were laid out by the Committee. The first golf house was a tiny tin hut that measured 5 feet 4 inches across. A year later the membership was presented with plans for a new and more ambitious clubhouse, 12 feet by 10 feet. These specifications were promptly amended to 15 feet by 11 feet, which, one suspects, allowed for four golfers to occupy it simultaneously, at least if they remained standing. In keeping with what was a continuing expansionist bent, John Sutherland came over from Dornoch to enlarge the links to eighteen holes. Alterations were subsequently effected by Sutherland and J. H. Taylor. Then, in 1924, Braid paid two visits to the club, one in January and one in December. The result was substantive change.

ON THE COURSE

This is as fine an example of James Braid's work at the sea as we are likely to find today. The course was built on a relatively narrow stretch of linksland just two holes wide, the sea on our right all the way out and in view on almost every hole. Cattle regularly graze the links, and sheep sometimes do. A club promotional flyer may exaggerate the case, but it is probably close to the truth: "Eighteen greens as the glacier left them; swings and borrows to gladden the heart." There is gorse but no heather. And the rough is light, which makes the course enjoyable for the high handicapper.

The holes range from good to great, with water in the form of sinuous burns intruding on five holes. The two best holes on the first nine are,

as it happens, also the two hardest, both par 4s. At the 447-yard 3rd, the very long second shot, fired over a ridge as well as hummocky ground, must be held skillfully up to the left because the ground slopes away toward the sea on the right. At the 428-yard 5th, a burn must be crossed on the second shot, and the partially concealed green is defended at the right front by a big sand hill cloaked in long rough grasses. A ravine behind the green discourages the bold second shot. Waves crashing on the rocks behind the green of the 162-yard 9th are an exhilarating distraction.

Now we turn about and head for home, one first-class hole after another, with the final four not likely to improve our score. The fairway on the 430-yard 15th—a blind drive over a high ridge, a boundary edging in unseen on the right, gorse tight on the left—is elusive on what is a strong and original hole. At the 16th, 345 yards, the climb to the putting surface is so steep that the hole plays 385, and the rough hollow, far below green level on the left, is cruelly cautionary.

Opposite: Brora, 17th. Above: 3rd.

Golspie, 12th.

The 17th, 438 yards, is one of Scotland's best par 4s, and it was Braid's favorite at Brora. It is named Tarbatness for the lighthouse down the coast that signals the optimum line of play. Braid designed the hole for two drawn shots, the first being the drive from a moderately elevated tee over rough ground into the neck of the fairway, and the second, also from right to left, to an adroitly bunkered green in a little hollow on the far hillside. It is all there before us and it is all quite splendid, another indisputably great hole requiring two excellent swings.

The final hole is 201 yards long, tending uphill all the way. The depression in the forepart of the green, certainly meant to summon the Valley of Sin, may just be overkill, especially since the clubhouse is all but cantilevered over the green, so that any shortcoming will be duly noted.

Brora is holiday golf at its best—a full measure of Darwin's "pleasurable excitement," a seaside setting of inordinate beauty, and the genuine warmth of the welcome accorded to visitors.

NEARBY COURSES

Founded in 1889, the **Golspie Golf Club**, some six or seven miles south of Brora on the indispensable A9, has a delightful course that is largely seaside. Even shorter than Brora (5,836 yards, par 68) and also with revisions by Braid, it has four first-class holes: the 530-yard 4th, which ripples along as it skirts the beach; the 8th and 9th, each over 400 yards long and rising, where heather constricts the shots and the prevailing wind is against us: and the grand 16th, 176 yards, which, from a lofty tee, plays over a valley to a two-tier green backdropped by the sea. The views at Golspie, mountains and meadows and water, are consistently captivating.

An hour north brings us to **Wick Golf Club**. An authentic links, easy-walking Wick measures almost 6,000 yards against a par of 69 and is laid out along a ridge of dunes, with sandy beach beyond. The small greens, which putt beautifully, make scoring difficult, as does the wind.

There are three attractive places to stay in Brora, all of them on Golf Road and within steps of the links:

- The **Royal Marine Hotel**, formerly a private country house, has handsome fireplaces, a grand staircase and reception hall, and rich paneling. Guest accommodations provide modern comfort at what is a full-facilities hotel: heated indoor swimming pool, sauna, steam room, Jacuzzi, tennis, curling, croquet, and fly-fishing on Loch Brora. The "Taste of Scotland" cuisine is altogether satisfying.
- Two four-star B&Bs here—the three guest rooms in each of these houses have private bathrooms—are also quite comfortable. **Tigh Fada**, a haven for non-smokers, has a large garden with croquet, pitch and putt, and a gate to the golf course and the beach. The more upscale **Glenaveron** is a luxurious Edwardian house set amid extensive mature gardens.

As far as nongolf activities are concerned, Hunter's Woolen Mill and the Clynelish Whisky Distillery, both in Brora, nicely repay a visit. However, the outstanding nearby attraction is Dunrobin Castle. Dating to the early 1300s, the ancestral home of the Duke of Sutherland contains impressive period furniture and furnishings, a Victorian museum featuring Pictish stones and wildlife specimens, and magnificent formal gardens, all of it in a setting high above the sea that is an integral part of its grandeur.

From left: Royal Marine Hotel (top) and a view of Brora; the gardens at Dunrobin Castle; the castle (top) and a falconer on the grounds.

LOCH LOMOND AND AYRSHIRE,
KINTYRE AND THE ISLES

LOCH LOMOND

Not thirty minutes north of Glasgow on the A82 lies Scotland's only private golf club in the strict (i.e., American) sense of the term. You cannot play either of the Loch Lomond Golf Club's two courses, one here on the storied lake, the other an hour's drive south, unless you are the guest of a member and in his company. No other Scottish club, not even the Honourable Company or the several "Royals," imposes so sweeping a stricture. Since Loch Lomond's membership is heavily American, it's possible that readers of this book may have a friend or acquaintance who belongs to the club and might be willing to host a game.

In 1992 Tom Weiskopf and Jay Morrish laid out an eighteen here on a six-hundred-acre tract bordering Loch Lomond and near the village of Luss, in Dunbartonshire. Many who had the opportunity to play the course in its early months called it great—and, as it turned out, appropriately so. Weiskopf, scarcely objective, said: "Jay Morrish and I firmly believe that Loch Lomond Golf Club has the best eighteen holes of golf that we have ever created—or quite possibly may ever create."

The course has made its mark in the polls: eighth among the top hundred courses in Britain and Ireland (*Golf World,* a British monthly magazine); sixty-sixth among the top hundred courses in the world (*Golf Magazine*). It is regularly referred to as the "best inland course in the British Isles." It is also kiddingly called—but this is kidding on the square—the "best American course in Europe." In truth, it is very much an American beauty: gorgeously green, lovingly manicured, pristine, its style of bunkering owing nothing to the birthplace of the game.

Beginning in 1996, the European Tour has stopped annually at Loch Lomond. Ernie Els has won here twice (2000 and 2003). Among the other victors have been Retief Goosen, Colin Montgomerie, Tom Lehman, Lee Westwood, and Thomas Bjorn. In 2000 the Solheim Cup was held here.

ON THE LOCH LOMOND COURSE

The course measures 7,100 yards from the championship tees, 6,350 from the regular markers. Par is 72. The first nine has little in the way of elevation change; the second nine is rolling. A single hole may well display

oak, copper beech, silver birch, maple, chestnut, larch, holly, Scotch pine, and Douglas fir. A tree in this veritable arboretum sometimes dictates the line of play, as on the par-4 15th, where the green is defended on the left by an immense silver birch.

The holes fall with perfect naturalness on the terrain; nothing is forced or gimmicky here. The demands on the swing are fair, shot values are of a high order, and the holes are attractively varied. The bunkering is consistently functional but nonetheless elegant, often with peninsulas of turf breaking up the expanses of sand. No revetted pots here. As for the

Opposite: Loch Lomond Course, 5th. Above: 6th. Previous spread: Loch Lomond Dundonald Course, 9th.

greens, they are brilliant—endlessly varied in size, shape, and contouring, spacious when the shot to them is long, less generous when it is short, swift and silken surfaces for a ball to skim across. Fairway lies delight the pure ball striker (they are tight), and the overall condition of the course is impeccable.

No hole at Loch Lomond is less than good, and at least half a dozen are genuinely great. The 5th, 6th, and 10th have been selected for *The 500 World's Greatest Golf Holes,* and it might be well to focus on them. The 5th, which we play at 152 yards and the professionals at 190, is essentially level. It is also breathtaking, presaging the full majesty of Loch Lomond. The tightly bunkered green is set against the shimmering backcloth of the lake, with low hills looming on the far side of the water. Weiskopf's words of caution are in stark contrast to the beauty of the setting: "Never, ever miss this green in the bunkers left or you are as good as dead."

The next hole is called Long Loch Lomond. In both senses of the word *long* is this true, for the hole is a 500-yarder (625 yards from the tips and as such the longest hole in Scottish golf) and it plays along the loch. An energetic slice on any stroke will find the water. Determined to make

Opposite: Loch Lomond Course, 10th. Above: 9th.

It is at the 10th that we enter new territory, a lot of it quite rolling and much of it with water squarely in the center of things—a stream here, a pond there, wetlands here and there. The second nine may possess a little more pepper, a little more flair and surprise and zing, than the consistently excellent but a shade more passive outward half. The loch itself is now at a considerable remove, but great golf continues to be much at hand.

Hole after hole glitters, perhaps none more so than the 14th, a sharp right, 310 to 345 yards. The player who believes he can carry his drive an honest 270 yards will be tempted to go straight for the flag across a bog. The rest of us will play safely out to the left, leaving a ticklish little pitch to an elevated green on the far side of a stream and beyond a deep bunker. This hole almost cost Tom Weiskopf his life during construction. Shortly after dawn one morning, when there was no one within hailing distance and he was reconnoitering the green site, he lost his balance and was sucked down into the bog. Very slowly sinking, he fought desperately for several hours to get free, finally gaining hold of a root and painfully inching his way out of the clutching muck, minus Wellington boots, socks, and trousers, but alive and able to bring the great course to completion.

ON THE DUNDONALD COURSE

In 2003 the club acquired a second eighteen, this one a links course an hour south of Loch Lomond in an area dominated by Prestwick, Royal Troon, and Western Gailes. Called Dundonald, it is another example of the skill of Kyle Phillips, architect of Kingsbarns, who has fashioned here a second modern links. Sand-based, it has low dunes covered in fescue and gorse framing many of the fairways, steep-faced revetted bunkers, and an assortment of exquisitely sculpted greens that are actually more natural than many at Kingsbarns. A burn meanders across half a dozen holes. The waters of the Firth of Clyde are rarely in view; not so the Isle of Arran. Admittedly, there is not the majesty of Kingsbarns—the views are altogether more ordinary—but the golf holes themselves sometimes approach that masterpiece in terms of originality and shot values.

Dundonald measures 7,300 yards from the championship tees, 5,580 yards from the forward markers, and 6,410 yards from the middle tees. Two level par 4s on the second nine are especially fine: the 365-yard 13th, out-of-bounds tight all the way on the left; and the 400-yard 17th: sweeping dogleg left; three bunkers at the inside of the bend to swallow the overly aggressive tee shot, low runoffs at the left and right sides of the green that demand deft chipping—or putting.

Above: Loch Lomond Course, 18th. Opposite: Dundonald Course, 9th.

this hole a legitimate three-shotter, Weiskopf and Morrish have plunked down a large and fanciful cross bunker smack in the center of the fairway 120 yards short of the green.

The third and final contribution to the seminal book is the 10th—richly scenic, rigorously exacting, 405 yards from the daily markers, 455 from all the way back. The tee is elevated, and our drive toward Glen Fruin hangs suspended against the wooded mountainside. Said Tom Lehman, "You face a tough downhill tee shot with 'stuff' both left and right—bad 'stuff.'" Moreover, crossing the fairway on the diagonal in the driving area is a burn. How much risk will we assume on the tee in order to shorten the long second shot? A pond lurks at the left of the green, which slants from the front right, where there is sand, to the back left, where the water is. It's not surprising that this hole was named one of the one hundred greatest in the 500 *World's Greatest* book.

SCOTLAND

Top-notch also are a couple of the par 5s, both for the same reason. On the level 3rd, 510 to 560 yards, a burn haunts us much of the way, to devour first the pushed drive and then the weak or pulled second shot. On the 18th, 550 to 585 yards and also level, low dunes flank much of the hole, but in the end it is a waterless burn, a ditch, edging in from the left to cross just short of the green and then skirt the right side of it, that gives the hole its sting. That leaves only the one-shotters, and what a quartet they are! A dune boldly intrudes at the left front of the 170-yard 4th; a burn unnervingly close on the left guards the spectacularly contoured green of the 6th; a marsh must be crossed to gain the elevated green on the 125-yard 11th; and on the 15th, 190 yards, the elevated green is defended by two "in-over-your-head" pits at the front and at the left, and the railroad track is not far behind the putting surface. A very demanding test, Dundonald is, I suspect, more than most of us can handle in a 30-miles-per-hour wind.

The members of Loch Lomond now have a choice of exceptional courses, parkland or links. There will be occasions when rain at the one will send them scurrying to the other. And occasions when they will play one in the morning and the other in the afternoon. Now that's a *day* of golf.

By the time this book is published, the club's third eighteen should be well along, though probably not open for play. Jack Nicklaus has designed a course on Loch Lomond to take its place beside the Weiskopf-Morrish jewel. When I followed the proposed routing in mid-2004, the tees, greens, and center lines were clearly marked. But I'm not about to advance an opinion based on what I could make out. I will say that Tom and Jay did not lay claim to all the trees on the property—not by a long shot—and that Jack may intend to incorporate the great loch into his layout even more extensively than they did. At any event, count on it to be a worthy companion.

Opposite: Loch Lomond
Dundonald Course, 3rd.
Above: 18th.

We cannot leave Loch Lomond Golf Club, however private it may be, without a word or two about **Rossdhu House**, the eighteenth-century manor that is the clubhouse. It is magnificent. An imposing and symmetrical Georgian structure built of a warm beige sandstone, it is a procession of noble spaces, virtually all with fireplaces: the main hall, the drawing room, the cocktail lounge, the library, the spike bar (just the place for breakfast as well as lunch), the dining rooms, the locker rooms, and, up the grand staircase out of the main hall, the six accommodations, which vie, in luxury and comfort and style and view, with the accommodations at Skibo Castle. As for the cooking, it is marvelously creative and contemporary. Presentation, service, and wine list are also exceptional, in a period setting that calls up an age of opulence.

Set on the southern shore of Loch Lomond and not five minutes from the golf club is one of Scotland's foremost country-house hotels, **Cameron House**. Traditionally decorated, this nineteenth-century former residence is noted for its elegance, warmth, and cuisine. The hotel has long had a nine-hole golf course, the Wee Demon, which measures just 2,266 yards. As this book goes to press, however, Cameron House is building a full-length eighteen on land bordering Loch Lomond: The Carrick on

Loch Lomond, a name that takes its cue from this Carrick area of Scotland, not from the architect, Doug Carrick. He is the designer of twenty-four courses in his native land, including Osprey Valley, northwest of Toronto, which, with its echoes of North Berwick and Prestwick, is a hymn to old-style British golf. Several holes here run right beside the grand loch, and 14 holes provide generous views of it. An effort is being made to see to it that this course will play firm and fast, with vigorous roll on the ball that brings the game along the ground much into play.

Opposite: Kilchurn Castle. This page, clockwise from above: Rossdhu House; Loch Lomond; Cameron House; Balloch Castle.

THE MACHRIE

Single-malt whiskey and traditional links golf—no more need be claimed for the Isle of Islay (pronounced eye-la). Islay lies eighteen miles off the southwestern coast of the Scottish mainland. It is the home of eight distilleries and The Machrie Hotel and Golf Links.

Regularly scheduled flights from Glasgow take us there in thirty minutes. Or we can drive and use the car ferry. This will require a good five and a half hours, but what a rewarding trip it is! The run south on the A83 through Argyll is endlessly beautiful—the great fjord Loch Fine, the starkly rugged mountains and lonely wooded glens, the inviting lochside villages of Inverary, Fornace, and Lochgilphead. At Kennecraig we board the ferry for a nonstop two-hour cruise on a commodious and comfortable ship (bar, cafeteria, lounges, gift shop) to dock at either Port Ascaig or Port Ellen. The latter is only a few miles from The Machrie.

For golfers, the question is a simple one: Is this links worth getting to? The answer is equally simple: Yes. Oh yes, indeed.

The course was laid out in 1891 by Willie Campbell of Musselburgh. Ten years later, in an effort to attract attention to this western outpost, the owners held a professional match-play tournament with an unignorable first prize of one hundred pounds. Many leading players made the arduous two-day trip to The Machrie immediately following the Open Championship at Muirfield. J. H. Taylor nipped James Braid in the final on the last hole to pocket the winnings.

ON THE COURSE

The word *unforgettable* is likely to surface with some frequency in a book of this nature. It is an adjective that can fairly be applied to The Machrie, which is riddled with blind shots. Par is 71. The low-handicap golfer thus gets to play 35 full shots. And of these 35, at least 18, probably 19, will be blind. The Machrie is truly unforgettable. You may be inclined to insist that it must also be unknowable and unmanageable. I urge you to play here and make your own judgment.

To begin with, this is splendid golfing country. The grass-cloaked dunes, which constitute the dominant feature of this 260-acre tract, are

often colossal. Within this turbulent landscape are a number of obvious green sites: amphitheaters, plateaus, ridge tops, punch bowls. An architect might start by identifying the eighteen best green sites, then work out a route back to the potential tee for each. Given ground of The Machrie's exuberance and, 115 years ago, given the absence of equipment for altering this topography, the result would necessarily be blind shots. For between tee and green, sand hills, whether modest or mighty, would intervene again and again to produce a series of holes that are marked by the thrill of the unknown. Concealed targets would be the order of the day.

The Machrie wastes no time in making this clear. The first hole on this 6,292-yard course is a mere 308 yards, but since the ground rises in front of the tee and since a hollow at the foot of a ridge hides the green, both drive and pitch turn out to be blind. Only the drive is blind on the

Opposite: The Machrie, 7th.
Above: 8th.

508-yard 2nd, which doglegs abruptly left as it skirts the bank of a fast-flowing stream. On the climbing 3rd, 319 yards, with its tee commanding our first view of the broad, tawny beach, both shots are blind, the hole climaxing in an outlandishly terraced green just beyond a ridge. The 390-yard 4th plays from an elevated tee, our back to the sea, down to a fantastically billowing fairway that, somewhere in its abundance of hummocks and hollows, contains a landing area, then up and out of this secluded spot to a green concealed beyond yet another ridge. A marvelous hole by any yardstick, and a suspense-filled delight.

We are not prepared for the 5th. Why? Because all 163 yards of it, from the pulpit tee down over broken ground to the green, is in full view. The putting surface is defended by a large bunker and a small one. Bunkers are in very scarce supply at The Machrie. There is a grand total of six, with

two of them spent recklessly here on the short 5th, one each reserved for the 1st, 11th, 13th, and 17th. Willie Campbell and Donald Steel (Steel revised the course in 1979) were both reluctant to dig holes, preferring to rely on the natural contours of the greens themselves, which are generally undulating or wildly sloping (some are both), to say nothing of the green surrounds, which almost always contain cunning little folds and creases.

A stretch of four outstanding two-shotters completes the nine. Only the 7th will be described. A candidate for the title "Blind Hole of the World," it goes beyond the merely theatrical. The tee is tucked away in a tiny hollow on low ground. The fairway is nowhere to be seen. Then our perplexed gaze happens to light on an overgrown footpath working its way up the dune that towers some 40 to 50 feet above us, a good 150 yards out from the tee. The fairway, we conclude, must be somewhere on the far

side of this shaggy pyramid. A brief walk around its base confirms our instinct. The forced carry up and over has a value of not less than 185 yards (in the calm). Into the wind, the shot required to surmount the pinnacle is very like 220 yards. Fail to pull off this drive and we find ourselves—that's assuming we can find the ball—in deep and clinging grass on a slope so precipitous as to preclude any chance of making a swing.

Ah, but the drive that does clear this "Alps" plunges into a broad, rumpled fairway along and above Laggan Bay, where miles of deserted sand sweep away toward the horizon. Beyond the Rhinns of Islay, five or six miles across the bay to the west, lies the open Atlantic. To the northeast, the Paps of Jura soar twenty-five hundred feet above the water. What an inspiring amalgam of beauty and solitude, of tranquillity and spaciousness and freedom.

Now, having surmounted the giant sand hill, surely we deserve a clear shot at the green. No such luck. The green is out of sight, just over a low ridge. Nor do we catch a glimpse of the flag. We have no choice but to make our best guess and attempt our best swing.

The inbound nine, though at a slight remove from the sea, is nonetheless routed over characteristically heaving linksland, a patch of bracken here, of heather there, fierce rough flanking the broad fairways. The two par 3s could scarcely be less alike. The 156-yard 10th plays from a raised tee in low dunes beside the beach down to a green guarded by wetlands on the right and the wide Machrie Burn on the left. On the other hand, the 174-yard 12th is exposed and windswept, rising gently on a suggestion of ridge to a green that falls off to the left. Beyond this slope is a peat moor—Islay's whiskeys are noted for their distinctive peaty flavor—that stretches away toward dark low hills. The remoteness is palpable.

High tees continue to present compelling seascapes and landscapes. Blind shots—on the 13th, 14th, 15th, and 16th—continue to befuddle us. By now the disbelieving shake of the head may even be accompanied by a rueful smile.

Which brings us to the 352-yard 17th, almost certainly inspired by the 17th at Prestwick. Following a drive that must clear rough rising ground, we launch our 6- or 7-iron over a high dune, the shot disappearing out of sight toward a green far below in a pretty dell, a green defended in front by sand.

Now home at last, on a 374-yarder that, you will have guessed it and braced yourself, culminates with a totally blind approach shot. But this time, the green, in the lee of a broad ridge, welcomes our shot.

The Machrie, 17th.

If it is excessive, this nonpareil eighteen at The Machrie, it is an excess born of naturalness, an excess that produces more than its share of pure golfing joy. Could a claim for greatness be made? Probably not, though this links can usually be found in a ranking of the top seventy courses in Britain and Ireland. Still, there is perhaps too much of the dicey. More than half the shots are a lottery. But what should be kept in mind is that there is not a single prosaic hole, that there are four or five great holes (4th, 6th, 9th, 14th, 16th), and that Darwin's "pleasurable excitement" is present in full measure—all in a setting of uncommon beauty.

One other thing: Here is a course that is very rarely crowded. The five times I've played it, on three separate trips, I simply walked over to the 1st tee and hit off. Nobody ahead of me, nobody behind me, nobody with me, no starter. The Machrie may require a journey, but when you do make the effort, it's all yours and, even more to the point, it's terrific.

The hotel and the golf course are now owned by Graeme Ferguson Lacey, who seems to have a penchant for islands. He is also the owner of the admirable Castletown Golf Links and attendant hotel on the Isle of Man. Here at The Machrie he has a minor (possibly silent) partner, Peter de Savary, of Skibo Castle fame, the owner of the Bovey Castle country-house resort, in Devon, England.

The hotel dates to 1745, when it was built as a farmhouse. Guest rooms, each with private bath, have been freshly decorated. While in no sense fancy, they are comfortable. Public rooms are cheerful and relaxing. An open fire and a pool table make the Golfers' Bar inviting. As for the cooking, the seafood, beef, lamb, and game, all from Islay itself, are reliably flavorful. And the scallops on our last visit were as delicious as any we've eaten.

I spoke with the estimable Ian Brown, general manager, who is a sound golfer (almost a prerequisite for running The Machrie), about possible changes now that Mr. Lacey has the bit in his teeth. I expressed a concern that the very character of this plain-vanilla, get-away-from-it-all place, this simple haven for golfers, might be altered to give it an upmarket look and feel (and tariff). He assured me that such a transformation was not in the plan.

If you can tear yourself away briefly from the wonderful links, keep in mind that five single-malt distilleries are still in operation on Islay. Guided tours can be arranged by the hotel. There is a distinctive flavor and hue and character to each of these whiskeys, to say nothing of distinctive names such as Bruichladdich, Bunnahabhain, Caol Ila, Lagavulin, and Laphroaig.

Also worth a visit is the Museum of Islay Life, on the shores of Loch Indaal. The collection contains some sixteen hundred items, dating from 8000 B.C. to the 1950s. Among the displays are those showing life in a simple cottage and in a farmhouse bedroom during the Victorian Age. One other place might be mentioned, the Round Church, in the village of Bowmore. Built in the 1760s, it is said to have been designed so that there would be no corners where the devil could lurk.

MACHRIHANISH

Machrihanish is less than an hour's drive south from Kennecraig, the port on the mainland for the Islay ferry. If you are making the long land or over-the-sea trip to The Machrie, you will want to visit Machrihanish. But then, you will want to play Machrihanish (a twenty-five-minute flight from Glasgow, a four-hour drive from St. Andrews) regardless of your intentions regarding Machrie.

One thing is certain: The opening hole at Machrihanish is superior to its counterpart at The Machrie. It may also be superior to just about every other 1st hole in the world. The tee on this 423-yarder, tight beside the curving beach, is elevated 10 feet above it. Our drive is fired on the diagonal across the Atlantic's waves to an undulating fairway that skirts the shoreline. How much of Machrihanish Bay have we the courage to bite off on our first swing? The beach—perhaps with an oystercatcher strutting about on it—is very much in play. This is a thrilling, tempting, tantalizing business. So we pick a target, probably a low dune, and if our swing be rhythmic and unrushed, away we go on a round that will give us enormous pleasure not only as we play it but as we hark back to it again and again.

It was on March 20, 1876, here near the bottom of the Kintyre Peninsula, that four men (including a Presbyterian minister) laid out a ten-hole course and "cut the first sod." Then, having handled the easy part in the morning (i.e., designing and building the course), they got down to playing it that afternoon, and playing it a second time as well that same day!

Over the years that followed, the task of shaping or reshaping the course fell to Prestwick's Charles Hunter, then to Old Tom Morris, J. H. Taylor, and, following the Second World War, Sir Guy Campbell. Machrihanish today, though chiefly attributable to Sir Guy, still contains a few reminders of Old Tom and J. H. Taylor.

ON THE COURSE

The links measures 6,225 yards from the medal tees; par is 70. After the unique opener, the 2nd, 395 yards, is no letdown. The approach shot must first clear a very broad stream called the Machrihanish Water and then a bluff with two large bunkers in its face. The ball comes to rest out of sight—

in the best Machrie tradition, Machrihanish has seven or eight blind shots of its own—on an astonishingly large and shapely putting surface. On the 3rd hole, the green swoops through a dune-framed dell to a length of 144 feet. By whatever yardstick—novelty, artistry, fascination, test, smoothness, pace—the Machrihanish greens rank with the very best in Britain and Ireland.

Now we are deep in the duneland: platform tees with intoxicating views across soaring and shaggy sand hills; fairways tossing and tilting or

Opposite: Machrihanish, 3rd.
Above: 7th.

FARAWAY PLACE WITH A GRAND SCOTTISH NAME

- Play **Machrihanish**, Scotland's most remote great links (or is The Machrie?) and worth whatever it takes to get there.

- Have lunch in the modest **clubhouse**, perhaps with your caddie, who just may be the captain of the club.

- Play the **splendid course** again; anybody who gets here deserves at least 36 holes.

- Drive twenty minutes south to **Mull Lighthouse**, here to take in the gorgeous views across the sea to Northern Ireland.

- Book dinner and an overnight stay in nearby **Campbeltown's White Hart Hotel**, where the rooms are merely acceptable but the cooking is exceptional.

doglegging around pyramidal dunes or twisting along snaking dune-lined valleys; now a hidden punch bowl green, now an exposed green on a ridge, now a breezy plateau green with steep falloffs right and left. We are called upon to draw the ball, fade the ball, knock it down into the teeth of the wind that comes funneling along a valley floor, lift it up to sail with the wind in order to gain a green high on a knob. The game here is inordinately rich and complex and involving. The sea is sometimes in view, at other times shut off by the massive sand hills, but the sound of it, which may range from a murmur to a roar, is always with us.

Though it steadily challenges the scratch player, Machrihanish does not discourage the high handicapper, who is not being overpowered (the last six holes on the outbound nine measure 122 yards, 385, 301, 428, 339, 353) or intimidated. The game here is joyous in this rough-and-tumble, enticingly natural—in truth, this magical—expanse of linksland that is the first nine.

If the inbound half lacks the grandeur of the huge sand hills, it still provides the vigorous movement of sand-based terrain. And the prevailing wind seems to be perpetually hostile: Virtually every stroke is played into it or across it. Among the numerous outstanding holes are the 513-yard 12th (a pair of deep bunkers hidden in a swale just short of the green awaits the aggressive second shot that just fails to get up) and the 231-yard 16th, a brutally long one-shotter that must traverse broken ground and rough country.

The record must show that the home hole, a 313-yarder over dull ground to an ill-defended green, disappoints, but let's just be grateful for

Opposite: Machrihanish, 5th.

this birdie chance and say no more about it. Besides, we may take the opportunity on the green to turn around and see just where we've been, perhaps even spotting the tilled land on higher ground immediately beyond the links. For a number of years the second farm belonged to Beatle Paul McCartney, whose attachment to this corner of Scotland—the sea, the lovely green hills of Kintyre, the panoramas that include the islands of Islay and Gigha and Jura—was powerful. In 1977 he composed a song called "Mull of Kintyre," and recorded it with the Campbeltown Pipe Band. Wistfully evoking this idyllic place, it enjoyed worldwide success.

Of all Scotland's notable golf clubs, Machrihanish must be the most egalitarian. So don't be surprised if your caddie is a member, is a first-rate player with a keen knowledge not only of the golf holes but of the club's history, and is an unpaid officer in the club administration, perhaps even captain. He might also be a philosophical humanist. I recall being caught once in a pitiless rain here, a downpour so drenching that our heaviest waterproofs utterly failed to be waterproof. One of our caddies muttered, "The rain can only go so far—it has to stop at the skin."

I was not surprised to find my friend Michael Bamberger writing in his classic *To the Linksland,* "If I were allowed to play only one course for the rest of my life, Machrihanish would be the place." I might not go quite that far, but taken all in all, links and club and remote, appealing Kintyre, Machrihanish has also gained an enduring hold on my affections.

It's worth noting that golf and lodgings at Machrihanish are soon to get a big boost. Next door to the much-loved eighteen, golf photographer Brian Morgan is building an upscale hotel and a links course designed by Kyle Phillips. Both are scheduled to open in 2007.

DUNAVERTY

All of fifteen minutes south of Machrihanish is the appropriately named Southend, a holiday village on the Mull of Kintyre. Northern Ireland, often in full view across the North Channel of the Irish Sea, is only twelve miles away.

Tiny Southend has its own tiny golf course, Dunaverty, measuring just 4,597 yards and playing to a par of 64. It is a cow pasture—literally: The first time I played it, more than twenty-five years ago, I had to nudge two Ayrshires aside in order to begin the round. They were chewing their cud squarely between the markers on the 1st tee. Sheep contend with the cattle for pride of place.

You get a good idea of the golf at Dunaverty simply by reading the local rules on the scorecard: "SUNKEN LIES. A ball lying in a rabbit scrape, rabbit hole, sheep path, hoofmark, or cart road [the reference is not to a golf cart] may be dropped without penalty. . . . When a ball lies in or touching DUNG, or if dung interferes with a player's stroke or stance, the ball may be lifted and dropped without penalty. The ball may be cleaned. . . ."

The views, of Dunaverty's Rock and the island of Sanda and the coast of Northern Ireland, are enormously winning. The course has no hole as long as 400 yards, but several holes are testing, including the 240-yard 6th, a stout par 3, and the 387-yard 17th, where the green is fronted by a fifty-foot-wide stream. The club's lone greenkeeper mows the greens twice a week and the fairways about ten times a year. It is a beguiling primitive, this links, and there's a chance you would get a kick out of it.

Opposite: Machrihanish, 8th.
Below: 6th.

The lower end of the Kintyre Peninsula, for all its natural beauty, is not full of important sightseeing opportunities. The village of Machrihanish is little other than the golf club, though there is good windsurfing near the RAF base at the end of the long beach. In nearby Campbeltown, which has a population of about seven thousand, the waterfront is a pleasant place to walk. Facing the harbor is the fifteenth-century Campbeltown Cross, with its elaborate ornamentation. In the bay lies Davaar Island, where a cave painting of the Crucifixion, which was completed in 1877, can be seen. Back in town are the Campbeltown Museum, with its geological and archaeological exhibits, and the Campbeltown Cemetery, of necessity somewhat less lively but still intriguing, situated as it is at the end of a row of grand houses (once occupied by merchants and ship owners now buried next door) and rising up the terraces of a steep overhanging bank.

From left: the Kintyre Peninsula; Shore Cottage (top) and the White Hart Hotel; the shoreline.

A hilly, winding, and scenic coastal road runs from Campbeltown to Southend. Beyond Keil Point, a minor road across the Mull of Kintyre leads to Mull Lighthouse, built in 1788. As from Dunaverty, the views across the sea—this is the meeting place of the Atlantic Ocean, the Firth of Clyde, and the Irish Sea—to Northern Ireland are enthralling.

I'll suggest a few places to stay in Kintyre:

- Overlooking the golf links and Machrihanish Bay is **Ardell House**, a B&B with eleven bedrooms, eight in the sturdy Victorian stone dwelling, three in the converted stables. Those in the house itself are more spacious and have the views.
- In the center of Campbeltown is the **White Hart Hotel**, more than 150 years old. The rooms are decently appointed, and the cooking on our most recent visit was exceptional, particularly the seafood dishes and most particularly mussels in a cream sauce. A sign near the reception desk is worth quoting: THE GROUND FLOOR OF THE HOTEL IS A MAZE OF EATING AREAS. PLEASE FEEL FREE TO WALK AROUND AND VIEW AT YOUR LEISURE BEFORE CHOOSING A TABLE.
- Five or six miles north of Campbeltown lies the hamlet of Saddell, its ruins of a Cistercian abbey dating to the twelfth century. But, for us, it is not the abbey ruins that are the lure; **Shore Cottage** is. This Landmark Trust property is one of more than one hundred eighty structures of historic interest or architectural importance to which the Trust has given new life and a future by restoring them and making them available to vacationers. Almost all are in the United Kingdom, though there are a few outlanders, in Rome, Venice, Florence, and even four in Vermont, one a house where Rudyard Kipling lived for a time.

A number of years ago, Harriet and I occupied Shore Cottage on two occasions. It was built in 1870 and sleeps six. In Saddell, we drive briefly along an embowered lane, past Saddell Castle (it dates to 1508 and sleeps eight; in a cove perhaps a quarter of a mile farther on is Cul na Shee, a pine-paneled bungalow that sleeps four), and proceed through a low stone archway in a garden wall. Directly ahead, no more than 150 yards away and at the water's edge, sits Shore Cottage. Thanks to the surrounding trees and rocks, the whitewashed house, with its slate roof, has a sheltered look, this despite its situation on a spit of land where Saddell Bay meets Kilbrannon Sound. The Isle of Arran lies just six miles away across the water.

It is not easy to imagine a finer day than the morning and afternoon rounds at Machrihanish, followed by a home-cooked meal with a good bottle of wine in front of the fireplace at Shore Cottage. On one of our stays here we were joined by our second son, John, then twenty-three and working in Belfast to bring a little cheer into the lives of the ghetto children there, Protestants and Catholics. At our urging, he related some of his experiences. The contrast between serene Kintyre and deadly Belfast was stark. After he went off to bed and the glow of the last embers had died away, I pulled Alisdair Kilmichael's *Kintyre* from the bookshelf and read for a while. Then I put the book down and went outside. A few steps took me to the water's edge, beside the rivulets and the rock pools. There was no breeze, no moon, and only a scattering of stars. I looked across to Arran, its pastures sloping down to the sound. There was no sign of life, but I could make out the ghostly silhouette of its peaks. Or was I imagining them? I went back inside. Machrihanish and Shore Cottage: No combination in this book of a place to play and a place to stay could hope to surpass them.

Above: The town of Tarbert in night and day. Left: fields near Campbeltown.

SHISKINE

If you are heading for the Isle of Arran from Ayrshire (Troon, Prestwick, Irvine, and the like), you will take the ferry from Ardrossan over to Brodick, a fifty-five-minute crossing. Arran is sometimes referred to as "Scotland in miniature," with its mountains, heather-clad glens, rolling farmland, sea cliffs, and rock-ribbed beaches.

The delightful old 12-hole Shiskine links is the best—actually, the best and only—12-hole layout I've ever played. And of the seven courses on the island, only Shiskine is a links. The club was founded in 1896, and St. Andrews–born Willie Fernie (1883 Open champion, architect of the original Ailsa and Arran at Turnberry) was brought in to design nine holes. In 1910 and 1912 a total of nine more holes were laid out by Willie Park Sr., but six of them, wearyingly high on Drumadoon Hill, fell into disrepair during the Great War and were abandoned. Thus the 12-hole course.

The Shiskine Golf & Tennis Club today, located at Blackwaterfoot, is a reflection of the two Fionas. Fiona Crawford is the club manager; Fiona Brown runs the golf shop, collecting green fees and telling you when to hit away. The manager's office is up at the clubhouse, opposite the 18th green. Fiona Crawford is a gracious and kindly woman and an avid golfer. She will be most pleased to make your acquaintance and, if she has the time, to take a cup of tea with you in the clubhouse tearoom (the club has no liquor license), calling up the early years of Shiskine and spelling out the makeup of its membership today. She may tell you that there used to be three tennis courts, but that some fifteen years ago one of them was converted into a bowling green. (I'm a little surprised that this move did not call for a change in the club name: Shiskine Golf & Tennis & Lawn Bowling Club.)

The irrepressible Fiona Brown, in her simple quarters beside the 1st tee, will accept your modest green fee and, beyond congeniality and hospitality, exude nothing short of delight about the pleasure in store for you. She will put in your hands a hole-by-hole commentary, which she wrote, and then review it with you. A typical entry: "8th. Hades. Don't let the name put you off! . . . you can see the green from the tee. (Just pretend that the big hollow is not there)!!"

ON THE COURSE

The course, on its broad seaside shelf, measures 2,996 yards from the tips; par is 42. There are seven one-shotters, ranging from 128 to 243 yards; four two-shotters, ranging from 249 to 391 yards; and one long hole, the 506-yard 9th. Clearly, power is not the point. With the ball on this firm and rolling—and sometimes hilly—terrain often seeming to have a mind of its own, control is everything. There are boundaries and burns and blind shots (by the time we put behind us The Machrie and Machrihanish and Shiskine, we will surely have the blind staggers) but no crisscross holes. The seascapes are stunning and Kintyre itself is often in view across Kilbrannon Sound. And if your instinct is to think that the game here is not

Opposite: Shiskine, 4th.
Above: 2nd and 3rd.

to be taken all that seriously, you are doubtless right. Still, it is just possible that there are three great holes: the 243-yard 5th, a one-shotter along and above the sea from a giddily high perch to an ill-defined green on somewhat lower ground; the 275-yard 6th, a par 4 with the sea slamming into the rocks beside the tee, the blind drive gently downhill and the second shot seeking the hollow where the green is hidden; and the blind 209-yard 11th, improbably up and down from tee to concealed punch bowl green, a case of having to trust your swing and your luck.

I should mention the winds, anything from the sweet caress of a zephyr to the savage battering of a gale. The last time I played Shiskine—and while I was still out on the course—the greenkeeper stopped at Fiona Brown's shop to advise her that some madman (me) had driven from the pinnacle tee on the 5th with the anemometer at the equipment shed registering 72 miles per hour. In relaying this news to me, Fiona laughingly added, "I could only hope you wouldn't find yourself back on the mainland sooner than you'd planned."

Opposite: Shiskine, 6th.
Below: 11th.

We've not stayed in Blackwaterfoot, where Shiskine is situated, but we've looked at two places there, both attractive:

- The **Kinloch Hotel**, within paces of the sea, is a nicely decorated modern hotel with plenty of leisure facilities: heated indoor swimming pool, sauna, solarium, squash, and snooker.
- The **Greannan**, on the other hand, is a five-room B&B in an elevated position that affords panoramic views over the village to the Mull of Kintyre. All rooms have private bath and color TV.

The finest hotel on Arran is 17th-century **Kilmichael Country House**, just outside the port of Brodick and a very beautiful twenty-five-minute drive from Blackwaterfoot. The oldest house on the island, it is the only Arran hotel to merit five stars ("world class, exceptional") from the Scottish Tourist Board. Each of the seven accommodations is luxurious and tastefully appointed. Fresh flowers and fruit welcome you on arrival. We occupied the Garden Suite, whose bright yellow sitting room overlooks the garden (giant sequoias here courtesy of California). And the island's premier hotel is its premier restaurant as well. Coffee and petits fours are served in the antiques-filled drawing room with its log fire and baby grand piano.

Roughly twenty miles long and ten miles wide, Arran is mainly moor and mountains. The best way to experience it is simply to get in the car and roam. It is boundlessly scenic. Worth seeking out are Brodick Castle, which dates in part from the thirteenth century and contains much in the way of fine furniture, silver, and paintings. Goatfell, at 2,866 feet Arran's highest peak; Corris, a sweet seaside village; Glenashdale Falls, a series of cascades in a rocky gorge (swimming is paradise), about three miles from Whiting Bay; and the plain village of Shiskine, which claims to be the burial place of St. Malaise. Pious legend has it that despite deliberately contracting thirty diseases in order to make amends for his sins, the good man managed to live to the age of 120.

Above: the view of Holy Island, from Lamlash. Right: Brodick Castle. Opposite: the Mauchrie Stones, on Arran.

WESTERN GAILES

Of approximately 170 genuine links courses in the world (seaside, sea level, undulating terrain, sand-based turf), 14 of them are to be found an hour south of Glasgow along the Firth of Clyde, on a twelve-mile stretch of Ayrshire coastline between the city of Irvine and the town of Prestwick. Two of the 14, Prestwick and Royal Troon, are world renowned, and they tend to overshadow most of the nearby courses. Most, but not all. Western Gailes is the exception.

The club was founded in 1897 by four Glasgwegians who had been playing parkland golf in the city. To attract golfers who, like themselves, were already members of other clubs, they set the annual dues at ten shillings and sixpence and, for those who took the long view of things, lifetime dues for just one payment of five pounds.

The new club leased a long, narrow strip of linksland between the Glasgow and Southwestern Railway line and the Firth of Clyde. The club tells us in its "Strokesaver" booklet that it was the first greenkeeper who laid out the course.

ON THE COURSE

For the habitual slicer, it is entirely possible to bend northbound drives onto the railway tracks and southbound drives onto the beach. And for all of us tackling this great and classic links, there are dunes and heather and gorse and long, spiky marram grass. The overall elevation change can hardly be twelve feet; the walk itself is an easy one. There are raised tees, and greens in dune-framed dells and on plateaus exposed to the wind. Burns give pause, as do bunkers—one hundred of them, steep-faced revetted pots where, in most instances, a stroke is lost. The course can be stretched to more than 6,700 yards; the regular markers come to a bit under 6,200. Don't be put off by the shortness of Western Gailes—this test is very real.

Three of the first four holes are short par 4s, all with quite enough going on in the lively green complexes, but perhaps still offering the opportunity for a birdie. The 2nd, 412 yards, offers no such opportunity. It curves left, and the long second shot presents an appreciable drop to a blind punch bowl green. This is a tough-as-nails beauty, and we dearly love it.

Now we walk over to the shoreline and do an about-face. If the wind is out of the southwest—and that is the prevailing wind—we play the next nine holes dead into it. Like the first four holes, these nine are routed over what can fairly be called perfect linksland for golf: undulating, full of hillocks and hummocks and hollows, rising here, tumbling there, the greens strikingly sited, the fairways uncomfortably narrow at times but always neatly defined by the low dunes and the wild grasses

Opposite: Western Gailes, 7th. Above: 6th.

and the heather. Superb—and superbly natural—holes pop up again and again: the short par-5 6th, doglegging right, its second shot fired through a broad "cartgate" in the dunes, the fairway dipping at the last to a green in a hollow; the 7th, 145 yards from a pulpit tee to a green in a dune-framed amphitheater; the 8th and 10th, a pair of shortish two-shotters, each defended by a burn across the face of the green; and the 11th, 415 yards, curving smoothly right to an exposed plateau green. The 13th, a short par 3 down at the end of the property, its green ringed by seven bunkers, marks the end of what is probably the longest straight run along the strand in Scottish golf.

Another 180-degree turnabout and it's time to head for home, inside, along the railway, on the 525-yard 14th, 562 from the medal tees. One of the chosen in *The 500 World's Greatest Golf Holes,* it often plays downwind, tempting big hitters to open their shoulders in order to get

home in two, but ten bunkers spread over the final third of the hole encourage prudence. The short and level 15th is also stoutly defended by sand, and the 16th, 364 yards, is crossed by a burn about 30 yards short of the green to swallow a flubbed second shot. Seventeen, 404 yards (443 from the medal tees) is the course's final feature hole, and what a memorable one it is! A long diagonal ridge, six or seven feet high, dominates the driving area. If we can place our tee shot on top of it, we have a clear view of the flag on a green tucked away among hillocks and hollows. On the other hand, forced to play from the base of the ridge, we not only have a blind shot to contend with but we must get our fairway metal or long iron up very quickly. This is an original golf hole and a great one.

Over the years, Western Gailes has hosted the Scottish Amateur, the Scottish PGA, the British Seniors, and both the British and Scottish Boys' Championships. It was also the venue in 1972 for the Curtis Cup

Below, left: Western Gailes, 9th; right: 10th.
Opposite: 17th.

Match, which the U.S. team, led by Hollis Stacy (who would go on to win three U.S. Women's Opens) and Laura Baugh, won in a squeaker, 10–8.

The graceful clubhouse, white and with a red tile roof, has exactly the interior we would expect: old paneling (the lockers have a wonderful antique patina), old leather, old pictures, old silver. And the view from the clubhouse is the same captivating panorama one enjoys from the elevated tees at 6, 7, and 9: across the Clyde to the hills of Arran and to the bold outline of Ailsa Craig. The course was ranked thirty-eighth by the UK's *Golf World* in its most recent list of the top one hundred courses in the British Isles. The late Sam McKinlay, long Scotland's most astute commentator on the game, coined a simple encomium for this superlative, links. It is, he said, "full of golfing goodness."

NEARBY COURSES

Glasgow Golf Club's Gailes Links, on the other side of the railway line, is a basically level and straightforward course with views of the Arran hills but no sight of the sea. Visitors are likely to play it at 6,300 yards; par is 71. Five par 4s, ranging from 409 to 425 yards, call for hitting. Gorse and bunkers, all of them revetted, must be avoided; even more so the vast acreage of fierce calluna heather. Among the best holes are the 530-yard 5th, with its shrinking fairway and its green in a dell just over a rise; and the 18th, 409 yards, sand at the four corners of the green but open across the front. In recent years this worthy test has been the venue for the Scottish PGA Match Play and the Scottish Amateur.

The **Barassie Links of Kilmarnock Golf Club**, also next door to Western Gailes, has plenty of gentle ups and downs. This links measures just under 6,500 yards from the regular markers; par is 72. The beautifully contoured greens look quite natural. Gorse, heather, revetted bunkers, low dunes, old stone walls, and stands of pine all lend character. So do burns, which threaten to snare the mis-hit on half a dozen holes. Memorable is the double-dogleg 8th, 519 yards, dunes and gorse corseting the sinuous route as we get closer to the green.

Nearly 120 years old, the **Irvine Golf Club**, **Bogside**, is packed with sport and spine from the tough rollercoaster opening hole (418 yards, blind second shot) to the delightful finishing hole (337 yards, stiff forced carry from the tee over two of the deepest boarded bunkers we're likely to encounter outside of Royal West Norfolk). And in between are sixteen diverse holes, not one of them dull.

The course measures 6,408 yards (par 71) or 5,687 yards (par 72). The collection of par 4s is sterling. The 289-yard 4th, for instance, is a quirky little gem: a mildly elevated tee, a narrowing fairway with gorse tight on the right, a railway embankment (OB on the tracks) even tighter on the left, a stone wall so close to the left edge of the green that it could impede your takeaway when putting, and a stream at the foot of a sharp falloff behind the green. The 465-yard 11th, on the other hand, is textbook: gently rising and curving smoothly left, four pits in the crook of the dogleg to catch the pulled and underhit drive, sand right and left at the green to menace what is a very long second shot. This links owes much of its distinction to the design work in 1926 of none other than James Braid.

Opposite: Western Gailes, 18th. Above: Barassie Links of Kilmarnock Golf Club.

ROYAL TROON

Like Western Gailes, Royal Troon, with its championship course and its Portland eighteen, occupies linksland between the railway line and the Firth of Clyde. All the holes along the sea belong to the championship layout. The club was founded in 1878, and Prestwick's Charles Hunter laid out the first golf holes, just five of them. It was Willie Fernie, in 1900, who lengthened the course to eighteen.

Royal Troon has hosted the British Amateur and the British Ladies' Championships five times each, and it has served as the venue for the Open Championship eight times. England's Arthur Havers won the first Open at Troon, in 1923, edging defending champion Walter Hagen by a stroke. Hagen seized this occasion to dramatize his distaste for the treatment too often accorded golf professionals, particularly Americans, by British private clubs. He recounted the moment in his autobiography, *The Walter Hagen Story*:

> After my bunker shot missed and Arthur Havers became the new British Open champion, the secretary . . . insisted that I come into the clubhouse with Havers for the presentation of the trophy. . . . At the doorway I stopped and turned to the enthusiastic gallery.
>
> "I'm sorry I didn't win," I told them. "I've been asked to come to the clubhouse with Arthur Havers for the presentation. . . . But at no time have we Americans been admitted to the clubhouse, not even to pick up our mail. At this particular time I'd like to thank you all for the many courtesies you've extended to us. And . . . I'd like to invite all of you to come over to the pub where we've been so welcome, so that all the boys can meet you and thank you personally. If the Committee likes, they can present the trophy to the new champion over there."
>
> I turned and walked away with . . . the gallery following me to the pub, leaving only the Committee and Arthur Havers at the clubhouse.

In 1950 South African Bobby Locke won the second of his four Opens with a final-round 68 here for a 279 total, the first time 280 was broken in the championship. In 1962 Arnold Palmer captured the claret jug for the second straight year—he had won at Royal Birkdale in 1961—with a record-setting aggregate of 12-under-par 276 (71-69-67-69) that left second-place finisher Kel Nagle 6 strokes back. Only six rounds under 70 were shot in the entire championship, and three of them were by Palmer.

Eleven years later, Tom Weiskopf, on record for disliking the course, tied Palmer's 276 and finished 3 strokes to the good on Johnny Miller and Neil Coles for what would be his only victory in a major. In 1982 Tom Watson's 284 total gave him the fourth of his five Open Championships as twenty-five-year-old Nick Price, up by 3 shots with six holes to play, stumbled to a pair of bogeys and a double bogey. And in 1989 Mark Calcavecchia beat Greg Norman and Wayne Grady in the Championship's first four-hole playoff by completing the four extra holes 2 under par. In the final round of the 1997 Open, Justin Leonard uncorked a glittering 65 to wipe out Jesper Parnevik's 5-stroke lead and win by 3 with 272 (69-66-72-65). And in 2004 an American won here for the sixth consecutive time as Todd Hamilton, a thirty-eight-year-old PGA Tour rookie, edged Ernie Els in a four hole playoff by a stroke after they had tied at ten-under-par 274.

ON THE COURSE

Troon is as classic an example of links golf as is to be found: an out-and-in design with rumpled fairways, grass-covered sand hills, punishing rough, gorse, and remorseless revetted bunkering. Just under 7,200 yards for the 2004 Open, the course is likely to be set up at just over 6,200 yards for visitor play; par is 71. The prevailing wind, which can be counted on about 75 percent of the time, helps going out and hurts coming in. This is another way of saying that we need to get our figures on the first nine, because the second nine is downright hostile.

Having tried to provide a general picture of this links in the preceding two paragraphs, I have little choice now but to spell out a basic aspect of

Opposite: Royal Troon, 11th.

it that will come as an unpleasant surprise for many: Troon is too frequently dull. The first six holes, more or less level, march straight out. The last six holes, also more or less level, march straight in. Despite the necessary differences in length (the 6th, chosen as one of the 500 *Worlds Greatest*, measures 601 yards from the tips), the holes are too much of a piece. There is a sameness about them that borders on monotony. Understand, they are challenging, rigorously so more often than not. But exhilaration is hard to come by.

As for the "middle six," ah, they are another matter altogether. Here we find originality, character, drama. In a couple of instances, they are unnerving simply to look at. But even more to the point they are a delight to play.

At the 355-yard 7th, after six holes paralleling the shore, we turn our back to the sea and, from a raised tee, drive inland. Pot bunkers and a sand hill in the elbow of the gentle right-hand dogleg dare us to cut the corner. Then our second shot must carry a dune and a deep dip to gain the elevated, sand-defended green.

The 8th, called Postage Stamp, measures 123 yards from the back (113 from the regular markers) and is the shortest hole on any Open course. It is honored in *The 500 World's Greatest Golf Holes* as one of the top one hundred. Isolated in the dunes, it has a sharply plateaued, mesa-like green. Birdies are common, but so are double bogeys. The extremely narrow putting surface, about 11 paces wide at the middle, is guarded by five cavernous pits, one at the front, two at each side. The wind may require us to play any club from a 5-metal to a sand wedge. When he triumphed in 1962, Palmer had to go with a 5-iron in one round. In 1997, after just making the cut, Tiger shot 64 in the third round to climb back into the competition. On Sunday, birdies at the 4th and 5th further brightened his chances, but a triple-bogey 6 on the Postage Stamp sent him reeling to 74 and a tie for twenty-fourth. On the other hand, at the age of seventy-one Gene Sarazen came back to Troon for the 1973 Open, fifty years after his initial appearance in the championship, which was also at Troon, and in the opening round notched a hole-in-one here. But my favorite 8th-hole tale is the one about the woman who hit her driver into the bunker short of the green. Even as it plunked into the pit, she wrathfully denounced her caddie: "You underclubbed me!"

Both 9 and 10 measure about 370 yards from the daily markers. Two bunkers threaten the drive on the 9th. Because of high sand hills, only a patch of the 10th fairway is visible from the tee and the shot to the

Opposite: Royal Troon, 8th.

green is blind. There is no greenside sand on either of these sporty and inviting holes, but low dunes flank the putting surface at 9, and gaining the 10th green, with its embankment of gorse on the left and steep falloffs on the right, is a demanding task. In the third round of his Open, Weiskopf was relieved to escape the 9th with no worse than a double bogey after hooking his drive nearly 100 yards off line into a stand of gorse and choosing to drop the ball 125 yards behind the spot where he found it. Later, claret jug safely in his clutches, he laughingly called this strategic decision "one of the longest drops in history."

Play the 11th at 357 yards (regular markers) and you may wonder what all the hullabaloo is about—after all, the 11th is one of the top hundred among "the world's 500," where it is also singled out as one of the 18 most difficult holes and one of the 18 most penal holes. But from the medal tees (421 yards), both danger and drama rear their heads, and from the championship markers (490 yards), well, it can be said that there it takes courage even to place your ball on a wooden peg, not to mention taking a swing at it.

This hole is a story of railway and gorse. The railway runs ominously close along the right for the length of the hole, warning that a slice means a 2-stroke penalty. Our drive, from a small tee up the hillside, involves a fierce forced carry of at least 185 yards over a sea of strangling grasses, heather, and gorse to an angled fairway about 30 yards wide, where gorse awaits both left and right to wreck our card. The drive is blind and claustrophobic. We incline to aim left, away from the cruel combination of railway and gorse. And we incline to steer the tee shot, ideally with a view to a soft fade. The fade may not materialize. So if, in fact, the ball hangs left when it should slide right, it now vanishes, horrifyingly, into what may well be the densest thicket—no, jungle—of shoulder-high gorse in the game.

As for the long second shot, the need to slot it between gorse and railway continues, only now the railway's encroachment is even more pressing, for the green nestles in the very shadow of the low stone wall that separates it from the tracks.

When Palmer won here in 1962, the 11th was a par 5. It is the same length today, 490 yards, but now it is a par 4 in the Open. In the course of the 1962 championship, Palmer posted one eagle, two birdies, and a par here. Nevertheless, he called the 11th "the most dangerous hole I have ever seen." Jack Nicklaus probably agreed. He flew into Troon on the wings of his victory at Oakmont in the U.S. Open, where he had defeated

Opposite: Royal Troon, 12th.

Left: Royal Troon, 17th.
Right: 18th.

Palmer in a playoff. In the first round Nicklaus took a 10 on the 11th. He finished 29 strokes behind the "champion golfer of the year."

The last of Troon's marvelous "middle six" is the 380-yard 12th. There is the merest suggestion of bending right. The fairway pitches and heaves characteristically. A sand-hills ridge renders the drive blind. Every foot of the way is menaced on both sides by throttling rough. The slightly raised green is defended by a bunker tight on the right and a sharp little falloff at the left, where another bunker lurks. It is a superb hole.

Now we head home, essentially on the straight and level and, sad to say, too often on the prosaic. The holes—there are two one-shotters, one par 5, and three par 4s—are testing enough, particularly into the prevailing wind. Sand threatens almost every stroke. A burn crosses the fairway on the par-5 16th, but it should be of no consequence. There is little of an arresting or inspiring nature.

Colin Montgomerie, whose father was club secretary from 1987 to 1997, knows the course better than any other top player. "Royal Troon," he has said, "is more difficult than good." It is a carefully phrased—and pointed—assessment. Troon is solid stuff, offering all the basic ingredients of championship links golf. It is honest, straightforward, stalwart. Over more than eighty years, it has hosted eight Open Championships, so you will certainly want to tackle it. But if you do so in the knowledge that it is not full of flair and fascination, you will probably get more pleasure out of your round.

The club's second eighteen, called Troon Portland, measures 6,274 yards against a par of 70. Laid out by Willie Fernie in 1906, it has not been greatly altered. It offers the challenge of traditional links golf, especially when it comes to the importance of the game along the ground. And the inbound nine has the attractive diversity of three par 3s, par 4s, and par 5s.

Ayrshire is chock-a-block with rewarding places to stay, and Troon is particularly rich:

- **Lochgreen House**, set amid thirty acres of woodlands and gardens, has public spaces with paneling, period paintings, fine furniture, and log fires. Its guest rooms are individually and stylishly appointed (lovely floral chintzes, king-size canopy beds, rugs in the Aubusson manner), and the table d'hôte dinner is superb.

- Overlooking the 18th hole of the championship course and providing marvelous views across the Clyde to Arran and Ailsa Craig, the **Marine** is a golf hotel in the Scottish baronial style. Renovations and redecoration in 2003 and 2004 have upgraded the hotel's appearance and comforts (families particularly appreciate the leisure center with indoor pool), and the menu in the **Fairways Restaurant** is extensive.

- Just across the road from Royal Troon's clubhouse is **Piersland House Hotel**, built in 1899 for the grandson of Johnnie Walker (of Scotch whiskey fame). The original features remain, including oak paneling, stone fireplaces, carved millwork, and a Jacobean embroidery frieze worked by the tapestriere to King George V. The exquisitely landscaped grounds contain a Japanese water garden, and the guest rooms, decorated in period styles with muted colorings, retain their Edwardian charm. The **Brasserie**'s cuisine is imaginative.

- One of only two five-star B&Bs in Ayrshire is **Harford House**, overlooking Troon Darley, a municipal course. The two guest rooms, with a king-size four-poster bed in one, are handsomely appointed, each with its own bath. The welcome by Linda and Steve Ford is a notably warm one, and Steve, a commercial pilot, will even give you an aerial view of the region.

If by some chance you're looking for a Troon pub where golf is king, drop into the **Anchorage Hotel**. When it comes to talking the game, customers compete with bartenders—no amateurs here.

At the Scottish Maritime Museum, in Irvine, the history of seafaring and boat building in Scotland can be explored. Also to be seen here are historic vessels, including the oldest clipper ship in the world, a shipyard worker's tenement home, and a shop where engines were built. In nearby Kilwinning is the Dalgarven Mill, a restored water mill that houses a museum of Ayrshire country life, with costume displays.

PRESTWICK

Next door to Prestwick International Airport lies the Prestwick Golf Club, twenty-seven years older than Royal Troon. It was founded in 1851 by men of means and leisure, many of them landed gentry. More than a century and a half later, there is still a somewhat elitist aura about the great Ayrshire club, although, paradoxically, there is also a notably hospitable attitude toward the unsponsored visitor.

Within weeks of the club's founding, Tom Morris—he was not "Old Tom" then, being all of thirty—was induced to leave St. Andrews and take the post of professional and greenkeeper at the fledgling club. His first assignment was to lay out a twelve-hole course. (The final six holes, also his work, were not added till 1882.)

Here at 12-hole Prestwick, in 1860, was born the Open Championship, the world's first national golf championship and still the most important of all golf competitions. Musselburgh's Willie Park Sr. won the 36-hole event, three rounds of 12 holes, with a 174 total (55-59-60), two strokes better than Tom Morris's.

The championship was played solely at Prestwick through 1872, when St. Andrews and Musselburgh began to take their turns. Prestwick hosted the Open twenty-four times. Among the winners here were, in addition to Park, who also won in 1863 and 1866, Tom Morris Sr. (four times) and Tom Morris Jr. (four times); Willie Park Jr.; Hoylake's celebrated amateur John Ball (eight-time winner of the Amateur Championship); Harry Vardon (three of his six Open victories came at Prestwick); and Jim Barnes, Cornish-born but by 1925, when he won the last Open played at Prestwick, a U.S. citizen. It was the conduct of that championship that spelled the end of the premier event at Prestwick. Carnoustie-born-and-bred Macdonald Smith, the crowd favorite, teed off in the final round with a 5-stroke lead over Barnes. But Smith's thousands of unruly fans (there were no marshals then)—cheering and whooping and rushing about uncontrollably, crowding their hero so that he scarcely had room to take the club back and was rarely in position to see a shot finish—so disturbed him that, as Herbert Warren Wind memorably phrased it in *The Story of American Golf,* "they killed old Mac with their ardor." Smith collapsed to an 82 and a fourth-place finish,

3 strokes behind Barnes, who had closed with a solid 74. It was not long after this tragic debacle that Prestwick was deemed too confined and too short for the Open championship.

ON THE COURSE

Prestwick currently can measure as much as 6,678 yards, but we will play it at 6,544, with a par of 71. The 1st is one of the game's truly lethal opening holes, portentously named Railway. Level, straightaway, and only 346 yards long, it presents a high stone wall running tight along the right side of the fairway from tee to green, the Glasgow–Ayrshire train tracks immediately beyond it. Intruding from the left in the driving area as the fairway narrows sharply is low duneland full of sand, gorse, and heather. The green, with a bunker at the left front, actually extends to within two feet of the wall on the right. There is no breathing space here on the drive or the approach. A fade on either—the wind off the sea encourages just such a miscue—sends our ball over the wall and onto the rails. A pull or hook will not trigger penalty strokes, merely a plunge into penalizing vegetation or sand. This may *not* be a place to trust your swing. At any rate, Railway surfaces in the 500 *World's Greatest Golf Holes* book as one of the top hundred and one of the eighteen most penal. You may be amused by the story—very probably apocryphal—of the woman who sliced her tee shot and hit a passing train's engine, the ball then sailing back over the wall and onto the fairway. Leaning out of his cab, the engineer called to the woman, "If it will be of any help to you, I'll be here at the same time tomorrow."

Well, this is only the beginning of a seaside golf experience that offers towering sand hills, fairways that call up a moonscape, dramatically undulating greens, perhaps the world's two most storied blind holes, and a fabled burn, not to mention one of the game's truly astonishing bunkers. There is so much to defy and delight us here that sometimes we have to remind ourselves how studded with superlative golf holes Prestwick is.

Following the dropping 167-yard 2nd comes a par 5 of only 482 yards that was named one of the five hundred greatest holes. The infamous Cardinal Bunker is its centerpiece. It is a tripartite business: first

Opposite: Prestwick, 11th.

Above: Prestwick, 3rd.
Opposite, left: 17th;
right: 12th.

some 200 yards off the tee, a pair of good-size pits side by side crossing the fairway, then an island of turf, and finally a vast excavation of sand at least forty yards wide and some ten feet deep, its forward ramparts "paneled" with huge timbers standing on end and stretching from one side of the hole to the other. Harry Vardon called this bunker "an ugly brute that gives a sickening feeling to the man who is off his game." There is no way around this hazard—it must be carried. Into a stiff wind, clearing it on our second shot cannot be taken for granted. In the 1908 Open, Braid took eight on the hole after, as Bernard Darwin described it, "playing a

game of rackets against these ominous black boards," but somehow pulled himself together and went on to win the fourth of his five Open Championships. Blame the Cardinal for the railroad ties that Pete Dye installed in bunkers on some of his courses after he first saw this old-world feature here in 1963.

The Pow Burn edges scarily close to the right side of the Cardinal Bunker (as though that blackguard needed reinforcement!), and it sticks with us even more adhesively for the entire length of the 382-yard 4th, which curves gently right. (Some golf historians point to it as having introduced the principle of the dogleg.) The wind off the sea will send even the mildest fade into the Pow on both drive and approach.

The 5th, called Himalayas, is another of Prestwick's legendary holes. For sheer suspense, there is scarcely anything quite like a blind 206-yarder over a twenty-five-foot-high sand hill smothered in wild grasses. Optimistic—perhaps foolishly so—that our shot will scale the Himalayas and float down somewhere onto the concealed putting surface, we have no choice but to swing away. Six greenside pot bunkers—one at the right front, a second at the left front, and four along the left side—make the obstructing sand hill seem almost incidental.

Five consecutive rolling and sternly demanding par 4s now follow: 362 yards, 430 yards, 431, 444, and 454. Sand imperils every swing. That 454-yarder, the 10th, is another of Prestwick's great holes. It plays

directly toward the sea. Our drive, launched from the Himalayas ridge of sand hills, must first clear the Pow Burn. The rather spacious uphill landing area is defined by pits left and right. The hole continues to climb into the prevailing wind as sand brackets the fairway and we struggle—most of us in vain—to reach in two an elevated green that, appropriately, has no sand, just steep falloffs. This is a hole not simply of character but of majesty.

There is no elevation change on the 11th. This 195-yarder plays over broken ground beside the beach to a green ringed by six deep pots. A well-nigh perfect stroke is called for.

The 12th also parallels the beach, but the 513 yards play along a little valley where we are slightly sheltered from the sea winds by low dunes on the right. Despite the string of bunkers down the left, a birdie is pos-

sible here. Which is more than can be said about the par-4 13th. One lonely pot bunker, hidden in the middle of the fairway about 240 yards from the tee, is all the sand there is. But there is length and to spare here, 460 yards, routed over uneven ground. The small green, angled to the fairway, is marked by convolutions and falloffs that make it unreceptive even to a short pitch or chip, to say nothing of an all-stops-out fairway metal. An inarguably great hole of both style and distinction, the 13th is, for many, the finest hole on the links.

Fourteen, 15, and 16 are all short or shortish two-shotters, but none of them is a snap. The 15th (falloffs, low dunes, sand right and left) and 16 (this 288-yarder can be driven by the prodigious hitter willing to run the very real risk of finishing in the Cardinal Bunker) create equal opportunity for birdies and double bogeys.

The 17th may be Prestwick's most unforgettable hole. Going back many decades, world-class players who conquered it, even in merely companionable games, pointed proudly to their achievement. In 1912 Philadelphia's Johnny McDermott, the first American-born-and-bred U.S. Open champion and at that time the holder of the crown, made his initial visit to Britain. In a letter home to fellow Philadelphian A. J. Tillinghast, McDermott boasted of having birdied the "Alps."

down. Our astonished gaze encompasses a vast and cavernous sandpit, with the green on the far side of it. This first view from the pinnacle of the Alps down to the depths of the Sahara Bunker—how would any club dare employ the names of two famous topographical features on one hole?—is one of golf's indelible moments.

The 18th is anticlimactic, a 284-yard par 4 where we aim on the clubhouse clock and strive to stay clear of the sand that awaits right and left 215 yards out as well as greenside. The chance of making a birdie here is obviously a good one. But the green is 141 feet deep, and the indifferent little pitch that meanders away can result in a three-putt bogey.

Little changed over more than a century, Prestwick may indeed be old-fashioned, a "museum," a monument to the era of the gutta percha ball. But say what you will, on this marvelously natural golfing terrain, the game is still vital. In truth, you have not played golf in Scotland unless you have played this great and inimitable course.

NEARBY COURSES

No distance down the road is the **Prestwick St. Nicholas Golf Club**, only four months younger than what some have taken to calling Old Prestwick and counting among its twenty-eight founding members none other than Tom Morris himself. It was an artisan club (caddies were members here from the outset), and the links, laid out between the railway and the sea by Charles Hunter, is the authentic undulating and sand-based stuff, just under 6,000 yards, par 69. Fairways that incline to be narrow and framed by gorse and heather add up to a stern test of driving. Bunkers are not easily avoided. This is a sporty layout that plays firm and fast and offers unimpeded views over the Clyde to Arran and Ailsa Craig.

Some seven or eight miles south, in Ayr, lies **Belleisle**, a very beautiful parkland course laid out by Braid in 1927 and widely viewed as one of Britain's finest inland public courses. Somewhat sheltered, it can be an attractive alternative to windswept links. It is long on the card (6,540 yards, par 70) and long underfoot (relatively little run on the ball). Only two of the par 4s are less than 400 yards. The remaining nine two-shotters are not only more than 400 yards, but, in most instances, much more. And the four par 3s are challenging, particularly the long uphill 3rd and the tricky 17th, played across a burn. Belleisle is all the golf most of us can handle.

This 391-yarder is blind. The green is not in sight on either the drive or on the second shot. There is a big forced carry from the tee over rough ground to a liberal fairway flanked by sand hills. A steep mound about 220 yards out gives way to another level stretch. And then the fun begins. The fairway now climbs abruptly and, along the way, shrinks scandalously, becoming little more than 25 feet wide as it crests this immense sand hill. All we can be sure of is that the green is somewhere on the far side. To have any chance of successfully executing this blind second shot, we must climb the hill and, gaining its peak, look down, straight

Worthy accommodations all but crowd in upon Prestwick Golf Club:

- The **Parkstone Hotel** is on the Esplanade, with wonderful views to Arran. The twenty-two guest rooms in this modern three-star facility are nicely decorated, and the hotel, a member of the Taste of Scotland association, prides itself on its cooking.
- The **Golf View Private Hotel** on Links Road is an intimate four-star guest house with coastal and golf-course views from generous windows; breakfast is the only meal served.
- The **North Beach Hotel**, also on Links Road, has thirteen rooms, many of them with views over the links to the Firth of Clyde. The cooking has a reputation for consistent quality.

A number of sightseeing attractions are distinclty worthwhile. Ayrshire is the land of Robert Burns, Scotland's national poet ("O my Love's like a red, red rose, / That's newly sprung in June: / O my Love's like the melodie, / That's sweetly play'd in tune."). Among the most important sites on the Burns Heritage Trail are the thatched-roof cottage in Alloway where the poet was born in 1759 and which contains the foremost collection of Burns manuscripts and memorabilia; Alloway's Auld Kirk, where he was christened; the Brig o' Doon, scene of Tam o' Shanter's dramatic escape from the hellish witches; the

Burns House Museum, in Mauchline, where Burns lived after his marriage to Jean Armour; Souter Johnnie's Cottage, in Kirkoswald; and the Mount Oliphant, Lochlie, and Mossgiel Farms, where at various times Burns eked out a living.

Shopper alert: Little known to traveling golfers is the Begg of Scotland Mill Shop, in the town of Ayr, which offers a large selection of high-quality ladies' and men's cashmere knitwear at factory prices. The Scots themselves find bargains here.

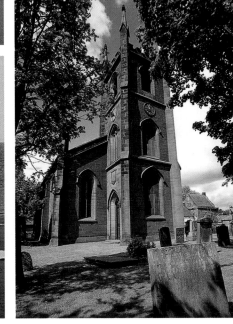

Clockwise from above: near Mauchline; the Mauchline parish church; beach near Alloway; the Robert Burns birthplace.

TURNBERRY

It could be claimed that the Royal & Ancient club was dilatory in waiting till 1977 to assign the Open to Turnberry's Ailsa Course for the first time. The majestic links had for twenty-five years been conceded to be the best course in the west of Scotland. In any event, the Ailsa finally got its due, however long overdue, and the result was the titanic Watson-Nicklaus mano a mano (they were paired on both the third and fourth day) that produced one of the very greatest Open Championships in history. Watson was twenty-seven, Nicklaus ten years his senior. Remarkably, the two posted the same score in each of the first three rounds, 68-70-65. Watson fired another 65 on the last day. Nicklaus, missing a breaking downhill four-footer on the 71st hole, had to be content with 66. Michael Corcoran's book *Duel in the Sun* is the definitive and enthralling account of this open.

Greg Norman, the only player to equal the par of 280 in a championship cursed by vile weather for the first three days, left the field behind in 1986 to win by 5 strokes. There was no runaway in 1994, as Nick Price birdied 16, eagled the par-5 17th (a fifty-foot downhill curler somehow found its way to the cup!), and parred the home hole to post a 268 total that nipped Jesper Parnevik (bogey on 18) by a stroke.

Some fifty miles south of Glasgow on the A77, Turnberry is the only golf resort on the British Open rota. Of the other eight courses that serve as venues for the championship, two are municipal (St. Andrews and Carnoustie) and six belong to private clubs (Royal Birkdale, Royal Liverpool, Royal Lytham & St. Annes, Royal St. George's, Royal Troon, and the Honourable Company of Edinburgh Golfers, Muirfield).

Golf has been played at Turnberry for a hundred years. Concrete runways to accommodate military aircraft scarred many of the holes on both eighteens (Turnberry long had a relief course called Arran) during the two World Wars. Philip Mackenzie Ross (Royal Guernsey and Club de Campo de Malaga are two of his better-known courses) was hired in 1949 to undertake the restoration, which in the case of the Ailsa might better be thought of as a resuscitation, so near to expiring was it. Using modern earth-moving equipment such as the bulldozer, he rerouted a number of holes on the Ailsa, preserving its natural features and bringing boldly to the fore the range of sand hills skirting the shore. The result was a links with a nobility and challenge it had never possessed.

ON THE AILSA COURSE

The Ailsa measures 6,976 yards from the championship tees (par 70), 6,440 from the regular markers (par 69), and 5,757 from the forward tees. The first three holes (358 yards, 381, 409) are a bit of to-and-fro-ing, with minimal elevation change. There is sand right and left at the green on all three and sand in the driving area on the 1st and 2nd.

The next eight holes are strung out like a necklace, along and above the sea. If there is any other links course where eight consecutive holes are able to produce challenge of this level and pleasure of this depth, I don't know where it might be. For what we are talking about here are golf holes so splendid that they actually measure up to the splendor of the scenery. Consider the setting first, as the Firth of Clyde at long last melds into the Irish Sea, with Arran's mountains looming across the water to the north, the curving outline of the Mull of Kintyre due west, and, popping out of the deep in the foreground to claim our attention, rocky, turtle-backed Ailsa Craig, the plug of an extinct volcano. It is a panorama of surpassing fascination and one made all the richer when the day is crystalline, for then we are able to make out, on a southwesterly heading, even Northern Ireland's Antrim Coast, by the Giant's Causeway.

The parade of great golf holes accompanying this riveting seascape begins with the 165-yard 4th, "Woe-Be-Tide," a witty play on words that stems from the presence of the beach along the left. The shot is played uphill across rough ground to a small and strikingly sited plateau green with a long, steep falloff left and a bunker backed by a sand hill at the right. Any kind of wind is a mischief. This is one of the best medium-length one-shotters you will ever play.

The 415-yard 5th curves left along a dune-framed valley, the tee shot falling, the second shot rising, all of it difficult—greenside bunkers front, left, and right—and all of it beautiful. Another great hole.

Opposite: Turnberry Ailsa Course, 9th.

The 6th is the second of the Ailsa's four superlative short holes. It is 221 yards long, hill to hill, three pits tight on the left, a big bunker out front in a sharp rise, a steep falloff right. The shot is all carry. Into a headwind or a left-to-right crosswind, few ordinary mortals can make it. Unveil your best swing and pray! Greatness yet again.

The great 7th is a cousin of the 5th, only a much longer par 4: 475 yards, turning emphatically left ("roon the ben") through the tall sand hills, down off the tee, up to the green. From the championship markers it is a par 5 of 529 yards. Watson hit driver/driver to reach the green and make 4 in the last round of the 1977 Open.

Eight, 431 yards, runs steadily uphill to a sand-defended green that is one of the highest points on the links. Played with a fairway-metal or a long iron, this is one of the most taxing second shots on the course: It must be perfectly struck—line, power, trajectory—or it will fail. The views over Turnberry Bay from the green are entrancing.

The same can be said of the spectacle that awaits at the 9th, which measures 411 yards from the regular markers, 454 from the tips. I urge you to walk out to the championship tee, unless you are subject to vertigo. The teeing ground is a mere scrap of turf atop a crag that towers above the rocky shore. For all the thrill, it is a lonely spot and so starkly exposed to the wind that there will be days when it will be all we can do to hold our position at the ball. The drive from this perch must carry 200 yards over the abyss, past the landmark white lighthouse and the remains of Robert the Bruce's castle, to reach the haven of the far slope. Glorious indeed, but how fierce! The green, subtly angled to the fairway and sand-free, with humpy shoulders on both sides, inclines to shunt away our long second shot. From tee to cup, a powerful experience. You will not be surprised to find this hole one of the top hundred in *The 500 World's Greatest Golf Holes*.

Now comes one final display of seaside grandeur coupled with drama, on the 429-yard 10th. From the headland heights, the drive floats down to a generous fairway, the sea thrashing at the base of the cliff on our left. The long second shot must traverse a large bunker in the center of the fairway, this hazard containing an island of turf ringed by sand.

This magnificent coastal run, which inevitably summons images of Pebble Beach, concludes with the 161-yard 11th, playing along the cliff top to a mildly raised green, sand right and left. A left-to-right crosswind off the water raises hob with any stroke that is less than solid.

Time to turn inland now and surrender the pleasure of shot-making along the shore but not the rewards of tackling first-rate golf

holes all the way home. Two of the remaining seven are among the world's five-hundred greatest. The green at the 380-yard 16th—the hole is called Wee Burn—is fronted by a deep, precipitously sloping swale with a trickle of water at the bottom. There is no penalty-stroke hazard on the preceding hole, the last of the par 3s, which measures 170 yards from the regular markers, 210 from the championship tees. The cavernous drop at the right into broken ground must be avoided at all costs. It was on this hole that Watson, trailing Nicklaus by a stroke in their epic Sunday-afternoon struggle and electing to use a putter from just off the green and 60 feet from the hole, gave the ball a characteristically crisp rap. Off the hardpan it skipped, over the collar, true to the unattended flagstick, and, miraculously, into the cup.

"Was it," I asked Nicklaus three years later (and two years before Watson holed the little pitch of perhaps half that distance on the 17th at Pebble Beach to steal the 1982 Open from Jack), "the most unexpected shot ever hit against you at a critical moment in a major championship?"

"Well," he replied, "that one was a big surprise. I thought there was a chance I might add to my lead, and suddenly we were even. But I got an awful lot out of my short game that week. I'm not sure I hit the ball all that well. Watson obviously played fantastically, and he played one stroke better than I did."

For me, the Ailsa is one of the three best courses in Scotland. And from the standpoint of pure delight in the game, it may well provide the single most satisfying round in the game's birthplace.

Opposite: Turnberry Ailsa Course, 8th. Above, left: 10th; right: 11th.

ON THE KINTYRE COURSE

The Arran Course was reconstructed in 2001—so sweepingly, in fact, that it was even given a new name: Kintyre. Donald Steel was the man behind this wholesale makeover. There are six new holes; there are twelve new greens; the bunkers, all of them revetted, have been carefully reworked. From the championship tees, the Kintyre measures 6,861 yards. (It was used for final qualifying in the 2004 Open, held at Royal Troon.) It is set up regularly at about 6,370 yards, par 71.

The old holes, down their well-remembered channels of menacing gorse, have been freshened, and the new holes are bona fide sparklers. Two of the newcomers, the 8th and 9th, are routed over Bains Hill. The 8th is mysterious. It plays straight out to sea and measures only 298 yards. The tee is high, but there is no sign of the green. It turns out to be hidden, just over a narrow ridge and down in a cove that seems to merge with the rocky strand beyond. This green can be driven, provided you are willing to take on the two nasty pot bunkers that, like the putting surface they defend, are totally concealed. I can't think of a hole that either looks or plays like the Kintyre's 8th. It is an original, and the degree of golfing fun that it provides is incalculable.

The stimulating tee shot on the 9th, a short par 5 playing from high ground into the prevailing southwesterly, actually crosses the approach to the 8th green as it wings away against Turnberry's two symbols, the light-house and Ailsa Craig. The fairway, running parallel to the coast on land that had just been waiting to be pressed into service, is at first well above the water; then it drops, by way of a grassy buffer zone, to the shore.

Make no mistake about it: The Kintyre is a treat. It will be interesting to see whether, like the New Course at St. Andrews, it finds a place in the top hundred courses of the British Isles.

Opposite: Turnberry Kintyre Course, 8th. Below: 9th.

Remarkably, the hotel itself at Turnberry—the long white Edwardian structure stretched out on the crest of a hill, monarch of all it surveys—manages the difficult feat of living up to the superlative golf. It is luxurious yet relaxed, the epitome of Old World graciousness. Public rooms are welcoming, stylish, comfortable, and blessed with those nearly incomparable land-and-sea vistas. Much the same can be said of the guest accommodations, which reflect a thoughtful attention to detail (heated towel racks, terrycloth slippers to match the robes). Rooms on the front, looking out over the links to the sea, are especially bright and spacious, and it is not uncommon to find two crystal chandeliers, one over the beds, the other over the sitting area.

The spa boasts a glass-fronted indoor swimming pool more than 60 feet long that embraces the sea views. There are also steam rooms, sauna, a plunge pool, the latest fitness equipment, twelve treatment rooms, and a staff trained to provide hydrotherapy, aromatherapy, massage, mud wrap, and holistic ministrations.

The hotel's cooking is sublime. Among the dishes served regularly at the **Turnberry** are a haddock and saffron risotto with poached egg, fennel cream, and Parmesan; smoked and seared medallions of Scottish beef with mushrooms, creamed spinach, caramelized butter onions, and a malt whiskey jus; and, for dessert, warm apple *vol au vent* with cinnamon cream, honey syrup, and Calvados ice cream. The wine list is carefully chosen, comprehensive, and provocative to peruse (just under a thousand dollars for a bottle of Château d'Yquem, 1983, a very good dessert wine indeed). But as though to prove that the best things in life are free, we find ourselves mesmerized by the magic of a pink-tinted golden sunset suffusing the western sky beyond Ailsa Craig.

For more informal and less expensive dining, the **Terrace Brasserie** at the spa presents a selection of lighter dishes, with the emphasis on natural ingredients and Mediterranean flavors.

About a hundred yards from the hotel building itself is the outdoor activity center. Among its offerings are trout fishing in the resort's own loch, clay-target shooting, archery, falconry, off-road driving, mountain biking, and horseback riding (gallop down the beach in the very shadow of those seaside holes on the Ailsa's first nine, where pars are so dearly bought).

What it all adds up to is a transcendent golf resort, a cornucopia of the good life with the game as its soul. Turnberry is without peer at the sea, not simply in Scotland but anywhere in the British Isles.

Virtually next door to Turnberry and high above the sea on tree-clad cliffs is **Culzean Castle**, a magnificent late-eighteenth-century castellated mansion designed by Robert Adam that is now a museum open to the public. General Eisenhower occupied it as his headquarters prior to the Normandy invasion, and the top floor was later presented to him for his lifetime use. This large accommodation has been converted by the National Trust for Scotland into six beautifully appointed guest apartments. We've not stayed here, but friends who have say that it was a unique and thoroughly enjoyable experience.

A few miles east of Culzean Castle, on the A77, is Crossraguel Abbey, whose ruins evoke the life of Cluniac monks here from the thirteenth through sixteenth centuries. More intact and extensive than most such ruins,

Crossraguel includes a turreted gatehouse, a dovecote, and a rectangular chapter house with groined vaulting.

Purely for fun, and nearby, is a section of the road to Danure that is famous for an optical illusion known as the Electric Brae. You would wager your favorite putter that the car you're driving is heading uphill, when in truth it is going downhill.

Top row, from left: Girvan shore; Crossraguel Abbey arch. Bottom row: Culzean Castle views and a gatehouse at Crossraguel.

LANARK

Just where is the Lanark Golf Club? In Strathclyde, southeast of Glasgow and a very pretty two-hour drive from Turnberry across meadows and over hills. A good forty miles from the sea, Lanark is a moorland course. It is built on washed glacial sand and gravel, which produce not only terrain that drains quickly but topography full of hummocks and wrinkles and ripples. Fairways in season are firm and fast, encouraging us to play much of the game along the ground. As at Boat of Garten and Edzell, you would swear this is links golf.

Founded in 1851, Lanark is among the twenty-five oldest golf clubs in the world, the same age as Prestwick and Prestwick St. Nicholas. It was in 1851 that Old Tom Morris laid out an eighteen here, charging the club £3.50 for his services. North Berwick's Ben Sayers lengthened and toughened the Morris design fifteen years later. The course we play today, however, is largely the offspring of the ubiquitous Braid and his partner John Stutt, who in 1927 substantively modified the layout, even building new holes at the 13th and 14th.

In 2001, to mark its 150th anniversary, the club published an addendum to the history of its first hundred years. Here are a few of the moments that lightened this new chronicle: In 1953 the club considered removing the sheep from the course, but this would have meant giving up annual income of £85 for grazing rights. . . . Watering the greens in 1953 was a matter of persuading the local fire department to carry out a hose exercise on the golf course. . . . Sunday golf was turned down in 1960, but the vote to permit it carried by a large majority the next year. . . . In 1981 the club bought its first TV set, with the stipulation that "it was only to be used for important occasions." . . . In 1985 there was consternation when the need to renew the club liquor license was overlooked by the secretary, precluding the sale of whiskey for almost a month.

ON THE COURSE

Gently rolling Lanark insists that we keep our wits about us or pay the price exacted by bunkers and burns and boundaries, thick, tussocky rough, spinneys of pines and stands of gorse, and the characterful greens.

The imaginative routing plan sees to it that consecutive holes never run in the same direction, thus introducing again and again the element of surprise into the round, not to mention the constant adjustments needed to combat the wind. And speaking of surprise, there are three pairs of crisscross holes: 1 and 18, 2 and 15, 9 and 10.

Don't expect greatness here, where the back tees add up to a length of 6,428 yards (par 70). There are a couple of humdrum holes and a handful of birdie opportunities. But nine or ten holes are very good, including four strong two-shotters. The 459-yard 2nd calls for both hitting

Opposite: Lanark, 14th.
Above: 4th.

Lanark, 18th.

and control as it doglegs nicely right, presents frustrating fairway hummocks early, middle, and late, and serves up a green defended by sand, falloffs, and mounds. The 4th is almost as muscular, 446 yards, a case of down, up, down, and up to an elevated green. The 12th, 357 yards, bends smoothly right (sand tight at the right in the tee-shot landing area) to reveal a beautifully sited narrow plateau green bunkered at the left and with steep falloffs at the front and the right. Our approach shot has to be perfect. On the 388-yard 14th, a rising drive is followed by a shot that must carry a deep hollow just short of another plateau green.

The 18th is a tester and, as it happens, also a charmer. It is that rarity for a finishing hole, a one-shotter, in this instance 207 yards long and downhill ever so slightly. What makes the hole memorable is the location of the stone clubhouse, no more than 20 feet from the right side of the green. Twenty feet is close—seven paces. Still, I was assured that the clubhouse is not struck by a ball as often as twice a year and that never has a window been broken.

You will enjoy a game at Lanark, with its panorama of distant hills, some of them wooded, some of them farmland in shades of beige and green. The linkslike topography so far from the sea is a delight, and the club is most hospitable. Be sure to look at the trophies, particularly the Silver Claret Jug, remarkably similar to the Open Championship claret jug and, dating to 1857, actually fifteen years older.

If you are overnighting in Lanark, a good bet is **Cartland Bridge Country House**, an imposing structure little changed since its days a century ago as the home of a rich Clyde shipbuilder. Though the hotel is not luxurious, public spaces and guest rooms have a stately air about them. Fireplaces, paneling, old gilt-frame oil paintings, and intricate plasterwork all contribute to the feeling of a more tranquil age. Views over the wooded and hilly property are enchanting. As for the cooking, the menu is likely to be limited—such staples as salmon, chicken, and beef, prepared simply—but the ingredients are fresh and the net of it on our stay was satisfying.

Unlike Ayrshire, Strathclyde is not full of tourist attractions, but it does boast the Falls of Clyde, dramatic waterfalls in a long gorge of the Clyde River, and New Lanark. In 1820, with the Industrial Revolution shifting into high gear, factory owner Robert Owen, a visionary humanitarian, recognized the need for safe working conditions complemented by decent housing. So on the Clyde River he built New Lanark, a then pioneering industrial town that provided a school system (including the world's first nursery school) and free health care. New Lanark, with its uniform look, is today a living museum and a UNESCO World Heritage Site. You would find a visit memorable.

Below: in New Lanark.
Right: the Falls of Clyde.

MUIRFIELD AND
THE EAST LOTHIAN COAST

MUSSELBURGH

A level, slightly scruffy, somewhat weedy, and largely featureless nine-hole course inside a racetrack is not why we cross an ocean. Yet Musselburgh Links, The Old Golf Course (its formal designation), should not be ignored. For this is truly sacred ground: Six Open Championships were contested here, between 1874 and 1889, on holes akin to the ones we play today.

The course is six miles east of Edinburgh, in East Lothian. Mary Queen of Scots is said to have played on the Musselburgh links in 1567. James VI of Scotland (James I of England) is supposed to have played here in 1603. Rather more important, the first golf tournament strictly for women was held at Musselburgh in 1810, when the town's fishwives teed off, the prize being a new creel (a small fish basket) and scull.

By 1875 the nine-hole course was shared among four clubs—Musselburgh (later Royal) Golf Club, the Honourable Company of Edinburgh Golfers, Bruntsfield Links Golfing Society, and Edinburgh Burgess (now the Royal Burgess Golfing Society of Edinburgh)—to say nothing of the general public. For roughly half a century, Musselburgh—with its prestigious clubs, its wealth of outstanding local players (most of them professionals/caddies), its golf equipment makers (the Gourlay family for balls and the McEwan family for clubs), and its role as a six-time venue for the Open Championship—could claim to having eclipsed mighty St. Andrews.

Musselburgh's Mungo Park, Willie Jr.'s brother, won the first Open contested on his home turf, in 1874, with a 36-hole total of 159, two strokes better than Young Tom Morris. Bob Ferguson, also of Musselburgh, won the Open there in 1880. Like most of the leading players of the age, Ferguson was a professional/caddie, so I suppose we should not be surprised to find Bernard Darwin writing in 1910, thirty years after Ferguson's first Open victory: "At Musselburgh there is a right line and a wrong line [for shots] and if we are very fortunate, or very highly honoured, we may have it pointed out to us and our clubs carried for us by Bob Ferguson, who won the championship three times running. . . ."

It was fitting that the final Open at Musselburgh, in 1889, was won by perhaps the town's most illustrious golfing son, Willie Park Jr. This was his second Open victory, his first having come two years earlier at Prestwick. An accomplished putter—it was he who said that "the man who can putt is a match for anyone"—Willie Jr. also carved out a reputation in golf course architecture on both sides of the Atlantic. Among his outstanding courses are Sunningdale's Old Course, Formby, and Huntercombe, all in England, and the North Course at suburban Chicago's Olympia Fields, the venue for the 2003 U.S. Open.

ON THE COURSE

Having shamelessly managed to pass by Musselburgh over a period of thirty years, I finally could live with myself no longer. Shortly before ten o'clock on Thursday, July 26, 2001, I presented myself, alone, at the golf house, which contains small and spartan changing rooms and a space for the green-fee-collector/starter to do business. I teamed up with two local ladies, Felicity (short and well into her seventies) and Joan (tall and in her early sixties). They vowed to show me the way, though it would not be easy to go off the prescribed path on this straightforward and very compact layout that appears to be routed over less than thirty acres.

The mile-long racetrack has been here since 1816. Today only four shots begin or end outside the white rails. All others take place within the infield. The par-35 course measures 2,808 yards.

It was a pleasure to play with the ladies, who seemed to relish my good shots every bit as much as their own. Joan got the ball airborne with some regularity and probably scored in the low 50s. Felicity's efforts were not so, well, felicitous, and she did not break 60. Still, both enjoyed themselves.

The nine begins with a par 3 named, aptly, the Short Hole. It is 160 yards long and simplicity itself. A matched pair of pot bunkers, one at the right front and one at the left front, make clear the requirements of the shot. Almost all the bunkers are penal: steep-faced and revetted, in the classic links tradition. The rough, often fiercely thick, is also penal.

There are no trees, gorse is scarce, and holes often lack definition. The fairways on this sand-based terrain were weed infested, but we did not play preferred lies. The greens, small to medium and with little

Opposite: Musselburgh, 4th.
Previous spread: North
Berwick East Course, 13th.

some complex contouring has to stay clear of the sand right and left. Strong stuff, indeed, like Mrs. Forman's libations.

If you do make it a point to play The Old Golf Course, consider using a set of hickory-shaft clubs, which you can rent right here.

NEARBY COURSES

While we're within hailing distance of the capital, a light once-over of a handful of Edinburgh courses and two other Musselburgh courses might be in order. **Royal Musselburgh**, designed by Braid in 1924, is a solid, tree-lined layout with five long par 4s. What may be most memorable here is the mansion that is the clubhouse, one of the most impressive in the United Kingdom. Less than fifteen minutes away is the **Musselburgh Golf Club**, at Monktonhall. Another worthy test, the eighteen here is laid out over ground ranging from level to gently rolling. There is plenty of room off the tee, but sand consistently threatens the shots to the green.

Ronnie David Bell Mitchell Shade, a five-time Scottish Amateur champion and a four-time Walker Cupper in the 1960s, grew up at **Duddingston Golf Club**. The uncanny straightness of his shots prompted one journalist to suggest that the initials R.D.B.M. really stood for "Right Down the Bloody Middle." This kind of accuracy is essential at Duddingston, where the bunkering is almost as menacing as the burn, which comes between player and target eleven times in the course of the round.

Unlike Duddingston, **Dalmahoy**, three miles from Edinburgh Airport, is not a golf club; it is a full golf resort with two eighteens and 151 accommodations. The golf on these gently rolling meadowlands courses is good but, by and large, lacking in excitement. The par-68 West Course is only 5,200 yards long. The par-72 East Course, however, laid out by Braid in 1926, is 6,670 yards. There is a good birdie opportunity on the wide-open 505-yard 1st hole and an excellent chance to follow that illusory start with bogeys on the 2nd (435 yards), 3rd (446 yards), 4th (430 yards), and 5th (461 yards).

The upper echelon of Edinburgh private golf clubs consists of the **Royal Burgess Society of Edinburgh** and the **Bruntsfield Links Golfing Society**. Founded in 1735, Royal Burgess may thus claim to be the oldest continuously established golfing society or club in the world; Bruntsfield incorporated in 1761. Both clubs first played their golf on the Bruntsfield Links itself, a common not far from the city center, and then, in the last quarter of the nineteenth century, at Musselburgh. But the explosive popularity of the game forced another move, shortly before the

character, were slow. A sprinkler plagued us at three of the greens, but I had to smile: This was not the kind of problem that Bob Ferguson or Willie Park Jr. ever had to deal with. Nonetheless, the day was sunny and warm, the company was convivial, and the game was golf. I was delighted to be abroad on this storied links.

The 2nd and 3rd holes, a pair of short par 4s, play in front of the grandstand, reminding us that 150 years ago the Honourable Company found a couple of rooms somewhere in the back to serve as a makeshift clubhouse, and also reminding me that when the Thoroughbreds are running and the crowds are cheering, the golfers are sidelined.

The nine has four good holes: 1, 5 (called the Sea Hole, though the Firth of Forth, once quite near the back of the green, has by now retreated more than the length of a football field), 6, and 9. And there is one hole that is terrific, the 424-yard 4th. (It is called Mrs. Forman's, the name of the old whitewashed tavern right behind the green. For decades, a pass-through cut out of a wall in the pub saw to it that the game could proceed apace even while the players savored their pint. Now you have to use the door if you're thirsty.) The hole doglegs right, around the race-track starting gate, and the long second shot to an angled green with

Above: Royal Musselburgh, 18th. Opposite: Bruntsfield, 9th.

turn of the nineteenth century. With Royal Burgess taking the lead, the clubs each bought ground in Edinburgh's Barnton district, built fine clubhouses, and, for the first time, constructed golf courses. Both clubs radiate an atmosphere of welcome and warmth and well-being. The two eighteens are pretty parkland layouts: rolling, tree-studded, manicured, each with its quota of good holes. Strategically sited trees and an innocent-looking low-cut rough that will snuff a thin hit—it is these elements that give Burgess and Bruntsfield a measure of test. Like the clubs themselves, the two courses can be viewed as gentlemanly.

And then there is **Braid Hills**, specifically Braids No. 1 (the No. 2 Course is too short and too altitudinous to be taken seriously). Hundreds—perhaps thousands—of trees have been planted here in recent years, threatening to spoil this treasure. It is doubtful that the philistines can be forced to retreat, but meanwhile, with their depredations not fully in flower, we continue to play what has long been one of the world's grandest municipal courses, where Tommy Armour and James Braid won club championships; where the length from the back tees is all of 6,172 yards (par 70) and the green fee is not all of £18; where the views of the capital, including the castle on its crag, are of breathtaking grandeur; and where the round inevitably calls up Royal Dornoch and Ballybunion and Royal County Down. There are narrow plateau fairways to be hit—and held; gorse-covered hillsides (à la Dornoch, a golden blaze in May) to be given a wide berth; the occasional rock outcropping; the more than occasional humps and hillocks and hollows and mounds and swales; tees high and cruelly exposed to the winds (after all, this is the "breezy Braids"); greens in wonderfully natural dell-like settings that call for precisely struck irons or, failing that, highly creative chipping; and, it need hardly be said, feature holes aplenty.

I think of the 202-yard 13th, which rises modestly over broken ground to a tightly bunkered green where nothing less than a perfect swing, sometimes with a driver if the wind is at us, will suffice. Be prepared to repeat that perfect driver swing immediately. Reminiscent of the 9th at Royal County Down, the 378-yard 14th calls for a long forced carry from an elevated tee across a gorse-covered hillside to the safety of a blind landing area in the valley below. Accomplish that and you are left with a medium-length iron over another expanse of gorse to the shelter of the green. The great James Braid (this facility, dating to 1889, is not named after him) once characterized Braids No. 1 as "absolutely rich in sporting quality . . . scenery from every point that is romantically beautiful, and air that makes one feel a good few years younger while playing."

Opposite: Braid Hills
No. 1, 16th.

Vibrant and graspable and fascinating Edinburgh is full of things to see and do that need scarcely be noted in this book (with the possible exception of the vast putting green at the heart of the sunken gardens in Princes Street). The city also offers an assortment of outstanding hotels, including:

- The **Balmoral**, luxe in every respect and towering over the Waverly Street train station, in the center of town.
- The **Caledonian Hilton**, also five star, around the corner from the Castle and boasting a bar that is a popular meeting spot and a spa that is a rare amenity.
- **Channings**, quiet and stylish, five period town houses cheek-by-jowl in the West End.
- The **Howard**, a five-minute walk from Princes Street, fifteen generous rooms and three suites, no bar or restaurant.

There is one other accommodation, in truth not all that comfortable and not actually in the city. But it is unique.

Long ago we spent a week no more than twenty minutes' drive from downtown in a fragment of a fifteenth-century castle. It sleeps seven. There was and is no housekeeper, no cook, no help of any kind. Still, it is wonderfully atmospheric, isolated on a wooded and rocky promontory high above the River North Esk. Next door, on even higher ground, is a striking stone church, also dating from the fifteenth century. We rented the castle from the Landmark Trust, proprietor of Kintyre's Shore Cottage. Over the years since, our thoughts have gone back to this extraordinary accommodation, but it was never in the forefront of our minds. Not until some seventeen years later, that is, when we read the novel that all the world seemed to be devouring, *The Da Vinci Code*. Imagine our astonishment at finding this high-speed potboiler ending in Rosslyn Chapel, mere paces from **Rosslyn Castle**, where we had stayed in 1986. Our Christmas card that year had shown the hauntingly beautiful church.

Views of Edinburgh, including the castle from West Princes Street Gardens (above), Rosslyn Castle (bottom), Doune Castle (right), and the Royal Mile buildings (opposite).

NORTH BERWICK

About thirty minutes east on the coast road from Musselburgh lies North Berwick, with its two widely curving bays, its little sheltering harbor, and its two seaside eighteens. The West Links is for me one of the seven or eight best courses in Scotland and one of my very favorites in all the world.

It was in 1850 that the railway first reached North Berwick, from Edinburgh and via Musselburgh. With the trains came vacationers, many of them people of means and prominence, so many that fashionable hotels and handsome villas sprang up right and left in the latter part of that century. Golf was a principal element in the town's appeal, and two individuals were in the forefront of the boom.

A.J. (Arthur James) Balfour, a Member of Parliament whose ancestral home was in nearby Whittinghame, would serve variously as Chief Secretary to Ireland, Home Secretary, and Prime Minister. Balfour seemed at times to live for golf, which he took up at the age of thirty-six. He was captain of North Berwick Golf Club in 1891 and 1892. In his excellent history *Golf: Scotland's Game*, David Hamilton quotes from the prime minister's memoirs:

> I spent each September at North Berwick, at the Bass Rock Hotel, or in later years at Bradbury's, in rooms which looked down on the seventeenth green and the first tee. . . . I lived a solitary and well-filled life, playing two rounds of golf or more a day, and in the evening carrying on my official work, and such philosophical and literary undertakings as I happened to be engaged on. Each Friday after my morning's round I drove to Whittinghame . . . in a brougham, with a pair of horses, and spent the weekend with my family and guests.

In 1898 *The Times* noted with a touch of sarcasm Balfour's role in the game that had fairly recently become so popular in England: "Mr. Balfour has insensibly attained to a sort of grandmastership of golf players in this country. . . . A new golf club can hardly be satisfactorily set on foot without his assistance.

The correct thing to do is either to make him President [of the new club] or . . . an honorary member and then induce him to play over the new course, or to make a little speech to the players or better still to do both."

The other man who helped put North Berwick front and center was Mr. Balfour's frequent foursomes (alternate stroke) partner, Bernard "Ben" Sayers. All of five feet three inches tall and 130 pounds, "Wee Ben" made golf clubs and balls, gave lessons, and played in every tournament of consequence (winning 24, in Scotland and England), to say nothing of big-money challenge matches. It is said that he once worked in a circus as an acrobat, and there are accounts of his executing a series of cartwheels and handsprings on the green after holing a 45-foot putt. He also climbed 40 feet off the ground to the roof of Wemyss Castle, club in hand, to fire a recovery shot 150 yards down the fairway.

Sayers was consistently sunny, his cheerful disposition laced with a ready wit. Often partnered in foursomes with Andra Kirkaldy, Ben also faced off against the dour St. Andrean in high visibility "brag matches." In one such contest he wore an unidentifiable contraption over his shoulder and attached to the grip of a pitching club. When asked afterward how much this curio had helped him, he replied, "Not a bit. I just used it to frighten Andra." And when he sent a postcard to Andra from the United States (Sayers was visiting his son George, then the professional at Merion), he addressed it "Andra, Hell Bunker, St. Andrews, Scotland." It did reach Kirkaldy, who at the next Open buttonholed Ben to ask what he meant "by sending a postcard like that." Ben answered, "I lost your address and this was the only one I thocht on."

Nothing contributed more to Wee Ben's celebrity than his role as golf professional to the royal family. He gave lessons, sometimes playing lessons, at Windsor Castle to King Edward VII, King George V, Queen Alexandra, Princess Victoria, and others. He also made a set of clubs for King Edward, whom he had first met at North Berwick. The king asked him on that occasion how Grand Duke Michael of Russia, one of Ben's pupils, was progressing. The ever candid Sayers replied, "I am sorry to inform your majesty that he is one of the keenest and one of the worst."

Opposite: North Berwick West Course, 15th.

ON THE EAST COURSE

North Berwick has continued to thrive chiefly because its courses have steadily attracted golfers from all over the world. The East (or Glen) Links is the lesser of the two. It is strictly holiday golf, but that in no sense detracts from the pleasure—if not the challenge—in playing it. Total yardage is just under 6,100 yards; par is 69. It was Sayers who designed the first nine, in 1894, and it was he and James Braid who collaborated on the second nine in 1906. Following the Second World War, Philip Mackenzie Ross made certain revisions.

Laid out on clifftops high above the sea, the East presents enthralling views. Into the prevailing wind, half a dozen of the par 4s are quite testing. And in any kind of breeze, so are all four of the one-shotters: the 4th (190 yards), 9th (250 yards), 13th (a blind 146-yarder with the green in a hollow a good 100 feet below the tee), and 16th (200 yards).

ON THE WEST COURSE

It is the West Links, however, that has drawn knowledgeable golfers to North Berwick for 150 years. The combination of authentic links golf, inarguably great holes, and ravishing sea views—Bass Rock, the islets of Fidra, the Lamb, and Craigleith, and the coast of Fife—makes the game here a joyous occasion every step of the way.

Though we're inclined to think of this course as having simply evolved over many decades, one individual ought to be given a measure of credit for it. David Strath, a St. Andrean, accepted the greenkeeper job here in 1876. In less than three years, as Geoffrey Cornish and Ronald Whitten relate in *The Architects of Golf,* he formalized the course, extended it from nine to eighteen holes, and so thoroughly revised the 14th (Perfection) and 15th (Redan) that these holes gained worldwide renown. In years to come, first Tom Dunn and then Sir Guy Campbell would make limited revisions, but for well over a hundred years the best holes have been very little changed. Like Prestwick, the West Links is, if you will, a museum of the game, taking us back to the latter half of the nineteenth century.

The course, measuring 6,317 yards against a par of 71, is laid out on undulating linksland that lies 10 to 30 feet above sea level. Dunes, beach, burns, long rough grasses, blind shots, and stone walls are all critical elements. Thanks to the elongated figure-8 design, both the outbound and inbound nines have their share of seaside holes. There is a beguiling unpredictability about the routing plan, but then, the West Links has rather more than its share of surprises, beginning with the opening hole.

Called Point Garry Out (the 17th is Point Garry In), the 1st measures just 328 yards. The breeze, however, is generally into us, and the beach is unsettlingly close. The anticipated flow of the hole is interrupted about 190 yards from the tee by a vast sandy area that isolates the well-elevated green from the fairway. We have no choice but to lay up, then play a little longer approach than we would like, the green perched 20 feet above us. The concealed green, which can be counted on to be fast, slopes perilously toward the rocks and the sea. This is an entirely natural hole and a nonpareil. It is also potentially lethal. Once, in an important medal competition, Mr. Balfour took 8 here.

The next two holes, both great two-shotters (more like three-shotters into a west wind), are straightforward. The 435-yard 2nd, named Sea, begins from an elevated tee. The shoreline eats into the fairway on the right; the merest push or cut sends us down onto the beach, a hazard from which the ball may be played but in which the club may not be grounded. The left side of the fairway is studded with giant hillocks that sometimes obstruct our view to the green. On the 3rd, 460 yards, the

beach is less magnetic, but the long second shot, almost always a fairway metal, must clear a low stone wall. A thin hit here rebounds from the wall or, worse, huddles in its shadow. To play this pair of par 4s, into the prevailing wind, in a total of 8 strokes is beyond dreaming.

The next six holes head inland, and though not so thrilling as the opening trio, are very testing. Two of them were chosen for the 500 *World's Greatest Golf Holes* book. At the 353-yard 7th, the Eil Burn fronts the green, which is also tightly bunkered on the right, bounded by a wall on the left, and backed by high grass. On the 496-yard 9th, it is the drive that teases. The hole turns left in the tee-shot landing area; an out-of-bounds wall on the left forces us right, where two bunkers, solidly in the fairway, await. The daring player who can slot his drive into the gap between wall and sand has a chance to reach the elevated green in 2. Boldness and accuracy on this classic risk–reward hole can produce a birdie.

Following three good holes near the sea—the 161-yard 10th, played from high in the sand hills, is particularly worthy—the inbound nine unveils a fine and thrilling long run home.

Opposite, top: North Berwick East Course, 13th; bottom: 16th. Above, left: North Berwick West Course, 1st; right: 4th.

The 355-yard 13th doglegs smoothly left to a green that is shoehorned into a hollow, one blockaded by a low stone wall and backstopped by a high sand hill. Delicately clearing the wall, which is less than three feet short of the putting surface, on our 125-yard approach shot—almost like a high-jumper slithering over the bar!—calls for very pure ball-striking.

On the 14th, 382 yards long, both shots are blind; the drive is into wickedly choppy terrain with sand right and tousled rough left. Our iron is then fired over a high diagonal ridge, the ball disappearing downhill toward a bunkered low-plateau green scarcely two paces from the beach. We are hitting straight out to sea on this second shot, desperately hoping that somewhere down there we will find a safe harbor. Just choosing the right club—never mind swinging it well—prompts fearful indecision. A brilliant and unique hole.

We now putt out, ring the all-clear bell, and proceed to the 15th, Redan, a military term that refers to a type of guarding parapet. This is one of the most copied holes in the world, and in the 500 *World's Greatest Golf Holes* book it is one of the top one hundred. On this 190-yarder, the flag can be seen but not the green. Angled away beyond a deep bunker under its left

front flank, the green also slopes downward to the left and the rear. More-over, there is a high shoulder at the right front of the green, plus three pits awaiting the shot that misses on that side. On a given day, depending on the wind and the location of the cup, the shot called for may be a draw, a fade, or a low, straight "chaser" that dashes onto the green.

There is a lot going on here, and that is surely the chief appeal of this great one-shotter. Charles Blair Macdonald simulated it—he may even have improved on it—at the 4th hole of the National Golf Links of America, in Southampton, New York, the first great American course. And next door, at Shinnecock Hills, a close look at the 7th (which caused calamity in the final round of the 2004 U.S. Open) reveals another Redan hole, this one the effort of William Flynn and Dick Wilson, which was also inspired by the granddaddy of them all, the 15th at North Berwick.

Macdonald comes to mind again at the next hole, where our drive on this level 403-yarder must clear a stone wall and, about 200 yards out, a ditch. As for the green, is there another quite like it in the British Isles? This long, narrow surface is divided into three discrete parts, from front to rear: plateau, trough, plateau. Fail to place your second shot on the

part where the hole is cut and the likelihood of three putts is imminent. This green obviously prompted the even more eye-popping 9th green at Macdonald's great Yale University course.

The 17th has always seemed to me to be one of the very best holes on a course that has more than its share of "very best holes." At 422 yards, level for the first half and uphill for the second, it is long. We can well employ the frequently helping breeze. The broad and tumbling and naturally sculpted fairway makes a grand platform for the long uphill second shot. The green cannot be seen, but the flagstick can.

The 18th, a 275-yard par 4 and in that respect similar to the last hole at Prestwick, is the best birdie chance on the course. Today's power hitters can easily reach the large, bunker-free green, a plateau with a hollow in front and gentle falloffs at the sides. The only hazard is the road bordering the right side of the fairway, which is always lined with parked cars (St. Andrews). Hundreds of dents must be incurred here in the course of a year. Still, there is ample room to drive left (St. Andrews again). Back-dropping the green is the handsome and comfortable stone clubhouse of the North Berwick Golf Club, where visiting players are welcome for a drink or a meal or some good talk about this sublime links.

For pure golfing pleasure—a pleasure bred of diversity, challenge, unpredictability, proximity to the sea, and the satisfaction of true links shot-making—few courses can equal North Berwick's West Links. Is it a candidate for the one course to play, day in and day out, for the rest of your life? Oh my, yes.

Opposite: North Berwick West Course, 14th.

The hotel choices in East Lothian are nearly limitless:

- The **Marine**, just off the 16th fairway of North Berwick's West Links, was extensively refurbished in 2005 and 2006. A stately turreted pile, it offers eighty-three rooms and suites (half of them with sea views), a sauna, heated outdoor swimming pool, tennis, and billiards. The bar is especially welcoming and the cooking is creative.

- **Blenheim House**, a small hotel that caters to golfers, is a two-minute walk from the 1st tee of the West Links. It is quiet, professionally run, moderately priced. Room 15 is a spacious accommodation (double bed and single bed) with a large bay window overlooking the municipal putting green, the strand, the harbor, the 1st tee and 18th green of the West Links, and the Firth itself.

- **Glebe House**, a centrally located Georgian mansion behind a garden wall, lacks the views provided by the Marine and Blenheim House, but its furniture (many antiques) and furnishings are superior. It is almost certainly North Berwick's best B&B and surely an excellent value.

Roughly halfway between North Berwick and Gullane on the coast road lies Dirleton, one of the prettiest villages in Scotland. There are two triangular village greens and a ruined thirteenth-century castle that encompasses a garden and a seventeenth-century bowling lawn. Guest rooms at the **Open Arms**, though smallish, are tastefully decorated, and some have a view of the ancient castle. A particularly delicious entrée in the inn's intimate **Library Restaurant** is the saddle of wild venison wrapped in pancetta and presented on a bed of chive mash with roast parsnips.

Another dining spot worth keeping in mind is the **Waterside Bistro**, in Haddington, an atmospheric pub and restaurant that serves bar snacks as well as complete meals. Go for lunch on a lovely day, when you can sit outside, on the bank of the River Tyne and in the lee of an old triple-arched stone bridge, gazing idly across the water at fourteenth-century St. Mary's Collegiate Church and enjoying a toasted ham and cheese sandwich and a pint of lager. Such an idyllic setting, which calls up Constable or Turner and which surfaces with considerable frequency across the face of England, is a rarity in Scotland.

Opposite: Dirleton Castle. Left: Bass Rock. Middle column, from top: the Open Arms; Tantallon Castle; the Marine. Above: Tantallon Castle.

DUNBAR

Less than twenty minutes east along the coast road from North Berwick, lies the seaside resort of Dunbar, a historic fortress-port and royal burgh where once again we find that the game, or some rudimentary form of it, has been played for more than 350 years. As early as 1640, a local clergyman was disciplined and held up to public disgrace "for playing gowfe" on Sunday.

The Dunbar Golfing Society was formed in 1794, but it had disappeared from the scene by the time the Dunbar Golf Club was organized in 1856. The new club's founders immediately called in Old Tom Morris to lay out fifteen holes. In 1880 Willie Park Sr. added three holes to bring the links up to what had become the accepted standard. Like North Berwick, Dunbar is little changed since then.

ON THE COURSE

The course is set up for daily play at about 6,200 yards, par 70. The start of the round is not promising: a couple of level and humdrum short par 5s that run back and forth beside each other, with the result that we soon find ourselves where we began: outside the golf shop. These two holes are inland in character, as is the 3rd, a falling 170-yarder to a heavily bunkered green by the spiffy white clubhouse. But it plays straight toward the sea, and we know without being told that the golf we have come for must be just around the corner—or, more precisely, just on the other side of the stone wall that backdrops the green.

The 4th hole marks the beginning of what might be called the real Dunbar. This shortish two-shotter and the thirteen holes that follow are laid out—sometimes squeezed in—between the wall and the sea. On the inland side of this fieldstone barrier lay for many decades the Duke of Roxburghe's deer park. Since the seaward side also belonged to him, whoever succeeded to that eminence became president of the club.

The slicer must negotiate these fourteen holes warily. The boundary wall nags all the way out on the right, and the rocky beach threatens virtually all the way in on the right. The net of it is out-of-bounds on ten holes and the sea a worry on nine. The round can be stressful.

This long strip of land beside a crescent bay has a pleasantly rolling character. Bunkering is light; gorse imperils the shot on occasion. And the deceptively short rough turns out to be penal.

The 386-yard 7th, one of the two best holes on the first nine, doglegs smoothly right to follow the wall and calls for a semiblind second shot over rising ground down to a green set between the wall and a beautiful old barn called Mill Stone Den. Following the uphill 8th, 365 yards long and with a large green sloping emphatically down from back to front, comes the other top-notch hole, the 9th, 507 yards long. A blind

Opposite: Dunbar, 7th.
Above: 9th.

Ironically, however, it is possible that the beauty of the setting rather than the rigors of the test may be what colors the memory of most visitors. It is difficult to call up any stretch of holes in Scotland with lovelier views than those at Dunbar. On a sparkling day, the blue of the sea is a brilliant reflection of the blue of the sky, the fishing smacks slowly ply the waters not a mile offshore, the chatter of the oystercatchers as they hop, stiff-legged, from rock to rock delights our ear, and Bass Rock and May Island and the distant outline of the Fife coast all vie for our attention. And on the way in, the spires and roofs of the town extend the same warm invitation to us as do those at St. Andrews.

NEARBY COURSES

There is a second eighteen in Dunbar, at the opposite end of town. It is also seaside. Only 5,200 yards long and with a par of 64, **Winterfield**, atop the cliffs, is nothing if not sporty, or so it looks to me. I say *looks* because I must confess to never having played it. But I've stood on the 1st tee, and if that hole is any indication—an unnerving shot over a deep, grassy swale—this little course has to be fun.

Located midway between North Berwick and Dunbar is the **Whitekirk Golf Course**, which opened in 1995. A public course that welcomes everybody at all times, it was laid out by a Scot, Cameron Sinclair, whose design experience had previously been confined to the Far East. Whitekirk measures 6,200 yards from the regular markers, 6,420 from the medal tees; it wanders over 160 acres of high, hilly, and treeless land. Though laid out several miles from the coast, this delightful eighteen has a linkslike feeling, thanks to its openness, its panoramic sea views, its broad and undulating fairways, its festive greens, and the naturalness that imbues it all. The holes are never less than good, and one hole can fairly be called great: The 420-yard 5th climbs, bends left in the driving area (three bunkers here), and then plunges into a hollow only to rise almost vertically to a shelf of green angled to the line of the long second shot. The numerous lofty tees at Whitekirk provide 360-degree views of the world of East Lothian, with rich farmland ringing the course, an occasional village catching our eye, Berwick Law and Bass Rock in the middle ground, and, as ever, Fife on the horizon across the broad Firth. And as we stand on the noble 18th tee, Tantallon Castle (built in 1375 and reduced to ruins in 1651 by twelve days of Oliver Cromwell's bombardment) lies far below on our left, Dunbar off in the distance to our right.

uphill drive puts us on the flat and within sight of the distant Barus Ness Lighthouse. A solid 3-metal now, sailing high above the sloping fairway, should get within a short pitch of the green far below.

The excellent 200-yard 10th brings us to the far end of the links. Six of the remaining eight holes play along and modestly above the sea. Seven of them often play into a westerly wind, which for most of us means a losing battle, since four of the two-shotters measure 417, 459, 433, and 437 yards. And three of those are perilous, with the greens at 12, 14, and 15 perched in lonely splendor above the rocky strand. The pitch on the short par-4 17th must carry a burn, and the 437-yard home hole (we are now back inside the great wall) is one of those par 4s that calls for two stout blows into the wind if we are to have any chance of gaining the green in regulation.

Whitekirk Golf Course, 5th.

Dunbar's ivy-clad **Bayswell House** gets a lot of repeat business from golfers. Guest rooms are comfortable but in no sense luxurious, the clifftop setting affords spectacular sea views, the food is good, and the tariffs are reasonable. At nearby **Creel Restaurant**, in an old smuggler's house, the emphasis is on locally caught fish.

Difficult as it may sometimes be to believe, there is much more to East Lothian than the royal and ancient game. Twenty-six miles of beaches beckon (some locals insist that the water reaches 60 degrees at least twice a summer!). Among the beguiling harbors are those at Dunbar and North Berwick, with the latter town offering antiques shops, art galleries, and, on the outskirts, Berwick Law, an extinct volcano.

Dunbar may lack the refinement of North Berwick, but this ancient fortress port and royal burgh has witnessed important moments in British history. In 1295 England's Edward I suppressed a Scottish revolt here. And it was outside the town in 1650 that Oliver Cromwell, whose forces had been encamped on the links for six weeks, crushed the Scottish supporters of Charles II. Since Cromwell then used the castle stones to reinforce the harbor, there is little of this once imposing structure to be seen today.

The steepled seventeenth-century Town House, Scotland's oldest civic building in continuous use, is of interest. Also, John Muir, father of America's national parks, was born in this town. His birthplace is a little museum on the High Street. Not far outside town to the north is the John Muir Country Park. South of Dunbar, on the coast, are picturesque Cove and Eyemouth, where the harbor, stretching up the river, is a bustling scene. The Eyemouth Museum, in Market Place, presents informative displays about fishing and farming in this district.

At the foot of the hill over which many of the Whitekirk golf holes are routed is the hamlet of the same name, with its large fifteenth-century church and its two-story sixteenth-century barn, both built of a rust-brown stone. In pre-Reformation times Whitekirk possessed a miraculous crucifix and a holy well, which attracted thousands of the faithful annually, including the man who became Pope Pius II. The future pontiff is supposed to have walked here barefoot from Dunbar, thus contracting the rheumatism that would plague him the rest of his life.

Lenoxlove House, home of the Duke of Hamilton, and Gosford, the residence of the Earl of Wemyss, are two stately homes open to visitors. For a change of pace, pop into the Myreton Motor Museum (a knockout collection of vintage cars), just outside Aberlady, and the Museum of Flight, in East Fortune, with its Concorde, the supersonic jet that's no longer in the skies.

In addition to Dirleton (page 231), the county is dotted with endearing villages such as Preston (here are Preston Tower, a fifteenth-century fortress house, and Northfield House, a sixteenth-century tower house with turreted stairs); East Linton, site of Preston Mill, a working water mill, and of a six-hundred-year-old stone bridge that spans the Linn River; Gifford, a planned estate village that is the gateway to the Lammermuir Hills; and a trio of old stone-walled villages, Garvald, Morham, and Saltown. It is quite possible that a stay in East Lothian would turn out to be golf in the morning and sightseeing in the afternoon.

Along the shore, Dunbar.

GULLANE

T ouring golfers are sometimes surprised to find that Muirfield is just one of five 18-hole courses in Gullane. The other four in this small town given over entirely to the game (its population is about 4,200), are Gullane Golf Club's three eighteens and Luffness New. All five are endowed with the crisp sand-based turf of a true links, and three of them—Gullane No. 1, No. 2, and No. 3—play up and down, over and around Gullane Hill.

In his charming book *Golf on Gullane Hill,* published in 1982, Archie Baird celebrates the game here, and on the opening page he singles out the unlikely heroes: rabbits. It was rabbits that cropped the grass "to a lawn-like smoothness." Perhaps even more important, "If they found a succulent new shoot of hawthorn or buckthorn had taken root, they applied their sharp little incisors and 'nipped it in the bud.'"

Golf was played over the Gullane links as early as 1650, probably on three or four very rudimentary holes near the ancient church, which dates to 1150. A close look at one of the headstones in the graveyard there will reveal—if revelation be needed—the value placed on the services provided by those who work for golfers:

> Erected by the Gullane Golf Club
> to the Memory of James Dobson 1853–1924
> in Grateful Appreciation of Thirty Years
> of Faithful Service as Starter on the Links

Two golf clubs were formed in 1854, but it was in 1882, spurred by the need to improve the course ("in very poor order, mole hills being numerous and grass very rank"), that Gullane Golf Club was formed and Willie Park Sr. was called in for extensive revisions. By 1898 play was so heavy that a second eighteen was fashioned by Willie Park Jr. Eleven years later, he also laid out Gullane No. 3. So Gullane Golf Club has had three eighteens in play for very nearly a hundred years.

I first played over Gullane Hill in 1971. On my many visits during the years since, I have been conscious of almost no change (except for the construction of a handsome clubhouse specifically for visitors) in this timeless place—not to the town nor to the golf club nor to the courses. In more recent years, most of my games on Gullane No. 1 have been with Archie Baird, an RAF pilot in the Second World War and a practicing veterinary surgeon from 1954 to 1980. Captain of Gullane Golf Club in 1976 and 1977, Archie is also a member of the Honourable Company of Edinburgh Golfers and of Kilspindie Golf Club, in his home village of Aberlady, some three miles west of Gullane. Of compact build and a shade under average height, he is easily met, and you sense at once that the twinkle is never far from his eye. His handicap, once as low as 6, has crept up over the years, but he continues to make an aggressive pass at the ball, fearlessly employing his driver "off the deck" ten or twelve times in a round with the hope of reducing the mileage on those two-shotters that he now needs three shots to reach.

Archie's wife, Sheila Park Baird, a retired veterinarian as well and a former ladies' captain at Kilspindie, is the great-grandaughter of Willie Park Sr. Sheila and Archie used to visit the United States during the winter to play golf in Florida, but they no longer do. They stick to East Lothian, with its dozen links courses. Archie now plays only links golf, even declining to join his son-in-law, a member at nearby Haddington, for a game at that perfectly acceptable parkland course.

Archie's faithful golfing companion of more than a dozen years, an obedient Border terrier named Niblick, died in 2001, to be replaced by an equally endearing Border terrier called Brody, whose conduct is also impeccable.

Over the years, Gullane No. 1 has been the scene of the Scottish Amateur, final qualifying for the Open Championship when it is held at Muirfield, and, on three occasions, the British Ladies' Championship.

ON THE NO. 1 COURSE

The No. 1 Course measures 6,466 yards from the medal tees and 6,100 yards from the regular markers; par is 71. The level and straightforward opening hole, all of 287 yards from the regular tees, is a likely par or better. But the 2nd, warningly dubbed Windygate, is a likely bogey or

Opposite: Gullane No. 1, 9th.

worse. The card says 334 yards, but I have never known the 2nd to play less than 400. It climbs straight up Gullane Hill every foot of the way. Don't be misled by the sheltered look of the hole, which follows a natural cut in the hillside. The prevailing wind funnels so powerfully down this cut and into us that climbing is a chore and standing solidly over the ball on our second shot can be difficult. What's more, the fairway is narrow, the rough is throttlingly thick, and the skimpy sand-free green is cunningly framed by little falloffs. Two very straight and cleanly struck shots will do the job, but nothing less.

Now, having jotted 5 on the card, we hoist ourselves up onto the tee of a shortish three-shotter that, even into the prevailing breeze, should be manageable. The elevated tee reveals a good deal of the vast golfing landscape, to say nothing of the Firth of Forth itself. Power is no prerequisite on this 479-yarder, but precision is. Again, the fairway is not wide. Eight pot

bunkers along the way and four at the green combine with the rough to give this hole punch. What ought to be an automatic par turns out to require 3 sound strokes, and we end up conceding, however grudgingly, the appropriateness of the 3rd's selection to *The 500 World's Greatest Golf Holes*.

For some of us, the 5th merited this honor but, inexplicably, did not receive it. A 436-yarder, it bends smartly left around deep pits in the elbow of the dogleg, then climbs to a large green carved out of the hillside. To reach the green in regulation calls for two first-rate swings. And to get down in two putts is almost as difficult a feat, so steeply sloping from back to front is this putting surface. Which may be a good time to add that Gullane's greens are among the finest in Scotland.

The 300-yard 6th, also uphill, brings us to the storied 7th tee, on the pinnacle of Gullane Hill. Here is the downhill hole of the world. The pulse races as we strive to take it all in. Popping up in profusion far below are innumerable flagsticks. Who can possibly keep straight the holes on the three Gullane eighteens and Luffness New from this aerie? Back-dropping them is a vast nature preserve and then the waters of Aberlady Bay. Turn some 90 degrees to the right and the elegant tracery of the Forth Road Bridge catches the eye. So do Arthur's Seat and glimpses of fair Edinburgh itself. Now turn east to command the pale green fairways of Muirfield and, beyond them, Bass Rock and Berwick Law. Finally, take a deep breath, the keen fresh sea breeze suddenly expanding your lungs, and come back to earth. The 400-yard 7th plunges all but vertically from tee to green. Shoulders open, we swing mightily, then watch in almost childlike rapture the prodigious hang time of this shot. And despite the downhill lie for our approach, which may be no more than 120 yards, we play it confidently and come away with 4, maybe 3.

The 8th, a short par 4 heading straight toward the sea, is followed by a pretty 141-yarder, paralleling the cliff edge and perhaps fifteen paces from it, our 7- or 8-iron drifting down to a spacious green ringed by eight bunkers.

The inbound half calls for stronger hitting. More than 400 yards longer than the first nine, it starts with a couple of testers, the uphill 434-yard 10th and, right beside it, the downhill 427-yard 11th, sweeping majestically toward the sea. The tees on the short par-5 12th, bending quietly right, and the 160-yard 13th, knob to knob, are both set high above the beach. Serving as unignorable reminders of the Second World War are massive gray concrete blocks, which were lodged in the thickets above the beach some sixty-five years ago to thwart the German tanks that never came.

The 409-yard 14th, straight and almost indiscernibly rising, is serious stuff, and so is the 15th, which reminds us of Babe Didrickson

Zaharias's dominance of the 1947 British Ladies' here. The first American ever to win this championship, Babe was not only larger than life, she was also longer by a country mile than any woman who had ever struck a golf ball. The 15th measured 535 yards for the championship. The first 350 yards are level; the hole then climbs steeply to a hillside green. In one of her matches, Babe, assisted by a moderate breeze, followed a crushing drive with a bullet 4-iron shot that rolled to a stop at the back of the green. A few locals, very elderly now, recall with awe that display of unbridled—and unladylike—power. It was also on this occasion that Babe's costume was declared unfit. When she appeared for one of her matches sporting red-and-white-checked shorts, officials politely requested that she change her attire. Babe graciously complied.

After 14 holes on the sea side of Gullane Hill, we turn our back on the water and tee it up on the 17th to head for home, gazing out now from this spectacular height over golden beige fields, if it be an August evening,

awaiting the harvest. And at last we even the score for that punishing climb we endured on the 2nd. The 17th goes straight downhill, with the wind, our drive quite possibly a clout of 310 yards. The 80-yard pitch that's left just may result in birdie, something that is not out of the question on the rolling 340-yard final hole as well. Talk about finishing with a flourish—the irresistible Gullane No. 1 gives us every chance to do just that.

OTHER GULLANE COURSES

The **No. 2 Course** measures 6,244 yards against a par of 71. It has several quite forgettable holes and not enough holes like the terrific 13th, which edges right as it climbs to a two-tier plateau green. As for **Gullane No. 3**, it is much too short—5,166 yards, par 66—but it is not without charm and spirit. A number of hillside and dell green sites are particularly attractive. And the 169-yard 15th is the most steeply plunging one-shotter in my experience: sheer fun!

Above: Gullane No. 1, 8th.
Opposite: 13th.

NEARBY COURSES

Luffness New, laid out along the lower flanks of Gullane Hill, had Old Tom Morris as its originator, in 1894, and Willie Park Jr. and Tom Simpson as its remodelers. The fairways are ribbons of green framed by waving wheat-colored rough; the bunkers feature nearly vertical revetted faces; and the greens—Bobby Locke, who knew something about putting, believed there were none better anywhere—are firm, fast, and reliably true. Though total yardage is only 6,122 (par 69), there are five par 4s comfortably over 420 yards. This easy-walking course, which often looks out over Aberlady Bay, turns out to be more testing than we might have expected.

Three miles away, on a low headland between Aberlady Bay and Gosford Bay, lies **Kilspindie**, laid out by Willie Park Jr. in 1898. Only 5,500 yards long, par 69, it is not a challenge unless a brisk breeze is blowing. But it is a delightful place for the game, with the sea in view on seventeen holes and in play, to catch the push or slice, on four of them. Two holes are memorable, both along the strand: the 513-yard 2nd, a "par 6" into a westerly, and the 162-yard 8th, where the shot must often be started out over the beach if there is to be any chance of holding the green.

Abutting Kilspindie is newcomer **Craigielaw**, laid out by Donald Steel's associate Tom McKenzie. It measures 6,601 yards from the medal tees, 6,043 yards from the regular markers (par 71), and it reveals gorgeous views of Aberlady Bay and Gosford Bay. The green complexes border on the tumultuous, with the result that we find ourselves, hole after hole, pitching and chipping and putting out of hollows and over knobs to teasingly spotted cups. On a man-made course that is not a true links, the fun—and occasional frustration—of true links golf is with us here at every turn.

Above, left: Luffness New, 4th; right: 1st. Opposite: Longniddry, 13th.

Just five minutes from Craigielaw, along the coast road toward Edinburgh, lies **Longniddry**, designed by Harry Colt in 1921. It is a hybrid, an appealing mix of links and parkland golf, the broad fairways often framed by tall umbrella pines. Only 6,260 yards from all the way back and with a par of just 68, Longniddry has no par 5s. What it does have is eight two-shotters over 400 yards. Once aboard, it can be very difficult to get off the dreaded bogey train.

Archie Baird plays regularly for Gullane in the winter club match against Longniddry. A couple of years back, when Longniddry was the venue, tee markers were rather too far forward to suit the visitors. Called upon, as he often is, for after-dinner remarks, Archie congratulated the hosts on the excellence of the wine and the cooking and on their victory in the competition. Then he added, "But perhaps the next time the match is here a way might be found to set up the course so that we do not play *Short*niddry."

At Gullane No. 1 there is a one-room museum next to the pro shop, and I urge you to visit it. Archie Baird is its founder, owner, curator, and conductor of what turns out to be a forty-minute tour of his Heritage of Golf Museum. The exhibition contains the fruits of his half century of collecting golf memorabilia. Through a skillfully arranged—and utterly absorbing—selection of old paintings, prints, postcards, and photographs, of old balls (including priceless featheries) and clubs and bags and costumes, of antique medals of silver and antique buttons of brass, and of so much more, Archie presents the evolution of golf from its origin some 550 years ago down till today. Listening to him and examining his acquisitions close up is a once-in-a-lifetime experience. Visits are by appointment only. A telephone call to the maestro (0875–870–277) is all that is needed to open this treasure chest.

A word of caution: If you should elect to embark on this marvelous guided tour courtesy of Scotland's quintessential golf purist, be prepared to come away conceding that golf was *not* born in Scotland.

LODGING AND DINING

In recent years the **Golf Inn**, on Gullane's Main Street, has earned a good following. The guest rooms, some small, are cheerful and up-to-date. No views, but the cooking is top-notch, with a menu full of appetizing dishes.

Aberlady is all of five minutes from Gullane. On the main street is the hospitable **Old Aberlady Inn**. Rooms are modest and modestly priced, the atmosphere might be called "olde worlde," and both bar (crackling log fire) and beer garden are well patronized by the locals.

Two Gullane restaurants of note:

- The **Old Clubhouse** (the original golf clubhouse) is a large and lively spot, very bistro in feeling, with a strong sense of times long past (high beam ceiling, dark paneling, old fireplaces) and good food at what is sometimes called "popular" prices.
- **La Potiniere** is small and smart. The choices are quite limited, but the cooking is imaginative.

Archie Baird's Heritage of Golf Museum.

MUIRFIELD

O n September 1, 1971, I played Muirfield for the first time. With me were my two sons, seventeen-year-old Jim and sixteen-year-old John. At the east end of Gullane, the one driveway leading left off the main street had only a tiny gray-blue sign with the letters H.C.E.G. peeping up out of the grass. Ignoring it as of no consequence, I drove on, perhaps half a mile farther. Since we knew where the course lay, having looked down on it from atop Gullane Hill the day before, this inability to get to it was maddening. There was no point in continuing toward Dirleton, so I turned around and headed back. This time the minuscule sign communicated: H.C.E.G. stands for Honourable Company of Edinburgh Golfers.

Down the driveway to Muirfield we sped—it was now 9:22 and our tee time was 9:30—and zipped into the extensive parking garage. Shoes and clubs in hand, the three of us now sprinted along the tarmac to the clubhouse. An official-looking man in a navy blazer, ruddy-cheeked, solidly built, in his early fifties, came out of the clubhouse and intercepted us. His face wore no welcoming smile.

"James Finegan?" he asked peremptorily.

"Yes," I said. "Yes, sir."

"And these, I presume, are your sons. No time for introductions."

He did not volunteer to shake hands. "Do you see that two-ball?" Three pairs of eyes followed his finger as he pointed beyond a nearby green and a short distance down the fairway leading to it. "They started on the tenth and are now finishing their first nine right there, on the eighteenth. They will then proceed to the first tee"—he pointed some thirty yards to our left—"and if you have not driven off before they get there, it is entirely possible that you will not play golf at Muirfield today. I suggest you put on your golf shoes at once. That door leads to the changing room. You can pay your green fee when you finish—that is, if you start." The legendary curmudgeon Captain P.W.T. Hanmer (H. M. Royal Navy, retired,) pointed the way with that imperious finger toward a clubhouse door, and we fled on the prescribed line.

Not ninety seconds later we were back, breathless, discombobulated, but nonetheless determined to beat the looming twosome to the 1st tee, fishing our gloves and balls and tees from our golf bags as we scurried and stumbled toward the markers. A powerful, shrieking wind—55 miles per hour may not be storm force, but it is ruinous where the golf swing is concerned—was raking the links. And the level, straightaway 1st hole, measuring 425 yards, played dead into it. I caught my drive flush and advanced it about 110 yards, precisely half the distance of my normal tee shot in those days. We all laughed. The boys outhit me, both off somewhere in Muirfield's infamous tall rough. Heads down and leaning fiercely forward, wind whistling past our ears, we set out toward the distant flag.

My ball had gained the fairway by no more than a pace. I pulled out my brassie (2-wood). At 130 pounds and standing a fraction under six feet, I was no match for a fifty-five-mile-an-hour wind. Now, having anchored myself as solidly as possible, I had no choice but to swing. As I drew the club back, a particularly violent guest rocked me. Throwing the club from the top in a desperate effort to bring it back to the ball, I slammed the wood into the firm turf about eight inches behind the ball and, to my horror, felt the club bounce up and fly cleanly over the ball as I followed through.

"I missed it!" I screamed into the wind. "I whiffed it! I never touched it!"

The boys, out ahead of me in the rough on the right, turned as my voice reached them. The wind made it impossible for them to understand me. I pointed to the ball and shouted again, mimicking my swing. Now they understood, and the wind carried their laughter back to me in a rush.

I tried again. This time the ball, thinly struck, stayed low, burrowing its way a bit farther than my drive had traveled. I finished the hole with a 7. John also had a 7 and Jim nipped us with a heroic double-bogey 6.

Nothing would be gained by describing this round in detail. It was an unremitting struggle, and, for the most part, details were lost in the conflict. I remember realizing, as we walked from the 2nd green to the 3rd tee, that the faint clicking sound reminiscent of hail tapping on a window pane was actually grains of sand ricocheting off the slats of a sand fence. Without that barrier, we would have been stung repeatedly by particles blown off the dune behind the 3rd tee. I also recall Jim's choosing a pitching wedge on

Opposite: Muirfield, 4th.

the tee of the 187-yard 4th and then begging the ball to stop as it ran 35 feet past the cup. And I recall making an easy 4 on the 516-yard 5th by chipping *back* from just over the green, where my *second* shot had finished—this by the same player whose drive on the 1st had eaten up all of 110 yards. Still, that birdie 4 was twice as many strokes as Johnny Miller needed here in 1972 (the hole measured 560 yards for the Open), when he followed a 280-yard drive by holing a 280-yard 3-wood for an albatross (double eagle).

The final tallies were ludicrous: 110 for John, 101 for Jim, 96 for me (48 each way). There was nothing to do now but pay the green fee: £1.50 (just under $3), change our shoes, and retreat.

A year after this harrowing round, the Open Championship was held at Muirfield for the eleventh time. Lee Trevino, victor at Royal Birkdale in 1971, carried off the claret jug for the second straight year. This win was astonishing. Three times in the last 21 holes, he holed out from somewhere off the green. Scrambling for the lead late in the third round, he pulled his 6-iron on the par-3 16th into a bunker, the ball coming to rest on a downslope and too close to the back of the pit to permit a full swing. Off balance as he chopped awkwardly to make contact, he almost fell down as the ball, skulled, flew across the green, bounced once, and disappeared into the cup for a 2. His opinion was that a 5 seemed likely as the ball left the clubface. Twenty minutes later, after his 5-iron shot on the 18th rolled over the green into thick rough, he pitched in from thirty feet for a 4 and a 66 that gave him a 1-stroke lead over Tony Jacklin.

When Trevino and Jacklin, paired in the final round, came to the 71st hole, they were tied at the top. Jacklin hit a couple of very good woods on this 528-yarder, followed by an indifferent chip from just in front of the green that came up about 18 feet short of the hole. Trevino pulled his drive into a bunker, then made three more bad swings—there is no other way to say it—which left him lying 4 in a troublesome spot halfway down the low, grassy mound that rings the 17th green. Hurriedly—in truth, it appeared to this TV viewer, carelessly, even halfheartedly—he jabbed at the ball, and it raced some fifty feet across the green and neatly into the cup as though no other conclusion to the shot were imaginable. Later Trevino would say candidly that he had believed he had no chance with the shot: "I thought I might have given up. I felt like I had."

Jacklin then did what you and I might have done in the circumstances: he three-putted, this despite the eighteen-foot stretch he had to negotiate being flat, presenting no problem of pace or borrow. The first putt exploded to three feet past the cup, and the jittery comebacker never looked

like going in. Shattered, Jacklin had to accept a 6, falling a stroke behind Trevino. Then, needing a birdie on the home hole to tie (the Texan would par it) and still shaken by the cruel turnabout on the 71st, he could do no better than bogey. The man who had captured the Open Championship in 1969 at Royal Lytham and the U.S. Open in 1970 at Hazeltine, and here had walked onto the green of the penultimate hole with every expectation of winning his third major, would never again contend in either the British or U.S. Open.

John and I returned to Muirfield in September of 1973. This time the day was pretty and our golf was sound. He posted an 82, I a 76. But neither score was quite so gratifying to me as the brief exchange after the round with Captain Hanmer. I noted that grandstands had been erected at the 18th green.

"Yes, yes," he said. "The preparations for the Ryder Cup are well in hand." He paused, then added, "Were you thinking of playing the afternoon round?"

"I was," I said, "but John thinks he's had enough for today."

"Perhaps you might want to play from the Ryder Cup tees," said the secretary, "to see firsthand what they'll be up against. It's a lot more length than you're used to here, much the same as the Open, a little over sixty-nine hundred yards, but I think you'd find it interesting."

I said I'd be delighted to try and that I was much in his debt for the kindness.

There was no sign of Captain Hanmer that afternoon when I teed off, blithely shouldered my light canvas bag, and, however overmatched, headed down the 1st in high spirits, my 215-yard tee shot making certain that I could not reach the green on this 447-yarder in regulation.

By Scottish standards, Muirfield, twenty miles east of Edinburgh and built in 1891, is not an old course. It is actually about the same age as the first American courses, such as Shinnecock Hills, Newport, Philadelphia Country Club's original eighteen, and Chicago Golf Club. The Honourable Company of Edinburgh Golfers was founded in 1744. The club minutes have been kept ever since and constitute the oldest continuous record of any golf club. Shortly after its founding, the Honourable Company drew up the first "Rules of Golf."

Following long stays at Leith (only five holes) and Musselburgh, the club headed farther east, finding its way to Muirfield. None other than Old Tom Morris gets credit for the basic design of the new course, a highly unusual scheme for the time, and one that in its general outline

Opposite: Muirfield, 17th.

was maintained even when the course was drastically reconstituted some thirty years later: The first nine moves in a clockwise arc outside the counterclockwise pattern of the second nine. The golfer's struggle with the winds off the Firth is thus a constantly shifting one.

The 1892 Open was a milestone. It was the first to be played at Muirfield, itself only a year old, and the first at 72 holes (instead of 36). Prize money, formerly £20, soared to £110. But the winner didn't get a farthing, because he was an amateur: Harold Hilton, a twenty-three-year-old Englishman who went on to claim the claret jug again five years later and won the Amateur Championship in 1900, 1901, and 1911, and the U.S. Amateur in 1911.

In the years to come, the Opens at Muirfield would be won by many of the greatest players in the game: Lee Trevino, Jack Nicklaus, Harry Vardon, James Braid twice, Walter Hagen, Henry Cotton, Gary Player (in 1959, the first of his three British Opens—despite a double bogey on the final hole!), Tom Watson, Nick Faldo (1987 and 1992, the 1987 victory by dint of 18 pars in the final round), and Ernie Els.

ON THE COURSE

The course sits splendidly above the Firth of Forth and at rather a remove from it. Still, the nobility, remoteness, and tranquillity of its location are enormously appealing. Herbert Warren Wind characterizes Muirfield as "a linksland course with a touch of meadowlands about it." And in *The Golf Courses of the British Isles,* Bernard Darwin comes at it with the sensibility of a poet: "There is a fine view of the sea and a delightful sea wood, with the trees all bent and twisted by the wind; then, too, it is a solitary and peaceful spot, and a great haunt of the curlews, whom one may see hovering over a championship crowd and crying eerily amid a religious silence."

Though Old Tom Morris was the initial architect of the links, the course today is more appropriately attributed to Harry Colt (Royal Portrush, Wentworth's West and East Courses, Sunningdale New, Swinley Forest, not to mention counseling with George Crump on the routing of Pine Valley). In 1925 Colt, one of the towering figures in the history of golf course architecture, extensively revised eleven holes here and created seven new ones. The result of his efforts was indisputable greatness, although it is, almost curiously, of a quite orderly sort. For in the pantheon of great courses—and Muirfield is unfailingly ranked in the world's top ten, on occasion as high as third—Muirfield is neither thrilling (Pebble Beach is) nor spectacular (Ballybunion Old is) nor breathtaking (Royal County Down is) nor dramatic (Pine Valley is). There are no hills, no trees, no water hazards, no unnerving forced carries over gorse- or heather-studded ravines. "Death or glory" shots are absent. Nonetheless, there is a rightness about the holes that adds up to excellence, so much so that we never find ourselves longing for attributes that are not present.

At the root of this excellence is what Ben Crenshaw calls "its beautiful honesty as a test of golf." Each hole states its requirements with unfailing frankness: no surprises, no tricks. Except for the drive on 11, there are no blind shots. Except on the 9th, there is no out-of-bounds. As targets, the greens are clearly etched and staunchly sand-defended. As putting surfaces, they are readable and manageable: They have character but are never excessively contoured. On terrain that very gently undulates, there is essentially nothing in the way of hillocks and hummocks to send the ball skittering crazily—confoundingly—off line. Muirfield is less mysterious, less "foreign" in feeling than other British seaside courses. Here we get exactly what the shot is worth—the good shot is properly rewarded, the poor shot is properly punished—and it all takes place within full view. Small wonder that whenever the world's best golfers are polled, Muirfield emerges as the favorite course on the Open rota.

Wherein, then, lies the challenge? The answer is simple: You have to hit the ball long and straight while, more often than not, battling a stiff breeze. From the regular markers, the course measures nearly 6,700 yards against a par of 70. That's a lot of golf. Then there is the bunkering: 165 meticulously crafted and stringently penal sod-wall sandpits (an average of more than nine per hole), every bit as intimidating when they patrol the fairways as when they defend the greens. Finally, there is the rough, deep, throttling, often mattresslike to walk on and to hack out of, that puts intense pressure on the swing by duping the player into believing the fairways to be narrower than they actually are. Muirfield is one of the game's most rigorous tests of driving.

Among the half dozen or so truly great holes are three long par 4s, all of them unyielding except to full-blooded strokes of genuine precision. The 443-yard 6th, swinging left, presents a nest of gathering bunkers (all Muirfield bunkers strike us as voracious) in the crook of the dogleg and a deceptive dip—dead ground—in front of the green to complicate club selection. The 8th, also 443 yards, bends right: Set in the elbow of the dogleg this time are six bunkers, three of them actually in the right side of the fairway itself, three in the adjacent rough, all lurking to snare the push or slice. Equally superlative is the 18th. It is 415 yards long for daily play (448 for the Open or the Ryder Cup), it is level, and it edges almost imperceptibly left. It is blockaded across the front and bracketed by sand. A nerveless second shot is demanded here, the type of shot summoned by Nicklaus in 1966, Trevino in 1972, and Faldo in 1987, when anything other than a pure stroke might well have cost the title. This hole was chosen for *The 500 World's Greatest Golf Holes.*

Still, on a course noted for its two-shotters, we don't want to ignore the par 3s and the par 5s. Two of them, the 9th (a two-shotter at 465 yards for member play, a three-shotter at 505 yards for the Open and the Ryder Cup), and the one-shotter 13th have been singled out in the *500 World's Greatest* volume as among the hundred best. The level 9th, more often than not played into the breeze, may show par 4 on the card when you tackle it, but you will not be upset to walk away with a 5 on a hole that demands strict control from start to finish. The fairway, which moves a shade right in the tee-shot landing area, is pinched there to about 20 yards by two bunkers on the left and tenacious rough on the right. Running the entire length of the hole on the left and becoming increasingly intrusive as we draw closer to the green is a stone boundary wall not quite five feet high. A pulled or hooked second shot—into a stiff headwind, even a third shot—can easily sail over the wall. A long second with even a suggestion of cut is likely to be wolfed down by any of four pits. And in the middle of the fairway, 65 yards short of the green and exactly where many a soundly struck second shot will come to rest, awaits Simpson's Bunker, Tom Simpson's sole contribution to Muirfield, and what an indelible memento it is! Played as a par 5, the hole yields its share of birdies and, in the Open, eagles as well from time to time. For instance, in the 1972 championship's final round, Jacklin and Trevino, head to head, drove into the right rough but reached the green comfortably with long irons and holed for eagles. On the other hand, in 1959 Peter Thomson, seeking his fifth Open (he would gain it in 1965) and squarely in the hunt, squandered his chances by hooking his 3-wood second shot over the wall in the last round.

The 13th, 160 yards, plays uphill to a long, narrow green perfectly sited in a cleft between two dunes—and zealously guarded by five deep pits eating into the putting surface, three on the right, two on the left. This green slopes maliciously down from back to front. It was here in 2002 that Ernie Els played one of the most brilliant shots of his career, somehow lifting the ball almost vertically from the very base of the mas-

sive forward wall of the larger left-hand pit and watching calmly—but doubtless relievedly—as it touched down perhaps a dozen feet from the hole and trickled to within 18 inches for a certain par.

For the record, that afternoon in 1973 I shot 80 from the Ryder Cup tees. The Match, contested three weeks later, saw the visitors field what must have looked to be an impregnable team, headed by Nicklaus, Trevino, Palmer, Casper, and Weiskopf. At the end of the first day the British/Irish side led 5½ to 2½. The U.S. squad reversed this score on the second day, and on the final day whipped the home team to retain the cup. The Honourable Company has also hosted the Walker Cup (twice), the Curtis Cup (twice), and the Amateur Championship (seven times).

As I walked up the 18th that day, I spotted Captain Hanmer standing in front of the clubhouse, scanning the links with his binoculars as he might have scanned the sea from the bridge of a warship during his years of service in the royal navy. Now, however, he was focusing on a dilatory foursome approaching the 12th green as the explanation for the holdup on the second nine. He intercepted me as I left the home green to point out that I had neglected to pay the green fee for my second round and that he would accept it now. The tariff was £2. (Today it is £125.) Visitors unaccompanied by a member are permitted to play only on Tuesdays and Thursdays. Muirfield must strike some sort of balance between the need to protect the rights of members and the obligation, acknowledged by The Honourable Company, to permit the faithful to come and worship at

the shrine. Somehow, and not without a touch of asperity from time to time, the secretaries have managed to walk this tightrope with considerable success and without compromising the principles of how a great golf club should be run. Still, a couple of them, Captain Hanmer and Colonel Brian Evans-Lombe, could fairly be labeled dictatorial.

Evans-Lombe, a retired cavalry officer, "reigned" from 1947 to 1964. Among the stories illustrative of his style is the one that finds him, on a Sunday morning, noting an unfamiliar figure sitting alone in the smoking room. When he inquired of the chap whose guest he might be, Evans-Lombe was sharply informed that he was speaking to a member of twenty years' standing. "In that event," the secretary replied, "you should come more often; then I would recognize you."

Evans-Lombe was not merely astringent. He could also be witty, as in this light verse he composed for a meeting of the Monks of St. Giles, a group of amateur versifiers:

Club Members to me, I think you'll agree,
Are as to a shepherd, his sheep;
I chase them off here and pen them in there,
And I count them as I go to sleep.

I have to listen as their eyes glisten
And they tell me of marvelous putts.
All I've seen them sink is a great deal of drink;
It's gradually driving me nuts.

They tell me with force what to do with the course
And how drinks are cheaper in pubs.
I'd like to suggest, if I ever was pressed,
What they could do with their clubs.

And when at last the ultimate blast
Of the dear old trumpet calls,
They'll all expect me on the first fiery tee
With a box of asbestos balls

Captain Hanmer ("Paddy," I'm told, to his friends) was Muirfield's secretary from 1968 till 1983. I played the course five or six times during that period but actually had only a couple of brief, pleasant exchanges with him (after the first one, that is). In 1993 I ran into him at the house of a mutual friend in Gullane. Privately, he told me that he had regretted being forced out at Muirfield after fifteen years' service ("I suppose there were those who believed I had become too powerful"), particularly since he had aimed to hold the position three more years and eclipse the seventeen-year tenure of Evans-Lombe, the record for an Honourable Company secretary. He went on to say that he never really considered his activities at Muirfield a job but rather a nice pastime, something to occupy him that he enjoyed and could do well. "My compensation was less than the girls' in the dining room," he said. "I made it clear to the committee when I took the post that I did not require more."

Often portrayed as an ogre who took keen pleasure in turning away visiting golfers, he claimed, on the contrary, that he strove to make Muirfield more accessible to them, especially Americans. He took credit for the special arrangement now in effect with Greywalls (to be covered shortly) and made unaccompanied visitors feel at home by encouraging local members to join the visitors in the evening for a drink. He seemed surprised that I, a golf writer, was not aware of what he had done.

I recall that he told an Augusta National story with considerable relish: "One of our members," he said, "was not only turned away at the gates of Augusta National but was even refused permission to use the guard's telephone so that he might try to reach Hord Hardin, a friend of his, and have Mr. Hardin tell the guard to let him in.

"A year later," Captain Hanmer continued, "four Augusta members arrived at my office requesting the privilege of playing. They had not contacted me in advance to reserve a tee time. I carefully detailed the sorry experience of the Honourable Company member at their club and concluded by regretting that they would not be permitted to play Muirfield. I suggested that they try Gullane Number Three. They laughed. They thought I must be joking. When I made it clear that I was in dead earnest, they uneasily shuffled out of my office and headed toward their car. I let them get almost out of sight and then called out, inviting them to return. I said that they could indeed play here now that they understood what their club had put a Muirfield man through."

I never saw Captain Hanmer again, not at Muirfield nor at Pine Valley, where he had become an overseas member in 1983. He died in 2000.

Opposite: Muirfield, 13th.

H.C.E.G.

- Play the great **Muirfield**, the favorite Scottish course of many knowledgeable Americans.

- Down the storied five-course lunch with wine in the **club dining room** amid the spirited camaraderie of its members.

- Make a day of it here by **playing the links again**, after lunch, this time in a swift-paced foursomes (alternate stroke) match.

- Dine in **Gullane at La Potiniere**, where the cooking is creative.

- Spend the night just off the 10th tee at clubby **Greywalls**, the favorite Scottish inn of many knowledgeable Americans.

Muirfield, 18th.

airborne for all of 40 yards, vanished into the right rough. Said the perpetrator with an easy smile, "If you don't mind, I'll play a mulligan."

Replied Archie, "You, sir, may play whatever you wish—I'm playing golf."

On those occasions when visitors are authorized to play two rounds in a day, the second round will, by edict of the secretary, almost always be foursomes (two balls, alternate stroke). Such a game takes about two and a half hours, a circumstance that pleases the secretary—and his constituents—no end. Slow play, which some Scots incline to view as America's principal contribution to the game, is not tolerated at Muirfield.

Off the northeastern boundary of the club's property, near the 6th, 7th, and 8th holes, loom the gnarled trees of Archerfield Wood, where, in 1882, Robert Louis Stevenson set his suspenseful novella *The Pavilion on the Links*. "On summer days," Stevenson wrote, "the outlook was bright and even gladsome, but at sundown in September, with a high wind, and a heavy surf rolling in close along the links, the place told of nothing but dead mariners and sea disasters." That was 125 years ago. Today it tells of nothing but new golf courses, two of them, on a six-hundred-acre site nestled along the strand between the corner of Muirfield and the 9th hole at North Berwick.

For this sand-based tract, it is actually a return to golf. Years ago there were two courses here, Archerfield and Fidra. Some claim that the first Archerfield holes—just six—were laid out in the sixteenth century. Not till the late 1800s would there be eighteen. Fidra was not created until the 1930s; the villagers of Dirleton fashioned the nine, with each hole built and maintained by a different family. Both the eighteen and the nine fell victim to the Second World War, when they were plowed up in order to grow vegetables.

The man behind this ambitious undertaking today is Kevin Doyle, a local businessman/entrepreneur, who also has plans for housing and a hotel here. Turning his back on the marquee names in golf course architecture, he entrusted the design of the two links eighteens to a little-known architect, David Williams, and a little-known professional golfer, D. J. Russell. As for the clubhouse, that honor falls to Archerfield House itself, an impressive pile that once housed Winston Churchill and Franklin D. Roosevelt as they planned the Normandy invasion but much more recently has functioned as a hay shed. Restoring it was almost as ambitious a task as building the two courses. Fidra opened in 2004, Dirleton, as the second course is now called, in 2006. And if The Honourable Company is keeping an eye on its new neighbors, it is surely not with bated breath.

In recent years my games at Muirfield have been with Archie Baird. About six or seven years ago, he and I had set a date for a round there well in advance, expecting that just the two of us would play. But when I arrived shortly before nine o'clock, he took me aside to say that there would be a three-ball. The other player was also a visiting American. Archie had not met him before this morning, but had felt compelled to have him join us when one of his Muirfield clubmates, a friend of this American, had asked Archie to let him come along, adding that the fellow, an avid golfer who had never played Muirfield, would have no other opportunity to do so till the next time he came to Scotland, which might not be for several years. I sensed that Archie had only grudgingly acquiesced. On the 1st tee he insisted that his two guests precede him, naming me to go first. I hit off. Now it was the unknown quantity's turn. He took a couple of practice swings (just one such preliminary would normally be enough to set Archie's teeth on edge), teed his ball up, stepped carefully back to sight down the intended line, set his stance and his grip, and swung. The half-topped shot,

Regrettably, the clubhouse is off limits to women, though the links is not. This mock-Tudor structure is the very image of what most golfers hope it to be: aging wooden lockers, handsome paneling, antique silver, oil paintings of revered golfing or club figures, an abundance of golf books, and grand views over the links. Upstairs are a half-dozen guest rooms, for members.

Frank Hannigan, former senior executive director of the USGA, once wrote: "Muirfield has everything desirable in golf—a fascinating mixture of holes, history, wind, stunning scenery and a great lunch." How enthusiastically, following the morning round, we tuck into that great lunch, in a spacious, bright, high-ceilinged dining room that will accommodate sixty to seventy golfers and a corresponding decibel level. We sit at long club tables—this promotes camaraderie and we are thus likely to talk with a member or two seated opposite or beside us. I might mention that the law is well represented in The Honourable Company—solicitors, barristers, judges—which may help to account for the lively talk, the ribbing, and the ripostes.

The choices on the luncheon menu are almost as daunting as the two-shotters on the great links. To start, trout in oatmeal and almonds or gazpacho or cullen skink, an especially hearty native cream soup featuring smoked haddock and potatoes; then sirloin of beef or loin of lamb or perhaps fillet of pork *en croûte*; five or six vegetables, often among them a delicious cauliflower au gratin; a selection of sweets that may include assorted meringues, chocolate cream pie, and a superb rhubarb crumble; and, finally, a variety of cheeses. The house wine, a chardonnay or a claret or both, will help sustain us through this trencherman's trove, and coffee at the conclusion will help restore our equilibrium, an especially useful development in the event that the secretary has approved our request for an afternoon foursome.

Is it, you may ask, a meal that measures up to the fabled luncheon at the National Golf Links of America,

which opens with cold half lobsters accompanied by a club-secret mayonnaise and works its way through three more courses, including shepherd's pie? Perhaps, perhaps. It is awfully good, this Muirfield meal.

GREYWALLS

Muirfield's next-door neighbor—they share the same driveway, off the main street—is Greywalls, backdropping the 10th tee. This twenty-two-room country-house hotel looks out in the rear over the links to the sea and in the front over the gardens to the distant Lammermuir Hills. It was in 1901 that Edward Lutyens, England's foremost residential architect in the early twentieth century, designed the graceful crescent-shape house of honeyed sandstone, and there is a sense of gentle embrace as, within the garden walls, we move down the pebbled drive to it. The equally redoubtable Gertrude Jekyll, often the architect's collaborator, fashioned the ravishing gardens, with their roses often in riotous bloom, their lavender borders and holly hedges, their long perspectives and secret nooks.

The house was built as a holiday home for a serious golfer who wanted to be within a mashie-niblick of the 1st tee. At one point over the years it was occupied by a woman who happened to catch King Edward VII's fancy. A charming story, possibly apocryphal, stems from one of the royal visits. In a bridge game one evening, the king took the lady, who was his partner, to task for her play. She replied, "To tell you the truth, sir, I am so tired that I can't tell the difference between a king and a knave!"

It was in 1948 that the private house became a hotel. How wonderfully it still echoes the Edwardian Age—the gardens, the open fires, the dark paneling, the snug bar. Photos of Nicklaus and Watson mix amiably with antiques and books and, one suspects, half the framed prints in Scotland. Neatly indicative of the overall ambience is, in the library, an old phonograph complete with a selection of early dance-band records. Clublike in feeling, Greywalls has both warmth and style.

Bedrooms, attractively appointed in traditional fashion (chintzes and faux antiques) can be very small, a drawback of a couple of those with links views. (Consider requesting Room 16, and avoid rooms over the kitchen.)

The cuisine is of a high standard, with cooking to match the excellence of the ingredients. Three dishes that might well be offered on a given evening: fish mousseline with a sauce of saffron and golden caviar to start, followed by breast of duck with a confit of the leg, and, for dessert, warm chocolate pithivier with espresso coffee sauce.

One final point about Greywalls: It can sometimes do for you what no letter, e-mail, fax, phone conversation with the secretary, or impassioned plea by an Honourable Company member of long standing can do: get you on Muirfield. Tee times for visitor play (Tuesday and Thursday only) are generally reserved a year in advance. But for the person who cannot commit that far ahead—and has very capacious pockets—Greywalls just may save the day. On certain Friday afternoons and Monday mornings, hotel guests have access to a limited number of Muirfield starting times.

The game in Ireland—Northern Ireland as well as the Republic—is much the same age as it is in the United States. In 1888 America's first club, the St. Andrews Golf Club, in Yonkers, New York, was founded, just seven years after Ireland's first, Royal Belfast. Here, we take a look at most of Ireland's links courses, beginning with Royal Dublin and ending with the European Club, and including Ballybunion, Lahinch, Waterville, Portmarnock, Royal County Down, and Royal Portrush. Then, too, there are those seaside courses less heralded, such as Portsalon, Carne, and

I R E L A N D

Narin & Portnoo, plus two dazzling newcomers, Greg Norman's Doonbeg and Pat Ruddy's Sandy Hills Links, at Rosapenna. All of these links are magnificent, offering aesthetic and shotmaking satisfaction of the highest order. And when we turn away from the sea we find an impressive array of inland layouts: the K Club's two eighteens, Adare Manor, and Mount Juliet. You don't have to stick to the coast to enjoy top-notch golf. Be assured that Ireland is indeed all you have dreamed, this land of the forty shades of green and a hundred thousand welcomes.

GREATER DUBLIN
AND A BIT BEYOND

ROYAL DUBLIN

I hope you'll agree that Royal Dublin Golf Club makes a good starting point for this exploration of Irish clubs and courses. It is the oldest club (formed in 1885) in the Republic; it is the only "Royal" in the Republic (so designated in 1891, thanks in large part to North Berwick's A. J. Balfour, then Chief Secretary to Ireland); and it offers authentic links golf. What's more, located within the city limits on Bull Island, it is scarcely four miles from the O'Connell Street Bridge. For the member whose office is in downtown Dublin, the temptation to skip lunch on a pretty day in favor of a quick nine holes must be difficult to resist.

The club was founded by John Lumsden, a Scot from Banffshire, and some of his friends. There seems to be no record of just who may have laid out the early golf holes here. After the First World War, the brilliant Harry Colt was brought in from England to thoroughly revamp the course. As this book goes to press, Martin Hawtree (more about him later) has embarked on a program of improvements, principally with a view to lending character to the green complexes.

When we first visited Royal Dublin, more than thirty years ago, this was a male-only club. Nevertheless, the clerk in the clubhouse who took my green fee then (two Irish pounds), learning that Harriet planned to walk around with me, said, "There aren't many on the links today, a mere handful. In the circumstances, I don't think the secretary would have any objection if your wife were to hit an occasional chip shot, ah, here and there, say, a little five-iron run-up if it should strike her fancy."

"No, no," I said. "You're very kind, but she really doesn't play golf—ever, anywhere. Just loves to walk along and enjoy the day."

Today, the club's attitude toward women is more enlightened. Wives of members as well as women visitors play regularly, and there is a comfortable locker room for them.

Royal Dublin is hospitable (what Irish club isn't?), and on our most recent visit the attendant in the men's locker room took me in tow. He ushered me into the vistors' locker room so I could put on my golf shoes, then escorted me over to the 1st tee. A threesome had just hit off and was quickly gone. A very elderly man now teed his ball up.

"You follow him," said the locker attendant. "You're next."

"But it's only ten-thirty," I said, "and my tee time is ten-fifty."

"No need to worry about that—you'll follow him. He's slow, but he won't hold you up because he won't be going to the second tee. He'll head off in some other direction so he can play just four or five holes and get back in. There, he's hit away. You get over there and tee up now and be ready to go."

ON THE COURSE

From the championship tees, Royal Dublin measures 6,920 yards (par 72); from the daily markers, 6,425 (par 70). The two nines are quite disparate in length—only 2,910 yards going out but 3,415 coming in. Also helping to emphasize the sharp contrast in length between the two nines

Opposite: Royal Dublin, 18th. Above: 1st. Previous spread: The K Club Smurfit Course, 18th.

is the prevailing wind. It is with us going out, on the short nine, against us coming in, on the much longer nine. Clearly, if we are going to make a decent score here, we'd better play well on the outbound half.

In addition to being compact, with the sea skirting the links on two sides, Royal Dublin is basically level. Not flat, you understand, because the fairways do undulate. Still, the overall elevation change can scarcely be more than seven or eight feet. We cheer every modest rise or dip, because it's obvious that there will be no hills; wrinkles and hummocks will have to do. As for the views over the water, they are not captivating, for this area of the Dublin harbor, occasionally punctuated by tall power-generation chimneys, is somewhat industrialized. All this being said, however, Royal Dublin is still an appealing course, altogether natural, straightforward, and testing. The crisp, tight fairways lend themselves beautifully to the running game that is the hallmark of a true links.

Accurate driving is consistently required. The fairways are not wide, the rough is strangling, and few days are anything like calm. On the first nine there are several occasions—the 1st, 2nd, 5th, 8th—when a sliced shot can sail off the club property to finish out-of-bounds on the strand along Dublin Bay. There are four or five equally good chances for a slicer to wind up beyond the white stakes on the incoming nine.

For the player with a penchant for hooking, Curley's Yard, the out-of-bounds between the 3rd and 13th, must be assiduously avoided. This old stone enclosure now serves as a museum center for what is an officially designated animal preserve. Prominent among the protected are the hares. It would be a rare round that did not find, on at least one occasion, a couple of these cousins of the jackrabbit—with their surprisingly long legs—zipping across our bow out of nowhere as, say, we attempt a 60-yard pitch.

Among the strong holes going out are the 465-yard par-4 2nd (it used to be a par 5), tightly bunkered in the tee shot landing area and at the green; the 370-yard 3rd, gently curving right, where the drive is blind and the narrow green is corseted by sand; and the 5th, another fine and classic par 4, this one 420 yards and framed by low dunes all the way.

The second nine, 500 yards longer, has a quintet of robust two-shotters (408 yards, 410, 445, 435, and 440) that, into the prevailing wind, often turn out to be three-shotters. An out-of-bounds ditch along the right side of the fairway on the dogleg right 515-yard 11th gives pause, as does a burn 50 yards short of the green on the 445-yard 14th.

Royal Dublin has hosted a number of important competitions, men's and women's, amateur and professional. Seve Ballesteros won the

Irish Open here in 1983 and 1985, Bernhard Langer in 1984. For high drama, however, perhaps no event has quite measured up to the 1966 Carrolls International, when Christy O'Connor, a supremely natural striker of the ball, came to the 16th tee in the final round needing to birdie the last three holes in order to gain a tie for the title. From the championship tees, the par-4 16th measured a paltry 267 yards. Sand straitjackets the green. O'Connor, a ten-time Ryder Cupper, drove it and holed an 18-foot putt for eagle. He birdied the 380-yard 17th. The famous 18th was then a par 5 of 478 yards. Today it is a par 4. A rather artificial

creation, it presents a 90-degree right turn in the driving area, where a boundary ditch tight along the right dares you to take a shortcut to the green. The intrepid O'Connor never hesitated, driving aggressively over the corner and then knocking a medium-iron into the heart of the green. He proceeded to roll the 25-footer in for yet another eagle. The crowd erupted. Not only was it a victory for Ireland, but this particular Irishman was Royal Dublin's own professional. He would hold the post for nearly thirty years. In the golf-playing public's consciousness, the two were synonymous: Christy O'Connor and Royal Dublin.

Opposite, top: Royal Dublin, 16th; bottom: 5th. Above: 3rd.

Dublin is awash in outstanding places to stay—luxury hotels, townhouse hotels, guesthouses, B&Bs, you name it:

- Leading the lineup is the flower-bedecked **Four Seasons Hotel Dublin**, in the Ballsbridge section of the city, with its gracious and historic residences. The 259 accommodations, including 67 suites, are sumptuously furnished in traditional fashion: crystal, marble, floral chintzes, inlays, one-of-a-kind carpets. Depending on your room's location, the view can reach to Dublin Bay or the Wicklow Mountains. In certain accommodations, French doors open onto balconies. Principal among the hotel amenities is the spa, with its forty-six-foot indoor pool and adjoining Jacuzzi pool. The elegant **Seasons Restaurant**, with its uninterrupted view here of the courtyard and gardens, daylight spilling through the tall conservatory windows, combines the best of Irish produce with contemporary Continental dishes.

- The **King Sitric**, which bills itself as a "fish restaurant and accommodation," is about as unlike the Four Seasons as any worthwhile place to stay could be. It is as a purveyor of seafood that the King Sitric, at the harbor in the picturesque village of Howth, has earned an international reputation. The pick of the morning's catch—sole, turbot, monkfish, lobster (from the restaurant's own pots in Balscadden Bay)—travels all of four hundred yards from Howth Pier to the kitchen here, where chef and co-owner Aidan MacManus works his magic. Complementing the extensive menu are sea views, which also come with each of the eight guestrooms. These rooms are cheerful and comfortable, but only the two on the top floor could claim to be spacious. The lady in charge is Aidan's wife, the effervescent Joan MacManus, who will be delighted to point the way to Royal Dublin or Portmarnock, both of which are a fifteen-minute drive. The drive into downtown Dublin takes about twenty-five minutes.

- The **Merrion Hotel** is the epitome of Georgian elegance (antiques and carved plasterwork), with a swimming pool and gym to boot.
- The luxurious **Berkeley Court Hotel**, traditional decor, is in Ballsbridge and near the U.S. Embassy.
- The **Shelbourne Hotel**, Dublin's dowager and an institution, on St. Stephen's Green, is true old world grace.
- The **Westbury Hotel**, a few steps off Grafton Street, is five-star luxury that attracts celebrities and politicians.
- The **Gresham**, on bustling O'Connell Street, has a nineteenth-century look and feel and a middle price range.
- The **Fitzwilliam** is a charming guesthouse near St. Stephen's Green, with generous rooms that are moderately priced.
- **Albany House**, an eighteenth-century residence, has period furnishings coupled with today's amenities; economical.

From left: Four Seasons Hotel Dublin; fish stand on Moore Street; the harbor at Howth.

Like Edinburgh, Dublin, with its population of about 575,000, can be readily grasped by even the first-time visitor. Wherever we happen to roam, we have a sense of where we are, at least in relation to our hotel and the most important sites. The Liffey flows through the city, but the structures lining its banks are not prepossessing. Which is to say that a stroll along this river, while certainly not to be avoided, is not to be equated with a stroll along the Seine or the Thames. On the plus side, the walking is easy in this largely level city.

By all means, seek out the landmarks: Trinity College, home of the Book of Kells, one of the most beautiful illuminated manuscripts in the world, and alma mater of Jonathan Swift, Oliver Goldsmith, Oscar Wilde, Bram Stoker, and Samuel Beckett; Dublin Castle; the cathedrals of Christ Church and of St. Patrick; the National Gallery (Italian, Dutch, French, and Spanish masters, together with outstanding Irish art); and the Dublin Spire, a nearly 400-foot-high stainless-steel column in the middle of O'Connell Street, completed in 2003, that is nothing more nor less than a monument to the astonishing vigor of the city and the country today. Another clue to that energy is lively Grafton Street, a shopping mall that is closed to automobile traffic and serves as a link for pedestrians between Trinity College and St. Stephen's Green. Which prompts me to say that Dublin's center-city parks are charmers: St. Stephen's Green, Merrion Square, Fitzwilliam Square. William Butler Yeats lived in a flat at No. 42 Fitzwilliam Square from 1928 to 1932.

Dublin is also the city of Joyce, Guinness, and the Abbey Theatre. The James Joyce Cultural Centre, in an eighteenth-century house, displays biographical details of fifty of the three hundred characters from *Ulysses* based on real Dubliners. The Guinness Storehouse, at the Guinness Brewery (on sixty-four acres, the largest brewery in Europe), offers a fascinating tour that concludes with a free pint of the creamy-headed black stuff in the Gravity Bar, with its splendid city views. The Abbey Theatre provides the chance to experience the great tradition of a national threater that got its start with Yeats and Synge and O'Casey and maintains its vitality today by presenting the new work of playwrights such as Brian Friel.

Top: Howth. Middle row, from left: Trinity College; Customs House; sculptures dedicated to the Great Famine. Left: Malahide Castle, north of Dublin.

263

PORTMARNOCK

Some five miles north on the coast from Royal Dublin, Portmarnock was also established on a solid Scottish foundation. Which is to say that two Scots, W. S. Pickeman and George Ross, both living in Dublin, founded the club in 1894, and that the first professional was Musselburgh's Mungo Park, the 1874 British Open champion. Pickeman, Ross, Park, and George Coburn, the first greenkeeper and yet another Scot, all shared the task of laying out the golf holes. Over the decades since, there have been revisions by Harry Colt, Harry Cairnes, Eddie Hackett, Fred Hawtree, and, in very recent years, by Fred's son Martin, but the holes still go pretty much where they always went.

The club's centenary history offers some delightful tales about the early days. A neighboring cottage was owned by one Maggie Leonard. Whenever a wayward ball sailed over the fence and into her garden, either her cow ate it or she pocketed it. One golf writer accounted for the balls Maggie kept by claiming that each winter a Portmarnock member gave her a half-ton of coal and she gave him the lost balls. What is certain is that any player trying to recover a ball from her garden did so at his peril. She once lashed out memorably at an eminent Dublin lawyer who was trespassing in search of his ball: "You are old enough and ugly enough to know better!"

Portmarnock is a slender peninsula in the Irish Sea, some eight miles from the center of Dublin. Water frames this linksland—sand-based, low dunes, overall elevation change of perhaps 12 feet—on three sides. A very narrow paved road gets us there, but we still have the feeling, once we've arrived, of being at sea. Here a player is alone with the terrain, the sea, the sky, and the oft-ruinous wind. Members, instinctively checking the anemometer on a clubhouse wall before heading to the 1st tee, are relieved to find it reading only 20 miles per hour.

Over the years, Portmarnock has been Ireland's premier stage for important competitions. The British Amateur has been contested only once in the Republic: in 1949 at Portmarnock, when (praise be!) an Irishman, Max McCreedy, who had beaten Frank Stranahan in the quarterfinals, rallied in the final to down Willie Turnesa on the 35th hole. The Walker Cup Match has been held only once in Ireland: in 1991 at Portmarnock,

when the U.S. team, led by Phil Mickelson, David Duval, Bob Tway, and Jay Sigel, triumphed 14–10 over a Great Britain and Ireland squad that included Padraig Harrington and Paul McGinley.

It is actually the many professional events that account for the course's international repute. The Dunlop Masters was held here twice, with Christy O'Connor winning in 1959. The Irish Open was inaugurated at Portmarnock in 1927 (1920 British Open champion George Duncan won, with brown paper wrapped around his body to insulate him from the wind and rain). Among the victors here over the years were Bobby Locke, Hubert Green, Ben Crenshaw, Seve Ballesteros, Bernhard Langer, Ian Woosnam, and José Maria Olazabal. It was at Portmarnock in 1960 that Arnold Palmer, competing for the first time in Europe, teamed up with Sam Snead to capture the Canada (now World) Cup.

Opposite: Portmarnock, 15th.
Above: 1st.

The first four holes move away from the clubhouse in a gentle left-hand arc around the tip of the peninsula. At the 5th, a medium-length two-shotter, we turn inland to play a particularly characterful hole where the rare blind drive must seek out a fairway basin in the low dunes as the hole drifts right; the green is blockaded by three bunkers.

Though both nines are demanding, the most memorable holes are in the second half, where 4 are great. The 129-yard 12th (160 from the tips) plays directly toward the sea, our shot modestly rising, often into the wind, to a green in the dunes that Hawtree has enlarged, boldly recontoured, and uncompromisingly bunkered. The backdrop for the flag is nothing but sky. The 375-yard 14th, chosen for *The 500 World's Greatest Golf Holes* book, also heads out to sea, the second shot played to a long plateau green in the dunes defended in the upslope that fronts it by twin devouring pits. Simple, superlative.

The 15th, 176 yards, is an unnerving beauty that runs smack along the shore to our immediate right. The pulpit tee affords a marvelous view of strand and sea. The two bunkers, on either side of the putting surface and just short of it, seem almost incidental. It is the obvious elusiveness of this narrow table of green, with its sheer little falloffs on both sides, that transfixes us. And if the wind off the water is a powerful one, blowing right to left, then we may well be called upon to take the brave line, out over the beach (itself out-of-bounds) and swing the ball back to the haven of the green. In his first competitive round on this side of the Atlantic, in the 1960 World Cup, Palmer fired a 3-iron here—into and across the wind—that came to a stop three feet past the hole. Crenshaw, Faldo, and Norman have joined him in saluting this hole as one of the greatest par 3s in the world.

The 432-yard 17th (472 from all the way back) strikes me as the hardest par 4 on a course full of hard par 4s. It is defended by fifteen bunkers, seemingly every foot of the way, to say nothing of a low ridge crossing just short of the green and a squeezed, skimpy entrance to that putting surface. Twice on the 36-hole final day of the 1959 Dunlop Masters, Christy O'Connor birdied it, the second time by flighting into the wind a majestic 4-wood that stopped eight feet from the hole and enabled "Himself" to edge the nonpareil amateur Joe Carr by a stroke. Carr, whose father had been the steward at Portmarnock, was born in the clubhouse. One of the handsomest clubhouses in Ireland, Portmarnock's boasts rooms with a strongly welcoming air about them. Fine leather, old wood, and crackling fires strike a note of comfort and cheer. This is a good place to lick our wounds or to weigh the advisability of tackling the third nine—Fred Hawtree laid it out in 1971, and some consider it at least as rigorous as either of the

ON THE COURSE

Like Muirfield—and for roughly the same reasons—Portmarnock is highly regarded by the professionals. Fairness is the reason—few blind shots, even fewer quirky bounces, and greens that rarely require local knowledge. The imaginative routing plan finds two consecutive holes running in the same direction only once (the 1st and 2nd). The wind is constantly shifting.

Portmarnock ranks eleventh in (British) *Golf World*'s top hundred courses in the British Isles, forty-third in *Golf Magazine*'s top hundred in the world. This is a superbly natural links, without a suggestion of artificiality. It is widely viewed as the most difficult course in Ireland. Length, the insistent need for accuracy, and the wind combine to make it more than most of us can handle. From the championship tees it measures 7,365 yards (only one par 4, a 370-yarder, under 400 yards; the three par 5s are 603, 565, and 577 yards). Par is 71. From the shortest tees for men, it comes in just under 6,700 yards. The forward markers add up to 5,840 yards. There are no water hazards. However, the 120 bunkers—invariably penal, often deep—menace all but a handful of swings. The rough is clinging, and driving frequently calls for long forced carries. Targets and hazards are fairly presented. The severity is uncomplicated.

Above: Portmarnock, 14th.
Opposite: 18th. Following page: 9th.

original nines—or to make the acquaintance of a member or two. The last time I played Portmarnock, in late summer of 2004, I did so in the company of Jim Harnett, a Dublin CPA who was captain in 1993, who claimed his handicap was 6 and who hit the ball like a 2. Before we headed out to the 1st tee, Jim introduced me to his father, Conn, a silver-haired man with a ready smile who said that it was not an easy day to make a score here, what with the wind blowing steadily at 25 miles per hour and gusting to 35. Nevertheless, he had enjoyed his round and hoped that I would enjoy mine, too.

Walking down the 1st fairway, I asked Jim his father's age.

"He's eighty-six. He's been a member for fifty-three years, captain in 1976. He was a good player for a long time."

"How often does he play?"

"Oh, three or four days a week."

"Eighteen holes?"

"Yes, of course. He walks and pulls the trolley."

I couldn't resist a final question. "What kind of a score does he make?"

"His age—or a little better—more often than not. That's from the regular markers, the same ones we'll be playing today, nearly 6,700 yards."

The world of golf is not full of Conn Harnetts. But you could safely wager that Portmarnock would have at least one of them.

PORTMARNOCK HOTEL AND GOLF LINKS

Almost near enough to be called next door is the Portmarnock Hotel and Golf Links, a golf resort. The course was designed by Bernhard Langer and Stan Eby, an American. It opened in 1995 and it is outstanding. A modern links routed over sand-based terrain, it can play as long as 6,850 yards, as short as 5,620. There is an engagingly natural look to this eighteen, but, like Kingsbarns and Dundonald, it is man-made. Considerable earth has been pushed around, the net of it being that the fairways have much more movement than those of its neighbor. When the ground here isn't rippling, it is tumbling, as is the case in the duneland that plays host to the closing holes. Though the overall elevation change is less than 20 feet, there are some attractive ups and downs. There are also about a hundred bunkers, all revetted and adroitly spotted. The greens are beautifully sited on low plateaus (the 9th) or in embracing dells (the 18th) or just beyond ticklish swales (the 8th). Portmarnock Links is a worthy companion to the legendary course next door.

The four-star **Portmarnock Hotel** has an intriguing pedigree. The ninety-eight-room hotel and the golf course were built on the former estate of the Jameson Whiskey family. William Jameson was a personal friend of the Prince of Wales, who became Kind Edward VII. (Edward, you may recall from the chapter on Muirfield, visited Greywalls from time to time when it was a private house at the turn of the century, to see a lady who had caught his fancy; one source claims that he brought the very same lady to Jameson House, here at Portmarnock.) An avid yachtsman, Willie Jameson, as he was known, gave the then Prince of Wales a yacht, which was renamed *Royal Britannia*. When subsequently offered a title, Willie declined, insisting that the name Jameson was already known worldwide by all who drank whiskey. Today, Portmarnock Hotel guests occupy sparkling contemporary accommodations constructed in 1996 as an addition to Jameson House itself. Most rooms look out over the links or the sea. Dinner in both the casual **Links Restaurant** and the more formal **Osborne Room** (top-quality Irish produce in dishes that frequently bow to France) is most enjoyable. The **Jameson Bar**, with its dark paneling, barreled ceiling, marble fireplace, and sense of times long past (it was at the heart of the great house), is ideal for a nightcap.

Up the 18th to the Portmarnock Hotel.

THE ISLAND

When I first played The Island, in 1994, it was with a member of the club's council, Frank Walshe, who in 1996 would serve as its captain. He warned me before we teed off that the course had one poor hole. "The tenth," he said, "is a par five that just doesn't have much to recommend it." His candor was spot-on. The 525-yarder was flat, featureless, a dull slog. "We've got to do something about it," he added, "and we will."

And they did, as my visit in late summer of 2004 made clear. The hole is still basically the same length. But it now bends gracefully right, and the new green, testingly contoured and 30 yards to the right of the original, is sited on the far side of an intimidating swale and just beyond a deep and ravenously gathering bunker.

What particularly distinguishes the course from Portmarnock and Portmarnock Links and Royal Dublin are the grand and massive dunes that the locals have long called The Hills. So irresistible was this dramatic terrain that the founding members were determined to play golf here even though the only access was by boat from Malahide, on the far side of the estuary. The trip, albeit brief, was often choppy and sometimes hazardous, but for very like eighty years, until the present clubhouse was built at the Donabate end of the links, that's how golfers got here.

The circumstances surrounding the formation of the club, in 1890, were unusual. There were ten founding members, most from either the law or banking. They were sometimes called The Bachelors, for the very good reason that at the time they established the club, none was married. In fact, only four of them ever did marry. These ten original members formed themselves into a syndicate that wholly owned and managed the club. They were, in truth, the club's *only* members during the early years. All others invited to play here regularly were merely holders of annual season tickets. Even they had to be scrupulously vetted, and no one who worked with his hands or who was a Roman Catholic could be extended this playing privilege.

The Island was just as elitist and exclusionary when it came to caddies and dogs. Regulation 9 read: "With a view to keeping the Links as private as possible, the club desires to discourage the use of caddies; they are strictly prohibited on Sundays . . . and on weekdays shall only be brought over [on club boats] when all other passengers are accommodated." In 1903 it was mandated "that no dog not belonging to a member of the syndicate of The Island Golf Club be allowed on the links on any competition day."

The Island, in short, was like no other Irish golf club. But over the years, as the original ten passed away, the club grew more egalitarian. In 1952 the syndicate resigned after handing over the course, clubhouse, boats, and equipment to those who had come to be known as the "associate members." A club council was promptly created, and The Island had at last found its way into the twentieth century.

Opposite: The Island, 13th.
Above: 14th.

It was in the late 1980s that Eddie Hackett, working from a plan by Fred Hawtree, developed seven new holes. They blended seamlessly with the best of the original eighteen (laid out by several founders) and eliminated most blind shots.

ON THE COURSE

The course measures 6,830 yards from the championship tees (the club hosted the Irish Amateur Close Championship in 1998), 6,540 yards from the regular markers, 5,940 from the forward tees. Par is 71. There are two long holes and three short holes; the other thirteen are par 4s. The round starts with a stiff and straightaway two-shotter of 420 yards that, from a low tee, rises gently through the dunes to an elevated green flanked by sand hills. The round concludes with an equally fine par 4 of much the same length, paralleling the opener but running in the opposite direction. This

time, however, the tee is high in the dunes and the hole plays down and then modestly up over the undulating linksland to a green as attractively sited as the 1st green. Between these two classic holes are sixteen that range from delightful through demanding to splendid and great.

There is not a prosaic hole on the property. The holes take full advantage of the topography. Time and again they meander along dune-framed valleys to cloistered greens, or descend abruptly off giant sand hills into tumbling terrain where only good luck can provide a level lie, or climb boldly over a dune ridge to gain the refuge of a shelf green, or curve around a high shoulder of sand hill to reveal the green on a teasing knob. Always there is challenge, exhilaration, surprise.

Bunkering is light. The contours of the land itself—the ripples and wrinkles, hummocks and hollows, dips and mounds—provide all the defenses necessary on a course that can be counted on, in season, to play fast.

The second nine possesses four consecutive holes that, taken together, convey the personality of this links. From a tee above the beach, the 13th plays 218 yards across the corner of the Broadmeadow Estuary to a green that is also high above the beach. The peril is palpable. The slightest fade will send the ball over the cliff and down into the water. Aim timidly left and the ball hit solidly on that line will dart down a steep slope into thick rough. In a stout breeze, the hole will be all but unplayable. In any circumstances, it is one of Ireland's great one-shotters.

Pause for a moment on the 14th tee to drink in the lovely view across the estuary to Malahide. The pilings of the old landing jetty for the club's boats can still be seen here. Now turn to the task at hand. The hole is 333 yards long. The fairway, generally regarded as the narrowest in Ireland, is not fifteen paces wide. On the left, deep grass and a low dune ridge are hostile. On the right, deep grass and an abrupt falloff into wetlands are even more threatening. It is imperative that we trust our swing.

The 15th is altogether magnificent, 525 yards commencing on a high tee, the blind drive floating down between tall dunes into an unruly fairway, our second and third shots played over terrain that climbs, drops, and finally levels out at an amphitheater green. As for the 145-yard 16th, the target here is a pure plateau green, surely one of the knobbiest in the world. It does not incline to embrace the ball; a revetted bunker at the right front does.

Though not filled with great holes—there may be no more than three—The Island is nonetheless a great course: Natural, imaginatively routed over ideal linksland, studded with diverse and demanding holes, it is unfailingly satisfying, shot after shot. It is solidly among Ireland's top fifteen courses. What's more, it is today a club that opens its arms to the visitor, which, you'll have to admit, is rather a turnabout.

ROGANSTOWN
GOLF & COUNTRY CLUB

Just outside the town of Swords and not fifteen minutes from The Island is Roganstown Golf & Country Club. The centerpiece of what is actually a golf resort is a first-rate parkland course designed by Christy O'Connor Jr., a nephew—not a son, despite his name—of "Himself." Roganstown opened in 2004. It can play as long as 7,000 yards, as short as 5,400. Whichever of the four sets of tees you choose, this gently rolling layout is a stimulating examination. Water is why. Whether in the form of streams or ponds, water imperils the shot on 12 holes. Particularly outstanding is the level one-

shotter 6th (196, 182, or 168 yards), where the play to an angled green is over water nearly every foot of the way. This hole is a beauty.

A handsome Georgian-style farmhouse, which for three generations was the home of the Roganstown resort's owning family, is now a central part of the clubhouse/hotel. Guest rooms—there are fifty-two, and though not spacious, neither are they cramped—are bright, comfortable, and carefully furnished in a contemporary fashion. The public spaces, which are more traditionally decorated, are very relaxing. As for the cooking on our visit, it was superb: succulent rack of lamb dressed with a thyme and garlic jus, delicious fillets of sea bream, presented on a lightly spiced risotto with red pepper.

THE K CLUB

Sometimes it is the smallest—indeed, the least significant—of moments that linger longest in memory. It was in 1994 that we first visited the Kildare Hotel & Country Club, better known as the K Club. The first evening at dinner, in the Byerley Turk Restaurant, Harriet sat down and promptly lowered her handbag onto the carpet beside her chair in this romantically lighted room. It had scarcely settled there, discreetly out of sight, when a staff member silently materialized at her elbow with a tiny square bench—in olden days, m'lady's footstool—upholstered in pale gray silk. He unobtrusively placed it next to her chair, put the handbag on it, bowed, and withdrew.

The K Club opened in 1991. It is the realization of the dream of billionaire Michael Smurfit, who was committed to creating in Ireland a world-class resort. Even before a ball was struck on the first of the two Arnold Palmer/Ed Seay eighteens here, he made a bid for the 1993 Ryder Cup. Perhaps a bit premature, the bid was rejected. In 1999 his proposal was accepted. And in September 2006, the Ryder Cup Match will be played in Ireland for the first time, at the K Club.

ON THE PALMER COURSE

The resort, less than an hour's drive from downtown Dublin and half an hour from the airport, is set on seven hundred acres of rolling woodland and meadowland. The River Liffey, which drifts for a mile through the estate, is very much in play on the 7th, 8th, and 17th. Fourteen other bodies of water—streams, lagoons, ponds, lakes—fill in where the Liffey leaves off. We seem to be playing in a vast water garden, albeit one with its share of flowers and mature trees (to say nothing of sand bunkers and clinging rough and imaginatively contoured greens). A million tons of earth were moved to build this eighteen.

From the forward markers, it measures 5,350 yards; from the championship tees, 7,360. Between the two extremes there are overall lengths of 6,200, 6,500, and 6,800 yards. Most visitors find the course to be unmistakably American. At any rate, it is full of terrific golf holes, including at least four that seem to me genuinely great.

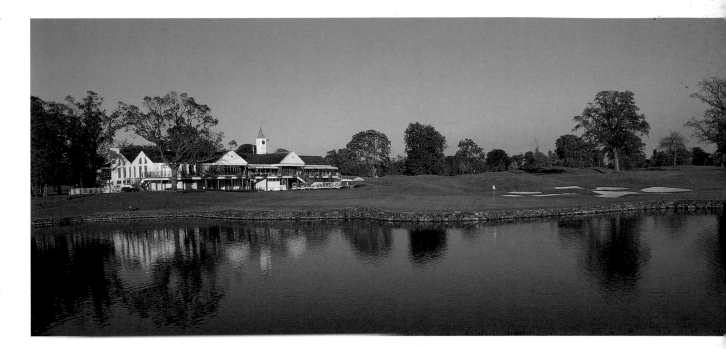

The first of that quartet is the 7th, a double dogleg par 5 that can play anywhere from 460 to 630 yards. The Liffey borders the fairway on the left, but it is concealed at first by trees along the bank. We actually hear its gentle flow before we see the broad stream. It does not come into view until about 120 yards from the green, which is on an island. But this is not an island green like Pete Dye's infamous one-shotter at TPC Sawgrass; here the island is actually much more than double the putting surface. Still, there is no margin for error short or right. Called Inish More (the very name seems to be urging us to take enough club), this is an altogether superlative hole—fair, challenging, very beautiful. A beguiling little white cast-iron suspension bridge, more than one hundred sixty years old, provides access to the island just beyond the green.

Two gems complete the nine. On the 330-yard 8th, the Liffey again flows along on the left, within a few paces of the fairway. The merest suggestion of a pull on either shot is lethal. The 400-yard 9th climbs toward the clubhouse, with bunkers on the left eating into the fairway to imperil the

Opposite: The K Club Palmer Course, 7th. Above: 18th.

drive. There is even less breathing room on the second shot, for three large pits frame the inhospitable green, which slants away from front to back.

If it is possible that there is no such thing as a free swing on the entire course, it is certain that there is none on the final four holes. The Daliesque water patterns astonish us on the downhill 15th (400 yards) and on the rather level 16th (375 yards), both calling for "death or glory" second shots. On the 120-yard 17th, the Liffey reappears within six or seven feet of the right edge of the green. A vast free-form expanse of sand awaits at left. The last hole continues to apply pressure. A patented Palmer/Seay double dogleg, this 485-yard par 5 displays just about everything that has harassed us during the first seventeen holes: sand, mounds, curves, trees, and water (the green juts into a lake). The long second shot over water is tempting. Most of us will virtuously resist, lay up short and right, pitch on from a hundred yards, and walk away with a 5.

In 1995 this course was, for the first time, the venue for the European Open. Bernhard Langer came to the 18th tee in the last round—the hole

Above, left: The K Club Palmer Course, 5th; right: 15th. Opposite: 16th.

measured 530 yards—needing an eagle to force a tie with England's Barry Lane. Two superb strikes put him on the putting surface but 90 feet from the cup. He now proceeded—not promptly, you understand, but following a thoughtful appraisal of the task (Langer is nothing if not deliberate)—to hole the 90-footer. And on the second extra hole he won the tournament.

ON THE SMURFIT COURSE

In 2004 the European Open moved to the K Club's new eighteen, called the Smurfit Course, where Retief Goosen, two weeks after his U.S. Open victory at Shinnecock Hills, won by five strokes with a 13-under-par 275. Largely treeless, the Smurfit Course may be less aesthetically pleasing than what is now known as the Palmer Course, but when it comes to arresting golf holes it is equally well supplied. Elevation changes are more frequent here than at the Palmer and, taken as a whole, more pronounced; the contouring of the immense and swift greens is more intricate, more daring. Sand may be even more confrontational: bunkers are

deeper and often steep-faced. Fairways, on the other hand, are broader. As for water, it awaits on 12 holes and 18 shots. The pressure on the swing for the ordinary player is not one whit less intense than on the original 18.

Because of the openness stemming from the absence of trees and because of the rough's tall, gold-tinted fescue grasses, some have labeled the Smurfit a links-style course. The look of it may suggest links golf, but the play of it assuredly does not. There is little or no room for the ground game, where the ball could run to the flagstick from 50 or 100 yards off the green. Quite the opposite. The term *forced carry* is commonly applied to tee shots. But on the Smurfit Course a forced carry is, again and again, what beleaguers us *on the shot to the green*. How many holes here are open across the front of the green? Two: the 3rd and the 6th. Otherwise, either sand or water (or both: e.g., 10 and 16) seal off the putting surface. There is no way on but *up* and on. We are thus required to hit the ball in the middle of the clubface with preternatural consistency. Otherwise, we'll come up short, which here means sandy or wet. This is not an unfair course, but once we've arrived at our drive, it is merciless.

Above: The K Club Smurfit Course, 4th. Opposite: 7th.

The Smurfit can measure as long as 7,300 yards, as short as 5,200; par is 72. Both nines are studded with exceptional holes. The brilliant knob-to-knob 2nd (146 yards), with a cavernous pit across the broad front compelling us to take more club than we think makes sense, is followed by a 555-yarder with plenty going on. Our gently rising drive traverses a water-filled quarry (surely ersatz), the ball then being propelled along on the level before heading downhill, threading its way between considerable sand, and finally turning sharply left to seek the safety of a bunker-framed green in a hollow. Strong stuff all the way, and as provocative as the unforgettable—in literal truth, unforgettable—7th, the first nine's other three-shotter, which is just over 500 yards from the daily markers, just over 600 yards from the tips. A high tee here invites an aggressive swing, but a broad lagoon down below along the right dissuades us, as it does on the second shot. Now comes the fun: At the greenside end of the lagoon looms Swallow Quarry, a huge man-made rock face that rises some 60 feet out of the water and comes complete with a series of waterfalls and cascades. The world is full of good golf courses that cost a lot less to build than this golf hole.

As on the Palmer Course, the finishing four holes here are intimidatingly wet. Consecutive "Cape" holes—bite off as much of the water hazard as you think you can chew—at 15 and 16 are packed with drama, especially the 422-yard 16th, where the long carry over water to the green on this, the number one stroke hole, calls for a near perfect swing. The falling 17th, 174 yards, finds the green bracketed front and rear by sand and defined on the left by water. As for the home hole, it's a beauty and, on every one of its 508 yards, heart-stopping. The high tee enables us to see much of the water. Another apparently endless lagoon hugs the left side of the hole all the way. The fairway bends emphatically left at about the halfway point and welcomes the carefully lined second shot—which looks squarely across the water at the island green. Imagine, if you will, trying to place a fairway-metal shot on a peninsula so that you will then be in position to hit a 9-iron onto an island.

My enthusiasm for the game at the K Club results in a simple admonition: Please don't limit your golf here to the Ryder Cup course. Whatever you have to do, find time for the new eighteen, as well.

CARTON HOUSE
GOLF CLUB

A ten-minute drive from the K Club brings us to the thousand-acre walled Carton Estate, with its 265-year-old Georgian manor house, one of the very greatest Irish country residences. Two eighteens welcome us to what is now the home of the Golfing Union of Ireland. The first course, designed by Mark O'Meara, opened in 2002. The architect made minimal alterations to the landscape, with its mature woodlands, moderate elevation changes, and the river Rye. The course can play as long as 7,006 yards, as short as 5,742; par is 72. A three-hole sequence on the second nine—13, 14, 15—is excellent by any standard. Water repeatedly stares us down here. The river crosses in front of the green on the 154-yard 13th (gently elevated tee), then swings left to threaten the pulled or hooked shot as well. On the par-5 14th, which curves right to follow the river, both drive and third shot must carry the water; it is sand that imperils the tee shot and second shot. And at the 15th, another medium-length one-shotter played from an elevated tee, a lake defends the front and the left side of the green. On these idyllic tree-framed holes, tranquillity and tension somehow manage to coexist side by side.

The second course, designed by Colin Montgomerie, opened in 2003. The vast meadowy tract for this eighteen was endowed with neither water nor trees nor much in the way of ups and downs. In the circumstances, what to do but fashion a so-called inland links? Well, the bunkering will have to be serious—and it is, with 140 pits, many of them deep—and the green complexes will have to be full of bold contours and frustrating hollows—and they are. Three holes on the second nine are quite good: the heavily bunkered 12th, 173 yards long, where only the precise stroke succeeds; the 303-yard 13th, with its narrow, knobby green angled to the pitch and threatening to transform a birdie into a bogey; and the 500-yard 15th, where three pits 100 yards short of the green and solidly in the fairway add up to a marvelous "cross bunker" and the putting surface is perched teasingly above us. This eighteen can play as long as 7,300 yards, as short as 5,655.

Not thirty minutes from Carton House and also in County Kildare is the new PGA National course at Palmerstown House, in Johnstown, which gives every promise of becoming one of the most beautiful inland courses in Ireland.

THE SUMPTUOUS K CLUB

- Play the superlative **Palmer Course**, venue for the 2006 Ryder Cup.

- Have lunch at the **Smurfit Course clubhouse**, an immense structure full of surprises.

- Don't fail to play the **Smurfit Course**, every bit as challenging as its more famous sibling.

- Spend a night or two in the nonpareil nineteenth-century chateau called **Straffan House**, where traditional luxury scales new heights.

- Dine in the opulent **Byerley Turk**—some of the very finest food in Ireland is served here.

- Outside Kildare Town, visit the **National Stud** and the adjoining **Irish Horse Museum**.

Each K Club course has its own clubhouse. The original clubhouse, at the Palmer (Ryder Cup) Course, has been expanded a couple of times and is now 36,000 square feet. The Smurfit clubhouse, 50,000 square feet, is thought to be Europe's largest. The architectural treatment—natural materials, sloping slate roofs, sandstone details, projecting gables, numerous chimneys, a three-story atrium topped by a glazed skylight that rises above the ridge of the main roof—is nothing if not surprising. This is an audaciously original structure to complement the exhilarating Smurfit Course itself.

But if the golf and its amenities at this five-star resort are extraordinary, the hotel itself is perhaps even more extraordinary. It is not large. At the core of the facility is **Straffan House**, an impeccably restored nineteenth-century chateau. There are sixty-nine accom-

modations here, plus twenty-five garden and courtyard suites. No two guest rooms in Straffan House are alike, and each is luxurious, soothingly so. Cut-crystal doorknobs are frequently at hand. Fabrics, furniture, furnishings, fireplaces—this is Irish country house on the grand scale, with a French influence (Louis XV here, Louis XVI there)—are fit for princes and princesses of the blood. The hushed and formal main dining room, called the **Byerley Turk** (a striking oil painting of the great stallion, one of three Arab progenitors in the male line of every Thoroughbred in the world, hangs prominently in the restaurant) purveys some of Ireland's best cooking. Two of the wonderful dishes on our most recent visit were black truffles with asparagus risotto, and a hot praline soufflé with Armagnac ice cream.

The public rooms display a number of pictures, not

to mention an occasional tapestry or bronze. Twentieth-century Russian, English, Colombian, and Irish artists are represented, including Jack B. Yeats, the poet's brother. *The Tinkers' Encampment,* a large oil painted in 1943 that reflects the effect of the Impressionists on Yeats's work, is particularly delightful. From the rear terrace there are views over formal gardens to the Liffey and beyond to the plains of Kildare. A leisurely stroll of some forty minutes will include the arboretum. Seasonal flowers charm us at every turn, but for many with a horticultural inclination, it is certain trees that are especially noteworthy: the Himalayan birch, the maidenhair ginkgo (a Chinese deciduous conifer), the cork oak (native to Spain and Portugal, where it is the source of cork for wine bottles), and a mighty tulip tree near the stables that is one of the finest specimens of this tree in Ireland.

From left: the Byerley Turk dining room (top) and a suite; St. Brigid's Cathedral; rooms in Castletown Palace.

Although golf is the principal K Club activity, there are also tennis (indoor courts), squash, clay-pigeon shooting, horseback riding, and boating. For the angler, there is a mile of fishing for trout and salmon on the Liffey, plus trout, carp, bream, and tench in five stocked lakes. At the heart of the spa is a beautiful fifty-two-foot indoor pool. There are also saunas, a Jacuzzi, a solarium, and compartments where a wide range of massages, therapies, and beauty treatments are administered.

When we put it all together—the setting, the golf, the accommodations, the cuisine, and the amenities— the K Club has a reasonable claim to being the single most luxurious golf-centered resort in Ireland.

COUNTY KILDARE

County Kildare is the heartland of Irish Thoroughbred breeding and racing. Three racetracks, the Curragh, Nass, and Punchestown, are here. Some of Ireland's most important races are run at the Curragh, including the Irish Derby (on the last Sunday of June or the first Sunday of July). Just outside Kildare Town is the National Stud. Visitors can tour it, as well as the adjoining Irish Horse Museum, where the principal exhibit is the skeleton of Arkle, one of the country's legendary race horses. Horses are auctioned off frequently at Goff's, in Kill.

The county is also noted for its splendid country houses. Carton House is not open to the public, but Castletown, at Celbridge, is. Built in 1722, it is the largest and greatest Palladian-style house in Ireland. Intricately carved plasterwork, priceless period furniture, silver, porcelains, and oil paintings all serve to evoke an aristocratic way of life that is long gone.

Ancient Kildare Town itself is noted for St. Brigid's Cathedral (Church of Ireland), which dates to the thirteenth century and is remarkable for the buttresses of its nave walls, connected by arches. Not far from the town is the Moone High Cross, one of the most striking medieval carved crosses in the land; its 51 sculptured panels show scenes from the Scriptures.

For shopping, Nass and Newbridge are best. The main street in both is lined with small craft shops that make for pleasant browsing and buying. At Tomolin, in the southern part of the county, the Irish Pewter Mill makes and sells all manner of pewterware.

Clockwise from top left: Black Abbey at the National Stud Farm; southern County Kildare; Japanese gardens at the National Stud Farm; Kilkea Castle.

GLASSON

Breda Reid (she and her husband, Tom, are the owner-developers of Glasson Golf Hotel & Country Club) pinpointed the beauty of the setting when she said, "I always considered this place to be heaven, even when it wasn't a golf course." Here, an hour and a half northwest of the K Club and six miles north of Athlone, water, hills, and sky merge into a tapestry so vast and glorious that the horizons can scarcely contain it. Inland golf in Ireland has rarely been better served.

Tom and Breda had been farming their 275 acres—turnips, cereals, cattle, sheep—for a number of years before converting the pasture and croplands into golf holes. It was a gamble, but the gamble has paid off. And it keeps not just Tom and Breda but their daughter, Fidelma, and son-in-law, Gareth Jones, who share the general manager responsibilities, very busy indeed. The course opened in 1993, the hotel in 2000. Glasson is now a full-fledged golf resort, with a three-hole teaching academy, a practice range, chipping and putting greens, and golf carts.

The Reids commissioned Christy O'Connor Jr. to lay out their eighteen. It is a winner, consistently measuring up to the gorgeous setting on the shores of seventeen-mile-long Lough Ree. One of its "arms" is Killinure Bay. The golf holes overlook the lake or the bay, which are parts of the Shannon River system. Players arrive by either car or boat; there is a jetty between the 15th and 17th greens, and a golf cart is dispatched from the clubhouse to pick up the sailors and whisk them up the hill to the 1st tee.

ON THE COURSE

Glasson is hilly, with an overall elevation change of not less than 120 feet. From the forward markers, the course measures 5,600 yards. From the championship tees, the length is 7,120 yards. Most golfers play it at 6,200 or 6,600.

A 350-yarder and a 500-yarder, both over rolling ground and with potentially uneven stances, enable us to get away to a comfortable start, but we know that rigorous tests must lie ahead. Immediately ahead, as it turns out.

The 3rd is a model of spectacle and simplicity: 190 yards from a modestly elevated tee across a swale to a plateau green backdropped in the distance by the shimmering immensity of Lough Ree. In full view is wooded

Hare Island, and the meadows of County Roscommon lie emerald on the far shore. The green, deep enough but a shade short on width, is defended by a pair of gathering bunkers that pinch the entrance. Into a stiff breeze off the lake, the shot can be at least a 3-metal, sometimes a driver.

Two other holes going out lodge securely in our memory. At the 500-yard 6th (560 from the tips), a boundary tight on the left all the way gives pause; so do two ponds on the right, waiting to swallow the pushed or cut second shot come sailing over the long steep hill that prompts the powerful to believe they can get home in two. Downhill again on the 8th, and more water, but this time on a 390-yarder that doglegs sharply left in the driving area (gorse left and right), then plunges to a green with steep little falloffs and, on the left, water that cunningly wraps itself around the back.

Fourteen, 15, and 18 are the equal of the first nine's three finest holes. The 14th is one of the most spectacular holes in Ireland, indeed in

Opposite: Glasson, 8th.
Above: 14th.

all of the British Isles. We can play it from 510, 521, or 566 yards. I urge you to climb to the top tee. A tiny launching pad of turf in the trees on this steep hillside, it is unsettlingly high, not less than 110 feet, above the green. From this aerie, the panorama over island-dotted Killinure Bay is improbably scenic. As for the golf hole itself, it is full of feature and fascination (and fear), plunging near vertically on the drive, then doglegging sharply right (sand in the crook of the bend), now dropping steeply again (a pond on the right to drown the errant fairway metal), and finally leveling out for the last 150 yards. The bay is some eighteen paces off the left flank of the green, which is also defended by sand in front and at the right.

At the marvelous 15th, which ranges from 127 to 185 yards, both tee and green nose into Killinure Bay. Into the prevailing left-to-right wind, the shot demands our soundest swing. The 360-yard 18th doesn't look like much on the card. On the course, however, it is plenty. Doglegging smoothly left, the hole climbs steeply to a narrow green—we can see the flag but not the putting surface—that is surrounded by a total of eight bunkers. It's hard to envision the day when this hole plays less than 400 yards.

Christy O'Connor Jr. may well have been Ireland's most prolific golf course architect over the last fifteen to twenty years, certainly since his heroics in the 1989 Ryder Cup, at The Belfry. On the final day he needed to

down Fred Couples in order to stave off a European defeat. Their match was even as they came to the great 18th: 474 yards, water, trees, sand. Couples detonated a 315-yard drive, leaving only a 9-iron. Christy's tee shot was short, and he now faced a 230-yard shot over the lake to the flagstick. "Coming down the fairway," he would recall, "Tony Jacklin said to me, 'If you put him under pressure, I promise you will win the hole and the match. Just have a good swing.' And that's all I thought about. I had a big two-iron, I made a good turn, and just hit it." The ball whistled over the water, then drew softly toward the hole to finish within three and a half feet of it. Couples, who responded by half-shanking his 9-iron, was forced to concede the putt and the contest. Christy's winning point turned out to be decisive, enabling Europe to retain the cup. With a single sublime swing, the Galway native had established himself forever as a folk hero in Irish golf.

On our most recent visit to Glasson, I played with Breda Reid, who seemed pleased to have a reason for getting out on the course. I asked whether Christy (when you are in Ireland and talking about golf, no surname is necessary for the great man: There is only one Christy; his late uncle was widely known as "Himself") ever came back to Glasson.

"Yes, he does come by from time to time," she answered. "He was here a few weeks ago and we played three holes before the rain drove us in. I was disappointed, but he wasn't. He had really come to see the new baby, Fidelma and Gareth's Alex. We had a nice visit, and the baby was on his best behavior." The small world of Irish golf is sometimes an endearing one.

MULLINGAR

There is another worthy course forty-five minutes away, at Mullingar. James Braid laid it out one day in 1937. With eighteen wooden pegs for tees and eighteen for greens, he moved briskly from point to point, collected his £25 fee, and set out that same afternoon for home near London. "Himself" won the Irish Professional Championship here in 1965.

Mullingar is a pretty, rolling parkland layout. The aspect, particularly on the first nine, is an open one, with the play on a vast and carefully maintained lawn. There are many wonderful old specimen trees, including some towering firs. Among the outstanding holes are a couple of par 3s on the first nine, the 182-yard 2nd and the 173-yard 5th, each playing from knob to knob, each requiring a precisely struck 3- or 4-iron (or perhaps a 7-metal) if we are to hold greens that are neither generous nor welcoming.

Overnighting at the **Glasson Golf Hotel** is a pleasure. The twenty-nine rooms are bright and comfortable; many overlook Killinure Bay. Drinking cocktails at the window is not likely to be forgotten. The plain dining room, with its old fireplace, is in 220-year-old Killinure House, which for decades was the Reids' home. The window tables have lovely views over the bay far below. The menu is simple. Harriet and I each had the grilled sole and, for dessert, champagne sorbet. Both were first-rate. The Glasson Golf Hotel & Country Club does not disappoint. Centrally located, it is an hour and a half's drive from Dublin, from Galway, and from Shannon. Of course, if you come by boat, it may take a little longer.

Adjacent to Mullingar Golf Club is Belvedere House, a mid-eighteenth-century structure built as a fishing villa. Today, it is derelict, but its glory is not quite extinguished. The setting, high above Lough Ennell, is a noble one. The formal and informal gardens continue to delight us. Somehow, the elegant carved stucco ceilings in the reception rooms are still intact. And then there is the folly, called the Jealous Wall, the grand facade of a manor house with nothing behind it. It was built to screen Belvedere House from nearby Tudenham Park,

another mansion that belonged to the same Rochfort family. This house, now in ruins, belonged to one of Lord Belvedere's brothers, who had not been properly sympathetic to Belvedere when the lord's wife ran off with yet a third Rochfort brother! By means of this monumental stone sham—and in order to dramatize the totality of the estrangement from the master of Tudenham Park—the wronged nobleman made it impossible for his brother to catch as much as a glimpse of Belvedere House from his residence.

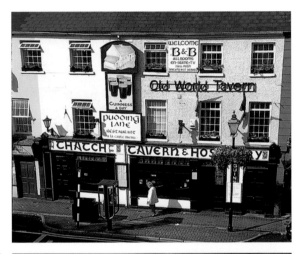

Clockwise from above: the Shannon River, in Athlone; blooming gorse along Lough Derravaragh; downtown Athlone; the Shannon River at dusk; up the 18th to the Glasson Golf Hotel & Country Club; on the square in Athlone.

COUNTY LOUTH

About an hour and a half's drive northeast of Glasson brings us to Baltray, home of the County Louth Golf Club. The seaside links here, a strikingly natural sand-hills layout, is one of Ireland's dozen best courses. It was the venue for the 2004 Irish Open, attracting a field that included Ryder Cuppers Padraig Harrington, Darren Clarke, Miguel Angel Jiminez, Paul McGinley, and Luke Donald. The winner, however, was little-known Brett Rumford.

The club was founded in 1892, when a transplanted Scot by the name of Thomas Gilroy—as we've seen, many of the early Irish golf clubs owed their formation to Scots—teamed up with a local barrister, George Henry Pentland, who had never struck a golf ball. As a boy, Gilroy learned the game at Carnoustie. Then, while a student at St. Andrews University, he played often with Young Tom Morris on the Old Course and brought his handicap down to plus 4. Here in Ireland he laid out 11 rudimentary holes at Mornington in 1889, just across the Boyne Estuary from Baltray, on rather unpromising terrain. But he ran into trouble with the neighbors, who were not sympathetic to this foreign game, and the course was soon abandoned. Pentland suggested the dunelands at Baltray. Astonished at what greeted him there, Gilroy said, "Here was I trying to make a course out of poor material when, less than a mile away, there was one of the best pieces of golfing ground in the world."

The first holes at Baltray were laid out by Gilroy and a Scottish professional with the curious name of A. Snowball. Though the club prospered from the start, it was not till the late 1930s that full advantage was taken of its superb linksland. Tom Simpson and his associate Molly Gourlay—English Ladies' champion and probably the first woman to earn money as a golf course architect—went well beyond mere updating. Pat Ruddy, some of whose achievements in golf course design this book presents, has written about Simpson: "Simpson's greatest strength as a designer was the ability to create greens that were great to look at but devils to play to. His work at Baltray is a prime example of his craft: pulpit tees and plateau greens abound, with surfaces that writhe as though some deeply troubled giant was having a bad sleep beneath these verdant quilts."

ON THE COURSE

From the first shot at Baltray, the game is on. This 415-yarder begins with a drive into hummocky ground corseted left and right by penal bunkers. Then, as it swings easily left, the hole calls for a long second shot over a gentle rise that conceals another pit, roughly 15 yards short of the green and solidly *in* the fairway, to snare the underhit long iron or fairway metal. The green falls off to the right. This rigorous opener is in a class with the 1st at Oakland Hills, Royal St. George's, Aberdovey, Pine Valley, and Oakmont.

The course, a par 72, measures 6,936 yards from the tips, 6,676 from the medal tees, 6,320 from the daily markers. In season, Baltray plays firm and fast; an adept ground game is essential to good scoring. With its sand-based fairways ranging from rippling to tumbling, its imaginative routing through the dunes, the remarkable diversity of its brilliant greens, and the number of truly great holes (no fewer than six), Baltray is all that a world-class links should be.

A pair of exceptional one-shotters on the outbound nine, the 5th (158 yards) and the 7th (153 yards), play from lofty windswept platforms across swales to plateau greens defended by gathering bunkers and steep falloffs. They bracket a thrilling par 5 that dipsy doodles its way for 521 yards to a green precariously sited on a knob with more of those dreaded falloffs.

A trio of par 4s on the inbound nine—12, 13, 14—weaves through tossing duneland beneath a range of towering sand hills along the Irish Sea. I still smile at the memory of our first visit to Baltray, in the mid-1990s. In a golf cart so that we could move quickly through the round and clear the way for an outing with a shotgun start at noon, we were struck by a number of corporate-sponsor signs decorating the course, and by the egalitarian nature of the placement of these signs: for example, the multinational corporation Becton Dickinson side by side with Monaghan's Poultry. Our favorite was the arrow-shape directional marker that greeted us as we left the 11th green. It unwittingly pointed the way into the tumbling dunes and read MCCABE'S GARAGE. We were entirely willing to believe it was in there somewhere.

Opposite: County Louth (Baltray), 14th.

The 12th and 13th, each well over 400 yards, call for a long second shot fired through a gap in the dunes to a partially hidden green. The 14th, though 100 yards shorter, purveys at least as much pure golf. From the pinnacle tee, our gaze encompasses the broad, tawny beach, the gray-green sea separating Ireland from Wales, and, on a crystalline day, the Mountains of Mourne, 40 miles north on the coast. Into the prevailing wind, the carry down to a riotously rumpled fairway is a stout one. Still, it is the pitch, likely to be less than a hundred yards, that sets the pulse racing. There is no sand, but the plateau green is partly hidden in the dunes. The wrinkled putting surface falls away into hollows as shallow as 6 feet, as deep as 15 feet.

The final stretch at Baltray includes two more very good par 3s and, at the last, a 541-yarder that is strong, though limited in visual appeal. A couple of pesky little pot bunkers smack in the middle of the fairway, one of them 100 yards short of the green, the other one 50 yards short, endanger the long second shot and can peremptorily transform the dream of a birdie into the reality of a bogey.

Some sixty to seventy years ago, two ladies and a brand-spanking-new men's amateur tournament went a long way toward putting Baltray in the front rank of Irish golf clubs. The ladies were Clarrie Tiernan and Philomena Garvey, who both learned the game as children on the links here. Clarrie won the Irish Ladies' Championship in 1936. In 1938 she became the first Irishwoman to be selected for the Curtis Cup team, and ten years later, she was chosen again. Philomena's record is considerably more impressive: six-time Curtis Cupper, between 1948 and 1960; winner of the 1957 British Ladies' Championship, at Gleneagles, and runner-up for the title four times; and fifteen-time Irish Ladies' champion, between 1946 and 1970.

It was in 1941 that the club founded the East of Ireland Amateur Championship, and it is here that this competition is held annually. Joe Carr, who died in 2004 and who was the greatest amateur in the annals of Irish golf—ten-time Walker Cupper and three-time British Amateur champion—managed to carry it off twelve times, between 1941 and 1969 (the 1970 winner was his son Roddy). Twenty-five years after his last East of Ireland victory, according to a story related by Donald Steel in his *Classic Golf Links of Great Britain and Ireland,* Carr, in a purely social game at Baltray, had on his bag a young caddie who was ignorant of his player's renown. The great man was struggling, which prompted the caddie to ask, "Ever played here before?"

"Yes," replied Carr, "as a matter of fact, I have."

"Did yer ever play in the East of Ireland Championship?"

Opposite: County Louth
(Baltray), 12th.

instance, on the 380-yard 4th, ponds both left and right of the green put fearsome pressure on the swing. The second nine, much nearer the sea, is generally routed over attractive linksland, starting with the par-5 10th, which plays along a gently falling dune-framed valley.

The final three holes make for a rousing finish. Sited high in the dunes, the tee on the 16th, a shortish par 4, enables us for the first time to take in the sea, with the fairway rippling away below, parallel to the shore, a range of low sand hills separating it from the beach. The 17th is a robust knob-to-knob 165-yarder solidly in the dunes, and the last hole, a short par 5 of only 460 yards, is a beauty that commences on yet another tee high above the beach. A gambling second shot will cut off some of the serpentine route that the fairway traces to the green, but failure to make this carry over hostile rough could result in 6 or worse. Clearly, Smyth and Brannigan have saved the best holes till last.

Not twenty minutes south is **Laytown & Bettystown Golf Club**, founded in 1909. Extensive alterations by Smyth and Brannigan in the 1990s have appreciably strengthened the old layout, a very compact par-71 test that can be set up at 6,440 yards, 6,270, and 5,610. Bunkering is light. It is the antic nature of the terrain coupled with the all-but-relentless wind that defends par here. Pulpit tees and plateau greens are common; so are narrow fairways framed by low dunes cloaked in long marram grass. The overall elevation change is scarcely 12 feet. Because the greens incline to be small and full of steep little falloffs, even our short irons, frequently from awkward stances, are a ticklish matter. There is an appealingly old-fashioned feel to the game here.

I happened to visit Laytown & Bettystown on an August morning in 2004 when fog enveloped the club. I spoke briefly with Bobby Browne, the professional since 1967. He told me that he had played the European Tour from 1962 to 1967 and "never pocketed so much as a bob." He suggested that this out-and-in course could fairly be compared to Royal Aberdeen, an assertion that left me dumbstruck. As the fog showed signs of lifting, he turned to three women waiting impatiently in his shop and delighted them—and me—with what was surely an old joke but a nonetheless serviceable one: "Get on up to the tee, girls—you'll drive it out of sight!" And then he urged me to follow him up to the 1st tee, an elevated platform, where, pointing as he turned, he pronounced, "North to Belfast, east to Liverpool, south to Dublin, west to Galway." It was as though Laytown & Bettystown were at the epicenter of all the world that mattered.

"Yes," said Carr.

"And did yer ever do any good?" insisted the boy.

"I won it twelve times," came the answer from Carr with a modest nonchalance, thinking he might have the last word.

"Well," concluded the boy, "the standard must have been much worse in your day."

NEARBY COURSES

For a hundred years, the County Louth Golf Club provided the only golf in this neck of the woods. Then, in 1993, the **Seapoint Golf Club** opened next door. Ryder Cupper Des Smyth (1979, 1981) and Declan Brannigan designed what cannot be considered a great course—it has very little of the ideal duneland with which Baltray is endowed—but is certainly quite a good one. It can be set up as long as 7,000 yards and as short as 5,000 yards.

The first nine, at some distance from the sea, has a rather meadowy feel to it. Water and boundaries lend a measure of menace. For

County Louth (Baltray), 13th.

The only place of real substance near Baltray, itself a fishing village with occasional thatched-roof cottages, is Drogheda. Just outside this bustling market town is the **Boyne Valley Hotel**, in its sixteen-acre park. This converted eighteenth-century mansion, though far from luxurious, is comfortable and well run. The cooking is good, the bar and the conservatory are convivial gathering places, and the guest rooms, which incline to be small, are suitable for a two-night stay.

In Termonfeckin, where Seapoint is located, is a B&B called **Highfield House**. A farmhouse on 120 acres, it dates to 1725 and is owned by the motherly Mrs. McEvoy, who knows that for a golfer the three most important things are a firm mattress, quiet, and getting to the 1st tee on time. There are just three guest rooms, all of them big, each with a double bed, a single bed, a private bathroom, and pleasant rural views. There is also a cozy sitting room with a fireplace. Breakfast is the only meal, but next door is the **Triple House**, where the cooking is first-rate.

One other place to stay could ring the bell with a foursome of men. At **County Louth Golf Club** the clubhouse itself, formerly the Golf Hotel, provides ten small and spartan rooms. There is hot and cold running water in the sink, but the bathroom is down the hall. And if a party is not going on downstairs, we sleep the sleep of the blessed, to be awakened the next morning by a knock on the door and word that breakfast is served. It turns out to be a full Irish breakfast of epic proportions, just what we need to fortify ourselves for another round on this great and noble links.

With a population of about twenty-five thousand, Drogheda, about seven miles west of Baltray, is a prosperous trading center that sprawls over the hilly banks of the Boyne River. Its motto, "God is our strength, merchandise our glory," may come off as a desperate attempt to reconcile the irreconcilable. "Over 300 shops cater for your every need," proclaims a chamber of commerce brochure, which then proceeds to spell out the richness

of the area's religious legacy: St. Peter's Roman Catholic Church (late nineteenth century), St. Peter's Church of Ireland (mid-eighteenth century), St. Laurance's Gate (thirteenth-century Magdalene Tower), St. Mary's Abbey (the ruins of a thirteenth-century Augustinian friary), Millifont (the ruins of a twelfth-century Cistercian monastery), and Monasterboice (three magnificently carved High Crosses, two of them among the finest of their kind; and the ruins of two medieval parish churches).

About a mile from Drogheda is the site of the Battle of the Boyne. Here, in 1690, William of Orange, commanding a force of approximately thirty-six thousand Dutch, Germans, Danes, and French Huguenots, defeated the deposed King of England, James II, leading twenty-five thousand Irishmen, in a battle that decided the fate of Ireland, to say nothing of the future of the English throne. History buffs come to tramp this ground and ponder.

A few miles west of Drogheda, on a ridge above the Boyne, is Newgrange, site of a remarkable passage grave that appears to have been constructed as long ago as 2800 B.C., and that, for size and decoration, is unsurpassed in Europe. The underground tomb itself, almost twenty feet high and roofed by beehive vaulting, contains three recesses, partially patterned. A small museum near the parking lot presents an explanation of what is to be seen here, as does the guide who conducts the tour.

Hill of Slane, in County Meath.

NORTHERN IRELAND

ROYAL COUNTY DOWN

Less than 45 minutes' drive due north from Baltray brings us into Northern Ireland. There is no sense of a border crossing, no checkpoint. In truth, were it not for the money changers and their signs proclaiming the opportunity to translate euros into pounds sterling, it might never occur to us that we are leaving the Republic of Ireland and entering the United Kingdom. We soon find ourselves heading into Newcastle and then down a tree-lined lane just off the main street to Royal County Down Golf Club, which is almost as close to the town center as the Old Course is to the heart of St. Andrews.

The first time I visited Royal County Down, more than twenty-five years ago, I was in a party of six touring Americans who were invited to join the members on hand, some forty to fifty of them, in what is a Saturday ritual here: the "Hat." First, you put your name in the hat. Then you down a couple (or three) drinks (pink gin or a pint of Guinness seem to be the potions of choice) amid a high and hilarious decibel level, while the Hat Man, off in a corner by himself and carefully analyzing the handicap and current form of each participant, draws up the foursomes and posts his list (instantaneous whooping and groaning and calling about to spread the news) under a small brass clock on the wall. Foursomes eat together, enabling them to sort out their better-ball matches while they wade through the three-course luncheon: hot soup from one of the grand old silver tureens, a roast with four vegetables (including the obligatory potatoes and cauliflower), cheese and crackers, coffee or tea. At long last, off to the 1st or 10th tee to begin the round of golf that, at least in theory, is the reason behind all this enviable camaraderie. Afterward, it's back to the bar to settle the bet and enjoy a libation (or two or three) before calling it a day. To my knowledge, no other golf club in Britain or Ireland puts on anything quite like County Down's Saturday "Hat."

The County Down Golf Club was formed in the spring of 1889 at a gathering in Newcastle of more than seventy-five men and women. Old Tom Morris made the voyage from Scotland in mid-July "to lay out the course at an expense not to exceed £4," according to the club council minutes. But the centenary history, published in 1988, says that Old Tom was paid this munificent sum "presumably to comment on the existing nine and make suggestions for a second nine." Substantial revisions were effected over the next twenty years, principally by Harry Vardon in 1908 and 1919. Except for lengthening, the course is little changed since Vardon's day. Over the years, it has served as the venue for the British Amateur Championship (1970 and 1999); countless Irish amateur and professional championships, including three Irish Opens; and three British Seniors (Nicklaus, Palmer, Player, and Watson in the field); but never the British Open. The Walker Cup will be played here in 2007.

Royal County Down—the "Royal" prefix was bestowed by King Edward VII in 1908—is a men's club, but it shares the links with The Ladies' Golf Club, which was founded in 1894. "Four years later," as John de St. Jorre writes in *Legendary Golf Clubs of Scotland, England, Wales, and Ireland,* ". . . the club held its first mixed foursomes, during which one bold lady, noting it was leap year, proposed to her partner on the back of the programme. She ended her carefully drafted letter thus: 'If I am wrong, let the matter rest, you keep your counsel and I'll keep mine, and if no answer upon the subject, I suppose I shall be at liberty to "Pop the question" elsewhere.'" We don't know whether her partner accepted this offer of marriage. In the decades to come, Royal County Down would be the venue for ten Irish Ladies' Close Championships, seven British Ladies' Championships, and, in 1968, the Curtis Cup. The ladies have their own clubhouse, and they often choose to play the delightful and much shorter second eighteen.

ON THE COURSE

The championship course, laid out along a curve of Dundrum Bay, is one of the glories of world golf. For many discerning and widely traveled golfers, it is their single favorite course. We are struck at the outset by the sublime views, the massive nature of the sand hills, the profusion of gorse (a blaze of gold in spring, impenetrable at all times), the multitude of bunkers (130) and their ferocity. These deep pits are generally fringed with long marram grass; in some instances they are heather bewhiskered. The mandate is simple: *If you get in, get out.*

Opposite: Royal County Down, 9th. Previous spread: 4th.

bends en route to a green framed by bunkers and low dunes. The greens have less contour than those of many other great courses. A player with a sound stroke can make putts here.

County Down's 9th, a 486-yard par 4 from the championship tees (425 from the daily markers) is one of the most celebrated holes in the game and one of the eighteen greatest holes in the 500 book. From its hilltop tee, the loftiest point on the course, a solid drive sails over a direction pole and floats down to the unseen fairway some 80 feet below. The view from the summit is spellbinding. Beyond the red-roofed white clubhouse and the redbrick steeple of the adjacent Slieve Donard Hotel are the rooftops of Newcastle and then the Mountains of Mourne, a faded purple, their tallest peak often wreathed in clouds. Our gaze also encompasses miles and miles of green countryside skirting the Irish Sea, which morphs from leaden through azure to cobalt whenever the wind, dispersing the clouds, makes way for the sun to take charge of this heart-stopping panorama. It may be the most aesthetically thrilling moment in all of golf.

Then there is the business of playing the hole. The fairway is lined on both sides with sand hills clad in gorse, heather, bracken, and marram grass. Two sentinel bunkers, one smack in the middle of the fairway, one at the left, are deftly spotted in the face of a slope some 40 yards short of the green. Clear these pits and your long second shot will skip onto the putting surface if the course is playing fast. The combination of test and beauty presented by the 9th at County Down is imperishable.

If the second nine does not quite measure up to the first—an impossible task on the face of it—it still offers a number of superlative holes, such as the 429-yard 11th, doglegging right through gorse and sand, and the 13th, much the same length and reminiscent of Sandwich as it enjoys the seclusion of a smoothly curving dune-lined valley all its own. Here, a blind second shot must be struck over the corner of a high right-hand sand hill if we are to have any hope of gaining the harbor of the green.

County Down ranked ninth in the world in the 2005 *Golf Magazine* top one hundred, second in the British Isles according to the *Golf World* (Britain) panel in 2004. More overall skill in shot-making, along the ground as well as through the air, and more intelligence in shot analysis are called for here than just about anywhere in Ireland. This is an immensely sophisticated test. Harry McCaw, twice captain of the club and once captain of the Royal & Ancient, expresses a sentiment that would surely be seconded by every golfer with a respect for the game's storied venues: "We are the custodians of one of the great golf courses of the world. We have an obligation to share it."

Above: Royal County Down, 4th. Opposite: 11th.

We must also be prepared to live with quirky bounces (this classic links terrain is endlessly rumpled) and blind shots: The 2nd, 5th, 6th, 9th, 11th, and 15th all call for blind driving over dunes to gain what may well be a narrow fairway. And there are three or four times when the green itself—or a large part of it—is hidden.

A handful of indisputably great holes may be taken as representative of the challenge on this par-71 course, which measures nearly 7,000 yards from the tips and over 6,500 yards from the regular markers. The 2nd, 374 yards, calls for a blind drive over a ridge, followed by a second shot that must be guided through a cut in another ridge to a green on a low plateau and bunkered at the left. The 4th, included in *The 500 World's Greatest Golf Holes*—174 yards from the members' tees, 217 from the championship markers—is a forced carry over gorse from high ground down to a green patrolled by ten sandpits. The equally superlative 5th, 409 yards and also commencing from an elevated tee, tempts us to bite off as much as we dare of a heathery outcrop on the right, around which the hole

MALONE

A number of Royal County Down members who live in Belfast also belong to Malone Golf Club, which was founded in 1895 and is four miles south of the city. The course here, designed by John Harris, is often spoken of as the best inland layout in Ulster. It's a spacious beauty (on 270 acres), with an abundance of mature oaks, sycamores, and pines, rolling terrain, the river Lagan bordering it on the east, and 27-acre Ballydrain Lake the centerpiece of the second nine. Black Mountain and the checkered fields of the Antrim Plateau provide a stirring vista from the 10th, one of the half dozen par 4s measuring well over 400 yards on this par-71, 6,642-yard eighteen.

The 13th, 14th, and 15th are especially arresting, thanks to the lake. The drive on the 403-yard 13th must carry a corner of the water; the stout uphill second shot curves from left to right. Fourteen plays shorter than its 418 measured yards because the second shot is downhill, but a combination of sand short, left, and right of the green, plus water at the rear of it, makes clear why this is the number two stroke hole. At 15, only 136 yards, the left side of the putting surface juts into the lake.

ARDGLASS

A thirty-five-minute drive north from Newcastle, some of it with sea views, all of it with hairpin turns, brings us to the historic fishing village of Ardglass and what may well be the world's oldest golf clubhouse. Formerly Ardglass Castle, the blocky stone structure, which dates to the fourteenth century, has a fortresslike look to it, there at the cliff edge some thirty feet above the water. Behind the clubhouse is the picturesque harbor.

The Ardglass Golf Club was founded in 1896, but it was not till 1970 that the course was extended from nine holes to eighteen. No more than six holes are authentic undulating linksland; the other dozen are rather meadowy. But virtually the entire eighteen is routed over high ground, with the result that the views—across the Irish Sea to the Isle of Man, down over Coney Island Bay, and south to the Mountains of Mourne—are intoxicating. Simply to be abroad on Ardglass is a delight.

This is a short layout, only 6,260 yards from the back tees, par 70. But when the wind blows—and the wind seems ever to be whipping across this clifftop—the yardages have little meaning, beginning with the first hole, all of 335 yards. Skirting the craggy cliff, it curves as it climbs. So

steep is this ascent that there must be many days when, into a headwind, the playing value is no less than 450 yards! A single bunker seals off the front of the long, narrow, dune-framed green.

Next is a great one-shotter. Its tee tight beside the cliff edge, this 170-yarder is played across a deep fissure in the sheer cliff face—the water rushes in at the bottom of this cleft, but it's so far below us that we never actually see it—to a smallish green a bit above eye level, with sand left, a dune right. This is supremely natural, and unforgettable.

The next 4 holes also tee off at the cliff edge, but they lack the drama and distinction of the opening pair. The 7th, 8th, and 9th—219, 439, and 527 yards—all require very solid ball striking.

A stretch of 4 outstanding holes starts at the 205-yard 10th, where, from a high tee, we launch a falling shot to a green sited beside the rocky foreshore of Coney Island Bay. On the terrific 11th, a steadily rising 488-yard par 5 with a lighthouse in the distance off the starboard bow, the beach borders the hole on the right every foot of the way, a rough-clad sand hill serves the same purpose on the left, a long forced carry to a narrowing fairway intimidates us on the tee, a burn must be traversed on our second shot, and the green slopes markedly from left to right.

Opposite: Ardglass, 2nd.
Above: 18th.

The grand 12th is a cousin of the grand 10th, a downhill 200-yarder from a high tee, this one at the cliff edge, to a heavily bunkered green beside the shore. In a heavy left-to-right wind, we could well find ourselves starting the ball out a full green to the left of the green!

At the 13th, a dogleg left 397-yarder, the drive, with a stiff forced carry to a fairway bordered on the right by gorse, is followed by a husky second shot over a little hollow short of the green. The prevailing wind is into us. This is the number one stroke hole.

We are heading for the clubhouse now: 16 (a wee whitewashed cottage in the elbow of the left-hand dogleg) and 17 (riotously tumbling terrain leading to an elevated green) are both strong. As for the home hole—361 yards, and downhill—the drive floats and carries, then bounces and skates. The long walk down the slope to reach it enables us to drink in the harbor in the background, colorful sailboats and plain old fishing smacks catching our eye. The moment is magical.

Admittedly, Ardglass is not a great course. But the game here is nonetheless rewarding, studded with Bernard Darwin's "pleasurable excite-

ment" in a setting of surpassing beauty. I cannot imagine playing at Royal County Down and not finding the time for a game at Ardglass.

KIRKISTOWN CASTLE

Very like an hour's drive up the coast, yet still in County Down, brings us to another 6,200-yard course, Kirkistown Castle, a par-69 layout in the village of Cloughey. Some insist that James Braid extensively revised the original eighteen in 1932 (the club was founded thirty years earlier), but hard evidence is lacking. At any rate, this is very good links golf—a turf base of sandy loam makes it quick to dry—with substantive elevation changes, a number of greens on the high ground that are fearfully exposed to the wind, plenty of revetted pot bunkers to add spice to the round, and a handful of par 4s over the 400-yard mark. Since the round concludes with the longest—and strongest—holes on the links, the 445-yard 17th and the 530-yard 18th, we're not likely to compensate at the close for any of our earlier shortcomings. A pleasure to play, Kirkistown Castle is also a worthy test.

Above: Ardglass, 3rd.
Opposite: 11th.

LODGING AND DINING

Next door to Royal County Down is the **Slieve Donard Hotel**, an imposing red sandstone Victorian pile that opened in 1898, in the golden age of railway hotels. This four-star hotel sits in six acres of gardens that give directly onto a sweep of tawny beach along Dundrum Bay. Of the 126 accommodations, many are quite spacious and enjoy stunning sea and/or mountain views; all have recently been refurbished to a high standard. The public spaces—crystal chandeliers, oriental rugs, elegant architectural details—are opulent and, with their open fires, wonderfully welcoming. The Elysium Health and Leisure Centre has a heated swimming pool and up-to-the-minute fitness facilities. As for dining, choose the informal and atmospheric **Percy French** (French wrote the enduring ballad "Where the Mountains of Mourne Sweep Down to the Sea") in the gardens or the **Oak**, with its fine paneling, hand-carved oak fireplace, and engaging views over the bay.

A few miles south of Newcastle and just off the A2 coast road, outside the village of Annalong, is intimate **Glassdrumman Lodge**, now close to twenty-five years old. In the foothills of the mountains, this stylishly renovated farmhouse stands about a mile back from the sea, which it views. There are eight rooms and two suites. On our most recent visit we had a corner room called Knockree. The very broad windows provided a sea, but not mountain, view, and the gas-fueled fireplace (imitation logs and coals) made sure we were comfortable. Twenty-four-hour room service is one of the amenities. Glassdrumman is noted for its cuisine, which features fish dishes and vegetables from its own walled kitchen garden. Georgina Campbell's book *Irish Country House Cooking* presents the recipes for two of the inn's specialties, monkfish in red wine and white chocolate mousse.

Some fifteen miles north of Ardglass, in the village of Portaferry and on Strangford Lough, is the **Portaferry Hotel**, squarely on the harbor. Public spaces and guest rooms in this eighteenth-century structure are bright and cheerful, with an old-fashioned coziness. The first-rate cooking puts the emphasis on fish and shellfish brought in daily at Ardglass and Portavogie.

NEWCASTLE

With its good beach, its harbor for pleasure craft, and its setting in the very lee of the mountains, Newcastle is the leading seaside resort in County Down. More bustling than picturesque, and a magnet for Belfast day-trippers, it has a pleasant promenade along the seafront. The little Glen River leads up from the center of town through Donard Park, itself rising on the slopes of majestic Slieve Donard Mountain, into the forest. And the equally unassuming Shimna River, with its trout and salmon, flows down through Tollymore Park to enter the sea in the heart of Newcastle.

Away from the town and well out in the country are three National Trust properties—two stately homes and

Below: Slieve Donard Hotel.
Right: Silent Valley, in County Down.

one splendid garden—that reward a visit. Eighteenth-century Castleward, with its Palladian southwest front and its Gothic northeast front (bit of schizophrenia here), is set on six hundred acres of woodland, park, and gardens running down to Strangford Lough. Two-hundred-year-old Mount Stewart House has an octagonal "Temple of the Winds" that is an excellent copy of the Athenian original. The formal and informal gardens here contain rare plants, trees, and shrubs from all over the world. And at Saintfield, Rowallane Garden, on fifty acres, is noted for its rhododendrons and azaleas, as well as its magnolia and flowering cherry trees.

Or you can simply get in the car and meander through County Down, with its hills and valleys, its wooded glens, its lakes and rivers, its fishing villages and magnificent coastal scenery. Who knows? You may even stumble upon a spot that appeals to you as much as the non-pareil Royal County Down.

Far left: View from Inch Abbey. Middle column, from top: Tollymore Forest Park, near Newcastle; Inch Abbey; Ballynoe Stone Circle. Above: Slieve Donard towering over the beach at Murloough Park.

ROYAL PORTRUSH

To get from Newcastle, in the south of Ulster, to Portrush, in the far north, I implore you to take the Antrim Coast Road, which gets its start in Larne, rolls north through Carnlough to Cushendall, then on to Cushendun, where it heads inland briefly, returning to the sea at Ballycastle and staying there through Ballintoy and Portballintrae to Portrush. Whether down at sea level or high on the headlands, this is one of the resplendent passages of motoring: the unfolding majesty of mountains, glens (every one of the nine glens of Antrim spilling down to this two-lane road), and sea, and the remarkable assortment of colors—brown moorlands, green glens, white limestone, black basalt, red sandstone, and yellow ocher from iron ore. Soon after passing the ruins of ancient Dunluce Castle, the road bends sharply to disclose, with dramatic suddenness, the entire sweep of Royal Portrush's championship links spread out below. The course cascades wildly from the high ground on our left through mighty dune country, slashes of emerald fairway in bold relief against the shaggy golden sand hills, down to the cliffs above the broad beach. Brake the car and pause in an effort to absorb it. Then hurry on to the club, where a very warm welcome awaits.

Royal Portrush is the fourth oldest golf club in Ireland. Founded in 1888, when it was called the County Club, it became the Royal Portrush Golf Club in 1895, with the ever agreeable Prince of Wales (later King Edward VII) as its patron. Today this busy facility is run by Wilma Erskine, secretary-manager and the first woman to hold this post at a royal golf club. Many golf clubs in Britain and Ireland provide separate changing rooms and bar/restaurants for visitors. Not Royal Portrush. Says the hospitable Ms. Erskine, "We treat visitors as though they were members. We don't segregate them, because they're such an important part of our club."

More than fifty national championships, British and Irish, amateur and professional, men's and women's, have been held here, among them the Irish Amateur (inaugurated in 1892 at Portrush, where Tommy Armour lost in the final in 1919), the British Amateur (Joe Carr won here in 1960), the British Ladies' eight times, the Senior British Open five times, and the British Open itself.

In its nearly 150-year history, the British Open has been played outside Scotland and England only once, in 1951, at Portrush. The winner was five-time Ryder Cupper Max Faulkner, uninhibited, dazzlingly caparisoned (golden plus-fours were a feature of his wardrobe), and supremely self-confident. Despite holding a mere two-stroke lead with thirty-six holes still to be played, he was already signing autographs "Max Faulkner Open Champion 1951." He managed to live up to his presumptuous "billing," finishing the 72 holes two strokes ahead of Argentina's Antonio Cerda.

ON THE DUNLUCE LINKS

The championship course, called Dunluce, is the work of Harry Colt, who laid it out in 1932. It is little changed since then except for length: It can now measure almost 7,400 yards for a professional event, but daily play for this par 72 is more like 6,400.

Opposite: Royal Portrush
Dunluce Course, 5th.
Above: 4th.

Above: Royal Portrush
Dunluce Course, 8th.
Opposite: 11th.

A DAY JAM-PACKED WITH PLEASURE

- In the morning tackle the **Dunluce Links**, the only eighteen outside Scotland and England ever to host the British Open.

- Eat lunch in the spacious and spiffy **clubhouse**, with its views over the links.

- Play the afternoon round on the **Valley Links**—shorter, secluded, superb.

- Be sure to see the nearby **Giant's Causeway**, one of the world's natural wonders.

- Spend the night at **Ardtara Country House**, superior cooking and a comfortable bedroom guaranteed to have a working fireplace.

A few facts make clear why this has turned out to be one of the very greatest of links courses: The terrain is spirited—rippling, tossing, heaving—from start to finish; the sand hills, mantled in the long rough grasses, range from mere mounds to massive; blind shots are a rarity; the overall elevation change is ideal, about 60 feet; natural sites for both greens and tees abound; gorse pops up now and again to imperil the shot; out-of-bounds is a factor on just four holes (but heaven knows it's an unignorable menace, both left and right on, of all holes, the 1st!); and the views are stupendous. Given these features, Colt could be relied upon to produce a masterpiece. And it is a masterpiece characterized by diversity—no two holes are even cousins, much less sisters.

The agreeable 370-yard opener plays moderately downhill from the tee (we must ignore those white stakes on both sides of what is a broad fairway) and moderately uphill to a plateau green. Next, a 480-yard par 5 works its essentially level way along a secluded corridor in the dunes, the tension here stemming from three bunkers clustered in the left side of the fairway 30 to 60 yards short of the green—precisely where the attacking second shot may land. At Portrush the term *fairway bunker,* which is used on most courses to refer to a sand hazard *in the rough adjacent to the fairway,* more often than not means a sand hazard solidly *in* the fairway, where it can function at its most unsettling.

The 3rd, with its knobby green, is a good 140-yarder, and it is succeeded by two of Ireland's finest par 4s. On the 442-yard 4th, which the club rightly calls "a real par 4½," we drive over a burn to a fairway with a boundary tight on the right and a bunker in its left side. There is no sand at the green, but low dunes squeeze the entrance and a steep falloff at the left lurks to carry away our long second shot, likely to be at least a 5-metal, if it should come in low and drawing.

The 5th, 380 yards, is less rigorous but more memorable. It is majestic. The short climb to the tee brings us to the highest point of the course, the holes weaving through the sand hills below. Much of the eighteen now lies exposed to our mesmerized gaze. Beyond, to the east, our eye is caught by the White Rocks, limestone cliffs that lead to the Wishing Arch, an unusual rock formation hollowed out by the battering of sea and wind. Above are the evocative ruins of sixteenth-century Dunluce Castle. On the west, the dark bulk of Inishowen Head rears out of the sea. Straight ahead, backdropping the links and actually within swimming distance, is the long line of the Skerries, a series of low islets that serve as a breakwater. On a clear day—and with regrets to Alan Jay

Lerner—we cannot see forever, but, across the North Channel, we can indeed make out the coast of Scotland. Machrihanish is there, on the Kintyre Peninsula, and just west of it, on the island of Islay, lies The Machrie. Perhaps we can be forgiven for imagining that we discern at least a hint of one or the other.

Now to play this hole, which has neither bunkers nor burns. But the dune-flanked fairway is not broad, and it bends right just beyond a high sand hill about 200 yards out. Dare we, from our encouragingly lofty perch, swing aggressively in the hope of carrying this dune to set up a shorter approach for a possible birdie? Or is the reward really not worth the risk? The gambling tee shot that fails to get up will be choked, perhaps even lost, in the tall, tangled rough, which is no more forgiving because of the beguiling presence in it of primrose and bluebell, of buttercups and purple thistles and red-berried sea buckthorn. At any rate—and whether we choose the brave or timid line—we are totally exposed to the force and vagaries of the wind and compelled to launch a shot heading out to sea that must sail, must hang, must float weightlessly as it seeks the refuge of the fairway concealed below, just beyond the great dune.

The shot that now remains, about 155 yards long, is a modestly rising one over uneven ground to a green set nobly above the beach. Natural mounds and hollows defend this target, as does a steep right-side falloff that ends in punitive rough. The slope at the left is a gentle one that the deft chipper can handle. The iron shot that is too forceful will plunge over a sandy precipice and down to the beach, with its bathers and strollers and even, on occasion, its horsemen.

The middle holes contain a couple of excellent one-shotters: the 180-yard 6th, playing uphill to a sand-free plateau green, and the 160-yard 11th, playing downhill to a sand-ringed gathering green. This 11th turns out to be historic. In the 2004 Senior British Open, Graham Marsh knocked a 9-iron into the hole in the first round and an 8-iron into the hole in the last round. Never before had a player in a professional tournament made an ace twice on one hole in the same tournament.

If the 11th goes down in the record books, it is the 14th that is the most celebrated hole at Portrush. The shot here can be simply described: 200 yards long, over the corner of a 75-foot-deep chasm that skirts the right side of the green, troubling hillocks just left of the green. Depending on the wind, a driver must be used on what has been selected as one of the top one hundred holes for *The 500 World's Greatest Golf Holes*. The Dunluce Links ranked twelfth in the world on the 2005 *Golf Magazine* list, fifth in the British Isles according to the *Golf World* (Britain) panel in 2004.

In *The Golf Courses of the British Isles,* Bernard Darwin wrote almost a century ago of Portrush: "The air is so fine that the temptation to play three rounds [in a day] is very hard to overcome, while I may quote, solely on the authority of a friend, this further testimonial to it, that it has the unique property of enabling one to drink a bottle of champagne every night and feel the better for it."

ON THE VALLEY LINKS

The Valley Links, also Colt's handiwork, is no relief course. Nor should it be viewed as the ladies' course, even though its clubhouse is the head-quarters of the Ladies' Branch of the golf club. Women have played at Portrush since the game's earliest days here. The *Coleraine Chronicle* reported on a game that took place on July 13, 1888: "On Friday evening at Portrush . . . two ladies played an interesting and breathtaking 'single,' and it was a touching and beautiful thing to see the meek devotion of the attendant husbands, who kept the score and carried the clubs."

The Valley Links, as its name suggests, is tucked away, down in the lower reaches of the club property, tall sand hills enclosing the acreage and blocking out any view of the sea. A sheltered quality, an attractive snugness, if you will, characterizes the course, which measures just 6,304 yards from all the way back against a par of 69. There are only twenty-two bunkers. But the restless nature of this perfect linksland, the constricting dunes that produce narrow fairways, and the small, cleverly sited greens (on plateaus, in dells) all demand accurate shot-making—so much so, in fact, that the course is used annually for qualifying in the North of Ireland Amateur Championship.

Among the outstanding holes are the 6th, 17th, and 18th. Often a driver, the 237-yard 6th rises gently over heaving ground to a narrow green patrolled at the left front by a deep sandpit. A right-to-left cross-wind off the Atlantic Ocean, near but out of sight, often beleaguers us. The beguiling 17th, 384 yards, plays through a narrow neck of sand hills and along a corridor to a plateau green guarded by dunes and a lone bunker at the right, more dunes at the left, and a drop over the back to a big hollow. The home hole is unusual, a par 3, this one 193 yards from an elevated tee to a green with sand right and a steep swale front left. The Valley Links is full of very good golf holes. Even accomplished players are challenged—and all of us are charmed.

NEARBY COURSES

Roughly fifteen miles east of Portrush on the Antrim Coast Road is **Ballycastle**, at the foot of Glenshesk. The golf club was formed in 1890, and the course, only 5,660 yards long, is tough to categorize. The first five holes are routed over meadowland. The next five, as well as the 18th, occupy a cramped piece of linksland, with the 6th and 9th actually skirt-ing the beach. The other seven holes, 11 through 17, run up one side of a cliff, then along the top of it and down the other side. The game at Ballycastle—capricious, unpredictable, full of fun—comes with a num-ber of opportunities to gaze down on the fetching town itself or across the harbor and beyond to the Mull of Kintyre, not twenty miles away.

A championship-standard course by David Kidd is being built within three miles of Royal Portrush. The **Giant's Links at Bushmills**, to open in 2007 on high ground along the sea, will have holes that extend right to the Giant's Causeway.

Opposite: Royal Portrush Valley Links, 5th. Above: 6th.

Portrush, which came into favor among Ulster's people of means in the late nineteenth century, is splendidly situated on a peninsula jutting into the Atlantic. So striking is it with its terraces of brightly painted houses and its long beaches sweeping away on either side that it has been likened to an ocean liner heading out to sea.

Roughly seven miles east of Portrush on the coast road is Northern Ireland's most famous sight, the Giant's Causeway. An astonishing—and puzzling—natural wonder, it is a complex of nearly forty thousand basalt columns packed together, their tops forming "stepping stones" that lead away from the shore at the foot of the cliffs and disappear under the sea. Similar columns can be found on the Scottish island of Staffa, in the Hebrides, giving rise to the romantic myth that the Causeway was a road from Antrim to Staffa built by an Irish giant, one Finn McCool, whose sweetheart, a lady giant, lived on the Scottish isle.

Other nearby places that reward a visit, all of them on the coast east-southeast from Portrush, include Ballintoy, population less than three hundred and with a pretty white parish curch; Ballintoy Harbour, which is reached by a corkscrew road and where jagged volcanic stacks form an archipelago of islets, caves, and rocks for clambering; the swinging Carrick-a-Rede Rope Bridge, connecting a stack of basalt columns to the mainland over a seventy-eight-foot-deep sea chasm and more perilous in appearance than in fact; Whitepark Bay, with its half moon of perfect beach in a grassy bowl of dunes and cliffs and its tiny hamlet of Portbraddan tucked in a cleft of the cliffs like dice in a box; Ballycastle, population three thousand, an engaging seaside resort with many small Georgian and Victorian houses and old-fashioned pubs; Cushendun, a secluded beach village of Cornish-style cottages, the whole of it now protected by the National Trust; and nearby Cushendall, an equally picturesque village where three glens meet beneath a flat-topped mountain and where the river Dall enters the sea. (For lodging near Portrush, see the Portstewart chapter.)

Opposite: Carrick-a-Rede Bridge, in County Antrim. This page, clockwise from above: coastline at Ballintoy; the Giant's Causeway; Dunluce Castle; shoreline of Portrush.

PORTSTEWART

All of ten minutes' drive west on the coast road from Portrush, in County Londonderry, lies the seaside resort of Portstewart. Its golf club has three eighteens. The Old Course, where golf in Portstewart originated in 1889, at the east end of town, measures only 4,730 yards (par 64) and offers delightful holes along the sea. The club's other two eighteens are side by side in the west end of town, at Strand Head. The Riverside, 5,725 yards, par 68, is no more than a relief course, full of humdrum golf holes. The Strand, on the other hand, is a championship course, a genuinely great links.

Founded in 1894, Portstewart was fortunate in having as secretary during more than twenty-five years early in the twentieth century a retired Baptist minister, the Reverend P. H. Blaikie. Tall and powerfully built, and possessed of a stentorian voice, he was a man of energy and conviction. It was difficult to say no to him, as the minutes of the 1919 annual meeting illustrate: "So far as visitors were concerned, Mr. Blaikie gave them a hearty welcome, imparted all the knowledge possible about club and course, and, when going away, took them by the hand and asked them to come back, and they invariably did come back."

It was shortly after Rev. Blaikie took office that the club moved to the west end of town, where A. G. Gow, greenkeeper at Royal Portrush, laid out eighteen holes in 1908. The course we play today, however, is in large measure the result of a decision in 1986 by the club to build seven holes in the adjacent hilly and virgin duneland called Thistly Hollow and to incorporate these new holes into what is now the Strand Course.

Charged with designing the new holes was Des Giffin, the Greens Convener ("Chairman of the Greens Committee" in America), a math teacher at the Coleraine grammar school. Like George Crump at Pine Valley, Hugh Wilson at Merion, and Henry Clay Fownes at Oakmont, Des Giffin had no experience in course architecture. But he had vision, together with respect for the natural contours of the land, and a keen sense of what constituted a good golf hole. He wrote in the club history of "the sprawling wasteland of steep ridges and valleys, often covered with impenetrable sea buckthorn. . . . As a child I had spent many happy hours playing through this

magnificent wilderness and I knew the ground well. As far as possible I tried to work with the land rather than against it. . . . I hope that the course, with its elevated tees and sudden, unexpected vistas of sea, river, and mountain, allows the golfer to take as much satisfaction from the natural beauty with which he is surrounded as from the test of golf with which he is presented."

ON THE COURSE

The Strand Course can be set up at 5,860, 6,570, and 6,900 yards; par is 72. The two nines are quite different, the front nine weaving through the splendid sand hills, the second nine open, even pastoral, with the broad River Bann sometimes nearby and almost always in view.

The promise of Portstewart is stated—nay, proclaimed—on the 1st tee. This is a towering launching pad, and we are enthralled by what our eyes take in far below: on our right the frothing combers of the Atlantic Ocean rhythmically breaking upon the broad, golden beach; straight ahead a cluster of majestic, pyramidal sand hills; on our left the gentler holes along the lowlands of the Bann. In the far distance is the bluish outline of the Donegal hills. Our drive on this 417-yarder floats seemingly forever, touching down at last in a level landing area where the fairway bends right to seek a green cradled in colossal dunes that are cloaked in buckthorn and long grasses. This is an opening hole as sublime and unforgettable as the transatlantic 1st at Machrihanish.

The next seven holes are Des Giffin's legacy, more enduring than bronze, more precious than gold. Every aspect of seaside golf at its most compelling is here: sequestered holes swooping and bending and climbing through soaring sand hills; plateau greens with bedeviling falloffs and pulpit tees extending an invitation to swing for the fences; tumbling fairways and gathering bunkers; doglegs that range from subtle (the 2nd) to sharp (the 8th); not to mention the parade of hollows, hummocks, dips, and swales. And, withal, the sheer exhilaration of it.

Are there great holes here? Surely three, maybe four or five, beginning with the classic 360-yard 2nd (high tee, way down, then up to an elevated, dune-corseted green), and including the 6th, 135 yards (knob

Opposite: Portstewart, 1st.

IRELAND

tee, plateau green, a pair of ferocious pits sealing off the front of the green, a 30-foot falloff at the right), and the 516-yard 7th (another high tee, the hole doglegging right along a rumpled, dune-framed corridor, then climbing steeply to a narrow sand-free green). The first nine at Portstewart, with just nine bunkers, is one of the finest and most natural first nines in Ireland—and that's saying something.

If the second nine is a less exuberant canvas, we nevertheless play over beautifully rolling terrain. The round concludes with a trio of par 4s, the solid 16th and 18th, both 390 yards, and the great 17th, a rollercoaster 426 yards (double fall-and-rise) to a precariously sited plateau green with steep falloffs at the front, sides, and rear. Save your best swing for the long second shot here.

How good is the Strand Course at Portstewart? For my money, just one rung below County Down and Portrush and under no circumstances to be missed.

Make it a point to have either lunch or a drink in the clubhouse dining room, which reveals the same panorama of sea, strand, sand hills, and distant Inishowen Head that greeted us when we stepped out onto the

1st tee. When we were here in 2004, a few weeks after the Senior British Open at Royal Portrush, I spoke briefly with Michael Moss, the club's secretary-manager. He pointed out that qualifying for the championship was held here. I said that in view of the strength of the field—Tom Kite, Tom Watson, Dana Quigley, D. A. Weibring, Bob Gilder—the victory by Pete Oakley, an unknown club pro from Delaware, was astonishing.

"He had to qualify here," said Moss. "He pulled the trolley for the first nine—no caddies on hand. Then a local volunteered to caddie for him, so Oakley gave him the bag. And he stayed on the job right to the end." The secretary-manager smiled, then added, "A great win for Portstewart."

CASTLEROCK

It's a fifteen-minute run from Portstewart around the jagged coastline to the Castlerock Golf Club, with its modernist white clubhouse high above the sea. The club was founded in 1901, when the initial nine was laid out by a couple of Portrush greenkeepers, J. J. Coburn and Hugh MacNeill, here where the Bann enters the Atlantic. Ben Sayers came over from North Berwick seven years later to lay out a new eighteen-hole course on the site,

Opposite: Portstewart, 4th.
Above, left: 7th; right: 8th.

and in the years to come extensive modifications would be made to it by Harry Colt, Frank Pennink, and Eddie Hackett. Several Irish championships, both amateur and professional, have been held here, where the sand hills are not so lofty as those in Thistly Hollow at Portstewart.

The entire course lies neatly between the railway and the river and the sea. It can be stretched to 6,700 yards, but visitors generally play it at 6,250. Par is 73, with five par 5s, all of them on the short side. Many holes meander through inviting duneland, but equally many occupy less attractive ground, among them the famous and very much inland 4th. A 200-yarder played over meadowy ground, it is bordered by out-of-bounds on the right (the railway) and a little burn that first must be crossed and then avoided as it edges toward the left side of the green. This highly penal if rather ordinary-looking hole demands a straight, solid strike.

The 7th, 8th, and 9th, laid out in true linksland, show Castlerock at its best. A superb 407-yarder, the 7th ripples along over uneven ground before rising to a green exquisitely sited in the dunes. From a high tee, the 400-yard 8th doglegs right, with dunes on that side at the landing area, then climbs to a perfect shelf of green that, like the entire hole, is sand-

free. The exacting 193-yard 9th, also bunkerless, plays into the prevailing breeze to an amphitheater green framed by grass-mantled low dunes. An old quarry lurking off to the left is not out of play if the wind requires us to crack a 3-metal. The second nine on this links that has its share of gorgeous views, especially those across the water to Portstewart, is much like the first, with some holes nestled in the duneland, others out in the open.

As for the third nine, called the Bann Course, it is a jewel. Just under 3,000 yards and closer to the sea than the eighteen, it sticks resolutely to the duneland, its fairways and greens are elusive targets, and honest shot-making is called for (but not brawn) hole after hole.

I have a fond memory of our first visit to Castlerock, in 1994. The bartender, a strong-looking fellow in his late twenties, was taciturn. Between Harriet and me, we managed to pry out of him that he was a member of the club, that his handicap was 4, and that he had never been to America but was hoping to get there one day. When I paid the bill for lunch, he handed me the change and then fished out from under the bar a glass beer mug with the Castlerock Golf Club logo on it in blue. Awkwardly thrusting it into my hand, he said, "Here, so you'll remember us."

Below, left: Castlerock, 9th; right: 18th. Opposite: 17th.

It is likely that the two finest places to stay in County Antrim and County Londonderry are Ardtara Country House and Bushmills Inn.

Outside Coleraine, in the hamlet of Upperlands, within thirty minutes of Portrush and Portstewart and forty minutes of Castlerock, is **Ardtara Country House**. Built during the reign of Queen Victoria, it was for years the residence of one of Ulster's foremost linen families, the Clarks. Charles Clark Thompson, a signer of the Declaration of Independence and secretary to the first United States Congress, was born within a short stroll of Ardtara

(the name means "old house on the high hill"). This intimate hotel, in a heavily wooded setting, is elegant and comfortable. Antiques lend character and a sense of bygone days to the public spaces and the guest rooms. There are working fireplaces just about everywhere you turn, including all eight of the grand accommodations, with their king-size beds. I will admit that we are fireplace freaks. So when, on our most recent visit, our room, No. 3, turned out to have a fireplace in the bedroom *and* one in the bathroom, we were in paradise. The hospitality at Ardtara House is genuine and unforced.

Mary Breslin, one of the owners, and her staff are bent on making us feel very much at home.

Fortunately, dining at Ardtara is just as enjoyable as overnighting here. The dining room is rendered light and airy by an immense glass skylight. The dishes themselves—for example, mosaic of ham hock and wild mushrooms served with a pear and apple chutney—are innovative and consistently delicious. The good wine list is fairly evenly divided between French vintages and the rest of the world.

The town of Bushmills boasts the world's oldest distillery (also named Bushmills and dating to 1609),

The Strand, Portstewart.

where visitors are welcome for a guided tour. In the heart of town and not five minutes from the Giant's Causeway on the east and Royal Portrush on the west is **Bushmills Inn**. A remarkable re-creation of an old coaching inn and mill house, it is a thoroughgoing charmer, a combination of antiquity and warmth, rusticity and comfort. Beam ceilings, old fireplaces, nooks and crannies and pine paneling—all are features of the public spaces. You'll be sorely tempted to relax in a rocking chair beside a turf fire in the original old kitchen that adjoins the bar, itself illuminated by gaslight. There are thirty-two guest rooms, individually decorated. Most of the smaller rooms give on the village, with its active main street. The spacious Mill House bedrooms—whitewashed stone walls as well as dark paneling, some accommodations with four-poster beds—have a sitting area and a small dressing room.

The restaurant, with tables as well as booths (what the Irish call "snugs"), gets its appeal from mellow brick and well-aged timbers. The cooking is quite accomplished, blending "new Irish" cuisine with County Antrim produce. The onion and Guinness soup makes a wonderful starter, perhaps to be followed by pan-roasted salmon set on a cherry tomato confit with basil oil, and, for dessert, lemon soufflé. I find myself remembering what my uncle Pat (McGrath), a Pittsburgh lawyer, could be relied upon to say with a broad smile at the conclusion of one of my mother's most calorific dinners: "Thank God for that bite—many a man could have made a meal of it."

This is a particularly beautiful and interesting part of Northern Ireland. Portstewart has a sheltered harbor, a lively oceanfront promenade (everything from sausage snacks to old golf prints is for sale in the little shops), and a glorious beach. Cars have access to this two-mile-long stretch, which can be driven virtually from end to end. So attractive is Portstewart that, according to one historian, its well-bred nineteenth-century residents prohibited the building of a railway station for fear of bringing vulgar people to the town. Another source insists that the railway bypassed Portstewart mainly because the town's founding family, the Cromies (people who took the Sabbath very seriously), did not believe that trains should be permitted to run on Sunday.

Clockwise from top left: boat harbor at Portstewart; Portbradden; inside the Ardtara Country House; Portstewart at dusk; coastline of County Antrim; the Bushmills distillery.

THE NORTHWEST:
DONEGAL, SLIGO, AND MAYO

BALLYLIFFIN

I t's time now to leave Northern Ireland and head for "dear old Donegal." We have seen the vague outline of its hills on the western horizon, often a smoky bluish haze, more than once from high tees at Portrush and Portstewart and Castlerock. Now, via the car ferry across Lough Foyle from Magilligan Point, which is less than thirty minutes from Castlerock, we cross the fjord in less than ten minutes to Greencastle, in the Republic. Our goal is Ballyliffin, another half hour away, on the sinuous and hilly R238.

With a population of about five hundred, Ballyliffin is a plain-Jane village—three smallish hotels, a church, two grocery stores, a scattering of cottages—in a plain-Jane valley on the remote Inishowen Peninsula. It is scarcely conceivable that this backwater could be home to a thriving club with two eighteens, both of which have won the attention of itinerant golfers. The club property is framed by rolling sand hills, mountains, and the Atlantic Ocean's Pollan Bay, with its sweep of golden sands, at the north end of which lies the ruined tower of Carrieabragh Castle.

ON THE OLD COURSE

Golf came to Ballyliffin in 1947, when the Old Course (it seems we must call it that) opened; thus it is not old. A couple of greens committee members were responsible for the layout, which Eddie Hackett, godfather of golf course architecture in Ireland, extensively revised some twenty years later. Pat Ruddy, the foremost Irish golf architect today, said of Eddie Hackett: "He had no idea how to make money out of the game. He would visit your property, look it over carefully, give you a routing plan for eighteen holes, and wind up charging almost nothing beyond his travel expenses! Yet Ireland is in his debt, for he brought the game—and a good game it is—to tens of thousands who would never have had the chance to play a real course without him."

Over the last fifteen years, extravagant praise has been heaped on the Old Course. Nick Faldo called it "the most natural golf links I have ever seen." A widely respected golf photographer called it the finest golf course he had ever seen.

Well, it is not the finest golf course I have ever seen, nor is it even among Ireland's top forty. But it is an extraordinarily natural links, and if you approach it expecting to play some worthy holes in a duneland setting of indisputable grandeur—the sand hills, often colossal, stretch away to the north as far as the eye can see—you will be glad you got here.

Six holes, including five par 4s and the anemic 113-yard 9th (a little nothing if ever there was one), are ordinary. Two holes on the first nine are quite good: the smoothly uphill 2nd, a 497-yard three-shotter, and the climbing 5th, 186 yards, where a long iron or a fairway metal must be struck squarely to gain a shelf green ringed by dunes.

Routed nearer the shore, the second nine is better and stronger and a bit longer than the first. The 13th and 14th, both played from high tees, are

Opposite: Ballyliffin Glashedy Course, 7th. Above: 18th. Previous spread: Rosapenna Sandy Hills Course, 4th.

experience. Play the par-5 4th toward dusk on a long summer day and observe the magical effect that the locals call "the fairway of a thousand shadows." On a less romantic but more practical note, beware the temptation to take a golf cart: You do so at the risk of incurring cracked vertebrae.

ON THE GLASHEDY COURSE

On the adjacent eighteen, called the Glashedy Links, the corrugated terrain gives way to conventional undulation, this time with a mountainous sand hill at the heart of the layout. Pat Ruddy and Tom Craddock designed this course, which opened in 1995.

Two-time Walker Cupper Craddock won the Irish Open Amateur in 1958 and the Irish Close Amateur the following year. Ruddy was widely known as editor and publisher of two golf magazines, as a golf writer of immense charm and style, and as one of the most avid promoters of Irish golf. In 1992 they were called in to upgrade the Old Course. When Ruddy learned that the club owned 360 acres of duneland, he suggested that the first thing it ought to do is build a second eighteen, before the environmentalists—"those who have acquired the moral high ground by purloining the word to describe themselves, and thus turning anyone who holds a differing view into an antienvironmentalist"—could have laws enacted to freeze the development of duneland for golf. He was also able to guide the club toward a £365,000 grant from the Irish Tourist Board.

Fourteen of the eighteen holes are routed through the high duneland north of the original course, where the scenery is more stirring and the terrain provides more feature and elevation change. The course measures 5,860 yards from the forward markers, just over 7,200 yards from all the way back, 6,460 yards for daily play. On the brutally long second nine (3,845 yards, 3,700, and 3,460) only one of the six par 4s is less than 400 yards.

The opening three holes, each measuring about 390 yards from the regular tees, move away from the clubhouse on a northeasterly line. Lightly but effectively bunkered and framed by low dunes, they incline to rise very modestly, curving almost indiscernibly right. In August of 2004, on my most recent game over the Glashedy Links, I played with the honorary secretary, Desmond Kemmy, and two of his golfing pals, a mechanical engineering inspector and a retired schoolteacher. Des is a landscape photographer (he frames his pictures and sells them; three were up for sale on the clubhouse walls that day) and he is the owner-operator of the post office in the village. "If you want to post a letter from Ballyliffin," he said, with an engaging smile, "it has to go through me."

excellent, the former a short par 5 culminating on a knobby green in the sand hills, the latter—perhaps the best hole on the course—a 370-yarder doglegging energetically left through the dunes. The 18th, 556 yards long and often essayed in a left-to-right crosswind off the sea, curves left along a dune-framed corridor to a prettily sited green by the clubhouse.

All right, then, is there any reason why this eighteen should spark hosannas? Yes. You see, there is *no* level ground. The terrain ripples nonstop. Therein lies its singularity and a large measure of its appeal. Stances and lies comprise the principal challenge to scoring well here—not length, nor boundaries, nor water (there is none), nor convoluted greens, nor harshly penal bunkers (there are few sand hazards of any kind). However, so fantastically ruffled are these fairways, so unimaginably wavy and undulating, so rife with wrinkles and furrows, so akin to an endless scrub board, that a truly flat stance or a truly flat lie—to say nothing of the two in tandem!—is a very rare commodity, every bit as rare as a long bounce-and-run shot that behaves obligingly. No bulldozer was ever let loose on this unique topography.

Most of us are simply not equipped to digest this endless diet of tilts. Whatever the blandness of a number of holes, this links is a one-of-a-kind

Above: Ballyliffin Old Course, 4th. Opposite: Ballyliffin Glashedy Course, 5th.

Above: Ballyliffin Glashedy
Course, 13th. Opposite: 14th.

The wind blew steadily at 30 miles per hour, except when it gusted to 40. For me, the course was unmanageable, and my 85 was surely the result of "the kindness of strangers." Again and again I simply could not stay on solid footing at the ball. The inspector and the erstwhile schoolteacher also struggled. Not so the honorary secretary. A ruggedly built man in his late forties, Des settled comfortably into shot after shot, attacking the ball with a vengeance. The first three holes, heading straight into the wind, each had a playing value of 450 yards. He drove well on each and then hit the green on each with a 3-metal. Those were the three best consecutive approach shots by an amateur that I've ever seen. The odds on making even one of the three were long. He made them all, with a swing into the gale that repeated perfectly to produce a hard, low draw. He played superbly to the end, scrambling when scrambling was required, to finish with a 2-over-par 74.

The 4th hole, a very short par 5 of only 470 yards that is routed through a deep, dune-framed valley, offers a birdie opportunity and a grand view. A cross bunker on the second shot complicates our perception of the distance, and just short of the typically large green is a swale 15 feet deep. Backdropping the green is Glashedy Rock, out in the Atlantic, and we are reminded of playing a shot at Turnberry against the silhouette of Ailsa Craig.

Holes 4, 5, and 6 tack their way up one side of a mountainous sand hill to reveal, from the summit, the intoxicating 7th, a 165-yarder that plummets more than 100 feet to a green that looks no larger than a scorecard; a pond lurks scarily at its right to snare balls gone sailing on the wind.

This experience is simulated on the second nine, on the other side of this same mighty sand hill. Here it is the par-4 12th (green in a dell of dunes) and the par-5 13th (marvelous rollercoaster ride through a narrowing corridor in the dunes) that ascend to the top, and it is 14, the 140-yard cousin of 7, that drops to a lovely green on a platform—one deep pit squarely out front, a shallower one at the back—well down the hill. Pat Ruddy himself, in Laurence C. Lambrecht's monumental *Emerald Gems: The Links of Ireland*, tells the story behind the construction of the sublime 14th:

> *The plan called for No. 14 to be a par three from a tee on top of the long and tall sandhill to a green below. The problem was that a vociferous minority within the club liked that hill—which had been broken open into a magnificent jagged shape by the wind—just as it was. Civil war was threatened if the hill were touched.*
>
> *At last, the development committee gave the nod for the job to go ahead to a plan I had devised. Two bulldozer men, two excavator operators, and a dump-truck driver agreed to come into work at 11 p.m. on a wet and windy February night, and we worked by the lights of those machines right through the night. It was cold, it was crazy, and I was the only one standing out in the elements for ten hours of darkness. But when dawn broke, the hole had been built and nobody came out to complain. Indeed, nothing but praise has ever been heard for that hole, which is really a pretty picture, even though it can play like the devil—especially when those gentle Donegal breezes blow off the Atlantic!*

Ballyliffin Golf Club: truly in the middle of nowhere, yet providing a pair of links courses, one of them unique because of its naturally humpy terrain; the other less eccentric, sternly testing—surely one of the three or four hardest courses in Ireland—sprinkled with great holes as well as consistently high shot values every foot of the way. You will want to get up here one day soon.

Ballyliffin has more in the way of hotels than might be expected, given the size of the community:

- Accommodations at the thirty-six-room **Ballyliffin Hotel** are spiffy and comfortable but not individually decorated. Many have views looking toward the sea, though not necessarily encompassing it. The cooking is straightforward—chicken, roast beef, steak, salmon—and reliable. The **Rachtan Bar**, a favorite haunt of locals, offers good pub food and, on weekends, music.

- Just across the road is the twenty-room **Strand Hotel**. The carefully cultivated gardens are pretty; the rooms, which are individually decorated, incline to be small, but some have wide views to Pollan Strand and Malin Head. Cooking is confined pretty much to the staples—chicken, beef, surf 'n' turf, seafood—but there is also pub food,

including burgers, in the atmospheric bar. When "Irish Night" entertainment is on the docket, dancing, both old time and contemporary, will enliven the evening.

- At **Trasna House Hotel**, some of the thirteen rooms—all rooms are simply decorated and of modest size—have distant sea views. Again, you can eat in either the dining room or the pub, the latter winningly old-fashioned and the setting, at times, for traditional Irish music or modern rock.

- Thirty minutes south of Ballyliffin, in Fahan and on the shores of Lough Swilly, is **St. John's Country House and Restaurant**. The house, built in 1785 and restored by its present owners, Reg Ryan and Phyllis McAfee, enjoys striking views of Inch Island and the Donegal Highlands. On our visit in 2004

we occupied room No. 1 (there are five bedrooms, no suites), where Jean Kennedy Smith spent a night when she was ambassador to Ireland. The first thing she did was request that the gas fire be turned on. "You're sleeping in Jean Kennedy Smith's bed," said Phyl, with a twinkle, then added, "or should we say she was sleeping in yours?" A turf fire seems to burn perpetually in the inviting bar. The restaurant has garden and lough views and a very high standard of cooking—we had the impression that just about anything we might order here would be delicious, as was certainly the case with the duck liver pâté with caramelized onions, and the duo of fresh fish (brill and monkfish) in a white wine sauce. St. John's is one of Donegal's best places to stay and dine.

Below, from left: beach at Ballyliffin; boats at Greencastle. Opposite: scenes near Malin Head, in County Donegal.

Out on the Inishowen Peninsula, signs direct us to the Inis Eoighan 100 (or Inishowen 100), a drive that uncovers the most beautiful scenery in this area. Malin Head, at the tip of the peninsula and thus the most northerly point in Ireland, is only 220 feet high, but the cliff-and-rock views are riveting, not to mention the simple white rocks spelling EIRE that served as a much-needed landmark for pilots in the Second World War. Quite nearby is Glengad Head, where cliffs soaring nearly 500 feet present a view of Scotland's Kintyre Peninsula and the islands of Islay and Jura. Equally stirring are Mamore and the view over Five Finger Strand from Knockamany Bends.

Near Ballyliffin is the Doagh Visitors Centre, a purpose-built village of whitewashed thatched-roof cottages where we learn how life was lived in this corner of Donegal from the 1840s (the time of the terrible famine) to the 1970s. Nearly thirty miles south of Doagh is the Grianan of Ailech, the remains of a concentric fort roughly a thousand years old, with three stone ramparts and a circular wall 16 feet high, 12 feet thick at the base, and 224 feet around. Nobly crowning a hill, this is one of the most impressive examples of a concentric fort in Ireland.

PORTSALON

As the gull flies, Portsalon is only ten miles from Ballyliffin. In a car, the forty-five-mile drive takes almost an hour and a half. Portsalon is gloriously sited on Ballymastocker Bay, its crescent of beach one of the most beautiful in Ireland. The golf club's headquarters, a sprightly pavilion with generous bay windows, captures the enchanting views from the high ground.

The golf club was founded in 1891; the eighteen-hole course, about 5,000 yards long, was laid out by a Portrush professional named Thompson. The Irish Ladies' Championship has been played here three times, in 1905, 1912, and 2005. May Hezlett, who won this crown five times and the British Ladies' three times, was the 1905 winner. Shortly after her victory at Portsalon, she wrote of this special place in a magazine article:

> *The hotel [no longer in existence] is built upon the shore of Lough Swilly and commands an extensive view of the lake, whose name means "Lake of Shadows" and is aptly fitted to its character. The scene is constantly changing, the varying lights and shadows on the mountains conveying a new impression each hour. The effect is sometimes bright and glorious, sometimes dark and somber, sometimes wild, sometimes magnificent, but always beautiful in the extreme and possessing a nameless charm and wonderful attraction.*

ON THE COURSE

Although the setting remains the same, the course we play today is markedly different. We are now in the hands of Pat Ruddy. In 2001 and 2002 he executed a wholesale makeover of the links, adding a thousand yards, eliminating the weaknesses, reducing but not entirely eliminating the quirkiness, building eight new holes, improving almost all of the other ten, and seamlessly melding the whole. The result is a splendid links that can be set up as long as 7,100 yards. Regular play is usually at just under 6,300, ladies' tees adding up to 5,500; par is 72. No longer can Portsalon be viewed as nothing more than amiable holiday golf.

A marvelous start (the first two holes), a marvelous finish (the last two holes), and so much terrific stuff in between, over undulating linksland, that it makes our heads spin—that, in sum, is Portsalon. The 370-yard 1st gets us away from a high tee—ah, those ravishing sea-and-mountain panoramas!—our drive falling, our semiblind and suspenseful second shot rising over tumbling terrain to a green whose surface, but not its flag, is concealed. On the 400-yard 2nd another high tee encourages an aggressive swing despite the threat of a stream tight along the left far below. This stream soon bends right to cross the fairway 30 yards short of the green and imperil the long second shot. Both shots are thus

Opposite: Portsalon, 2nd.
Above: 5th.

in jeopardy on this great second hole. Imagine playing it from the championship tees, when it measures 495 yards and becomes one of the four or five most difficult two-shotters in Ireland.

The holes that follow on the outbound half range from stimulating to superlative. Solidly in the latter camp are the 185-yard 5th (straightaway through low dunes to a green, tilting left to right and all but unholdable); the 448-yard 6th (a narrow fairway curving gently left through a dune-corseted corridor to a low-plateau green ringed by little hollows, blue-tinted Knockalla Mountain a bewitching backdrop, the vast fjord shimmering on our left); the 9th, another 448-yard par 4 (from an elevated

tee down into a valley fairway that bends softly right en route to a green partially hidden behind a small dune).

The inbound half, 500 yards and two strokes shorter, may not be quite so sparkling as the first nine, but once we get past the first couple of holes, there is nothing of a prosaic nature here. The 13th, a short par 4 where our pitch must be played over violently broken ground to an angled and shallow green, is pure fun. So is the next hole, a 425-yarder called "Matterhorn" because of the pinnacle tee and the falling nature of the drive to a fairway that twists and turns and slopes dramatically downhill to the green. Three-hundred-yard drives are not uncommon here.

The village of Portsalon boasts an antiques-filled guest house called **Croaghross**, which looks down on Ballymastocker Strand. Guests frequently gather beside the fire in the lounge. John and Kay Deane are the proprietors, and Kay's excellent cooking is one reason that visitors come back regularly to Croaghross.

It could fairly be claimed that Donegal—the commonest surnames are O'Doherty, Gallagher, Boyle, Kelly, McLaughlin, McGinley, McSweeney, and McFadden—is the most Irish of the twenty-six counties that make up the Republic. The Republic's largest Gaelic-speaking population is to be met here, not to mention strongholds of Irish music, song, and dance. And no Irish fabric is quite so celebrated as handwoven Donegal tweed.

No place looks and feels more like the Ireland of our dreams than Donegal. Thinly populated, consistently rural, Donegal presents an extraordinary spectacle of landscapes and seascapes. The Atlantic seems to be everywhere, pounding the county relentlessly, and the result is a much indented coastline: peninsulas and bays, coves and cliffs, and the splendid fjords such as Lough Swilly and Lough Foyle slashing deep into the heartland. A day—just about any day—in this windswept land of scudding clouds, of steeply sloping sheep-dotted meadows and bald mountains framing lonely glens, is likely to bring with it surprising rain squalls followed by even more surprising rainbows.

Fifteen (a short one-shotter to a partially hidden green) and 16 (370 yards, steeply downhill, a burn sealing off the front of the green) are both good. Seventeen and 18 are outstanding, the former a 525-yarder curving left as we cross a broad stream with our tee shot and then climb to a treacherously fast plateau green. As for the home hole, just under 400 yards, it is even more testing; it drifts uphill, the long second shot having to carry a stream if it is to reach a green defended by sand and swales.

There is rarely a letup at Portsalon, in challenge or enjoyment. To play here is an exhilarating and haunting experience. On no account is this reborn links to be missed by anyone who comes to Donegal.

ROSAPENNA

osapenna, on the Rosguill Peninsula, has more golf than anywhere else in Donegal: 45 holes. To reach this feast from Portsalon calls for almost an hour's drive south, much of it along Mulroy Bay.

The story of how the first golf holes came into existence here is intriguing. In 1891 the fourth Earl of Leitrim, whose vast land holdings included this part of Donegal, invited Old Tom Morris to come over from St. Andrews to lay out nine holes in the parklands of his manor house at Carrigart. But before Old Tom undertook the task, the two men went out for a Sunday spin in a horse-drawn carriage. They crested a hill above Rosapenna to find themselves looking down upon hundreds of acres of tumbling duneland along Sheephaven Bay. Old Tom promptly said to his host, "This is where you must build your golf course." So naturally adaptable to the game was this tract that 15 of the 18 green sites were simply discovered by the Scot rather than constructed.

A grand hotel was built here in 1895, and, until the outbreak of the Second World War, Rosapenna regularly attracted a number of socially prominent golfers from England and Scotland. In 1962 fire razed the wood-frame structure in less than two hours. Helping to fight the flames was a local eighteen-year-old by the name of Frank Casey, who had caddied here and also tended bar in the hotel, where his father was the headwaiter. Two years later, a block of hotel rooms was built and the facility struggled along. In 1980 the headwaiter's son, back from stints at five-star hotels in Paris (the George V) and London (the Hyde Park), acquired the eight-hundred-acre Rosapenna property, including the golf course. From the outset, Frank Casey aimed to draw golfers not only from Britain and Ireland but from the Continent and America, as well. To accomplish this, he would need a larger and upgraded hotel, plus more and better golf.

ON THE MORRIS-RUDDY COURSE

The Morris course served as an enjoyable holiday layout for 115 years. And well it might have, for in addition to Old Tom's authoritative touch, it also benefited from the design skill of Harry Vardon, James Braid, and Harry Colt. The first nine works its way out through the low dune-framed valley bordering Sheephaven Bay. Here is seaside golf of supreme naturalness, born in a minimalist age when almost no earth was moved: rippling fairways, tees on convenient hillocks, generous greens on plateaus or in dells, the occasional deep sandpit at greenside, the occasional shallow bunker in the very heart of the fairway, the great gashes in the faces of sand hills that today go under the name "blowout bunkers." Among the best holes are the 4th, a 390-yarder that rises gently to a green spectacularly set in the dunes, and the knob-to-knob 6th, 167 yards, with its steep falloffs at the green.

Opposite: Rosapenna
Morris-Ruddy Course, 9th.
Above: 6th.

shot could be at the hole—or at the bottom of an unseen 20-foot falloff on the right. Equally memorable is the 8th, 530 yards long, its fairway at first on a high ridge curving right, then slanting steeply down to a green set beautifully in the dunes at the bottom. Even a 9-iron played to this narrow putting surface—only nine paces across the front—may not hold.

ON THE SANDY HILLS COURSE

All of which is by way of bringing us, at last, to the adjacent Sandy Hills, a bona fide masterpiece, not simply the jewel in the Rosapenna crown but one of the top ten courses in Ireland. Let it be said at once that this is a much more rigorous challenge than the Morris-Ruddy eighteen, that it is designed for the serious and, ideally, accomplished player, and that it is crammed with holes ranging from very good to great. In truth, at times Sandy Hills seems rather like a blur of greatness, and we almost suffer from sensory overload. The duneland topography itself—often beyond rolling to hilly and ranging from rumpled to heaving—is perfect for the construction of arresting golf holes. And Ruddy has unfailingly made the most of it.

Sandy Hills measures 7,155 yards from the championship tees, 6,356 from the whites, and only 4,868 from the ladies' tees; par is 71. The hallmarks of Ruddy's work are here at every turn: elevated tees, landing areas clearly in sight, graceful doglegs, light bunkering (the only bunker at the landing area for a drive pops up on the 9th), and large, stunningly sited greens, often on plateaus. These greens are admirably natural, understated, if you will, with little in the way of extravagant contours or slopes. It is as though the architect said to himself that the effort to gain the green is, hole after hole, such a demanding one that once the putting surface is reached, the player should have to struggle no more.

The fairways appear improbably narrow, especially from the high tees, but the actual landing areas, carved out of the dunes, are deceptively broad. There is room for the aggressive tee shot—if only we can make ourselves believe it. But to miss the fairway by even a few feet is to be swallowed by the deep, thick marram grass that cloaks the dunes. From beginning to end, the game here is through the dunes, the home of hollows, swales, craters, abysses.

The opening two holes—are they the finest starting pair on a links course in the world?—proclaim both the splendor and the seriousness of the eighteen. The length alone of these par 4s—495 and 463 yards, respectively, from the tips, 461 and 411 from the regular tees—is daunting. Into any kind of crosswind or headwind, both holes are more golf than any but powerful

The second nine that Morris, Vardon, Braid, and Colt shaped for us contrasts sharply with the first. Now the play is not on low duneland but up, down, over, and around a single mighty hill. Pinnacle tees, steep descents, wearying climbs, and some of the most majestic views in the world of golf await here. To stand on the towering tee of the 17th is to be staggered by the beauty of the 360-degree panorama that surrounds us—town and water, meadow and mountain.

This soaring nine is no longer on the rota. It has become the fifth nine, functioning as a key element of the teaching academy that has been established here. In place of the hill holes is a superlative nine designed and built by Pat Ruddy, who accepted a two-part task. One assignment was to fashion a nine to serve as a companion to the original duneland nine. These new holes are full of length and challenge and thrill, with the eighteen now measuring over 7,000 yards (Ruddy also introduced new tees to the Old Tom nine in order to add some needed length). One of the outstanding par 4s in the Ruddy canon is here, the 380-yard 6th, which, from a high tee, doglegs right along a turbulent fairway to a very naturalistic green half hidden behind a substantial dune. Your well-hit approach

Above: Rosapenna
Sandy Hills Course, 2nd.
Opposite: 6th.

hitters can handle, and the player in this losing battle finds himself recalling the rueful line that surely originated on a links somewhere in Britain or Ireland: "Aye, it'll take three good shots to get home in two today."

The 1st climbs steadily through the dunes, curving easily right as it heads toward a long (126 feet), narrow green corseted by sand hills. On the 2nd the fairway, again dune-lined all the way, rises gently from the tee, rumbles along pretty much on the level for a bit, then plunges into a deep swale just short of an abruptly elevated green in a dell of dunes. From start to finish, the ground is feverishly in motion on this natural wonder of a hole.

And so it goes, hole after flabbergastingly brilliant hole, the pressure on the swing intense, the drama nonstop, as are the ups and downs. We generally play in seclusion along high-banked corridors of sand hills, only occasionally breaking into the open, as on the intoxicating knob-to-knob par-3 11th. Most holes parallel the dune ridges, but there are those—the par-3 3rd; the downhill par-3 7th, where a mere scrap of green teases from beyond a dune; the par-5 8th—that run across the ridges, lending a change of pace to the test. The panoramas of sea and mountains—Mulroy Bay, Muckish Mountain, the stone promontory of Horn Head soaring 600 feet above the sea—are transfixing. But none of these grand vistas succeeds for more than a moment in taking our minds off the basic fact about Sandy Hills: This is a fiercely difficult course. There is no water, no out-of-bounds, no claustrophobic allées of trees; just turbulent ground, strangling rough grasses, and an endless succession of long and defiantly hard shots to be played in the wind. The golf is heroic, the struggle is epic.

And today, with its 45 holes of extraordinary golf in a setting of surpassing natural beauty, Rosapenna has become a truly world-class golf venue.

ST. PATRICK'S

There is more golf here, thirty-six holes more, but these two eighteens do not belong to Frank Casey. Another hotelier is the owner. His name is Dermot Walsh, and he's the proprietor of the Hotel Carrigart, in the tweed-weaving village of the same name. His 36 holes, called the St. Patrick's Golf Links, are next door to Sandy Hills and in the same range of colossal sand hills. Few people outside of Donegal have heard of St. Patrick's.

The principal eighteen, named **Magheramagorgan**, was designed by Eddie Hackett almost twenty-five years ago. He had not finished tweaking it at the time of his death, in 1996. This is a strong par-72 layout that can be stretched to 7,108 yards, though most men will find 6,550 yards enough to

digest; most ladies play it at 5,700 yards. There are a number of top-notch holes dipsy doodling through the dunes. Elevation changes are bold, doglegs abound, greens are often stunningly sited (the 15th is in an "amphitheater" and the 16th is a hilltopper with a grand view over Sheephaven Bay), and the challenge is stiff. Just noting the yardages from the regular markers on the first five holes of the inbound nine—419, 225, 566, 429, 577—makes it clear that Magheramagorgan means business. And the commentary on the scorecard underlines this point from time to time: concerning the 566-yard 12th, "You can be putting for a birdie on this par 5 if you hit a good drive, then back-to-back 3-woods"; on the uphill 577-yard 14th, "If you hit the ball 270 yards off the tee, you can cut out the dogleg and you may get on in two."

The second eighteen, called **Tra Mor**, was designed by Joanne O'Haire, who was an assistant professional at Royal County Down before joining Hackett here to help on the main course. From all the way back,

Opposite: Rosapenna Sandy Hills Course, 12th. Below: St. Patrick's Magheramagorgan, 18th.

Tra Mor measures 5,822 yards against a par of 69, and though short, it is still a worthy test, routed over more of the same animated terrain. Three two-shotters are more than 400 yards. On the other hand, the shortest hole I've ever played—77 yards—is here.

Now to come to what really distinguished St. Patrick's Links on my visit in late summer 2004. There was no clubhouse. A ramshackle tool shed the size of a one-car garage loomed out of a hollow near where I parked the car (on the grass; there was no parking lot). Nor was there a pro shop, for the very good reason that there was no pro. There was no starter and no green fee collector. Still, a member of the grounds crew—were there as many as four in total for the two eighteens?—did happen by to take my 25 euros, come up with a scorecard, and point me toward the 1st tee on the Hackett course.

At any rate, off I went. My first stroke emphasized the rudimentary nature of the course maintenance: The teeing ground was a model of clumpy unevenness. Fairways, a haven for sundry hostile growths, demanded preferred lies, and the scorecard concurred. Under the heading GROUND UNDER REPAIR, it read: "Any bare patches on fairway, lift and drop to the nearest point of relief." (You could find yourself heading to Sandy Hills in order to accomplish this!) Greens, many of them large and richly contoured, may not have been mowed in the last two or three weeks; they were slow and bumpy. Cups looked as though they were changed maybe twice a month.

In a conversation with Mr. Walsh, he conceded that he had never tried to get the word out about St. Patrick's because there was no club-

Opposite: St. Patrick's Tra Mor, 17th.

house and because the courses weren't maintained the way they should be. He said that Martin Hawtree had been up to look at them a couple of times and that it was his (Walsh's) hope to be able to retain Hawtree for some real upgrading. Then he paused and added, "Martin is confident he can bring the courses up to a very high standard, but he has also pointed out to me that, ironically, if he does so it will be at the cost of the primitive naturalness that is their hallmark, the very feature that helps to make them special. Right now they are largely a throwback to the game in Ireland a hundred and ten years ago."

St. Patrick's had a surreal quality. Perhaps one day the holes will be brought "up to a very high standard." While I was talking that afternoon with two members of the grounds crew, a man in his late sixties slowly approached from the sea. A black dog scampered around him. Of average height but slender almost to the point of frailty, the newcomer was leaning on a cane. He had a long and full snowy beard that made me think he could be a hermit. He was wearing a denim shirt, threadbare khaki slacks, and a red baseball cap with a distinctive white capital P on it. I recognized it at once as a Philadelphia Phillies cap. But was it? How could it possibly be, up here in remotest Donegal on the head of a man who struck me, at least before he opened his mouth, as surely having lived right here all his life? We introduced ourselves. His name was Barney Carr, and he had no brogue, no lilt, and very few teeth.

"Your cap," I said, pointing.

"The Phillies," he said. "I'm from South Philadelphia. I came over twelve years ago and got a room in the village. I stayed for five years, then went back, thinking I'd end my days in South Philly. It was good to get back to my family, but I kept thinking about Donegal, this part of it, with the sea and the dunes and the pace of the days. Finally, after several years at home, I just decided to come back here. This is my home now."

"Are you a golfer?" I asked.

"No, never played the game. But I take a walk over the links every day with my companion." He looked down, smiling at the frisky black dog. "There aren't that many players, so we don't get in anybody's way."

He spoke easily. He may have looked like the stereotypical recluse, with his long white beard and his cane and his dog, but there was nothing withdrawn about his manner. Was he a happy man, this former Philadelphian now a denizen of the Donegal dunes? Was he at peace with himself? I couldn't guess. It was safe to say only that he was going his own way.

DONEGAL GOLF AT ITS FINEST

- See how you stack up against Pat Ruddy's **Sandy Hills**, one of Ireland's ten greatest and three hardest courses.

- Be sure to play the altogether delightful **Old Tom Morris/Pat Ruddy eighteen**.

- At the very least, take a look at **St. Patrick's Golf Links**, next door—you may reluctantly decide not to play either eighteen.

- Settle in at either the **Rosapenna Golf Hotel** or, thirty-five minutes up the road and on the banks of Lough Swilly, **Rathmullan House**.

- Drive through magnificent **Glenveagh National Park**, stopping to visit the castle if possible.

The newer part of the **Rosapenna Golf Hotel**, which has a total of fifty-three accommodations, was built in 1993 and expanded in 2000. Here there are sixteen deluxe rooms and six suites, and although the rooms throughout are comfortable, there is a marked difference in size, decor, and view between the standard and deluxe accommodations. The public spaces are also attractively appointed. The main lounge itself, with its overstuffed sofas and settees, is spacious, and the bar, with its photographs of the game here going back more than a hundred years, has warmth and a nostalgic charm.

Your table in the restaurant could be one that looks out over a curving beach graced by an old whitewashed cottage with a scarlet door. On the four-course menu, you're likely to find smoked haddock chowder (a house specialty), poached fresh turbot, and baked Donegal ham and peaches in a cider sauce. The cooking is quite good; the wine list, while not extensive, has some attractive vintages and values; and the service is professional. Coffee and petits fours beside a fireplace in the lounge make a very agreeable way to bring the dinner and the day to a close.

In addition to golf, the hotel also offers a heated indoor swimming pool, sauna, steam room, body massage, tennis, billiards, and pony trekking. And just a short stroll down the road or along the beach brings us to the picturesque village of Downings, with its shop or two and its pub, where traditional Irish music can beguile the traveler long into the night.

Some thirty-five minutes from Rosapenna on a southeasterly heading, and set on the banks of Lough Swilly, is **Rathmullan House**. This Georgian-style mansion, which dates from the late nineteenth century, is practically an institution in northwest Donegal. There are twenty-five rooms, several with balconies and no two alike, and the preferred accommodations have a view over the gardens and through the ancient oak and elm trees to the sands of the lough and across it to the Inishowen Peninsula. Guest rooms are sunny, inviting, full of appealing old pieces and carefully chosen fabrics; but be wary of accepting a cramped double bed in order

Above: Fanad Head.
Right: Rathmullan House.

to gain a pretty outlook. The Wheeler family, who own and operate Rathmullan House, are thoughtful hosts. Log fires in the public rooms seem to burn all the time. I recall that on our first visit, in mid-April a dozen years ago, there were four fires blazing—two in sitting rooms, one in the drawing room, one in the bar—when we went in to dinner. Period furniture and oil paintings join crystal chandeliers to give the public spaces elegance and style. Dining in the conservatory-type restaurant, with its long, arched windows overlooking the lake and its exotic Arabian-silk-tented ceiling, is a treat.

To name only five of the many points of interest near Rosapenna: the village of Rathmelton, with imposing old warehouses at the harbor; six-hundred-year-old Doe Castle, outside Creeslough; the Fanad Peninsula, with its scenic forty-mile circuit; Glebe House, an exquisitely furnished nineteenth-century residence on Lough Gartan; and, above all, Glenveagh National Park, containing thousands of acres of glaciated valleys, Lough Beagh, and Glenveagh Castle, whose rhododendron gardens rival the great house itself for splendor.

Clockwise from above: beach at Bloody Foreland; low tide at Dunfanaghy; gardens at Glenveagh Castle.

NARIN & PORTNOO

In a desperate—and woefully uninspired—effort to avoid the cliché "hidden gem," I am calling the Narin & Portnoo course an "unheralded jewel." Though much better known than St. Patrick's, it is still not a magnet for nomadic golfers, not even, one suspects, for those bent on exploring Donegal. Yet here it awaits, an authentic links course, on Gweebarra Bay, an hour and a half's drive southwest from Rosapenna. The tiny village of Portnoo, a seaside resort strung out on the gentle hills above the water, has two attractions, the golf course and the beach.

Our first sighting of the clubhouse, nestled in the sand hills, discloses a surrounding armada of trailers, which the Irish and British call by the euphemism "caravans." It is obvious that we have not stumbled upon Shinnecock Hills.

The club was established in 1930. There were five founding members: Portnoo's postmaster, a couple of innkeepers, and two men of the cloth, one of them Church of Ireland, the other Roman Catholic (a nice ecumenical touch there). A "wee green hut" beside the 1st fairway served as the first clubhouse, to be succeeded by a "beautiful wooden structure . . . which opened on 3rd September, 1939, the day World War II was declared," as the club history tells us. The next ten to twelve years were lean; money, vacationers, and golf balls were all hard to come by, with the club teetering on the brink of dissolution. "The financial support received from the local Dramatic Club . . . proved vital to the survival of the golf club at this time. Funds were raised also from dances held in local halls. . . ."

But the Narin & Portnoo Golf Club somehow weathered these difficult years, and today, like Ireland itself, this modest enterprise thrives. One telling sign of prosperity is the little fleet of five golf carts at the ready, indeed, often all spoken for on a given day; so do reserve one in advance if you need it to get around.

ON THE COURSE

The golf holes today follow a classic out-and-in seaside pattern, in accordance with the plan the committee spelled out in 1930. This is a short course, 5,865 yards, par 69. There is not a lot of ground available, and, depending

on the location of the tee markers on the 1st hole, our opening shot may have to be fired over a corner of the 18th green. But away we go, invariably with a smile. The first four holes—two par 4s, a very short one and a very long one, a slightly falling 188-yarder with sand right and left and a burn lurking along the right side of the green, and a rather ordinary par 5 of 490 yards—do not add up to much. However, we put them behind us on the 5th tee, and the round gains steadily in interest. Routed through massive sand hills and over vigorously undulating ground, this is an altogether natural course. Little earth was ever moved here, and the bunkering is very light.

There are six par 3s, ranging in length from 123 to 206 yards and in quality from good to great. The three par 5s, all on the short side, provide opportunities to pick up a stroke or two. A succession of holes beginning at the 5th is of such test and tension and fascination and unpredictability that we find ourselves wondering how long it can possibly go on. Well, in point of fact it goes on for nine holes. I still rely on my scorecard jottings from our first visit, in 1994, to convey the pleasure derived from tackling

Opposite: Narin & Portnoo, 13th. Above: 12th.

Portnoo. The 392-yard 5th: "Splendid—fairway climbs over wildly heaving ground through draw to plateau green in dunes." The 144-yard 8th: "Exhilarating—from pinnacle tee to equally high shelf green and straight out to sea (shot can vary from driver to pitching wedge!)." The 325-yard 9th: "Drive floats forever down to hummocky fairway, then short pitch to tiny knob of green at land's end high above rocky shore." The 200-yard 11th: "Tee reveals entire world of Portnoo, endless golden beach far below, green atop a wind-whipped sandy ridge." The 190-yard 13th: "Terrorizing shot across abyss of broken ground to green sequestered in dunes."

And lest you think that marks the end of the wonderful golf here, let me add that the 123-yard 16th, called "High Altar," is a falling shot from above the strand that may call up the celebrated 7th at Pebble Beach, and the 17th, 415 yards, is a thriller, played from a high tee down into a rumpled landing area and then over wildly hummocky ground to a green partially concealed in the dunes.

Another indelible memory of our 1994 visit was the steward's response after I had sung Portnoo's praises in the small and cheerful clubhouse: "Aye, yes, it is quite good, quite good," he agreed, but I thought there was a certain restraint in his reply. Then he added, "You know, just a few weeks ago a group of us from here went over to the States to play, to play at Myrtle Beach. Ah, don't they have wonderful golf there! I loved it!"

Below: Narin & Portnoo, 9th.
Right: 8th.

IRELAND

DONEGAL

On a Thursday morning in mid-July 1999, I drove into the parking lot of the Donegal Golf Club a few minutes before eight o'clock. There was no one about and the clubhouse was locked. At 8:05 another car pulled in. A man whom I correctly guessed to be the secretary got out, dashed inside, reappeared in moments, and jumped back into his car. I stopped him before he could pull away.

He lowered the window and said, "I've got to get to Carnoustie for the Open."

I replied, "I've got to *watch* the Open on TV. But I want to play eighteen first and I need the key for a buggy."

Leaving the engine running, he leaped out of his car, darted into the clubhouse again, raced back out, handed me a key, a scorecard, and a pencil, smiled to suggest all was in order, jumped into his car, and shot out of the driveway—to Carnoustie.

I was dumbfounded. I stood there trying to make sense of the journey that lay ahead of him. Was he on his way to an airport? If so, what airport? If not, then he was driving from the west coast, here in southern Donegal, to the east coast, just above Belfast, at Larne, where he would get the car ferry in order to cross the North Channel of the Irish Sea to Cairnryan, on the southwest coast of Scotland, well below Turnberry. And then he would drive through Scotland on a northeasterly heading to Carnoustie, on the east coast. Could he do the entire trip in eight hours? I doubted it. Still, you had to like a secretary of the Donegal Golf Club who just had to see the Open at Carnoustie.

About nine miles south of Donegal Town on the N15 and nearly an hour on the road south of Portnoo, this course in the sand hills of the Murvagh Peninsula (the links is commonly known as Murvagh) was laid out in 1974 by Eddie Hackett, the great minimalist (he moved minimal dirt and he took minimal money). The club, with a membership of only eighty at the time, was struggling to keep afloat. John McBride, the secretary who had raced away to Carnoustie, told me, "Volunteer labor by members accounted for more than half the manpower used in constructing the course."

ON THE COURSE

The course opened in 1976. The measurement from the tips, 7,200 yards, enabled the club to boast that its course was the longest in Europe. The general routing plan echoes Muirfield's in an important respect: The first nine runs counterclockwise around the perimeter of the property, with the second nine running clockwise inside it. It is a scheme that makes the most of the views over Donegal Bay as well as of distant mountains.

Almost twenty-five years later, the club, recognizing that worthwhile improvements could be made and able to afford them now that the membership had grown to more than four hundred, invited Pat Ruddy to upgrade the links. In addition to introducing some strategically sited bunkers, he built seven new greens, reshaped four fairways, and rerouted burns on the 12th and 14th. His efforts now make it possible to set the course up at 7,400 yards, probably making it one of the three or four longest eighteens in Britain or Ireland today. Par is 73, thanks to the presence of five par 5s against four par 3s.

There is an alluring naturalness to the Murvagh links, a truly elemental quality, together with a remoteness—a barrier of dense woodlands cuts off this rugged, sandy peninsula from the world   all of it adding up to a beguiling haven of seaside golf.

A single adroitly sited bunker can sometimes make a golf hole. That is what happened on the heretofore flat and featureless 520-yard opener. Ruddy placed a lone bunker immediately in front of the green, on the center line of what is now a broad but shallow putting surface. Birdies are no longer commonplace. Whether your play to the green is long or short, and whether the cup is cut right, left, or in the middle, this sandpit cannot be ignored. A nothing hole has become a something hole. Perhaps worth mentioning, however ghoulish, is the discovery of a skeleton when the green was widened. The forensic experts concluded that the remains were those of an adult male and probably dated back a good 150 years, very likely to the time of the Great Famine.

The next three holes—the long par-4 2nd has been forced much nearer the boundary fence on the right—continue to carry us farther out

Opposite: Donegal, 5th.

When I played the course in 2004, it was in the company of John McBride (7 handicap) and his very good friend Eamon O'Connor (5 handicap), a retired high school teacher and one of the members who had helped build the course. Standing on the 6th tee, Eamon looked down on the 5th green and said with a suggestion of pride, "I was the first one ever to hit a ball onto this green. That was in 1975, months before the links was opened. I was out here with my scythe, cutting back the marram grass to clear a path for the 5th. I just happened to have a 4-iron and a ball or two with me. So I christened the hole."

On pinnacle tees above the broad beach, the 6th and 8th, 520 and 550 yards respectively, are sovereign in their command of Donegal Bay and unnerving as exposed platforms from which to launch drives into the wild dunescape below, where the marram grasses mantling the sand hills wait to ensnare the errant stroke. On the 7th, 380-yards, our drive soars away from yet another high tee to float down into the turbulent lower ground, leaving us perhaps a 6-iron from a hanging lie to a green cloistered in the dunes. What we have here is a four-hole stretch to rival the great quartet (4, 5, 6, 7) at Cruden Bay.

The second nine is not endowed with massive sand hills, but there are strong holes here as well, among them the 10th, doglegging decisively left to a green corseted by sand and low dunes, the 12th, 14th, and 18th. When it makes sense, Ruddy is not reluctant to acknowledge what he considers the most important contribution to golf course architecture by American practitioners: water. Thus, on the par-5 12th and 14th, serpentine burns must be cleared by the player striving to gain either green in 2. As for the 375-yard home hole, the dune ridge that runs across in front of the tee, creating a blind drive, has been shaved to provide a view of the landing area, which is stringently bunkered and mounded. This is the most demanding tee shot at Murvagh. The green, moderately raised to emphasize the depth of its bunkers, is sloped and contoured to put pressure on the putting stroke. An altogether wonderful finishing hole, from tee to cup, which, it might be noted, measures 440 yards from the championship tees.

Murvagh has been the venue on several occasions for Irish amateur national championships, men's and women's. And in the most recent rankings by *Golf World* (Britain) of the top hundred courses in Britain and Ireland, it was fifty-fifth. Given its length and the seriousness of the test, even more important events might well be held here. This Hackett-Ruddy layout would be a natural for the Irish Open if only it weren't so far from a population center.

Above: Donegal, 8th.
Opposite: 6th.

on the peninsula. At the 5th we enter the country of the majestic sand hills. The four holes commencing here are sublime. The 190-yard 5th, with the target just above eye level, requires nothing less than a perfect shot to hit and hold this narrow, perilously sited plateau green in the dunes: A deep pit awaits out front, and steep falloffs lurk along the right side. This is one of the very best one-shotters in Ireland.

LODGING AND DINING

Ten minutes closer to Donegal Town than the golf club is **St. Ernan's House**, a thirteen-room hotel on its own six-acre wooded tidal island in Donegal Bay. Access is by means of a two-hundred-yard-long causeway, and you fear that your eyes may be deceiving you when you first sight this graceful early-nineteenth-century house, perched on a low rise above its mirrorlike reflection in the water. You park on the stone-banked quay, some ten feet above the water, walk through an opening in a fieldstone wall and up glass-canopied steps, enter a sunny little flower-filled conservatory, then proceed into the paneled reception area. Brian O'Dowd may be on hand to greet you. He and his wife, Carmel, a skilled chef, own and run this intimate hotel, which is marked by a timeless serenity. There is little of a commercial fla-

vor here; each room is individually appointed, and the hand of an interior decorator is absent. In the dining room, with its brown marble fireplace and elaborately draped windows giving on the water, the delicious three-course prix-fixe dinner might include sauté of pigeon and quail with glazed shallots and a warm pear and almond tart with vanilla sauce for dessert.

Driving a few miles northwest of Donegal Town, on the N56 and within thirty minutes of Portnoo, brings us to **Bruckless House**, a B&B with four guest rooms (only two have a private bath). Set on high ground in nineteen acres overlooking Bruckless Bay, this eighteenth-century house, which is surrounded by azaleas and rhododendrons, has a traditional cobbled farmyard. Irish draft horses and Connemara ponies are bred here. If you occupy one of the front rooms, you will be able to observe

these animals, not to mention sheep, grazing in the meadow that runs down to the shore. The guest rooms, simply decorated and uncluttered, are inviting. Clive and Joan Evans, the proprietors, have no license for alcoholic beverages. He was a career officer in the British colonial police, and they spent twenty years in Hong Kong; the furnishings in the living and dining rooms reflect this. A peat fire in the dining room takes the chill off as guests gather around the long polished table for a full Irish breakfast, the only meal served at Bruckless House. I am forever in Clive Evans's debt: It was he, a nongolfer, who told me about Narin & Portnoo Golf Club.

On the wooded shore of Lough Eske, four miles from Donegal Town, is **Harvey's Point Country Hotel**, which opened in 1987. It is spruce and contemporary, with twenty carefully appointed bedrooms that offer

From left: Donegal Castle, outside and in-; St. Ernan's House, outside and in-. Opposite: Glen River, near Carrick.

satellite-TV, direct-dial telephone, and a mini bar. All rooms have a private bath, and most look out over the beautiful lake to the Donegal hills. The cooking is first-rate, and the piano bar is a welcoming spot for a nightcap.

DONEGAL TOWN

Donegal Town, population roughly two thousand, is situated where the river Eske enters Donegal Bay. However, its lively main square, called the Diamond, has no water view. Nor does it have an aura of antiquity, despite dating back four hundred years; the low commercial buildings that frame it, some of them gaily painted, are mostly late-nineteenth- and early-twentieth-century structures. There are small hotels, tea rooms, pubs, antiques shops, and clothing stores purveying Donegal tweeds (guaranteed to last longer than the wearer!).

At the center of the green is a twenty-two-foot-high granite obelisk in memory of the Four Masters. In the early seventeenth century four Irish Franciscan friars stationed in a nearby monastery compiled a history of the world, which came to be known as the "Annals of the Four Masters." Not far from the monastery is Donegal Castle, on the estuary. Its great square tower dates to 1505. About a hundred years later, Sir Basil Brooks, who laid out the Diamond, enlarged the castle. The graceful Jacobean structure well rewards a visit. A pleasant way of absorbing some of Donegal's scenery and history is by taking a guided tour of Donegal Bay on one of the ferries that depart in summer from the town pier.

If you head west out of Donegal Town on the N56 through Dunkineely and Bruckless, you will shortly find yourself in Killybegs, a lively fishing port. It's all but impossible to visit Killybegs without humming "How Are Things in Glocca Morra?": "Is that little brook still leaping there? / Does it still run down to Donny Cove / Through Killybegs, Kilkerry and Kildare?" Yip Harburg's lyric may be alliteratively irresistible, but it does play fast and loose with geography (Kildare is outside Dublin and Kilkerry is . . . well, where is Kilkerry, anyway?). Still, Killybegs is surely the place to pay tribute to *Finian's Rainbow,* the composer (Burton Lane), the lyricist, and their enchanting ballad. So let's hum or, better yet, sing the song. And we won't let the gulls drown us out.

COUNTY SLIGO

Five of the seven best courses in County Donegal reflect Pat Ruddy's gifted touch, sometimes as the originator of the layout, at other times as the remodeler. Let it be said at once that the golf holes at County Sligo Golf Club, familiarly known as Rosses Point, owe nothing to him. On the countrary, he owes them, from the standpoints of education and inspiration. Born and reared at nearby Ballymote (itself smaller than a speck on the map) and lucky to have a father who was a member at Rosses Point, Ruddy, nearly fifty years later, wrote a charmingly evocative essay about the links for Larry Lambrecht's *Emerald Gems*. The opening of the piece is pure Pat, a seventy-four-word sentence with a humorous twist in its tail: "One must be forgiven for waxing lyrical about golf at Rosses Point, the home of the proud County Sligo Golf Club, as this place enchants all who visit it, and it fairly enthralled those of us who were fortunate enough to spend thousands of idyllic childhood hours playing there at a time when fewer adults than today had developed the leisure time to get out and get in the way of kids at play!"

No golf course in Britain or Ireland is more splendidly situated than Rosses Point, on the heights between the Atlantic Ocean's Drumcliffe Bay and Sligo Bay, with wondrous views in every direction. Lording it over the entire scene is flat-topped Ben Bulben Mountain. To the west rises blocky Knocknarea; visible, on its summit, is the burial cairn of Queen Maeve, warrior queen of Connacht in the first century A.D. To the north it is Donegal Bay, towering Slieve League, and the mountains at which we gaze. And to the south the Curlew and Ox Mountains present yet another stirring panorama. The links itself, skirted by three broad beaches, is almost an afterthought in this scenic *embarras de richesses*. Every step we take here is freighted with overwhelming beauty—sea, strand, mountains, meadows, even the very roofs of Sligo Town.

The County Sligo Golf Club, some forty-five minutes' drive south on the N15 from Murvagh and four miles northwest of Sligo Town, was founded in 1894 by Lieutenant-Colonel James Campbell, a Scot. George Combe, the first secretary of the Golfing Union of Ireland, laid out the original nine, and the colonel's half-brother, Willie Campbell, added a second nine in

1907. The course we play on this site was fashioned by Harry Colt in 1927. Paid £50 plus expenses, Colt agreed to furnish plans and a report. He also promised "to visit the work on its starting, once during its progress, and when it is finished to ensure that the work is carried out."

The inaugural West of Ireland Championship was played at Rosses Point in 1923, and there this important Easter-weekend fixture has stayed. The weather in northwest Ireland in April (much less late March) is often vile, favoring the golfer who can somehow find a way to produce his good swing in gale-force winds. Cecil Ewing, one of the three or four greatest amateurs in the history of Irish golf, was born within a few paces of the links in 1910, and here he learned the game. Tall, husky, and endowed with massive forearms, he was noted for his ability to hit low, forcing long irons through even the most ferocious blasts. He won the West of Ireland ten times, between 1930 and 1950; won the Irish Open Amateur and the Irish Close Amateur twice each;

Opposite: County Sligo, 17th.
Above: 18th.

and six times, between 1936 and 1955, was chosen for the British and Irish Walker Cup team. In the 1938 Match, on the Old Course at St. Andrews, his victory over New York's Ray Billows (three-time finalist in the U.S. Amateur) was one of the keys to the only British and Irish triumph between 1922 (the year of the first Walker Cup) and 1971. The club feted its star on his homecoming from St. Andrews with a grand dinner, one highlight of which was a bit of doggerel (Yeats may have churned in his grave):

> The Garden of Eden's not vanished I say,
> For I know the way to it still;
> Go down to the Point and you're right on the way
> And there to the left of the hill
>
> In Sligo Golf Club you'll find tonight
> With the pals there's something doing:
> There's eating and drinking with joy and delight
> In honor of Cecil Ewing.
>
> So here's to you Cecil, of Walker Cup fame;
> To you we all doff our cap.
> In your match with Billows you played a great game
> And put Rosses Point on the map.

In truth, Cecil Ewing's enduring eminence, together with the influence of the County Sligo Golf Club itself, had much to do with the spread of the game in the west of Ireland.

Right: County Sligo, 4th.

ON THE COURSE

On the scorecard—against par of 71, just over 6,600 yards from the back tees, 6,280 from the regular markers, 5,830 from the forward tees—the course is certainly not long by contemporary standards. But the winds that rake it can make the hard holes impossibly hard and, paradoxically, fail to be of any real assistance on the four or five relatively easy holes. And though there is neither gorse nor heather, the rough is often a tangled proposition.

This links has a central topographical feature, a mighty hill. The first four holes and the 18th are on the clubhouse side of it. The other thirteen holes, out of sight as we commence the round, lie in the lower stretches of the course, which are closer to the sea. It is there that we find undulating fairways and essentially gentle dunes covered with wild grasses.

There is an attractive diversity to the holes themselves, and the routing is not predictable. Many holes parallel the shore, but a nearly equal number do not, so we joust with the wind from every direction: fore, aft, cross, quartering. And, surprising in a course so wonderfully natural, there are very few blind shots.

Of that opening quartet in view of the clubhouse, two holes are particularly good: the rollercoaster 3rd, 495 yards, and the 4th, 165 yards across a little valley to a sand-free plateau green with steep, short falloffs. Then comes The Jump, an even shorter par 5 than the 3rd and, if perhaps not quite so good a golf hole, an even more exhilarating business as we drive straight off the edge of a cliff—yet more in the way of heart-stopping views—down onto a level fairway some 70 to 80 feet below.

A couple of two-shotters on the outbound nine, 7 and 8, are especially strong. On the level 420-yard 7th, a burn crosses the fairway some 25 yards short of the green and then turns to skirt the right side of it. Only 10 yards shorter and generally played into the wind, the 8th doglegs right and calls for our second shot to clear another burn, as well as carry a steep falloff at the right front of the green.

The second nine is tougher than the first. The 375-yard 10th flows from a platform tee into a dune-framed valley—our gaze is trained on splendid Ben Bulben far in the distance—our second shot must carry a low ridge that conceals the green. The 13th, 170 yards, is dramatic, from a high tee down over a corner of the beach to a green defended by five bunkers and, at the right rear, by a pesky burn.

At the 14th we make it a point to climb a low hill to gain the championship tee (435 yards from here), which affords a stimulating view of the beach tight on the right, as well as of four holes skirting the strand. Cross

bunkers and then, some 70 yards short of the green, a burn intersecting the fairway contribute to the greatness of the 14th. The 410-yard 17th (455 from the tips) is Harry Colt at the top of his form and it is indomitable, climbing steadily through framing sand hills, doglegging left, the fairway narrowing as we go higher. The tee shot must be kept left if we are to have any chance of getting home in two. But the drive that has even a shade too much draw vanishes into a deep ravine, while the one played cautiously out to the right adds 20 to 30 yards to the trek, often converting the hole into a three-shotter. A second shot that gains only the front of the amphitheater green, which slopes boldly from back to front, will frequently retreat into the fairway; one that manages to roll past the cup sets up the peril of three-putting. Here is a hole that helps to establish Rosses Point among the top fifteen courses in Ireland and the top sixty in the British Isles.

The final hole, a short par 4 played over a dip and then along level ground to a manageable green, prompted a delightful story in the club history. A sign beside this green reads NO PRACTICE PUTTING. One summer

Opposite: County Sligo, 13th.
Above: 14th.

evening years ago found Father John Feeney, a 3-handicapper, practice-putting there. Just off the green, Father Tom Moran was walking up and down, reading his prayer book. Charlie Anderson, then chairman of the links committee, happened by. Both clergymen greeted him as he passed, and without turning his head the links officer responded: "It's amazing that one of you gentlemen can read Latin and the other cannot read English."

After the game you will want to relax—lunch or at least a drink—in the Tudor-style clubhouse, which affords some of the most beautiful views in all of golf. Yeats called Sligo "the land of heart's desire," and it inspired some of his most haunting verses, including these lines in which the nocturnal dancing of the "little people" is exquisitely evoked:

> *Where the wave of moonlight glosses*
> *The dim grey sands with light,*
> *Far off by furthest Rosses*
> *We foot it all the night.*

Below, Strandhill, 15th.
Opposite: 13th.

NEARBY COURSES

A brief digression and then we'll resume our southerly heading. Less than twenty minutes north on the N15 lies **Bundoran**, a popular seaside resort with an 18-hole course that is not laid out on sand-based terrain. Routed over a tract of land so cramped that it requires the tees at 14 and 17 to be protected by screens, the course was designed by C. S. Butchart, a Carnoustie native, in 1901. This is the same C. S. Butchart who, twenty-five years later, became the head professional at the palatial Westchester Biltmore Country Club (the "Biltmore" would later be dropped from the name of this suburban New York City enclave). Harry Vardon revised Bundoran in 1908.

There is not much here of a visual nature that is appealing, and, by and large, the holes have little distinction. Some holes are steeply hilly. The rough grows high in summer, which is also when the greens become hard and fast. Not till the 8th do we appreciate the nearness of the sea, in view here and from the high ground of 9 through 13. The 13th, a downhill 230-yarder, was the scene of one of Christy O'Connor's legendary exploits when he was the professional at Bundoran, in the 1950s. Playing in a foursome one day with three members, he hit his shot onto the green. So did one of the others, who asked the great man what club he had used. A 3-iron, answered "Himself."

"I went with a 4-iron," the fellow volunteered.

O'Connor then pulled 10 balls out of his bag and dropped them on the tee. Beginning with the 1-iron and working his way down to the pitching wedge, he proceeded to hit all 10 balls onto the green, 230 yards away, each ball with a different club.

Time to turn now and retrace our steps, past Rosses Point, through Sligo Town and then, in a matter of minutes, out along the coast to **Strandhill Golf Club**, where the game was first played in 1931. Boasting a succession of stunning sea-and-hill vistas and dramatic elevation changes, the links measures 6,245 yards against a par of 69. Three holes at the turn—9, 10, 11—are dull. The other fifteen are ripe with pleasure and test, rolling along over heaving and tumbling linksland, occasionally teasing us with a blind or semiblind shot. The 7th (elevated tee, sea backdropping the green) and the 13th (plunging from a high tee into a veritable maze of bold sand hills) are two of the finest par 4s in northwest Ireland. Strandhill's two sternest holes are the opener and the closer, a pair of backbreaking par 4s. The downhill 1st, 455 yards, bends left. The uphill 18th, 442 yards, bends right.

Eighteenth-century **Coopershill** is a superb limestone manor house that welcomes guests. Not thirty minutes south of Rosses Point and just off the Dublin Road (N4), in Riverstown, it stands secluded on high ground at the center of a 500-acre estate of farm and woodland. Winding its way through the property is the gentle River Arrow, which provides trout fishing and boating. Coopershill has been home to seven generations of the O'Hara family. Brian and Lindy O'Hara, who may fairly be called landed gentry, are your hosts today. Public spaces, retaining their original regal dimensions, are furnished in period style with antiques, old gilt-framed oil paintings, and hunting trophies. Six of the eight bedrooms—all eight are sunny, spacious, beautifully appointed, and endowed with entrancing rural views—have four-poster or canopy beds.

Fires are generally burning in the sitting room and the dining room. Ancestral portraits look down from the dining room walls, candles provide the illumination, and two massive eighteenth-century walnut sideboards dressed with family silver function as the serving tables. The cooking measures up to the setting, and we usually end the evening beside the fire in the sitting room with cappuccino and homemade fudge. Coopershill is a polished gem.

Five or six miles farther along the N4 toward Dublin, in the hills above Castlebaldwin, is **Cromleach Lodge Country House and Restaurant**, not yet a dozen years old but an established star in the Irish innkeeping firmament. There are ten guest rooms in this long, low, contemporary structure that crests a ridge commanding the stone-framed meadows that run down to island-dotted Lough Arrow. The prehistoric Carrowkeel Cairns (passage graves) are visible on the horizon. The view is yours to revel in from your bedroom, with its window-wall, your patio, the dining room, and the lounges. Guest rooms are large and comfortably furnished in traditional fashion (plenty of chintz). Fresh milk in the little refrigerator to accompany coffee or tea bespeaks the attention to detail here.

Having said all this, it is actually Moira Tighe's cooking that accounts above all for the regard in which international travelers hold Cromleach Lodge. A five-course gourmet tasting menu ("intense flavors—light portions" it says at the top of the menu) is offered every evening, but for overnight guests only. The à la carte menu is also sophisticated. In this flower-filled paradise, even the homemade petits fours that round off the evening are marvelous.

Cheek by jowl with the clubhouse at Rosses Point is the **Yeats Country Hotel**, with one hundred guest rooms (many with sea views), two dining rooms (formal and informal), two bars, a spa (seaweed baths, mud baths, Indian head massage, and more), and a leisure center with a heated fifty-five-foot indoor pool and up-to-the-minute fitness equipment. The cooking—likely to

Below: sea kayaking in Inishcrone. Below right: Coopershill.

be plain rather than fancy—is good, and the five-course table d'hôte dinner is a very decent value. All kinds of package deals are available. This is the place for those who like to roll out of bed and onto the 1st tee.

The very name Yeats Country Hotel makes it clear that it is not great golf but great poetry that gives this corner of Ireland world renown. When we first came to Sligo, more than thirty years ago, the scorecard at Rosses Point had, not numbers, but, as was once widely the case, a name for each hole. The 9th hole, called Cast a Cold Eye, aims toward the village of Drumcliff and in so doing reminds us that we should pay a visit to the church there (Church of Ireland), where Yeats's grandfather served as rector and where the poet is buried. Here, in the little tree-shaded graveyard, we see firsthand that Yeats's wish for a final resting place (he died in 1939) "under bare Ben Bulben's head" was granted. The sobering last lines of "Under Ben Bulben" were, as he ordered, inscribed on his headstone:

CAST A COLD EYE
ON LIFE, ON DEATH.
HORSEMAN, PASS BY.

On a slightly less somber note, consider visiting Lissadell (open May through September), where Yeats was a guest in 1894. It is a rare surviving example of the Irish manors that the poet referred to collectively as "the great gray houses."

One other nearby place closely linked to Yeats is Lough Gill, with its isle of Innisfree ("I will arise and go now and go to Innisfree.") Tiny, rocky, far from welcoming, the islet would not strike most of us as the ideal place "to live alone in the bee-loud glade."

In Sligo Town, a busy market center bisected by the Garavogue River, is the Yeats Society Building, at Douglas Hyde Bridge, with its collection of first editions of Yeats's work as well as memorabilia, including autograph letters. The nearby Model Arts Centre incorporates the Niland Gallery, which exhibits a number of paintings and drawings by the poet's brother Jack, who died in 1957. On O'Connell Street is Hargadon's Pub, a dark-beamed tavern with a maze of tiny rooms and benched "snugs." Like W. B. Yeats himself, Hargadon's is a Sligo institution.

Clockwise from top left: W. B. Yeats statue, Sligo; Yeats gravestone, Drumcliff; Glencar Falls; Ben Bluben Mountain.

ENNISCRONE

We now head west from Sligo Town, mainly on the gently rolling N59, through the villages of Dromard and Templebay and Owenbeg. Less than an hour's drive brings us to Enniscrone, a holiday resort where the River Moy reaches the sea at Killala Bay. We are still in County Sligo but very close to the Mayo border.

Enniscrone Golf Club was founded in 1918. A rather basic nine served for more than fifty years, till Eddie Hackett laid out a second nine in 1974. This eighteen, with nearly half the holes routed through ideal duneland, had its shortcomings, none of them so glaring as the 1st and 2nd holes, both par 5s out on a meadow, straightaway and flat and featureless, the greens mere extensions of the fairways. As usual, Hackett was working on a shoestring, and this regrettable start was a reflection of it.

Even more regrettable, acres of majestic duneland bordering the course remained untouched. Carving golf holes out of this rugged terrain would have been too costly. So it sat there for twenty-five years, teasing, beckoning, indeed all but begging the club to turn a golf architect loose here among these soaring, grass-covered sand hills—sometimes rising to heights of 75 feet—where golf holes were simply waiting to be discovered.

In 1999 Donald Steel was brought in to summon forth, if you will, six new holes. The twelve finest holes from the Hackett 18 were then allied with the Steel six to produce one of the greatest courses on the Irish landmass. And with the construction of three new holes to go with the six that were not chosen for inclusion in the principal eighteen, the club also had a relief nine.

ON THE COURSE

Par is 73—in large measure because four of Steel's six holes are par 5s—with the course measuring just under 6,900 yards from the championship tees, 6,300 from the daily markers, 5,570 from the forward tees. At first the opening hole, a 375-yarder, looks like the "same ol' same ol'." Dispirited, at least for the moment, we drive out into that deadly dull plain beside the clubhouse. Then, on reaching the ball, we find—hallelujah!—that the fairway neatly curves right, that we are gazing along it toward a tract

of mighty sand hills all of 150 yards away, and that our second shot will be played to a beautifully sited shelf green at the entrance to the dunes. No time is wasted getting us into the new Enniscrone, and suddenly a smile—maybe even a grin—lights up our faces. Award half a hole, the second half, to Donald Steel.

The double dogleg 2nd, a 500-yarder, is pure Steel, squirming and squirreling its way first right, then left, along the floor of a dune-framed valley, the approach to the low-plateau green providing one of the game's most striking vistas, with the Atlantic Ocean brilliantly backdropping the putting surface. A great hole and a supremely natural one. As on the 1st, no bunkering, for the very good reason that no bunkering is necessary to defend par: The ground will do it.

Opposite: Enniscrone, 2nd.
Above: 3rd.

The 3rd, 150 to 208 yards and solidly encased in high dunes, plays across rough country to a green slightly above us and fronted by a lone bunker that is deep and gathering. The green slopes treacherously from back down to front. If this is not a great hole, it is at least a perfect one.

We take the long road again on the 4th, another sand-free 500-yarder, this one commencing from an elevated tee and snaking along a dune-framed fairway that breathes in and out. The demanding little pitch is to a small, two-tiered, raised green. A classic hole with a simple magnificence about it from start to finish.

Now we emerge from the dramatic duneland and play the next four holes, each of them testing though perhaps not memorable, out in the open, low dunes and bunkers steadily requiring sound swings. The 9th and 10th are a pair of shortish and pretty two-shotters on low ground, the beach of the Moy estuary bordering both all the way on the left, plenty of mounds on the right to keep us honest.

And then we dive back into the great sand hills and begin a seven-hole stretch, 11 through 17—four of them old, three of them new—that is nonstop terrific. On the 170-yard 11th, with the green tightly framed in the

dunes above and only the flag itself showing, a grassy hollow lurks, more than 12 feet deep but hidden as we stand on the tee, ready to swallow any shot the least bit pushed or underhit. Two very sporty short par 4s follow, the 12th climbing and the 13th plummeting. The tee on 13, at very nearly the crest of this range of sand hills, looks out over the entire world of Enniscrone: the Moy entering the sea, the Ox Mountains, the miles of unspoiled beach that bound what is actually a peninsula; Killala Bay, its color—now steel gray, then foam green, then cobalt—at the mercy of the ever-changing skyscape as the bay itself blends into the limitless Atlantic. On a truly fine day we can see as far north as Donegal, perhaps glimpsing—or are we imagining it?—soaring Slieve League, just east of Mackras Head and Killybegs. As for this golf hole, it plunges almost vertically off a pinnacle tee into riotously heaving terrain, leaving only a short approach shot to a gathering green set perfectly in a dell of dunes.

Back now to three of the new holes: the majestic 14th rollercoastering for 500 yards to a heavily contoured green; the 380-yard 15th, tumbling as it closely parallels the beach on our left, the raised triple-tier green tucked left almost coyly beyond a sentinel dune; and the splendid 16th, 515

Opposite: Enniscrone, 4th.
Above, left: 11th; right: 12th.

yards, little overall elevation change, doglegging right around immense dunes mantled in the long marram grass. Club selection on the approach shot is critical because the broad green is very shallow and to be long is to find ourselves in what the affable club manager, Michael Staunton, perhaps in a bow to his American visitors, calls "Indian country."

Michael told me that so dense and uncharted—now he was laughing—is this territory that a four-ball from Brooklyn lost one of their party, a chap named Tony, in this jungle and that for more than five minutes cries of "Tony! Tony! Tony!" echoed across the links until, at last, the missing Tony was found and, like a golf ball, put back in play. The manager solemnly swore that this was true.

So, you ask, what remains? Just one of the best, and most rigorously demanding, 140-yard knob-to-knob holes in my experience (tiny green, steep falloffs front and right, dunes left and rear, sea in the distance) and the sturdy 400-yard finisher, from an elevated tee in the dunes, our back to the sea, down to a level fairway out in the open leading to a shapely green with sand at each of its four corners.

A question that may easily arise about what has been transformed into a truly monumental links: How many inarguably great holes are there here? Five at the absolute minimum, more likely six, very possibly seven. This is a links, characterized by both naturalness and nobility, that is not only worth a detour—as Michelin says about a particularly good restaurant—but worth a special trip.

If Nick Faldo has his way, there will be a second reason to get here. In Killala Bay, just beyond the mouth of the Moy and in view from Enniscrone's highest sand hill, is Bartra Island. In 2003 Faldo and an unnamed Irish partner bought the 365-acre island, most of it covered with dunes much like those at Enniscrone. I visited Bartra in 2004, and the potential for an outstanding links is certainly there. Faldo has developed a preliminary routing plan, but as this book goes to press he has not received planning permission. The six-time major champion, who has been much involved in golf course design for fifteen years now, is inordinately enthusiastic about the possibilities. "Quite soon after we drew up an initial layout," he wrote in *Links* magazine, "I got a little carried away and boasted to a journalist how I was about to create my 'dream golf course' and suggested that 'its worst hole will be as good as the best hole on any links course he might care to mention.' A man is allowed to dream, isn't he?"

Below, left: Enniscrone, 14th; right: 15th. Opposite: 16th.

From left: Moyne Abbey, County Mayo; Enniscoe House; hiking trail on Slieve League. Opposite: the cliffs of Slieve League.

Immediately south of Crossmolina, on the road to Pontoon and Castlebar, a pebbledash gatehouse on our left signals the entrance to **Enniscoe House**. A long, winding lane takes us to the manor house, first through a tunnel of trees and then across meadows where cattle graze. Enniscrone is half an hour east of Enniscoe House; Carne is an hour west.

Most visitors are taken aback at their first sighting of the Georgian manor, a masonry structure painted pink. Susan Kellett, the owner (she and her son D.J., both good cooks, run it), will assure you that pink is the color it was painted when it was built, nearly 220 years ago. It is a Heritage House of Ireland and "the last great house of North Mayo." Set in its own park surrounded by mature woodland through which a path runs down to vast Lough Conn, the place has its own jetty. Two Lough Conn islands, one with the ruins of a fifteenth-century castle, belong to Mrs. Kellett's 150-acre estate.

She is a direct descendant of the family that settled this land in the 1660s. The stately rooms with family portraits, antiques, and heirlooms, the oval staircase hall and fan-glazed dome ringed by plasterwork foliage and medallions of classical figures, the open fires, the pervasive sense of simpler, more leisurely times—in truth, no mere wandering golfer deserves any of it (though, of course, his nongolfing wife deserves it all). The larger bedrooms—there are only six guest rooms in all—look away over the park to the lake. In the room we occupied on our most recent visit, the makings of a fire were always freshly laid on the marble-framed hearth (and we never failed to light it before turning in).

Susan Kellett is diffident about the culinary skills she and her son possess. "This is country-house cooking, not fine restaurant cooking," she declares. Nevertheless, you are very likely to enjoy such dishes as wild salmon with a sauce of chives, white wine, and shallots; and, for dessert, an apple and almond pudding. You will want to take your coffee beside the fire in the sitting room.

Ballycastle, a thirty-minute drive north, is the location of another very attractive inn, **Stella Maris**, smack on the ocean and somewhat closer to Carne and Enniscrone than is Enniscoe House. The long and austerely graceful structure, three-story towers on either end of the two-story central element, has an interesting history. It was built in 1853 by Ireland's British rulers as a coast guard fortress and regional headquarters. In 1914 the Sisters of Mercy, who named it Stella Maris ("Star of the Sea"), acquired it for use as a convent, where they gave music lessons and taught lace making. The nuns sold it in 1960 to a Ballycastle couple who converted it into a hotel that hosted many a local *feis* (Gaelic for "party")—weddings, christenings, anniversaries, and yes, postfuneral gatherings.

Frances Kelly was born and reared in Ballycastle and as a teenager earned her spending money working

at the hotel. In 1980 she emigrated to the United States, where she attended college and later married Terence McSweeney, a newspaper sportswriter who became a PGA of America communications executive. She dreamed of returning to Ballycastle. In 1998 Frances and her Yank husband bought Stella Maris. Following a four-year renovation of this unique structure—twenty-four-inch-thick walls, Gothic arched windows, tiny gun turrets—they opened the doors of a stylish hotel with twelve accommodations (eleven doubles, one suite). Antiques are interspersed with leather pieces to create an atmosphere that exudes comfort, and open fires warm the inviting bar and the lounge. A remarkable feature of the house is the sunny conservatory, one hundred feet long, within steps of Bunatrihir Bay and with mesmerizing views of the coastline, including Downpatrick Head, one of Ireland's most photogenic sea stacks. Frances Kelly is the executive chef, overseeing the kitchen and her vegetable/herb garden.

You don't often hear of vacationers heading to Mayo for the sightseeing. Yet the county has its share of rewarding moments. At Enniscoe House itself are the Heritage Centre, with its wide-ranging collection of old farm machinery and household artifacts in restored farm buildings, and the Family History Research Centre, where research of names of Mayo origin (tens of thousands of Americans trace back to County Mayo) is conducted.

Five miles west of Ballycastle are the Ceide Fields. Preserved under what is called a blanket bog, which has been growing for about five thousand years, lies a farming countryside of stone-walled fields, the oldest enclosed landscape in Europe. These fields were already deserted before the Pyramids were built. An audiovisual show helps visitors make the most of this unusual experience. Less than half an hour's drive west along the same coast road is picturesque Portacloy, its miniature harbor all but walled in by high cliffs.

Immediately south of Ballina is Moyne Abbey, which overlooks the sand hills of Nick Faldo's Bartra Island. The monastic buildings are in ruins. Of the church, a lofty tower and good tracery in many of its windows remain, while miraculously—and if an ancient abbey can't produce a miracle, what can?—the cloisters are in very like perfect condition.

CARNE

Nearly an hour and a half west of Enniscrone (largely courtesy of the N59) lies the County Mayo village of Belmullet and, on its outskirts, the Carne Golf Links. Awaiting me on my first visit, in 1994, was Eamon Mangan, a co-owner, with his brother, of a furniture store and adjacent pub in Belmullet. Eamon was the moving force in the development of the new links and, at least as important, it was he who supervised the building of it. He had no experience in golf course construction, but he did have the course's architect, Eddie Hackett, as his mentor.

Dublin-born Hackett, who died in 1996, worked as a golf professional for more than forty years, beginning as an apprentice club maker at Royal Dublin, then moving on to become Henry Cotton's assistant at Royal Waterloo, in Belgium, and finally serving as head professional at Portmarnock for ten years. He learned the principles of golf course design under Cotton and Fred W. Hawtree, laying out his first course in 1964. Over the next thirty years he designed some thirty courses, a number of them nine-holers, and remodeled or expanded at least 120 others. His efforts were confined to Ireland.

Here at Carne he was offered the best tract of linksland that had ever come his way, and he seized upon it, at age seventy-seven, with the passion and delight of someone half his age.

"The first time Eddie saw this land," Eamon Mangan said, "he walked over it, up and down these giant sand hills, through the hollows and the dells, out to the sea and back to where the clubhouse would be built—there was nothing here then, absolutely nothing, just this virgin duneland—and when he had finished and made all his mental notes—I never saw him jot anything down—we suggested that we drive into town, have a cup of tea, and get him on the road for home. He said no, that what he wanted to do was go over the ground again, all of it. He was enthralled at the possibilities and he wanted to make sure that he had it all there, in his mind's eye. So, at seventy-seven, off he went again into the sand hills, with us traipsing along at his side. You had to believe it was going to be a wonderful course."

ON THE COURSE

And so it is. From the 1st tee to the 18th green, it is all that we could ever yearn for. No dunescape in Ireland—not Ballybunion nor The European Club, not Sandy Hills nor Royal County Down—is more majestic than this wild stretch along County Mayo's Atlantic coast. Eddie Hackett has routed his holes imaginatively, daringly—indeed, audaciously—in order to take full advantage of this tumultuous terrain and to challenge the player to the fullest.

The opening hole, 385 yards from the white tees—the par-72 course can be played at 5,200 yards, 5,750, 6,300, and 6,700—is not at all straightforward, but it does proclaim the thrills that lie in store. From an elevated tee we hit across a valley to the far hillside, the heaving fairway slanting left to right, the hole itself doglegging right. For most of us, the second shot is blind and fraught with tension, up over a crest and down to an intriguingly sited green with, at the right, a steep little falloff and low dunes. This hole cannot be everyone's cup of tea. Entirely too much going on, it will be insisted. Perhaps. And perhaps. Still, it is wonderfuly natural—no sand, no water, no out-of-bounds. And no need for power. All that is required are two sound swings, plus appropriate alignment on the blind second shot. And an eagerness to enter into the adventure.

In many instances it was the potential green sites that dictated the routing. Having spotted a plateau or a dell just crying out to be used for a putting surface, the architect must then have traced his way back—150 yards or 400 yards or 530 yards—to a possible teeing ground. This approach to design can produce some superlative holes, some surprising holes, and, if the topography is particularly churning, some holes that could be considered excessive. The 11th and 12th, two very short par 4s, are considered excessive, not to say wacky, by some. Both play from lofty tees that look out to sea. Both are doglegs, the 11th emphatically right, the 12th emphatically left. We drive from the high tee, troop down the long slope to the valley floor, and now start looking for a green. Sure enough, there it is, around the corner of a pyramidal dune and almost vertically above us on a shelf that serves enticingly as a place to cut a hole

Opposite: Carne, 17th.

and insert a flagstick. On a single 320-yard hole (in this case, on two such holes in a row), we have gone far down, turned a corner, and climbed far up. Darwin might have called it "jolly." At any rate, golf amid great sand hills, especially if the architect is reluctant to move earth, will have its share of unpredictable moments, to say nothing of stirring challenges.

"Once Eddie had laid out the holes," Eamon said as we wound our way along a dune-framed valley on the first nine, "and put the routing plan on paper, then detailed the size and contours of the greens, and once I'd agreed to take on the job of construction supervisor under his guidance, he got out here only rarely. His one worry was the bulldozer operator. Again and again he warned me to keep an eye on that fellow. 'Stay right with him,' he would say, 'otherwise he'll flatten it all out for you and ruin it. It's in his nature to want to level things. You'll see, but you must not let him.'

"The bulldozer operator was not my only worry. Many times over the months, the locals who were on the dole were brought in to work on the construction. They were paid twenty percent more than the dole would have provided them. I had to be alert all the time with them as well, and for the same reason. Many of them had a farming background and

they had that same instinct to want to flatten the land and get rid of all the wonderful natural ripples and hillocks and dips.

"Every once in a while Eddie would shape up a few low mounds around a green, and sometimes the two of us would be dissatisfied with the look of them, the artificial appearance. So then I would just turn over this sandy soil and let it sit there for a week, maybe two, while the wind worked its magic, fashioning it into mounds that looked for all the world as though they must have been created by nature."

Late in the round Eamon asked me if I'd noticed how few man-made hazards there were. I said yes, but that I'd not been keeping a count. "There are just eighteen sand bunkers," he said. "We're very proud of this. Eddie calls it a tribute to the character of the land he was given to work with. The great sand hills themselves and the natural configurations of this terrain—the pitching and the tumbling and the undulating—they are the course's defenses."

Like so much that has gone before, the finish at Carne is mighty. The 17th is one of the strongest and finest par 4s in Ireland. From a tee high in the sand hills, the drive on this 440-yarder calls for a long forced carry over a ravine to the opposing slope, where the hole curves modestly right and

Above, left: Carne, 8th; right: 9th. Opposite: 10th.

rises to a green set perfectly in the dunes; just short of the green on the right is a cavernous hollow. The 18th, 525 yards from a high tee, is sublime. It edges steadily left all the way over a dune-lined rollercoaster of a fairway that finishes in a deep swale immediately below the green. You may be able to see the flag on your little pitch from the bottom of this hollow, but you will not be able to see the vast putting surface well above your head.

Over the thirteen years since it opened, Carne has managed to build a solid fan base among traveling golfers. Scoffers and so-called purists spoke out first, declaring that it is frequently over-the-top and thus not to be taken seriously. But their voices faded, and soon the aye-sayers were heard singing the praises of this links. They seem to have prevailed. Ten years ago I called it "the single most remote great course in the British Isles." That summation may still be valid (assuming that it once was). What seems to me undeniable, in any event, is that Carne is remote and is great, a testament to the architect's living comfortably with the land as he found it. If it errs at all, it errs on the side of exuberance. As such, it is a no-holds-barred celebration of the joy of links golf, the challenge and the sport and the surprise and the sheer delight of the game in a setting of colossal sand hills. Eddie Hackett's last course is his best course. It is his epitaph, writ with a clear and uncompromising hand.

All right, what would you say to nine more holes of the same, right here in this magnificent tract? With any luck we are soon to have just that, thanks to Denver's Jim Engh. The majority of Engh's courses are in the West—for example, Sanctuary and Redlands Mesa (both Colorado) and The Club at Black Rock (Idaho). He has also laid out two courses in Michigan and one at Georgia's Reynolds Plantation. Still, it may not be stretching a point to suggest that nothing he's ever done has captivated him more than his assignment in County Mayo.

You may wonder how he came to get it. Well, Engh has long had a love of links courses; he worked for some time in Europe and actually took a hand in the design of Portmarnock Links. He found his way to Carne not long after it opened and was bowled over by it. Nothing would do but that he become a member of the golf club. Whenever possible, he got back there, studying it with the practiced eye of a professional, reveling in the sheer joy of playing links golf in its purest form. "I'd play it every day if it was close by," he told me.

Engh knew that the club had a lot more land than Eddie Hackett had used, but he did not know that more golf holes were a consideration.

When the committee, believing that additional golf holes would make Carne an even more attractive destination, decided to build a third nine, what more natural than that they should turn to the one club member with the talent and experience to lay it out?

Engh assured me that his work at Carne was also in the minimalist tradition, like Hackett's, that there would be the least possible disturbance of the duneland he was given. He spoke of "discovering holes that have always just lain there, not carving them out." He said, "Most of the green sites were there, most of the fairways were there. We had to spot them, and I think we have. The net of it will be a crazy ride through these giant sand hills, maybe, if you can believe it, even crazier than the Hackett eighteen!"

The nine is being built the way the initial course was, by men on the dole, with Eamon Mangan as boss. There is every reason to believe that this will guarantee the integrity and the excellence of the Jim Engh holes, which are expected to open in 2007.

WESTPORT

County Mayo has one more course of note, the Westport Golf Club's layout, down in the southwest corner of the county, just outside the engaging town of Westport. Fred W. and Martin Hawtree, father and son, laid it out in 1972, together with their partner A.H.F. Jiggens. This inland course measures almost 7,000 yards from the championship tees—the Irish Amateur Close Championship (no non-Irish need apply) has been contested here three times—and 6,600 yards from the daily markers. The first six holes disappoint us. The 7th, however, marks the start of what is from then on a thoroughly enjoyable game, thanks to an appealing diversity of good holes: three short holes (two of them not so short at 200 yards); four long ones, including the thrilling 515-yard 15th, where our drive from an elevated tee must carry a finger of Westport Bay; and five par 4s, three of them averaging 435 yards. On the 11th we take dead aim at Ireland's "holy mountain, Croagh Patrick," from the summit of which St. Patrick is believed to have banished all the reptiles from the land. Be that as it may, this outstanding hole climbs, turns right in the driving area and, at 420 yards, calls for two vigorous and accurate hits if we are to reach the adroitly bunkered green in regulation. Now we gain the heights that reveal a stunning panorama of water and mountains and meadows. It is all extraordinarily beautiful, and however often a vista of this grandeur unfolds on the courses of Ireland, we can never simply take it in stride.

Right: Carne, 18th.

The charm of Westport is not accidental. An architect—by some accounts, James Wyatt—laid out the town for the second Earl of Altamount. The Carrowbeg River flows through the very heart of it, its banks stone-framed to create a canal effect. Charming old limestone bridges arch over the Carrowbeg from time to time, and tree-lined pedestrian walkways flank it.

Just outside town is Westport House, an imposing Georgian mansion set on a cove of Clew Bay and open to the public. It is the seat of the Marquess of Sligo. The family has occupied it for 220 years. At the top of the marble staircase is a Holy Family by Rubens, and in the Long Gallery are two portraits by Joshua Reynolds. When it came to decorating the mansion, the second marquess allowed nothing to stand in his way. He wound up spending four months in an English jail after being found guilty of bribing British seamen in time of war to bring his ship, loaded with precious antiquities, from Greece to Westport.

Opposite: Achill Island (top); Dooncarton Stone Circle, near Belmullet (left). This page, left to right: Clare Island cliffs; sea stack along the north coast; old cottages on Achill Island.

THE WEST AND SOUTHWEST:
GALWAY AND CLARE,
LIMERICK AND KERRY

CONNEMARA

The drive to Ballyconneeley, home of the Connemara Golf Club—due south from Carne; southwest from Crossmolina, Ballycastle, and Enniscrone—will find us much of the time on the N59. Depending on our starting point in County Mayo, this beautiful run into County Galway takes between an hour and a half and two hours and a half. The last leg of it carries us from Clifden, the unofficial capital of Connemara, down to Ballyconneeley, as the golf club itself is generally referred to. The course opened in 1973. Behind the formation of the club was a local curate, Father Peter Waldron, and it was Eddie Hackett who laid out the first two nines, A and B, of the twenty-seven holes here.

The contemporary-style clubhouse, set on a modest rise and built with plenty of glass, affords lovely water views. The Atlantic Ocean never gets within a hundred yards of the golf holes, but it is in sight from the high ground on the B nine.

ON THE COURSE

Like many courses built in the 1970s, Ballyconneeley is a long and rather open par-72 layout that appears to have been designed with the big hitter in mind. Fairways and greens are generous, and though the rough is throttling, there is little reason to visit it. What gives this terrain its distinction, and much of its character, are the great gray limestone boulders and the rock outcroppings. According to Eddie Hackett, not a rock was moved. The look of this links is stern, flinty, like no other in my experience. The hospitality is confined to the clubhouse, repository of memorable homemade bran raisin muffins.

The course measures 7,055 yards from the championship markers, 6,666 yards from the medal tees, 6,235 from the daily markers, and 5,370 from all the way forward. The first nine, A, is no charmer, for, by and large, it is routed over listless ground. Still, there are some good holes here, such as the opener, a 360-yarder doglegging left and rising gently as our iron traverses a burn to gain a well-bunkered green on a little knob. Also testing are the 190-yard 6th, with sand and steep falloffs at the elusive green, and the 420-yard 8th, sand in front of a vigorously contoured green.

The second nine, B, rugged and dramatic, is mighty stuff. Par is 37, the topography is hilly, and three of the last five holes are par 5s. Then, too, the terrific uphill 12th, 430 yards culminating in a plateau green, plays more like 500 yards.

The 200-yard 13th is a delight: pulpit tee, broad green, and a surprising pond tucked into a hollow at the right. At the noble 14th, with an intoxicating view of the links and the Twelve Ben Mountains and the ocean from its lofty tee, the 500 yards is manageable enough, but the shelf

Opposite: Connemara, 13th.
Above: 14th. Previous spread:
Dromoland Castle, 11th.

green beckoning from the far side of a deep hollow makes club selection on the pitch a dicey business. The second shot on the 15th, 385 yards, must climb to another plateau green in the dunes, this one fronted by a steep bank. A stream swings across the fairway 35 yards short of the 16th green, imperiling a thinly struck second shot on this 405-yarder where the green is flanked by sand. The round concludes with a pair of three-shotters, 515 and 520 yards respectively, that begin from elevated tees. On 17 the green is adroitly cocked up in the sand hills. On the home hole, a burn crossing the fairway a hundred yards short of the green gives pause on the second shot, and the short uphill approach, if underhit, automatically retreats down the face of the slope into a pit. This eighteen is big

and demanding and, particularly on the second nine, full of that ideal combination of test and pleasure that we remember with affection.

In 1999 a third nine, by Tom Craddock, opened. Shorter than the other two nines—from the tips it is only 3,145 yards—the C nine plays to a par of 35. The opening hole is a harbinger of the fun and surprise in store as it rolls, bends crisply left, and leads us along a shrinking fairway to a shelf green beyond a little swale. Just about anything goes on this nine: greens that are spacious and festive; the occasional long forced carry off the tee; water (to be carried on both drive and pitch on the short par-4 2nd); very steep uphill climbs to greens (4, 6, 8); shelf greens and plateau greens; plenty of mounds and slopes; holes routed unpredictably

Connemara, 3rd.

and to every point of the compass. There is a playful nature to the entire nine, with its undulating fairways (sand-based linksland, as is the original eighteen) and dramatic elevation changes. The emphasis here is on precision and finesse rather than power. If you have time at Ballyconneeley for just 18 holes, you might want to consider playing the B and C nines.

GALWAY BAY

A good hour and a half's drive toward the city of Galway brings us out on the Renville Peninsula to Galway Bay Golf and Country Club (rousingly American-style nomenclature, that) and its rousingly American-style golf course by Christy. The course opened in 1993 amid fireworks, an ecumenical blessing by the Bishop of Galway and the Church of Ireland's

Rector of Galway, and skydivers swooping in from five thousand feet to bestow bouquets on the female dignitaries present.

The course is long (7,100 yards from all the way back), mildly rolling, and bunkered in the driving area as well as at greenside. Though the waters of Galway Bay wash three sides of the club property, this is not links golf, not sand-based terrain that was once covered by the sea. The land does not undulate and there are no dunes. Still, the sea is almost always in view and the wind is almost always a factor. There are half a dozen artificial water hazards, threatening the shot to the green on the 480-yard 6th and the drive on the 7th, 8th, 9th, and 12th. As Christy points out, "The *natural* water hazard is the Atlantic Ocean." Indeed, the ocean is there, along the full length of three of the par 5s and one par 4, admonishing the slicer as it froths over the rocky strand.

LODGING AND DINING

Due east of Ballyconneeley and about forty-five minutes away on the coast road, itself a serpentine fantasy of sea views studded with islets and meadows studded with boulders, is **Cashel House Hotel**, built in 1840 on fifty acres at the head of Cashel Bay. Because of the woodlands and gardens, only a few of the seventeen bedrooms and thirteen suites have sea views. The sense of seclusion and solitude is one of Cashel House's principal appeals. Britain's prime minister in the late 1950s and early 1960s, Harold Macmillan, was a guest on many occasions, when it was still a private country house. In 1968 it became a hotel, and within a year General and Madame de Gaulle spent two weeks at Cashel House on an extended Irish holiday. Guests take walks through the gardens (camellias, magnolias, rhododendrons, azaleas, roses), through wooded glades beside tranquil streams, and along the seashore. Connemara ponies are bred on the hotel's stud farm.

The house is neither smartly nor luxuriously decorated, but it is enormously relaxing and comfortable, with the emphasis on antiques, chintzes, old pictures, and turf-and-log fires. This is a place that invites settling in. And it rewards its visitors with excellent cooking. The sea provides a cornucopia of dishes day in and day out—lobster, crab, mussels, clams, oysters, scallops, salmon, sole, monkfish, turbot, trout (all likely to be on the menu on a given day) and it is not surprising that Cashel House has earned an international reputation.

North of Ballyconneeley and not a mile south of Clifden is **Rock Glen Hotel**, which has twenty-seven guest rooms. Rates that cover dinner—the cooking is excellent—as well as bed and breakfast are offered. Overstuffed chairs gathered around a turf fire in the lounge, and the spirited conversations of guests and locals in the bar, point up the convivial nature of this converted eighteenth-century hunting lodge. The bedrooms are smallish but nonetheless comfortable, and a few of them afford distant views of the sea.

On the eastern edge of Connemara, near the village of Cong, stands **Ashford Castle**, one of the three or four most opulent country-house hotels in Ireland. This stately nineteenth-century stone pile, for more than a hundred years the country residence of the Guinness family, is beautifully sited between the Cong River and Lough Corrib. It is the very embodiment of the term *castle hotel:* richly carved dark woodwork, imposing fireplaces, crystal chandeliers and parquet floors, furniture in scale and ornament of royal pedigree, suits of armor, period oil paintings. Ronald and Nancy Reagan stayed here on an official visit to Ireland in 1984. All eighty-three accommodations are luxurious, and the outstanding cuisine features Continental and nouvelle French dishes.

In 1984 Eddie Hackett laid out nine holes here over what was once the deer park. The course measures 3,000 yards against a par of 35. A rolling and perfectly mowed lawn—no rough to speak of, little definition between some holes, very few bunkers—it is punctuated by tees, greens, and trees. There are hard holes, easy holes, pretty holes; the 161-yard 9th offers the ravishing Lough Corrib as a backcloth. This nine proved irresistible to Tom Watson and Lee Trevino in 1994. They had stopped in Ireland for a few days, prior to going on to Scotland for the British Open, at Turnberry. It was not golf that had prompted them to stay at Ashford Castle, but when they learned of the nine here, off they went, towing the trolley (no caddies were available) and grinning with pleasure at what they obviously regarded as an unforeseen treat.

OTHER ATTRACTIONS

We never think of Connemara as a place containing specific sightseeing attractions (churches, castles, and the like) but rather as a place simply to roam across,

Clifden, County Galway.

basically barren yet austerely beautiful, bounded roughly by Clew Bay on the north, Galway Bay on the south, Lough Corrib on the east, and the Atlantic Ocean on the west. Harriet and I incline to begin the drive at Maam Cross, where, forty years ago, my search for the cottage from which my mother's mother emigrated to America in the 1890s proved futile. From Maam Cross we head toward Clifden on—you guessed it—the N59. In moments we plunge into the very heart of Connemara. Do not expect Ireland of "the forty shades of green." Oh, no. Much of it has a tawny tint, inspiring someone with a poetic touch to refer to this unpeopled landscape as "the golden silence of Connemara." The drive, sinuous but not hilly and with plenty of long and open views, uncovers a tapestry of lonely beauty, what with the pond-pocked bogs and the rippling rises, sometimes heather clad, the sharply soaring Maamturk Mountains, the boulders, the limestone meadows, the bleak moors, the absence—near total—of trees, and the absence—near total—of man. All of this under a canopy of shifting cloud-scapes that, with astonishing rapidity, present, and

then remove, and then restore the promise of a pretty day.

The sturdy Connemara ponies gallop into view from time to time, running wild and free, but it is the sheep that can make driving perilous. Be alert for them to appropriate this two-lane road. They are no problem when they sashay defiantly down the middle of the paving, for we see them in time and slow almost to a stop. But when what looks for all the world like yet another of the hundreds of limestone boulders beside the road suddenly rises and steps in front of the car, then there is danger and a shrieking of brakes and rubber that does violence to the stillness of this land, about which there is so much of the elemental.

Oliver St. John Gogarty, the physician-poet, tells a charming story that, like Connemara itself, has a touch of the surreal about it. He was once a passenger on a local bus heading toward Clifden in a torrential rain. Turning to the farmer seated beside him, he observed, "It is most extraordinary weather for this time of year."

The old man in the navy blue serge suit replied, "Ah, it isn't this time of year at all."

Top: Cashel House Hotel.
Above: central Connemara.
Right: beach at Laghee Bay,
and riding along
Ballyconneely Bay. Opposite:
Ashford Castle, County Mayo.

LAHINCH

Some years ago Tom Doak said that he thought Lahinch just might provide more golfing pleasure to the broadest spectrum of players—neophytes, scratch golfers, women as well as men, old folks, young children, and everybody in between—than any other course in the world. It seemed to me an insightful observation then, but the course may be a little too difficult today.

Driving south from Ballyconneeley (or Cashel House or Ashford Castle), we skirt Galway City on the east, then follow the N18 down to Ennis, where we take the N85 out to Lahinch. On the odometer, it's not all that far, but on the road it is very nearly two and a half hours. If you've taken a flight from the U.S. and have landed at Shannon, you are all of thirty miles south of Lahinch. An hour later, somehow refreshed and rejuvenated, you can tee off on a links that is one of the half dozen greatest in Ireland.

Lahinch Golf Club was founded in 1892 by two officials of the Limerick Golf Club who were looking for good duneland. The course we play today incorporates elements of the 1892 layout (half the holes were in the sand hills, the other half in much less satisfying terrain); of Old Tom Morris's design two years later (still half and half, but improved); of the design by Westward Ho!'s professional, Charles Gibson, in 1907 (thirteen holes now in the dunes, five on the wrong side of the tracks, if you will); of the Alister MacKenzie plan, in 1927 (all eighteen now in the glorious duneland); of the changes in the 1930s by the club's legendary amateur, John Burke; and of the remodeling in 2003 by Martin Hawtree.

John Burke, who died in 1974, was one of the greatest amateurs in the annals of Irish golf. Noted for the astonishing length he could produce with a wood out of strangling rough, Burke won the Irish Open Amateur in 1947; the Irish Close Amateur eight times, between 1930 and 1947; the West of Ireland Amateur (at Rosses Point) six times; and the South of Ireland Amateur (always held at Lahinch) eleven times. In 1932 he became the first golfer from the Republic to be named to the Walker Cup team. Shortly thereafter, the club gave him permission to "improve" the MacKenzie design, a project that saw Burke, whose putting was sometimes shaky, ruthlessly flatten the boldly contoured MacKenzie greens.

It might be mentioned that Lahinch has been the scene of the Irish Amateur Close Championship five times (Padraig Harrington the victor here in 1995); the 1961 Irish Professional Championship, Christy O'Connor the winner; and the 1975 Irish Matchplay Championship, Christy Jr. the winner.

In 1999 the club invited a number of golf architects to submit proposals for revising the course. The pivotal question put to each architect was this: "If we decide to go with you, what will you leave us with when you're finished?" Only Martin Hawtree came up with the answer that was sought: "A restored MacKenzie golf course." Hawtree, who reconfigured the greens at Royal Birkdale prior to the 1998 Open Championship, gave Lahinch all he had promised, and then some. For example, the old 3rd, a medium-length one-shotter near the parking lot, is gone. The 8th, also a medium-length one-shotter, is a brand-new and altogether splendid hole. The 12th, formerly a 418-yarder, is now 100 yards longer, with the tee moved high above the beach. At the 11th there are now two holes, 11 and 11a, side by side, both short/medium par 3s, this surprising development prompted by the wish to provide a second green that is much larger—and thus with more cup positions—than the original.

These are the most obvious changes, but there is no hole that has not benefited from Hawtree's touch. Half the holes have actually been reconstructed. The greens have been recontoured and, in many instances, enlarged. Bunkers, which had deteriorated, have been restored; a number of new bunkers have been built and some old ones have been removed. And a number of fairways have been realigned.

The result is, at the very least, a restoration of the "spirit" of the MacKenzie design. But it is certainly not a slavish reproduction of the great man's layout. Nor does Hawtree claim that it is. "The club has given me a free hand that has allowed me to use my imagination," he says, "to re-create what I believe was once there. . . . But I suspect I've gone beyond that. There's probably a fair bit of Hawtree there, too."

And welcome it is, for the net of this Englishman's total effort is a masterpiece, a course with no less than half a dozen inarguably great holes, a course that consistently awes and thrills and delights and challenges.

Opposite: Lahinch, 7th.

breeze, to a plateau green with a long, steep falloff on the right, where bunkers lurk. What on earth did he do? Why, he lowered the green two and a half feet so that, for the first time in seventy-five years, the putting surface itself is visible as we attempt to reach it with our medium-iron.

The 510-yard 2nd finds us turning about and heading down the hill past the clubhouse, with a total of ten bunkers right and left to catch any or all of our three shots. The 3rd, 401 yards, is the first of the great holes (and a selection for *The 500 World's Greatest Golf Holes*), the drive rising abruptly over a 30-foot-high dune—a terrible ravine waiting to swallow even a suggestion of pull—the fairway edging left along the high ground and drifting gently down to a green with a pit at the right front, a fiercely deep pit at the left front, and the sea as its backcloth.

Two of golf's most celebrated curios come next. Neither owes much, if anything, to Mr. Hawtree. Klondyke, a 465-yard par 5, is a shocker. About 350 yards from the tee, a colossal sand hill terminates the fairway, looming some 35 feet above us. This startling obstruction—is there any other moment in the game quite like it?—demands that we either fly blindly over it, perhaps with a 5-metal, or play blindly around it to the right, perhaps with a 5-iron. A wild business.

Maybe no wilder, though, than the equally improbable 5th, a 145-yarder called Dell. The green here is tucked away in a little natural amphitheater between two grand sand hills, one walling off the front of the green and the other backstopping the rear. There is no suggestion of a green, no sign of a flagstick. Admittedly unorthodox, it is an original Old Tom Morris hole, the only one that remains on the course. A white stone on the fronting hillside, moved whenever the cup is moved, marks the line of attack. To some, a frustratingly defective creation, this Dell; to most, terrific fun.

We now begin a virtually unbroken skein of superlative holes—surely five of the next eight are no less than great—that carry us higher and higher into these majestic and turbulent sand hills. The humdrum hole is nowhere to be found. On the contrary, every hole is arresting, a visual delight in a rough-and-tumble landscape culminating at a green that is so beautifully sited—on a plateau or in a dell, more often than not—that we wonder what, if any, role Martin Hawtree's artful bulldozing played here. Two holes in this triumphant procession are among my favorites anywhere. The 7th, 395 yards and curving left, calls for a rising blind drive to a generous expanse of fairway that, at about 250 yards, comes to a sudden stop when the terrain plunges into a cavernous hollow with a large sand bunker as its floor. This pit is to be avoided like the

My most recent round here took place in late summer of 2004, in the company of Martin Barrett, who had been captain of the club in 1999 and was a powerful voice in the club's decision to undertake the wholesale remodeling. Fifty-four years old and a schoolteacher for more than thirty years, Barrett is a 5-handicapper who knows both the game and his beloved Lahinch intimately. "Martin Hawtree came to Lahinch about seventy-five times over the five years," he told me. "That's how committed he was to this job. And on all but three of those visits I was at his side, counseling with him, serving as a kind of sounding board."

ON THE COURSE

Lahinch can now be set up as long as 6,950 yards, but it is regularly played at 6,350 (par 72), with the ladies' tees at 5,500. Right from the start Hawtree makes his presence felt, and in the simplest of ways. He has managed to improve on what I'd always thought of as the perfect start, a 365-yarder climbing up a great sand hill over hummocky terrain, into the prevailing

Above: Lahinch, 5th.
Opposite: 8th.

plague. From the safety of the high ground, the second shot is now launched down through the flanking dunes to the green—sand right, falloffs left—set strikingly above the sea. This is a hole of theatrical grandeur, to say nothing of insistent demands on our swing.

The 429-yard 14th plays from a slightly elevated tee down into a dune-framed landing area (a lone and gathering bunker at the right), then along this sheltered valley on our long second shot through a perfect "cart gate" gap to a rolling MacKenzie green, open across the front. Classic, fair, superb.

Lahinch has it all: a veritable dreamscape of the duneland that makes links golf the most natural and most rewarding expression of the game; panoramic views over Liscannor Bay that lend enormous exhilaration to the round; and, above all, a succession of varied and compelling and often great golf holes that test players of the highest rank (Phil Mickelson once called it his favorite links course) and still serve to gladden the heart of the unexceptional golfer. Lahinch ranked twenty-second in the most recent top hundred courses in the British Isles (*Golf World*, Britain) and sixty-seventh in the world's top hundred (*Golf Magazine*).

Alister MacKenzie, who could scarcely be relied upon for objectivity in this instance, once wrote that Lahinch might come to be regarded as "the finest and most popular course that I or, I believe, anyone else ever constructed." This from the man whose résumé includes Cypress Point, Crystal Downs, Augusta National, Royal Melbourne, and Pasatiempo.

On a purely personal note, I cannot name another course that, day in and day out, I would rather play. Surely here, in fullest measure, is Bernard Darwin's indispensable component: pleasurable excitement.

Right: Lahinch, 14th.

Poulnabrone Stone, in the Burren (left), and Moy House (right, top). Opposite: the Cliffs of Moher.

It is wonderful to be able to report that a course as great as Lahinch can point to a great country-house hotel all of a mile away. Its name is **Moy House**, and it was built of sea stone in the 1820s as the summerhouse on a nine-thousand-acre estate. In 1999 it was opened as the centerpiece of a fifteen-acre property adorned with mature woodlands, gardens, a pretty little river, and pastureland for cattle and horses that slopes gently down to Liscannor Bay. There are nine guest rooms— all spacious, individually decorated, and richly appointed, many with sea views, some with fireplaces—a paneled library, and an intimate dining room with top-notch cooking. Moy House and Lahinch add up to one of the very best stay-and-play combinations in the world of golf.

Thirty-five minutes north of Lahinch on the road to Ballyvaughn is **Gregans Castle** (not castellated in appearance), where you can count on tastefully appointed traditional rooms, first-rate cooking, lovely gardens, and captivating views. There are fifteen bedrooms and six suites. Peat fires in the public rooms are a welcome touch, and the absence of TV sets in the guest accommodations emphasizes the get-away-from-it-all feeling of this retreat. In a hotel four miles from the ocean, seafood dishes are prominent on the menu, and dinner here, on a fine evening as the sun sets over distant Galway Bay, can be unforgettable.

Back in the heart of Lahinch and on its main street are three moderately priced hotels:

- The **Aberdeen Arms**, which has been welcoming travelers since 1850 and golfers since 1892, has fifty-five bedrooms, most with views over the links to the beach.
- Smaller and more intimate, the **Atlantic Hotel** and the **Shamrock Inn** both have convivial bars that attract locals as well as tourists.
- And not ten minutes from Lahinch, in the village of Liscannor, is the fifty-four-room **Liscannor Bay Hotel**, situated at the water's edge. Many rooms have panoramic views over the sea to the links.

The plain little town of Lahinch is sometimes called the St. Andrews of Ireland, but this characterization misses the mark. For Lahinch has no university, no historical monuments, no handsome blocks of seventeenth- and eighteenth-century houses. In its single-minded focus on golf, Lahinch is actually much more like Gullane, which also exists solely for the game. Here, on the coast of County Clare, there are two eighteens, a handful of small hotels and B&Bs, some tweed and souvenir shops, and several convivial pubs (Irish folk music to be enjoyed). Even lovely Liscannor Bay, on which the town is set, seems to serve chiefly as a backdrop for golf holes. The game itself, more often than not, is the opening gambit in any conversation, and though other subjects may well be touched upon along the way, the talk will inevitably come full circle, back to what has brought us all together here.

Just north of Lahinch are two of Ireland's natural wonders. Only fifteen minutes' drive up the coast are the Cliffs of Moher, which stretch along the sea for almost five miles. A variety of seabirds, including puffins, razorbills, and shags, can be observed there, particularly in nesting season. The best view of the cliffs is from O'Brien's Tower, which is approached by a track that leads left off the main road. Beware gusting winds.

Roughly twenty minutes farther north, past the village of Lisdoonvarna, with its sulphur springs, lies the Burren. The word *burren* means "great rock" in Gaelic. This may well be the greatest rock formation many of us are likely to encounter, one hundred square miles of limestone. A lunarlike wonderland, it is a baffling and eerie plateau of grim gray stone that seems to stretch away limitlessly and contains within its bounds prehistoric graves and ring forts and ancient Celtic crosses. A favorite haunt of geologists and botanists, the Burren is, in a way, a cluster of vast natural rock gardens where an extraordinary variety of flowers grow, among them orchids and blue spring gentians, white anemones and yellow primroses.

Located in the Burren is Newtown Castle, a sixteenth-century fortified tower house that passed from the O'Briens into the possession of the O'Loghlens, who were known as "princes of the Burren." A guided tour of this remarkably intact structure takes us from the basement to the battlements.

DROMOLAND CASTLE

In May of 1968 we stayed for the first time at Dromoland Castle, in Newmarket-on-Fergus, less than an hour from Lahinch and not ten minutes from Shannon International Airport. Our room was smartly appointed and spacious, with a vaulted ceiling. From the moment we entered it, both of us had a sensation of déjà vu. At first we were unable to put our finger on it. A pretty wallpaper with oversize red roses set the right tone for a country-house guest room. There were two easy chairs, upholstered in scarlet tweed. A Chippendale-style mirror over a chest of drawers; a white opaline lamp on a dark round mahogany table; and a red satin quilt at the foot of each twin bed—all these somehow suggested another place. But where?

Then Harriet solved the mystery: "I've got it—the Greenbrier!"

"You're right," I agreed. "It's amazing, isn't it. What a coincidence. But wait, wait a minute—the man who owns this is an American and I'm pretty sure he's a West Virginian."

"But do you think he had Dorothy Draper also do Dromoland?" she speculated.

I quickly scanned the brochure, then looked up to announce the confirmation: "Here it is: 'All the pleasant accoutrements of luxurious comfort and convenience have been added with restrained good taste, created by Leon Hegwood and Carleton Varney of Dorothy Draper & Co.'"

I did not play golf here on that trip, nor on our next two stays at Dromoland. Then in 1995, with some misgivings, I decided to tackle this pretty parkland eighteen. Despite the very light bunkering, the even lighter rough, and the deceptively easy look of it all, the course, though lacking distinction, was not dismissable. With plenty of room, terrain that ranges from rolling to hilly, stands of mature hardwoods and evergreens, and a lovely lake at the heart of it, this clearly had the makings of a good course. But the makings would have to be employed in an extensive—if not extreme—makeover. In 2000 that task was entrusted to Joe Carr and Ron Kirby, both of whom had figured importantly in fashioning the Old Head of Kinsale. Kirby had built his reputation as an associate of Jack Nicklaus, Gary Player, and Robert Trent Jones.

ON THE COURSE

For the most part, Carr and Kirby stuck with the original routing plan. The holes go essentially where they have always gone. Some have been lengthened, others shortened. The 2nd, for instance, used to be a 520-yard par 5 that, sharply downhill, played only 470 yards; it is now a 432-yard par 4 and a sterner test. The result of these distance changes is to present a par-72 course that measures 6,845 yards from the back tees, 6,300 from the regular men's tees, and 5,300 from the forward markers.

The green complexes have been completely reconfigured. The greens themselves, now often angled to the line of flight of the incoming shot, are imaginatively shaped and contoured. Putting on these keen surfaces is demanding. So is chipping from just off them. Greenside bunkering, which is never

Opposite: Dromoland Castle, 7th. Above: 9th.

heavy (three greens have no sand), is so skillfully deployed that at times even a single pit serves effectively to defend the target. Fairways, which inhale and exhale now, also dogleg again and again, always with a winning naturalness. Nothing strikes us as forced, artificial.

We are not surprised to find water playing a more prominent role than it once did: It now endangers the shot on eight holes. But having said that, let it also be said that the use of water is in no sense excessive, and that a 16-handicapper will in most instances be able to negotiate these hazards. At times the fairways thread their way through large stands of oak, beech, and pine. At other times we must take on the marshes, the modest River Rine, and the formidable Lough Dromoland. The castle's crenelated towers can be glimpsed from different points on the course.

Shot values are of a consistently high order, and certain holes are memorable: holes such as the 7th, 160 yards from a dizzyingly high tee in the trees down to a narrow green that is flanked by a pond at the left and sand at the right and is backdropped first by Lough Dromoland and then, on the far side of the water, by the castle itself. Or the 400-yard 8th, a thrilling wooded rollercoaster of a hole. Or the short but spirited par-4 10th, only 270 yards but with the marsh threatening tight on the right every foot of the way. Or the home hole, 526 yards, swinging from left to right around the lough (and at a safe remove from it most of the way) to finish in the shadow of the castle, whose beige-gray walls rise nobly behind the green.

Carr and Kirby have transformed a not especially interesting layout into a rich, complex, and challenging course.

Dromoland Castle, 18th.

Though it occupies the lion's share of the estate, golf is not the only activity here. There is swimming in an indoor heated pool, tennis, clay-pigeon shooting, archery, cycling, and fishing from the banks of the Rine or on Lough Dromoland, which is stocked with pike, trout, and bream. There is also a health center. Here, in addition to a sauna, a steam room, and a well-equipped fitness gym, a spa offers an impressive array of beauty and body treatments, the latter including hot stone massage, aromatherapy, and reiki (an ancient Japanese approach to the laying on of hands).

Dating in part to the sixteenth century, **Dromoland Castle** was long the ancestral seat of the O'Briens, directly descended from Brian Boru, High King of Ireland in the tenth century. Virtually everywhere we find reminders of the castle's historic past: in the wood and stone carvings, the paneling, the old portraits and landscapes and still lifes, and the beguiling gardens and grounds. The gardens are based on designs by Andre Le Notre, of Versailles fame. A cut-stone gateway more than three hundred years old guards the entrance to the exquisite walled garden, where roses rule.

There is a total of ninety-five guest rooms, including eleven staterooms and six suites. Many rooms overlook the lake. All are very comfortable and stylish; some are luxurious to the point of opulence. The public rooms manage to be both stately and warm. And if afternoon tea in the drawing room evokes a more formal era, there is nothing at all hushed about the atmosphere. The guests, many of them American, obviously do not feel constrained: They are having a wonderful time.

The dining room, with its ecclesiastical Gothic leanings, is particularly beautiful: mahogany paneling below the chair rail, blue-and-gold antique velvet wallcovering above; three large crystal chandeliers; a marble fireplace; and lake views from every table. The cooking inclines more to the fancy than the plain, the wine list is appropriately extensive, and later, in the elegantly cozy bar, with a fire on the hearth, local artists regularly present traditional Irish music to accompany our nightcap.

It may not be easy to get used to living like landed gentry, but it is worth giving it a try.

ADARE MANOR

Robert Trent Jones was eighty-seven years old when, in 1994, his course at Adare Manor, in the village of Adare, County Limerick, opened for play. The father of modern golf course architecture may have been in the twilight of his long and brilliant career, but Adare exhibits no diminution of his gifts. It is superb, a fitting addition to a sixty-year roster of 440 courses (designed or remodeled) in twenty-nine countries, a roll call that includes The Dunes (at Myrtle Beach), Spyglass Hill, Mauna Kea, Peachtree (with Bobby Jones), Firestone South, and Valderrama. The hallmarks of his work are readily identifiable here: airport-runway tees, bunkers shaped like jigsaw puzzle pieces, immense and strikingly contoured greens, menacing water hazards.

Of all the settings for Trent Jones courses, perhaps none is more elegant than what Adare Manor provides. Here there are two centerpieces (if that is not a physical impossibility) on the 840-acre estate: the great course and the great manor house. Both are of such high excellence that neither puts the other in the shade.

ON THE COURSE

First, the golf course. Against a par of 72, it can be played at 5,400 yards, 6,200, 6,600, or 7,140. This is a spacious design, routed over 230 acres of gently rolling parkland. The overall elevation change may not reach 30 feet. Some holes are framed by mature trees (oak, elm, spruce, Scotch pine, and a three-hundred-year-old cedar of Lebanon); others play over relatively open ground. The great house itself comes into view on a handful of occasions during the round, not just at the beginning and end. Then there is the free-flowing River Maigue, which drifts beguilingly—and menacingly—through the very heart of the course, capturing not only our eye but our ear as well; on the 5th, 11th, 15th, 16th, and 18th we hear the water rushing over weirs. In addition to the river and a sly little tributary, two ponds and a fourteen-acre lake are also much in play.

Water threatens on twelve holes—twelve holes and no fewer than fifteen shots. Sometimes the danger is remote; more often it is tauntingly immediate. Right off the bat we must face up to it: The green on the dogleg-right 380-yard opener teases from only a few steps beyond a stream (that Maigue tributary). Our fragile golf swing from 165 yards out might prevail if this were the 7th or 8th hole, but having to call upon it on the 1st is rather too much to ask. The same stream pops up not all that far from the right side of the green on the 2nd hole, where again our approach may be something akin to 165 yards long.

No water on the next couple of holes, which means we can concentrate on avoiding the fanciful bunkers, generally large and sometimes deep, and on hitting the fanciful greens, also generally large, full of devilish cup positions, and unquestionably among Ireland's finest. Tension on the swing persists as it becomes obvious that unless our approach shot comes to rest in the proper sector of the green—the one hosting the hole—we will be consistently three-putting. That may be the only consistent aspect of our game on one of the country's most demanding courses.

The 7th is a Cape Hole in the grand tradition. The lake abuts this 510-yarder on the right from start to finish. Each of our 3 shots is endangered by the curving shoreline. How much of the water dare we attempt to cut off on the drive and then, if our aggressiveness has been successful, again on the long second shot in the hope of setting up a birdie? The weak-kneed among us can play down the left side, with its bunkers, trading the likelihood of death by drowning for the possibility of salvation by sand.

There are no indifferent holes. All deserve our respect. The final four constitute a lustrous finish, and they do so without resort to mileage. On the 350-yard 15th, both tee and green are sited at the river's edge, the fairway never gets far from it, and a tree on the left about 50 yards short of the green makes it impossible to take the water on the right out of play. At the 16th, 160 yards, a pond fronts a broad green that is heavily bunkered across the back; club selection is critical. The 17th, a straightaway 375-yarder through the trees and over lightly rising and falling ground, is no bear, but, with a three-leaved green that is tough to hit and tougher still to putt, neither is it a pussy cat.

Its author proudly called the 18th at Adare "the best finishing par 5 in the world." In truth, the world is not overrun with great finishing par 5s. One thinks instinctively of Pebble Beach, of Chantilly (outside Paris), and

Opposite: Adare Manor, 18th.

of the home hole on Trent Jones's course at Los Naranjos (on the Costa del Sol). At any rate, the 18th here, 510 yards from the regular tees, 544 from the tips, is a jewel. For about 440 yards the river all but hugs the left side of the fairway. It then swings right and ripples across in front of the green, which is sited in the shadow of the manor house itself. A couple of trees bordering the fairway on the right (Jones must have been thinking of Pebble's 18th) force our second shot left, thus intensifying the threat of the river there. And though our approach shot is a short one, still we must be up, and the green, cunningly, is not deep. This is a great hole, the very best on the course—beautiful, fraught with danger but nonetheless fair, demanding complete control of our swing and of our thinking each time we stand up to the ball. The round at Adare concludes with a crescendo.

Located less than thirty minutes from Dromoland Castle, not fifteen minutes south of Limerick, Adare Manor regularly pops up toward the top of many "best" lists, and in 2003 it was voted the number one European resort by the readers of *Condé Nast Traveler* magazine. An aerial photo of the manor house on a promotional brochure suggests a five-hundred-year-old French chateau on the banks of the Loire. In fact, construction of this magnificent structure was not begun until 1832. Its formal gardens in the French manner, its numerous chimneys and gables, and its overall grace of line promise rich architectural adornment within.

In 1988, following a painstakingly detailed restoration, it opened as a luxury hotel and soon was awarded the five-star designation. One's eye is constantly taken by the curved stonework—arches, gargoyles, mantels, bays,

Below: Adare Manor, 14th.
Opposite: 9th.

Golf is not the estate's only diversion. In addition to providing good mounts, the equestrian center has qualified instructors in dressage, show jumping, and cross-country riding. Arrangements can also be made to have resort guests ride with the prestigious Limerick Hunt. For the angler, the River Maigue offers salmon and brown trout. Also available is an indoor heated swimming pool and adjacent fitness center with the obligatory spa. For a resort that rarely accommodates more than 125 people, Adare Manor provides a remarkable variety of activities and services. And there is something refreshing about the fact that not all the guests are here for golf.

NEARBY COURSES

Coming along the 14th, you may have noticed golf holes off to the right through the trees and sensed that they do not belong to the course you're playing here at the Adare Manor resort. In fact, they are part of the **Adare Manor Golf Club**. That's right, the Adare Manor Golf Club is not the property of the Adare Manor resort. The club has been in existence for more than a hundred years. On what is an 84-acre tract are eighteen holes (5,706 yards long, par 69). Beeches, limes, elms, oaks, evergreen oaks (do not shed their leaves), and California redwoods create a perfect parkland setting. The walls of the medieval ruins of Desmond Castle, as well as of a fourteenth-century Augustinian priory and a fifteenth-century Franciscan priory, are all integral to the course. Lightly bunkered and very gently rolling, this layout, which has half a dozen par 3s, is actually more challenging than you might expect, thanks to its small greens. An old walled graveyard at the right of the 18th hole is still in use. A woman in the clubhouse on our last visit said, "That's where my bones are going to lie." She seemed to like the idea.

Some twenty minutes northeast of Adare is the **Limerick Golf and Country Club**, where the course opened in 1994. It is at the core of a housing development. Des Smith and Declan Brannigan (coauthors of Seapoint) designed the course, a par 72 that can measure as much as 6,900 yards and as little as 5,575. This is a hilly layout, with high tees offering gorgeous views over meadows and pastures. The generous greens are richly contoured. Water comes into play on ten holes, and doglegs abound. Large free-form bunkers defend virtually every green. Exceptional holes (the 420-yard 5th, for instance, with the long second shot plunging to a fiercely bunkered green) far outnumber the two or three rather ordinary ones. Though not great, Limerick is much more than merely pleasant.

window embrasures, and the like—and the carved plasterwork, including the numerous elaborately patterned ceilings. There are 365 leaded glass windows, 52 chimneys, 75 fireplaces. The interior spaces were conceived on a grand scale. The gallery, for instance, is 132 feet long, 26½ feet high, and lined on both of the long sides with seventeenth-century choir stalls. The 63 accommodations do not take a back seat to the public spaces, particularly if you are careful to specify a room in the oldest part of the manor, where the rooms are at their most spacious and luxurious. No. 406, which we've occupied, is an excellent example: Large, high-ceilinged, impeccably appointed with pieces that call up the eighteenth and nineteenth centuries, it possesses idyllic river, garden, and golf course views and also has two fireplaces, one in the bedroom and one in the bathroom.

As you would expect, dining is altogether wonderful. We prefer to eat in the candlelit glass-walled loggia, with its mesmerizing views of twilight stealing over the gardens. The cooking is marvelous and the wine list is all that it should be.

Adare Manor, 15th.

On the main road in Adare is the four-star **Dunraven Arms Hotel**, dating to 1792. It sixty-six accommodations, including eight suites, are attractively appointed, contain antique pieces, and provide a dressing room. Good cooking is offered in both the **Inn Between** (moderately priced, ideal for a soup and Irish soda bread lunch) and the highly regarded **Maigue** (the loin of rabbit baked in a pastry crust, with roasted garlic and its own juices, is delectable). The hotel's fitness facility has a fifty-five-foot heated indoor swimming pool.

Three Adare pubs—**Sean Collins**, **Lena's Bar**, and **Bill Chawke's Lounge Bar**—present traditional Irish music, to the enjoyment of both locals and visitors.

The Mustard Seed at Echo Lodge, fifteen minutes south of Adare in Ballingarry, is one of the finest restaurants in the west of Ireland. The dining room in this stylish Victorian former residence is marked by characterful furnishings, and the cooking, by sophistication and imagination. Worth noting: The Mustard Seed is a restaurant with rooms, and the rooms are luxurious.

Often called Ireland's prettiest village, Adare owes its picturesque appearance chiefly to the third Earl of Dunraven. In the 1830s, when landlords everywhere were replacing thatch with slate, he went against the trend and rebuilt Adare with larger thatched-roof houses. Today, ornate thatched cottages, alternating with old buildings of mellowed stone, line its streets. The River Maigue flows under a graceful arched bridge of stone and drifts past the ruins of a medieval monastery. The Adare Heritage Centre numbers among its tenants The Historical Exhibition (the village's unique past, from the arrival of the Normans to the hegemony of the abbeys in the Middle Ages, traced through realistic model enactments as well as audiovisual displays); the Kerry Woolen Mills outlet shop; Curran Heraldry (family crests, coats of arms, and the like); and Black Abbey Crafts (wide range of Irish handmade crafts).

Limerick, the Republic's fourth-largest city (population about sixty-three thousand), is, for the most part, a city of rather little interest to the traveler, this despite its setting on the Shannon. St. Mary's Cathedral, founded in the late twelfth century but frequently altered since, is large but not prepossessing. The tenement district, popularized by Frank McCourt's best-selling memoir of growing up impoverished here, *Angela's Ashes,* has its own celebrity today. There is also the occasional Georgian private house with a pleasing facade. But perhaps the most rewarding attraction is the Hunt Collection, a couple of miles from downtown and just off the Dublin Road (N7). Early Christian art and archaeology are its principal focus, ranging from a Late Bronze Age shield to a twelfth-century German statue of the Virgin.

About a twenty-minute drive from Dromoland Castle is fifteenth-century Bunratty Castle, which hosts a "candlelit medieval banquet" for tourists every evening. During the day the castle functions as a museum, having been restored to its original condition. There are tapestries and period furniture (fourteenth to seventeenth centuries), as well as nicely preserved seventeenth-century stucco work and a chapel.

Some five miles from Dromoland is the Craggaunowen Project, where, at the Castle of Craggaunowen, replicas of ancient dwellings have been built.

From left: King John's Castle, Limerick; Adare Manor Hotel; Dunraven Arms Hotel dining room and bedroom; Bunratty Castle.

DOONBEG

Because of the intervening Shannon estuary, the drive from Adare to Doonbeg takes more than two hours, including the car ferry ride from Tarbert to Killimer. Many golfers will be coming to Doonbeg from Lahinch, a direct run south on the N67 that takes no more than fifty minutes. And some will be coming north from Ballybunion by means of the Tarbert–Killimer ferry.

Greg Norman laid out Doonbeg, and though he surely has countless courses to design in the years to come, I suspect that Doonbeg will be his monument. Norman's love of links golf goes back to his boyhood, on Australia's northeast coast. "You'd learn to picture shots from start to finish, and not just through the air," he says. "You'd have to pick out a landing area, then trace [in your mind's eye] the path the ball would take along the ground. Landing a ball at the front edge, calculating there's another hundred and fifty feet of green to go and wondering if I can keep it on— that's a challenge." It is worth noting that his two major championships came on two of the world's greatest links courses, Turnberry's Ailsa, in 1986, and Royal St. George's, in 1993.

On his first visit to Doonbeg, in 1997, Norman was bowled over by the colossal sand hills, which seemed to declare the existence of golf holes before he had even so much as lifted a spade. He insisted that the naturalness of the terrain be maintained at all costs, that he was "not going to Americanize this course. Once we laid out the fairways, I just started mowing the grass that was there. The only major dirt we moved was for the clubhouse." He made a personal commitment to find at Doonbeg the best holes provided by nature rather than the best holes that could be contrived by machine. He uncovered 11 of the 18 simply by walking the land. "This course was built with shovels and lawnmowers, not bulldozers," he says.

During the two and a half years it took to fashion and seed the course, Norman couldn't keep his hands off it. Twenty-two times he visited the site, in the early days developing the plans and in the later days making sure his vision was being carried out. He personally tested how each hole would play, fine-tuning as he went, treating the project as though it were a once-in-a-lifetime opportunity. It probably was, authentic linksland being such a rare commodity. None of the thirty-five courses he had designed previously was kin to Doonbeg.

Ranging along Doughmore Bay, in County Clare, Doonbeg's grass-cloaked dunes soar some 80 feet above the sea beside a mile and a half of crescent beach. Through sand hills as spectacular as those at Ballybunion, Royal County Down, Cruden Bay, Rosapenna, and Lahinch, Norman has routed a succession of holes that are never less than good and that are often great (a minimum of seven or eight inarguably great holes). For almost every shot played fully through the air, another must be played—with imagination, with flair and feel and finesse—over the rumpled ground.

This is a traditional out-and-in links. Fairways meander along tranquil valleys flanked by tall sand hills. Greens perch defiantly two thirds of the way up the flanks of the dunes, or beckon from amphitheaterlike dells, or rest with supreme naturalness mere steps above the beach. Bunkers, whether sod-faced or ringed by shaggy tufts of wild grass, are sometimes unsparingly deep. And everywhere, long, throttling marram grass awaits to punish the wayward shot. Doonbeg was born tough. All that spirited topography that Norman was reluctant to alter has inevitably led to some daunting forced carries and some blind shots. When first unveiled, in late 2001, this layout went beyond stern to the point of harshness. But steps have been taken to make it more golfer friendly, and though it is still hugely challenging, especially in a heavy wind, the game here can be thoroughly enjoyed.

ON THE COURSE

Power is no prerequisite. From the championship tees, Doonbeg measures 6,834 yards, 6,268 from the regular markers, 4,665 from all the way forward. The par of 72 is derived in an uncommon fashion: five par 3s and five par 5s, only eight two-shotters.

The round begins with one of the best and most glorious openers in my experience, a par 5 of 544 yards that commences on a high tee. We are mesmerized by the vistas stretching away before us, majestic sand hills all but arm in arm with the exquisite crescent beach, the sea shimmering on

Opposite: Doonbeg, 6th.

the horizon. The dune-framed fairway lies far below, generous in the landing area as it edges right, somewhat less generous for our second shot as it edges left, with sand both right and left to swallow the errant fairway metal. The very large and strikingly contoured amphitheater green is encased on three sides by a single overpowering dune. It is likely that no other opening hole in Irish golf measures up to this one for its combination of grandeur, shot values, and pure pleasurable excitement.

The next three holes, gently rolling, play "inside," away from the sea and in full view of the cattle-grazing country. There is a vast and spectacular boomerang-shape green (2nd), a tiny and off-putting knob of a green (3rd), and a green tucked just beyond an old rock-and-sod wall that has been there for years (4th). On two of these three holes, the driving is blind.

On the 331-yard 5th we regain the sea—with a vengeance—driving uphill into a saddle between two tall dunes, the hole then opening up to reveal a green below us, sitting almost on the beach, the Atlantic Ocean breakers a dramatic backcloth for what, into the wind off the water, may prudently be a knockdown short iron that bounds its way onto the bunker-free

putting surface. This is a great short two-shotter, to rank with the 8th at Pine Valley and the 14th at Muirfield Village and the 12th on the Old Course.

The 6th, an even shorter par 4 at only 285 yards, is another stunner, skirting the sea from tee to cup, a blind drive from a high tee dropping into a tumbling fairway embraced by grass-cloaked dunes, the short pitch up to a skinny but 47-yard-deep green, sand right and left.

We go back inside for the 7th, a falling 195-yarder framed by modest dunes, and the 8th, a 546-yarder that plays a good 600 yards as it bends left into the wind, rises gently, and finishes at a sprawling and fiercely contoured green perhaps twenty paces from the sea. Dunes at the right on the 124-yard 9th force us to look warily at the left edge of the green, which is hard beside a low clifftop above the ocean.

Is the incoming nine just as extraordinary? At least. Five holes are world class, beginning with the 141-yard 11th out in the windswept open near the pastures, the elevated green defended by abrupt falloffs on three sides and by two pits, one concealed over the back 10 feet below the surface of the green (that's the easy one) and one at the right front, 15 feet deep and cavernous (that's the hard one). Choose your club carefully, inhale slowly, then make your very good swing.

Thirteen, 14, and 15, which find us back in the gigantic dunes, constitute one of the game's great trios. The 13th, a par 5 of only 451 yards but playing at least 500, climbs blindly over a ridge and down onto a broad fairway, swivels through low dunes for the next 200 yards as the fairway narrows, then turns emphatically right for a pitch to an elevated green dominated by tall dunes right and left. The ocean is close—we feel it but do not see it.

On the 14th we see it *and* feel it. The hole measures all of 106 yards, but there is, effectively, no margin for error. The tee is a platform well up a dune. On the far side of an abyss is the green, a narrow shelf carved out of the opposing dune at roughly eye level. This sand hill towers over the beach. The sea is the backdrop for the shot. A massive sand hill swaddled in marram grass defines the left side of the putting surface. The front, right, and rear are defined by long, steep falloffs into snarly rough. In the calm, a pitching wedge—a straight, solidly struck pitching wedge—will do. In the wind, heaven knows: Norman once had to hit a 5-iron here. This hole must stand alone among Ireland's very short par 3s.

The 400-yard 15th is sublime. From a tee high in the dunes, we take in almost all of it as it rolls along an ocean ridge, bending smoothly right, low dunes on both sides, the water much in view. The angled putting surface is cloistered in an immense "colosseum" of sand hills, a

Doonbeg, 15th.

picture-book setting that could have served no other purpose than as the haven for a green. From start to finish, the 15th takes our breath away.

The same can fairly be said of the climactic home hole, pressured by the importunate Atlantic on our right from tee to green. The safe drive on this 385-yarder, hit left over a dune into a concealed part of the fairway, leaves us with a vexing second shot. Timidly, we also incline to keep it left (a low sea cliff on the right is within paces of the green), which means having to carry a hollow and two bunkers at the left front of the large crowned green. You may want to play this triumphant hole from the

tips, at 440 yards, to experience the thrill of a championship finish on a great and noble links.

Well, it is over. We are exhausted, perhaps mentally more than physically, and yet we are exhilarated. The combination here of aesthetic delight and shot-making demands is a powerful one, indeed, a never-to-be-forgotten one.

I'm inclined to give Greg Norman the last word: "If I spent the rest of my life building courses, I don't think I'd find a comparable site anywhere. It's spectacular, land made by God. I'm the happiest man in the world."

There is no hotel *per se* at Doonbeg, but there is a wealth of truly five-star accommodations. These suites, complete with kitchen, living room, and as many as four bedrooms, are owned by members of the Doonbeg Golf Club (mostly Americans) and are available to visiting golfers for rental on a limited basis.

Just beyond the far side of the practice range at Doonbeg is **Links Lodge**, a B&B owned and run by the hospitable Tony and Maeve Prendegast. No more than three years old, it has ten guest rooms, all of them sunny and inviting, each with a private bath and a big picture window giving on the surrounding pastures and croplands. For a view of Doughmore Bay, you have to get one of the two accommodations on the second floor. A spacious lounge, a TV room with fireplace, and a dining room with fireplace complete the inviting picture.

In the village of Doonbeg is another charming B&B, called **An Tintean** ("our hearth"). Francis and Connie Killen are the proprietors of this seven-bedroom house.

Here, too, each room, spruce and pretty and comfortable, has its own bath. A peat fire regularly glows in the cozy parlor. Francis is a Doonbeg man, but Connie, her southern drawl a dead giveaway, was born and reared outside Atlanta. After studying at the University of Georgia, she took a job in Florida, where she met and married Francis. In the early nineties they came home—to his home—bought An Tintean, and now find themselves hosting a lot of Americans (surely even some Georgians), thanks to Doonbeg Golf Club.

Also in the village, with its population of about two hundred, is **Morrissey's Seafood Bar & Grill**. The ambience is bright and cheery, locals and travelers mingle happily, and the cooking is good.

The southwestern stretch of County Clare, including Doonbeg, is mainly a peninsula formed by the estuary of the Shannon and the Atlantic Ocean. It has very little in the way of must-see attractions, but it is a pleasant place in which to drive. Doonbeg itself has two picturesque elements, the stone Castle Bridge, with its five arches spanning the placid Doonbeg River, and the towerlike remains of four-hundred-year-old Doonbeg Castle.

A short drive north along the coast brings us to Spanish Point. Buried here are countless bodies that washed ashore when a number of vessels in the ill-starred Spanish Armada sank in 1588.

A drive south from Doonbeg soon reveals the starkly rocky Cliffs of Baltard, a dramatic contrast to the golf club's grass-clad dunes. Kilkee, with its bathing beach, comes next as we head toward remote Loop Head, passing here and there the ruins of a castle or a fort. The main reason for making this run down to land's end is the view. It astonishes, taking in, as it does, MacGillycuddy's Reeks to the south, just beyond Killarney; Brandon Head and Mount Brandon to the southwest, out on the Dingle Peninsula; to the north, the Aran Islands and, beyond, Connemara all the way to the Twelve Ben Mountains.

From left: Knappogue Castle, exterior and stained glass; Quinn Abbey, near Ennis.

BALLYBUNION

Leaving Doonbeg in order to complete the great seaside quartet—Lahinch, Doonbeg, Ballybunion Old and New—we follow the coast road, N67, south through Kilkee (reputedly delightful clifftop eighteen here, which, alas, I've never played) and Kilrush to Killimer and the ferry across the Shannon to Tarbert. Then, in less than thirty minutes, it's west on R551, through Ballylongford and Astee, to Ballybunion.

Golf has been played here, on this stretch of magnificent duneland where the River Shannon enters the Atlantic Ocean, since 1893. Today there are two of the world's truly great courses and a clubhouse that, if not great, is at the very least awe-inspiring.

It is not easy to say who designed the Old Course. Cornish and Whitten in *The Architects of Golf* name an M. Smyth and a P. Murphy as the first to lay out holes here, but the club history makes no mention of them. (Intriguing sidelight: A. Snowball, the Scot who, close readers of this book may recall, helped lay out the holes at Baltray in 1892, was Ballybunion's first professional, taking the post in 1896.) Lionel Hewson, editor of *Irish Golf* magazine, laid out nine holes in 1906; and Old Tom Morris, in the 1920s, and James Braid, in the 1930s, may each have had a hand in remodeling the links, but this is only speculation. On the other hand, there is no question but what Tom Simpson and Molly Gourlay, the two responsible for the major revamping of County Louth, made important and extensive modifications in 1936. In 1964 Eddie Hackett chimed in. And in the late 1990s Tom Watson revised the 18th as well as the 4th and 5th.

Over the fifty years between 1930 and 1980, the club hosted a number of national championships, men's and women's, amateur and professional; the Irish themselves knew what a jewel this links was. But the rest of the world had no knowledge even of its existence. Then, in 1971, following up on his 1964 Scotland piece, Herbert Warren Wind published a long story in *The New Yorker* dealing with six of the best Irish courses (Portmarnock, Royal County Down, Royal Portrush, Rosses Point, Lahinch, and Ballybunion). "Ballybunion," he wrote, "revealed itself to be nothing less than the finest seaside course I have ever seen." American golfers began to take notice. Ten years later, Tom Watson, who had won three

British Opens and would win two more, arrived at Ballybunion, to be thrilled at what he found. He wrote the introduction to the course's hole-by-hole guide, which opens with his saying that "after playing Ballybunion for the first time, a man would think that the game of golf originated here." His closing statement is also provocative: "Ballybunion is a course on which many golf architects should live and play before they build golf courses. I consider it a true test of golf." Watson accepted the honor of serving as the club's captain in the Millennium Year.

The sequence is obvious: first Wind, then Watson, and now the world. The roll call of well-known figures, golf and otherwise, who have made it a point to get to Ballybunion is impressive. To mention the most prominent: Jack Nicklaus, Tiger Woods, Byron Nelson, Lee Trevino, Peter Thomson, Nick Faldo, Seve Ballesteros ("It demands greater imagination and shot-making skills than anything I have ever known"), Ben Crenshaw, Payne Stewart, Mark O'Meara, Greg Norman (mere minutes by helicopter from Doonbeg), Ken Venturi, Ernie Els, Phil Mickleson, David Duval, Colin Montgomerie, Ian Baker-Finch, Bill Clinton, Dan Quayle, Tip O'Neill, Michael Jordan, Dan Merino, and Neil Armstrong. Down in County Kerry, they keep track of these things.

In 2000 the Irish Open was played at Ballybunion for the first and, thus far, the only time. A twenty-seven-year-old Swede by the name of Patrik Sjoland won with a total of 270. The course measured only 6,651 yards, against a par of 71. The field included Sergio Garcia (defending champion; two strokes off the pace going into the final round, he shot 77), José Maria Olazabal, Bernhard Langer, Adam Scott, Retief Goosen, Padraig Harrington, and Darren Clarke. On what was a very short course, all of these players posted at least one round over par.

ON THE OLD COURSE

From the regular tees the Old Course measures 6,200 yards; from the forward markers, 5,320. Standing on the elevated 1st tee, we are struck by the formidable nature of the landscape: the colossal grass-covered sand hills that, 70 feet high, disclose only an occasional patch of playable turf.

Opposite: Ballybunion Old Course, 15th.

Instead of paralleling the shoreline, these dunes often run at right angles to it. The result is a variety of dogleg holes carved through the sharply contoured land, as well as a number of straightaway holes where sand hills right and left patrol access to the greens in sentinel style. The round cannot be other than adventurous, though neither bunkers (the total is sixty-three, and the great majority are small) nor blind shots (can there be more than four?) will contribute to the eventful nature of the game.

There is an ominous quality to the first shot. A graveyard on the right, with its assortment of Celtic crosses, awaits the short slice, and who among us has not begun a round at least once with that very shot? Still, the hole, 366 yards long, is lightly downhill. A couple of bunkers 255 yards out on the left are unreachable by most players, and the green is open across the front. Not a great hole, but it is an ideal starter, while we get our sea legs under us.

The second hole *is* a great one, the first of nine such (not to mention one *greatest*). Just under 400 yards on the card and playing at least

440, the 2nd begins with a blind drive into a tumbling landing area bracketed by sand. Then comes one of the most demanding shots on the links—up, up, up through a gap in the dunes to a shelf green silhouetted against the sky, sand right and left. Anything less than a perfect strike fails. The green slopes wickedly down from back to front, and the approach shot that comes up short will often retreat 40 yards down the hill. Mighty stuff, and one of the 500 *World's Greatest*. The dramatically climbing shot to the green here points up something else Watson said about Ballybunion: "I love its vertical dimension, which creates a variety of shots second to none . . . there are uphill, downhill, and sidehill shots, uphill and downhill par threes. I've never been able to feel totally in control of my game here . . . especially in the wind."

The next three holes—a falling 211-yarder to a large green with a boundary tight on the left (the late Payne Stewart aced it in 1998), and then consecutive 500-yarders over rather featureless interior ground—are followed by the 345-yard 6th, which finds us back in the real dune country,

where the game will be played till the end of the round. The long, narrow, vaulting-horse green here inclines to reject any shot we fire at it, whether standard pitch, knockdown, or bump-and-run, sending the ball slip-sliding over the right edge, the left edge, or the back of this low plateau. There is no sand, just this small target with its pernicious little falloffs. Holding this crowned putting surface from even 20 yards is no sure thing. The ground will have its way, demonstrating forcefully what is the course's first defense against low scoring: elusive greens. Shots that seem to be well played somehow just miss, leaving extremely difficult chips or pitches or lobs or scuttles with a putter for a desperate effort to salvage par.

The great 7th measures 411 yards and plays along the ocean from tee to green, a good 70 feet above the broad golden beach. A fade—not a slice, just your ordinary garden-variety fade—sails right over the cliff and down onto the strand. Of course, if you steer the tee shot left you're in the grass-mantled dunes. Again a vaulting-horse green, a cousin of the one that just harassed us on the 6th, is obstinate. This hole is also one of the 500 *World's Greatest*.

The 8th, 140 yards down from a high tee, our back to the ocean this time, is another killer, and for the same reason: a long, narrow green, this one with pot bunkers alternating with abrupt little falloffs. The hole is one of Watson's particular favorites: "You must hit your shot within a 10–12-yard area or face bogey or double bogey! In a wind it's one of the most demanding shots I've ever faced."

The long par-4 9th, with its downhill drive and uphill second, is more greatness, and the short par-4 10th, slithering along a dune-framed valley, calls for another perfect pitch to hit and hold the green. Which brings us to the 11th, cast in the same heroic mold as the 8th at Pebble Beach, the 14th at Dornoch, and the 17th at St. Andrews, and chosen for *The 500 Greatest Golf Holes* as one of the eighteen greatest holes in the world. It measures 400 yards from the regular tees, 453 from the tips. A pinnacle tee towers above the beach, and the view is enthralling: the ocean's frothing combers, the arc of sandy bluffs gradually giving way in the distance to farmland, the mountains of the Dingle Peninsula claiming the southern horizon, and, depending on the moment, a school of dolphins breaking the surface of the sea far offshore. The fairway tumbles along below us, bordered on the right by the cliff edge; massive grass-mantled dunes stand guard tight along the left—no bailout area there, either. The fairway is actually broken into three separate steps, if you will: the landing area for the drive; then, about 100 yards farther on and on a

Left: Ballybunion Old Course, 11th.

lower level, a shelf; and finally, still lower, a path of cut grass threading its way between two sand hills till, on the far side of them, the green is revealed, an undulating carpet with a falloff on the right down to the beach and a bit of breathing room left. All this with the ocean cliffs tight on the right all the way. Such a combination of majesty and peril, of originality together with the integrity of the truly natural, is rare indeed. And so searching an examination is it that, on a customarily breezy day, no matter how you choose to plot your way, you cannot guarantee a bogey.

The pressure on the swing continues unabated to the end. So does the thrill inherent in the seven remaining holes, each arresting in its own way, six of them great by my reckoning. The two par 5s, neither measuring more than 475 yards, both, into the wind, playing like 575 yards, bend left, 13 softly, 16 emphatically. A burn 50 yards short of the green complicates life on the 13th, and on 16 it is the skinny fairway climbing through the dunes that sorely tests our resolve.

I recall standing on the 16th tee, a seaside raised platform, some years back and having my playing companion, a member, explain that the club's cliff erosion problem could largely be blamed on farmers hauling sand off the beach to provide bedding for their horses and cattle. "This," he said, "is now against the law. It's what has permitted the tide to rush right in . . . and undermine the golf course. That's why we are always having to shore up the holes along the sea with rocks and wood planking and metal caging pressed into the cliffside. Golfers think that playing the game here is a battle. But so is just keeping the links in place."

To come back to the one-shotters, there are three of them among the last seven holes, the play in each case dune-framed and over fear-

Opposite: Ballybunion Old Course, 17th.

some rough country. On 12 (180 yards, often a driver) and 14 (127 yards, sometimes a 4-iron), the plateau greens taunt us from high above. On the 200-yard 15th, there is a suggestion of fall to the shot. This hole, aiming out to sea, the target a broad double-tiered green encased in the dunes, is one of the game's most glorious par 3s.

The round ends with two par 4s. From a tee high in the dunes, the drive on the 360-yard 17th flies through a gap between giant sand hills. The temptation on this dogleg left to draw the ball around the left-hand dune is hard to resist. The 17th is the only green at the sea and at sea level.

If the 17th is boldly downhill, the 18th is just as boldly uphill, much the same length as its predecessor but playing a good 50 yards longer. The flag can be seen high above us against the sky, but not the putting surface, pinched by sand at the front, another of those long, narrow, elusive greens we've played to half a dozen times.

Ranked sixteenth in *Golf Magazine*'s listing of the world's top hundred courses and ninth in *Golf World*'s top hundred in the British Isles, Ballybunion may possess more great holes than any other eighteen in Ireland. It is unsurpassed for pure golfing pleasure, a remarkable balance of honest challenge, naturalness, aesthetic beauty, variety, originality, and exhilaration. A course to be cherished eternally, or so one player earnestly believed.

On New Year's Eve 1987, an avid American golfer by the name of Martin McDermott was buried in that cemetery beside the 1st hole. "It was the one wish he had," said his wife, who had the body of her forty-three-year-old husband flown six thousand miles from their home in Los Angeles in order to respect his last request. Martin McDermott had played Ballybunion Old twice, in 1984 and 1986. Father Michael Galvin, the local parish priest, officiated at the interment. The late Sean Walsh, longtime secretary of the club, said, "I really was not all that surprised. It is the kind of thing the Americans might do. They hold this course in very high esteem and come back year after year to play it. This man came back for good."

Well, after that sobering digression, it's time to head for the 19th hole in the imposing clubhouse. This architectural marvel opened in 1993, on high ground above the 1st tee and the 18th green. Nothing quite prepares us for it: a roofline full of massive and unexpected stone outcroppings, all manner of planes and angles and slopes and overhangs, vast windows giving on the sea, generous spaces for eating and drinking and showering and changing, a large, well-stocked pro shop, a terrace or two, and a big glass-ceilinged atrium at the heart of it all. It is the right place to ready yourself for the rigors of the game on the second eighteen.

A CLUB AND A CASTLE LINKED BY THE SHANNON

- Play **Ballybunion Old**—what other course in Ireland has so many inarguably great holes?

- Eat lunch in the nonpareil **clubhouse**, itself a bit of a shock.

- Under no circumstances should you pass up **Ballybunion's Cashen Course**, another triumph, though not everyone's cup of tea.

- Spend at least one night at **Glin Castle**, one of the four or five very finest Irish country houses that now accept paying guests.

ON THE CASHEN COURSE

Ballybunion's Cashen Course, named after the river on its southern border, opened in 1984. It is one of only two Robert Trent Jones Irish courses, ten years older than Adare and the only links course among his more than four hundred designs worldwide. Trent Jones was seventy-five years old when he routed this eighteen over land at least as magnificent as Ballybunion Old occupies. Unfortunately, however, the Cashen Course was greeted with disdain. It was viewed as contrived, unplayable, unwalkable, even outrageous. When I first played it, in 1990, Sean Walsh accompanied me to the 1st tee, saying, "The players . . . shy away from it. It's too hard and too tiring. They just don't like it. Perhaps if it were somewhere else, fifty or a hundred miles away, anywhere but here, next door to the Old Course, perhaps then it would be appreciated. Anyway, you can hit right off. It's not crowded."

Admittedly, there were excesses—four or five satanically contoured greens, some fairways too constricted by the encroaching sand hills, several forced carries that the average player simply could not make, and changes in elevation that resulted in exhausting climbs and staggeringly difficult shots. Over the years a number of modifications have been made and there has been a growing acceptance of the course, but it is still not so enthusiastically admired as the Old. Nonetheless, in my judgment it is one of Ireland's dozen greatest courses, a bona fide masterpiece. I last played it early on a sunny Saturday morning of August 2004. I was alone and riding in a cart. There was no one ahead of me.

Against a par of 72, this layout is a mere 6,300 yards from all the way back, just over 6,000 yards from the regular markers, and 5,030 from the ladies' tees; you'll want to play from the back tees. The par 5s measure 522 yards, 605, 478, 487, and 479. The short holes are also unintimidating on the card: 154 yards, 155, 146, 210, and 164; the eight two-shotters range from 314 to 400. Clearly, muscle is not called for. Essential are good judgment, because the endless parade of ups and downs makes choosing the correct club a frustrating exercise for most visitors, and accuracy, because shots even a hair off line are severely punished in the deep and tangled marram grass that mantles the dunes. Since there are only fifty sand hazards, bunkering is not much of a problem. But deep hollows—indeed, abysses—lurk at every turn. And more often than not, the wind beleaguers us, whipping across the links at 15, 25, 35 miles per hour, sometimes leaving our swing in tatters even before we've reached the 5th or 6th hole.

The entire eighteen is routed through duneland, gentle sand hills

on the opening three holes—a down-and-up par 5, a down-and-up par 4, and a slightly up par 3—and massive sand hills the rest of the way. The result of all these minimountains, with the land everlastingly in motion, is a stunning collection of rollercoaster holes, of tees on summits and tees in chutes, of shelf greens and plateau greens and amphitheater greens, of fairways tumbling and dipping and surging along cloistered dune-encased valleys, of every kind of exciting and pressure-filled shot that natural golf at the sea can provide.

Having just plodded, hole by hole and very like blow by blow, through Ballybunion Old in these pages, I am not about to do it again on the Cashen. But perhaps I can be forgiven for citing a handful of my favorites here. At the lovely 154-yard 3rd, its green, with two small pot bunkers out front, is cocked up beckoningly in the dunes. The strand-side 378-yard 7th is steeply uphill on the second shot, to a green on the heights perilously perched within three or four paces of a long vertical drop to the

Opposite: Ballybunion Cashen Course, 15th. Above: 16th.

beach on the left. The 210-yard 12th plays knob to knob in the very depths of this topsy-turvy linksland. At the 13th, 395 yards, the drive through a channel of low dunes and out into a generous fairway discloses an utterly heart-stopping prospect: the green well below, on the far side of a deep swale and on a shelf jutting from a grand pyramidal dune. And the short par-5 15th, 487 yards, calls for a semiblind drive followed by a second shot launched down into a scrawny neck of fairway claustrophobically enclosed by lofty sand hills, the pitch climbing abruptly to a plateau green. Are there five more holes here this marvelous? At least five.

During the two hours the round took on that August Saturday morning, I saw few players on the course. As I came down the 18th, it struck me that by this time on that Saturday morning the first dozen or so holes on the Old Course must be aswarm with golfers. More than twenty years since its debut, the Cashen still has not found the following it gen-

uinely deserves. All right, it does take some getting used to. Liam Higgins, the head professional at Waterville for years (his brother Ted held the same post at Ballybunion), once said to me, "When I first played the new course [Cashen], I shot sixty-eight and sixty-nine to win going away. I vowed never to play it again because I was convinced it was the worst course I'd ever seen. . . . Then I did play it again, and I did a complete flip-flop. I now believe it must be the single greatest course in the world and that it puts the Old in the shade."

Liam may have gone too far, but he was heading in the right direction. The Cashen is not only a worthy companion to the Old, it is a great course in its own right. And when we scan the world of outstanding 36-hole complexes—Royal Melbourne, Royal Portrush, Turnberry, Sunningdale, Walton Heath, Winged Foot, Baltusrol, Oakland Hills, Oak Hill, World Woods, Olympic—there may be none that can equal Ballybunion.

For the game at Ballybunion, you'll probably want to find lodgings on the south side of the Shannon estuary. The **Marine Hotel** in Ballybunion is two minutes from the golf club. Though not luxurious, it is comfortable. There are thirteen guest rooms, each with views over the Shannon and the ruins of Fitzmaurice Castle. The restaurant specializes in seafood, everything from mussels and cockles to black sole and turbot, all of it cooked to order.

Some thirty minutes east of Ballybunion, just beyond Tarbert and on the south bank of the River Shannon, is one of the great country-house hotels of Ireland, **Glin Castle**, more than two hundred years old. With its superb decorated plasterwork and its equally superb collection of Irish furniture and paintings, it is one of the Republic's most important Heritage Houses, on a property held for over seven hundred years by the Fitzgerald family, hereditary Knights of Glin. There are fifteen accommodations, including four rated deluxe, some with four-poster beds, some with fireplaces, some with both. On our visit in 2004 we occupied the Castle Room, with two broad windows looking down on the Shannon, plus twenty-three framed antique prints in the bathroom, sixteen in the bedroom, and, also on the bedroom walls, twenty-two pink-and-gold porcelain plates. In no sense either opulent or museumlike, the room—like the house, full of beautiful things—looks irresistibly lived-in as it calls up times long past.

We had cocktails in the library, where a log fire was burning on this chilly late-August evening and the secret door in the bookcase was certainly indiscernible to us. Then on to dinner in the formal dining room—silver candelabra, heavily carved neo-Jacobean furniture, red walls covered with family portraits—where both food and service were superlative. We took our coffee at the fireplace in the drawing room, with its eighteenth- and nineteenth-century pieces, porcelains, and pictures.

Breakfast the following morning was so bountiful a business that it ruled out any thought of lunch. The Knight of Glin and Madam Fitzgerald, Desmond and Olda, who make their home in the castle, were on hand for what was a very agreeable gathering. They made it a point to spend time with each of their guests. Desmond Fitzgerald, perhaps in his midsixties, is the twenty-ninth and last Knight of Glin: He and his wife have three daughters, no sons. An authority on Irish and English antiques—indeed, what other great house in Ireland can match the Glin Castle collection?—he serves as a consultant to Christie's. Two or three times a year find him in the United States to scout antique furniture and furnishings, which he continues to acquire for the castle, despite a visitor's instinct to think that there is little or no room for anything more.

Aware of my golf writing, the knight spoke to me of his concern for the aesthetic aspect of the natural environment. For him, there were too many houses of doubtful attractiveness being built and too many new golf courses, as well, both a blight upon the landscape. I could detect no trace of an Irish accent in his speech; it seemed pure Oxbridge to me.

We left Glin Castle shortly after breakfast, heading down the driveway toward the estuary of the Shannon with a twinge of regret. When would we be fortunate enough to return? In our Irish wanderings, it is a nonpareil. Hugh Montgomery Massingberd, in *Great Houses of Ireland,* summed up this extraordinary haven perfectly: "Glin is surely the beau ideal of an Irish country house, grand yet intimate."

Below left: Glin Castle, exterior and rooms. Below: ruins along the shoreline, Ballybunion.

TRALEE

His name was Wallace "Wally" McGee, and he was gangly and ruddy complexioned, with wavy brown hair parted in the middle matinee-idol style. Our parish always presented a musical entertainment on St. Patrick's Day, down in the low-ceilinged basement auditorium with its stage that served as the one classroom for grades three and four. And in his reedy Irish tenor Wally would sing, perfectly on key, a certain achingly sentimental old ballad. I can never return to the capital town of County Kerry without being reminded of him and the closing lines of the song:

> Though lovely and fair as the rose of the summer,
> Yet 'twas not her beauty alone that won me;
> Oh no, 'twas the truth in her eye ever beaming
> That made me love Mary, the Rose of Tralee.

I suspect that the song is older than the Tralee Golf Club, which, less than forty minutes south of Ballybunion, was founded in 1896 and offered nine holes of golf at three successive locations in the town before moving out to Barrow, fifteen minutes west on Tralee Bay, when its new course—its first eighteen—opened in 1984. Arnold Palmer and Ed Seay designed it, their initial assignment in Europe.

ON THE COURSE

Routed over 163 acres, the course measures 6,905 yards from the back tees, 5,480 from the ladies' markers. Men usually play it at just over 6,200 yards; par is 71. Bunkering is light, a grand total of thirty-nine sand hazards, most of them small pots, and four holes are sand-free. The greens are nothing if not festive: all shapes and sizes, full of beautiful and testing contours, consistently smooth and swift.

Barrow, as people commonly refer to it, is a headlands course laid out on sand-based links terrain. Much of the first nine runs along the clifftops high above the sea. Ireland's second-highest peak, Mount Brandon, is the backcloth. To the north, Kerry Head, a long promontory on the far

side of the water, is in view for almost the entire round. For sheer visual exaltation at the sea, Barrow measures up to County Down, Portstewart, Rosses Point, and Rosapenna.

The first nine, routed over erstwhile pastureland, is open, exposed, windswept. Palmer and Seay waste no time leading us away from the clubhouse to the cliff edge, which is where they have sited the green on this down-and-up 370-yard opener. The 550-yard 2nd, which calls up the 4th at Nefyn & District, in North Wales, bends left to right, high above the beach, toward a green with a pair of bunkers at the left. The beach here, called the Long Strand, is where David Lean (*Lawrence of Arabia, Dr. Zhivago*) filmed some of the epic scenes for *Ryan's Daughter,* in 1968.

The 3rd measures 158 yards from the white tees, tucked comfortably left, and 194 yards from the blue tees, spotted uncomfortably right, beside the cliff edge and calling for a 160-yard carry over the rocks and the

Opposite: Tralee, 3rd.
Above: 2nd.

oft-angry sea far below. The sensible decision from either white or blue is to aim left, on the thirteenth-century stone gun turret just down the slope at the left rear of the green. Local lore has it that Brendan the Navigator sailed from here to America a thousand years before Columbus.

Two other holes on the first nine are not easily forgotten. The 7th is a classic 150-yarder, the tee a scrap of turf perched above an inlet, the long, narrow green, with pot bunkers right and left, sited teasingly in a dell of low dunes. As for the 390-yard 8th, surely it is the finest hole on the first nine, defying us to risk a driver into a scarcely visible fairway that curves right to left along the cliff top every foot of the way, often disclosing errant golf balls on the beach far below.

In a sense, the first half is a warmup for the rollicking second half, which is one of Ireland's great seaside nines. Here, we are abroad in a convulsively wild stretch of mountainous sand hills cloaked in the long and throttling rough grasses. There are those who insist that this area was never meant to host golf holes. Called the Warren—we do run into hares here

TRALEE, SPRINGBOARD TO THE DINGLE PENINSULA

- Play the terrific **Tralee links**, its second half one of Ireland's most adventurous seaside nines.

- Have lunch in the **clubhouse's glass-walled lounge**, commanding the links, the sea, and the framing promontories.

- If you have time, drive far out on the beautiful **Dingle Peninsula** and play Europe's most westerly golf course, **Ceann Sibeal**.

- Come back from Dingle via vertiginous **Connor Pass**, one of the most dramatic moments in Irish motoring.

- Spend the night at comfortable **Brook Manor Lodge**, with its grand views over the countryside.

- Enjoy a delicious seafood dinner at family-run **West End Restaurant**.

from time to time—it possesses startling elevation changes, to say nothing of greens on all-but-inaccessible plateaus. Often must our drive traverse violently broken ground en route to constricted, crumpled fairways. Shots to the green are sometimes imperiled by treacherous falloffs that end not simply in hollows but in abysses. This is golf as high adventure.

The plateau green on the down-and-up 405-yard 10th leads us into the primitive dunescape that is the Warren. At the 560-yard 11th, Palmer and Seay demonstrate their penchant for double doglegs (remember the K Club) and their readiness to ascend to the heavens. This exhaustingly steep climb—up, up, up, with the second shot blind and only the sky backdropping the green—must, on days when the wind is in our face, play at least 700 yards. It can be a legitimate four-shotter!

Time now for a 180-degree turn and the course's number one stroke hole, the great 440-yard 12th. The near-vertical downhill drive is blind, a low stone wall close on the left, unplayable bracken and massive dunes on the right. The pitilessly long second shot plays boldly uphill, the fairway choked almost to extinction by bracken. Chasms short, left, and right claim the ball if our all-out swing from a demanding downhill lie should fail to scale the heights on which the smallish table-top green is set. This is an audacious and astonishing piece of business, unlike any other two-shotter in my experience.

The holes that follow keep the pressure on. The brilliant 150-yard 13th entails more cavernous crossing, this time to an immense amphitheater green. From a lofty tee on the 14th, 390 yards, we strike out over a dip to a fairway on the opposing hill, where our second shot is complicated

Opposite, left: Tralee, 8th; right: 12th. Below: 15th.

by a right-hand shoulder of dune at the green. On the short par-4 15th, the drive is from another elevated tee down to a generous patch of fairway in the sand hills, followed by an approach that, difficult to judge, rises to a hidden green almost completely ringed by dunes. The 165-yard 16th, playing out to sea, presents a spectacularly sited green barely clinging to the cliff edge above the beach on the right, the green itself the only haven. From the tee, sheltered in the dunes, a magnificent panorama unfolds: the bay and the notorious rocks on which several trading vessels were dashed over the years. The hole is called Shipwreck, and the slightest push will prove calamitous to the golfer.

As for the short par-4 17th, we face a chaotically heaving fairway that is extremely elusive from the elevated tee, a fairway that turns sharply right just beyond a mighty sand hill in order to reveal the green

high above us. Neither Seay nor Palmer would claim that this hole, chosen for the 500 *World's Greatest* book, falls naturally on the land.

At 443 yards, the last half of it smoothly uphill and with a bunker squarely in front of the green, the 18th—out on the open ground over which the first ten holes are routed—is rigorous in a perfectly straightforward fashion. There is nothing about it to suggest the drama and the danger of the warren.

Don't fail to have lunch or at least a refreshment in the glass-walled lounge of the clubhouse. From this expansive room you can take it all in: the links, the sweep of the Dingle Peninsula across the sea to the south, to the north Kerry Head, Ballyheigue, Banna, and Carrahane. Is it possible that for the avid golfer the Rose of Tralee is not Mary but Barrow?

Above: Tralee, 16th.
Opposite: 17th.

CEANN SIBEAL

Out on the tip of the Dingle Peninsula, a good fifteen miles beyond Dingle Town, at Sybil Head, is the most westerly golf course in Europe. Eddie Hackett laid out the Ceann Sibeal first nine in 1970, on his usual meager budget. In 1990 Christy O'Connor Jr., working with a more generous allotment, added a second nine.

The wide-open layout has little in the way of dunes or elevation changes. All of it is at a considerable remove from the sea. The par-72 course can measure as long as 6,650 yards, but it is usually played at about 6,200 yards by the men, 5,600 by the ladies. The linksland turf is quite good, and a narrow stream menaces the shot seven or eight times.

The first nine begins and ends with solid par 4s. Our approach on the 370-yard opener must carry the stream. The lovely 425-yard 9th is routed over undulating ground to a slightly elevated plateau green beneath the clubhouse windows. The second nine begins with an outstanding hole, a 185-yarder with a minimally raised green that is elongated and shapely, adroitly bunkered, and, for the most part, concealed beyond some mounding. The 11th and 13th, two good dogleg par 5s, take much of their character from the stream. On the 13th, which swings sharply right, water imperils both the drive and the pitch. At the beguiling 371-yard 16th, which moves slightly downhill and bends right, the ubiquitous stream must be carried on our approach.

The 506-yard finishing hole is the strongest hole on the course. The drive calls for a stout forced carry over rough country. Bunkers frame the landing area of the drive, the second shot, and the pitch to the green, the latter one of a number of lively putting surfaces on the second nine.

Ceann Sibeal is by no means a must-play, but it has some solid holes. And its views to the Blasket Islands in the south and Mount Brandon in the north are stirring.

Left: Ceann Sibeal, 2nd.
Right: 4th.

In Tralee town, some twenty minutes' drive from the golf club, and set in beautifully landscaped gardens, is the fifty-eight-room **Meadowlands Hotel**. Attractively furnished in traditional fashion, it offers three levels of accommodation: standard, executive, and suites (king-size bed, steam shower, and Jacuzzi, separate sitting room with fireplace). **Johnny Franks Bar,** on two floors, is noted for its excellent pub food (try the delicious braised lamb shank with scallion mash). On many nights live music is presented here, a particular treat when Irish folk songs are the choice. The fare in the main dining room benefits considerably from the fact that the hotel proprietor, Paddy O'Mahony, operates his own fishing boats and is thus able to put on the table seafood and shellfish that are truly "fresh caught."

A bit closer to the golf club is **Brook Manor Lodge,** on the Fenit Road in the captivating countryside. This B&B is one of only two four-star luxury guest houses in the Tralee district. Vincent and Margaret O'Sullivan purvey comfort and hospitality in equal measure. The sunny, spacious bedrooms are individually designed, and the communal living room features a peat fire. The cooked breakfast is such a hearty meal that you wonder whether you'll even be bothered with lunch. You can elect to eat in either the pretty dining room or the bright conservatory, a virtually all-glass enclosure that affords spectacular views of the nearby Slieve Mish mountains.

For dinner, a short drive down the road will bring you to the **West End Restaurant,** in tiny Fenit. It's an unpretentious seafood spot (no tablecloths). The proprietors, Dan and Madeline O'Keeffe (how about that double-F spelling?), are also the host and hostess, and the head chef is their son Bryan. The O'Keeffe family has been in business here since 1885. I'm recalling an exchange with our young waitress, whom I took to be an unworldly local colleen not yet twenty. When she lit the candle on our table, I said amiably, "Ah, a light goes on in Fenit." To which she dryly replied with the merest trace of an acknowledging smile, "How romantic." The West End wins no prize for ambience—it is bright and borders on noisy—but the welcome is warm and the cooking is terrific.

KILLARNEY

I was bent on beginning this unit with two of what Madison Avenue calls "unique selling propositions": (1) Killarney is Ireland's only golf and fishing club, and (2) Killarney is Ireland's only club with three eighteen-hole courses. Neither claim, put that baldly, holds water. Not thirty-five miles from Killarney is the Castlegregory Golf & Fishing Club. And up at the top of the "Emerald Isle" is Portstewart, with its three eighteens. Still, my instinct was not a bad one, for Castlegregory has only nine holes and Portstewart's Old Course measures a mere 4,730 yards against a par of 64. So where does all this leave Killarney today? Well, it can fairly be stated that it is Ireland's only golf and fishing club with three full-length eighteens. And that it is about thirty minutes southeast of Tralee, via the N22.

A half dozen skiffs and dinghies at the club await those who would cast a line on Lough Leane, but it's rare to see anyone so inclined. No, the lure here is golf. Two of the three courses are well known to American golfers, Killeen and Mahony's Point. Both touch the very shores of the largest and perhaps loveliest of the lakes of Killarney. Lough Leane, dotted with thirty islets, sparkles against a mountainous backdrop that metamorphoses from the forest green of wooded slopes near the water's edge through the soft rust brown of bracken to a suggestion of purple in the barren higher reaches. It is a paradisiacal scene, and never more bewitching than when, on a sunny day, white clouds dreamily wreath the highest peaks. This is one of the most beautiful settings in the world of inland golf, less dramatic than Banff or Jackson Hole or Crans sur Sierre, but magical nonetheless. The third eighteen, called Lackabane, is well away from Lough Leane and the other Killarney lakes, with the result that its setting is considerably less idyllic.

Golf has been played in Killarney since 1891 but for the first forty-eight years on a simple nine-hole course. In 1939, on land bordering Lough Leane, an eighteen opened. Largely the work of Sir Guy Campbell, it also benefited from the input of Lord Castlerosse, an enthusiastic golfer who, as it happened, was also a gossip columnist for one of the big-circulation London dailies. Castlerosse made a number of imaginative alterations to the Campbell layout, in the process improving the eighteen

markedly. But he could be eccentric, as witness his effort to gain publicity for the new course by planting trees in the middle of two greens! In 1964 Shell's *Wonderful World of Golf* pitted Al Geiberger against Joe Carr here (the trees were long gone from the greens), with Gene Sarazen handling the color commentary and declaring, "Never in forty-two years of golf have I seen such a beautiful course."

In 1969 Fred Hawtree was commissioned to lay out eighteen additional holes. Old and new holes were intermingled in 1971 to produce what could be called two new courses: Mahony's Point and Killeen.

ON THE MAHONY'S POINT COURSE

Just over 6,400 yards from the white tees, Mahony's Point gets under way with an essentially level 350-yarder that finds the fairway expansive and the green (five bunkers at the right) open across the front. But the next two holes, a rising 430-yarder curving right, sand bracketing the driving area, and a 440-yarder edging left and falling modestly, are tough and terrific. The holes that follow on the outbound nine, including a couple of one-shotters over dips, are quite manageable from the standpoint of hitting. Putting, however, is another matter on these vigorously contoured greens, which are often immense.

The second nine begins with a sharp dogleg-right par 4 that presents a holly tree smack in the middle of the fairway about a hundred yards short of the green (shades of Lord Castlerosse). Of the remaining holes, four are particularly good. Length (453 yards) and a triple-tier green on a little plateau combine to make the par-4 11th the number one stroke hole. The 13th and 16th, two short par 5s that don't look like much on the card, actually have spunk. Both require a stream to be carried on the long second shot. A knob of a green, well above us and with slick falloffs all around, complicates the pitch on 13. The 16th, downhill to a green just short of Lough Leane, offers a vista of lake and mountain that is jaw-droppingly beautiful. No wonder the hole is called Heaven's Reflex.

The level and straightaway 375-yard 17th, with the lakeshore along the right, brings us to what may well be the most photographed hole in Irish golf. The 18th is a 180-yarder with an inlet of the lake skirting the entire right side of the hole. The shot is actually not intimidating, but with the spacious green in a glade of rhododendrons and pines at the water's edge, the hole is an indelible reminder of the aesthetic charms of Mahony's Point, which ranks eightieth in *Golf World*'s most recent listing of the British Isles's top hundred.

ON THE KILLEEN COURSE

Eddie Hackett and the beloved Dr. Billy O'Sullivan (Killarney member Dr. Billy provided the club with its single most treasured moment when he won the Irish Open Amateur right here, in 1949) extensively revised the Killeen course in the 1980s. It was toughened even further in preparation for the Irish Open, serving as the venue for this championship in 1991 and 1992. In 1996 it was the site of the Curtis Cup Match, which saw Great Britain and Ireland win easily, 11½–6½. Among the U.S. players were Christie Kerr, Kelli Kuehne, and Carol Semple Thompson, who was making the ninth of her record-setting twelve appearances in the biennial competition.

Killeen measures 7,124 yards from the championship tees, just under 6,200 from the daily markers, and 5,420 from the ladies' tees. It has somewhat less in the way of elevation changes than Mahony's Point, and its fairways are noticeably narrower.

Below, left: Killarney Killeen Course, 3rd; right: 18th. Opposite: 10th.

While Mahony's Point saves Lough Leane for last (16, 17, 18) Killeen begins with it (1, 3, 4) and returns to it momentarily at the 10th green. The pretty opening hole, 335 yards, doglegs sharply to the right around an inlet of the lake, with the green tight to the water. The next three holes continue in the same general direction, with the 180-yard 3rd, often played into the breeze, calling for a long iron or 7-metal across a little corner of the lake.

The par-4 5th, bending strongly right, bushes and trees on both sides, is, at 465 yards, with its low-plateau green defended by sand at the right front and falloffs all around, a bona fide killer. It is also the number one stroke hole.

There is more heavy breathing at the 160-yard 6th (204 from the tips), thanks to a narrow, water-filled moat all but encircling the gently raised crown green. Water off the tee or at the green menaces the shot on the next four holes. The rough is deceptively low and choking; lost balls are not a problem, but lost strokes are.

The 13th at Killeen is probably the single best hole of the thirty-six here at Lough Leane. Measuring 430 yards from the white tees, it calls

for a drive to a stingy fairway, followed by a full-blooded second over a rough dip (the fairway has temporarily vanished) with a stream at the bottom. The raised green, minimally bunkered right and short left, awaits on the far slope. Hitting this green in regulation calls for a perfect blend, on both swings, of power and precision.

Seventeen and 18, both two-shotters, provide a grand finale. In the 1992 Irish Open, the defending champion, Nick Faldo, looked likely to relinquish the crown when he arrived at this hole late Sunday afternoon two strokes adrift of the leader, South Africa's Wayne Wester. But Wester, determined to be up on the steeply climbing second shot, knocked his short iron over the plateau green and bogeyed the hole. Now Faldo was only a stroke behind.

Measuring 430 yards from the regular markers and 450 from the tips, the 18th begins on a high tee that commands the panorama of lake and mountain. Water short and left of the green threatens the weak or pulled second shot. Wester played the hole well for a 4. Following a very

long drive, Faldo fired an 8-iron to 10 feet, then holed the putt to force a tie. On the fourth hole of sudden death, which turned out to be the 17th, Wester again failed to put his second shot (not to mention his third) on the inhospitable knob of a green, and Faldo won his second straight Irish Open. Killeen was ninety-ninth in *Golf World*'s most recent ranking of the top hundred courses in the British Isles.

ON THE LACKABANE COURSE

The Lackabane Course, which is the handiwork of Donald Steel and his chief associate, Tom Mackenzie, opened in 2000. Most of it is laid out on gently rolling terrain at the base of a high ridge. There is no sign of Lough Leane and almost no sign of the mountains.

But this is a layout with quite a bit going on. Specifically, there are seven holes where water endangers the shot and nine where out-of-bounds is a distinct possibility. Not to mention trees, gorse, and mounds. Now, all of this is not to suggest that there is unrelieved pressure on the

swing. But the careless play, or the daring shot that doesn't come off, or the truly wayward stroke—these will be costly.

Lackabane is long from all the way back, 7,065 yards. The daily markers add up to just under 6,200 yards; from the ladies' tees, it's 5,620 yards. The routing plan is attractively unpredictable, bunkering is light, greens are of good size and natural, and the fescue rough is not too punishing.

Among the best holes are a couple of frisky, short two-shotters and a couple of nifty par 5s. As it happens, water is the story on all four of them. The par 4s are cousins, each with two water hazards and mildly raised tees. On the 250-yard 3rd, a free-form lagoon on the left and a serpentine burn crossing the fairway conspire to jeopardize the drive; there is no bailout area. There is no margin for error on the 340-yard 12th, either, where the tee shot must avoid a pond at the left and a burn crossing the fairway on the diagonal and then bordering both the fairway and the green on the right. The two long holes are beauties. The 500-yard 11th, from an elevated tee, is a risk–reward double dogleg bending left around a pond that challenges us to carry it in order to set up a likely birdie. The 17th, only 480 yards, is straightaway, a burn crossing the fairway at 200 yards, plus three bunkers that effectively add up to one cross bunker, requiring a healthy carry on the second shot. Steel and Mackenzie used this cross-bunkering scheme at Peter de Savary's Carnegie Abbey, in Newport, Rhode Island, and Colin Montgomerie called on it once at Carton House. Lackabane is not a great course, but, with strategic demands that require sound thinking and hitting, it is a good one.

NEARBY COURSES

Ten minutes down the road and adjacent to the well-known shop at the Gap of Dunloe (tweeds, linens, sheepskin rugs, Waterford crystal, blackthorn walking sticks, shillelaghs, and more) is a nine-hole layout, called **Dunloe Golf Course** and a driving range. The course—2,500 yards long, par 34, and on less than forty acres—is a charmer. It is varied, it has some attractive ups and downs, and it is more testing than you would expect. It also affords splendid views of Lough Leane and the mountains, including Carrantuohill itself, the highest peak (3,414 feet) in Ireland. As for just when this nine might prove useful to an American golfer, perhaps late on his day of arrival in Ireland, after landing at Shannon, driving to Killarney, napping, and awakening that afternoon with an unquenchable thirst not for a Jameson's or a Bushmills or a Guinness but for a little golf.

Five miles due east of Killarney and routed over gently rolling pastureland is the **Beaufort Golf Club**'s course, which I've played just once, in 1995, shortly before the official opening. My companion was Arthur Spring, M.D., its architect, who looked to be about fifty then and who had been one of Ireland's best amateurs for nearly thirty years. On this cloudy and chilly morning, the willowy Dr. Spring, bundled up in a bulky, thigh-length kapok jacket and wielding borrowed clubs, gave a convincing demonstration of how his golf holes should be played: Each approach shot—a 210-yard 3-iron, a 165-yard 6-iron, a 110-yard pitching edge, and the like—was hit high and with a suggestion of draw, finishing within a 20-foot radius of the flagstick. A native of Tralee who had earned his M.D. at Cork University in 1969, he practiced medicine in Tralee for the next twenty years. During this time he had the chance to observe the construction of the Palmer-Seay course at Barrow and the Trent Jones course at Ballybunion. When the opportunity arose to lay out nine holes

Opposite: Killarney
Lackabane Course, 13th.
Above: Dooks, 4th.

Dooks, 11th.

in the dunes on the Dingle Peninsula for that *other* golf and fishing club, Castlegregory, he seized it and gave up healing the sick. A modern-day Dr. Alister MacKenzie, he has now designed a dozen or so courses.

Beaufort measures 6,620 yards from the back tees, just under 6,200 from the regular markers, and 5,300 from the ladies' tees; par is 71. Bunkering is moderate, there is very little water, and the narrowish fairways are corseted by thick marram grass. Among the especially good holes on the first nine are the falling 170-yard 2nd, where the large green, running diagonally across the line of the shot, actually plays small; the 330-yard 5th, a dogleg right with an exacting pitch to an elevated green; and the lovely 173-yard 8th, where the shot is hit out of a spinney of old oaks to a green in the open defined by bunkers and mounding.

The land must be much as the architect found it—much but not entirely. On the second nine, Dr. Spring did put a bulldozer to work, with the result that the course becomes more testing and more adventurous, the greens more creatively contoured. The 400-yard 16th boasts a triple-tier green that is 55 yards deep but only 16 yards wide. Particularly memorable on this nine are the par-5 12th, the last half of it played along a narrow, mound-framed corridor that creates a demanding second shot;

the romantic 165-yard 13th, with a tall, graceful fragment of 14th-century Castle Core off to the left of the green; and the 360-yard 15th, where our drive must carry a corner of a man-made lake to a fairway swinging right.

About twelve miles southeast of Beaufort and on the fabled Ring of Kerry (N70) as it heads down the Inveragh Peninsula is the village of Glenbeigh and **Dooks Golf Club**. The game has been played here since 1889. This is authentic links golf, and it comes with enthralling views of Dingle Bay, Inch Island, and MacGillycuddy's Reeks. For more than seventy years, Dooks was a nine-hole layout until, in 1967, the members set about building a second nine on their own. Bunkering is very light. Gorse, which is much in sight, is not much in play. Fairways heave and tumble. Greens, inclined to be small, are often sited on plateaus; holding them in the brisk breeze requires sensitivity to the bump-and-run seaside game.

The course, which now measures 6,150 yards against a par of 70, is studded with appealing holes. The 394-yard 6th doglegs left into a concealed fairway, then strikes out spiritedly uphill. At the 531-yard 11th, with the shore close beside it on the left, the hole curves right just where we would like to place our second shot, and a steep bank in front of the green renders our third shot blind. The small green on the uphill 150-yard 15th is exotically wrinkled and, as such, a shock. Equally shocking is the six-foot-deep barrier ditch that extends across the fairway some 30 yards short of the green on the 535-yard 18th, leaving the putting surface hidden in a punch bowl. This curious earthworks calls up trench warfare in the Great War and a foolhardy lieutenant shouting "Over the top, boys!"

A number of years ago I met Joe O'Dwyer, who had been captain of the club in its hundredth-anniversary year. I told him how much I enjoyed the course, particularly its plateau greens.

"Ah," he said, "I did the ninth green. And if you three-putted, you can blame me for it. . . . A number of us took the responsibility for returfing the greens, each man to handle one green. I took the ninth. A good friend of mine volunteered for the eighth. Now, with nine being a one-shotter, the eighth green happens to be fairly close by. Well, he thought nothing of hauling new turf all the way out to the eighth green to pile it up there for the creation of a grand new putting surface. And night after night—we worked mostly in the evenings—when he had gone, I would slip over to the eighth and help myself to some of that marvelous sod of his and lay it down on the ninth. So we got two very good greens in a row, eight and nine"—he was laughing now at the memory of it—"thanks to him. I don't think he ever knew."

LODGING AND DINING

Other than Dublin itself, Killarney is the most visited place in Ireland, so there are accommodations to suit every pocketbook:

- Quite near the golf and fishing club is **Killeen House**, a fifteen-room inn whose rooms incline to be small, but whose cooking is excellent.

- The **Great Southern**, a Killarney tradition going back more than 150 years, is a 180-room four-star hotel set in thirty-six acres of gardens, downtown and within an easy walk of everything (except golf courses). It offers not only Old World dignity and refinement but a leisure center with an indoor heated swimming pool, sauna and steam room, Jacuzzi and fitness facility, and a couple of tennis courts. There are two restaurants, the main dining room with its period architectural details and continental menu, and the intimate **Malton Room**, where the emphasis is on sophisticated French cuisine.

- The **Europe** is a five-star hotel on Lough Leane, its beautiful gardens running down to the water. Four out of five of the hotel's two hundred accommodations, which include a number of suites, overlook the lake, most of them from private balconies or terraces. Irish dishes—there are many seafood choices—as well as international cuisine are served in the **Panorama**. Afternoon tea is a particular pleasure when taken in the Lake View Room. The Europe is a full-facilities hotel: Olympic-size indoor heated pool, sauna with cold-water plunge pool, solarium, fitness gym, indoor tennis, stables. And next door is the golf and fishing club.

Not fifteen miles west of Killarney and only three or four miles from Dooks Golf Club is gemlike Caragh Lake, seven miles long, ringed by heavily wooded slopes, and backdropped in the east by the mountains of MacGillycuddy's Reeks. Two small and extremely attractive hotels are here:

- **Caragh Lodge** is a mid-Victorian country house secluded on high ground in award-winning gardens— palm trees, rhododendrons, azaleas, magnolias, camellias, and countless rare subtropical shrubs— that lead down to the lake shore. This is a four-star guest house with fifteen accommodations, seven of them garden rooms, charmingly decorated in antiques and chintz. The cooking is simple and superb, with vegetables fresh from the kitchen garden.

- Even higher above the shimmering lake is **Hotel Ard Na Sidhe** ("Hill of the Fairies"), a graceful beige-gray stone house dating to 1880. Antiques are featured in this stately but nonetheless inviting house with its fireplaces in the drawing room, study, and dining room. The superior cooking relies largely on local ingredients such as salmon, trout, and Kerry lamb. A couple of the twenty guest rooms, all individually furnished in traditional fashion, are quite small, though each has a king-size bed. Views of the lake beyond

Muckross House and other sights of Killarney town.

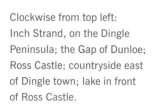

Clockwise from top left:
Inch Strand, on the Dingle
Peninsula; the Gap of Dunloe;
Ross Castle; countryside east
of Dingle town; lake in front
of Ross Castle.

the trees and far below are not easily come by from either the bedrooms or the public spaces, unless you are here in the off-season, when the leaves have fallen. It is the terraces—one grass, one paved—that offer the most rewarding views, and afternoon tea at the end of the grass terrace on a pretty day is a delight. You may want to follow it with a walk through the hillside gardens, twice winner of the National Gardens Competition. Among the many notable moments are the rock garden (on several levels), formal and informal gardens with some surprising tropical plants such as bamboo, walled gardens with a fetching little stream meandering through them, and even a carefully mowed lawn running all the way down to the lake. Ard Na Sidhe, so tranquil and at one with nature, is a special place.

The town of Killarney is not picturesque (the same can be said of Tralee). We do not seek it out for aesthetic, artistic, antique, or architectural appeal. But it does attract shoppers, and there is a youthful crowd to be seen after dark in the pubs (the **Laurels** is one, on a little lane off the High Street), where singing, professional or amateur, is a large part of the appeal. **Gaby's**, a fish restaurant on Killarney's High Street, and the **Cooperage**, a bar and restaurant on Old Market Lane, are quite popular.

Most of the sightseeing is in the environs. Immediately outside Killarney is Aghadoe Heights, which presents even more captivating panoramas of the lake-and-mountain scenery than do the Mahony's Point and Killeen courses, if you can believe it; Ross Castle, on Lough Leane, with its carefully restored seventeenth-century interior; Muckross House, an Elizabethan-style manor with fifty acres of gardens; and the Gap of Dunloe, a riveting mountain defile.

From either Tralee or Killarney, the wild and extravagantly beautiful Dingle Peninsula is within easy reach. We elect to take the low road out, along the southern coast. This is farming and grazing land, much of it gently rolling, silent, utterly devoid of people for long stretches. On the N86 we pass through tiny Inch (appropriately named) and Annascaul and Lispole and keep rolling along out to Dingle town, a thriving fishing port and a

magnet for tourists. Pastel-colored houses step up the steep streets leading from the harbor. Many pubs—the pub-to-people ratio here is said to be the highest in Ireland—provide traditional Irish music. Gaelic seems to be spoken by all the locals (is English the second language?) in what is a noted center for pottery and weaving. Among several very good restaurants are **Doyle's Seafood Bar** and **Aherne's Seafood Bar**, the latter with twelve nicely appointed bedrooms.

Beyond Dingle town the countryside gets hillier, and the Blasket Islands come into view as the road carries on toward Slea Head, another location used by David Lean in filming *Ryan's Daughter*. Close beside this narrow, twisting, lofty byway are the unique stone cells, shaped like beehives, that monks built for meditation more than twelve hundred years ago. The cliffs are sheer and high, the sea churning on the rocks and boiling up onto the strand. In a field just beyond Milltown, at the hamlet of Ballynana, stands the Oratory of Gallarus. Larger than the beehive-shape cells and probably built in the eighth century, it may well be the best-preserved early place of Christian prayer in Ireland. Twenty feet long, seventeen feet wide, and fifteen feet high, it is of dry-stone construction and is very nearly perfect. One small semicircular window and a narrow doorway provide light. For a community of monks, this was the place to pray together.

To leave the peninsula, I urge you to take the high road, the R560, out of Dingle town and north to Kilcummin. Inordinately hilly, this narrow, lightly traveled road, with its twists and elbows, its long dips into lonely glens and its abrupt climbs back out of them, seems almost whimsical, aimless. You are now heading toward Connor Pass. The ascent is dramatic, even tense, with the valley on the right slipping slowly away beneath you as the car labors to gain the pass. And then, quite suddenly, you are there. The road has crested and you have broken through the mountains. You have not scaled the peaks; this is a pass, a cut through them, though you had to climb a long way to reach it. And now you are poised, as on a high dive, gazing directly down on a pale green valley floor some fifteen hundred feet below and stretching away toward the north as far as the eye can see. There is nothing in sight but the eternal land—no cottages, no cattle, no sheep, and per-

haps, if you are lucky, not even another car. It is overpowering—simple and majestic and beautiful.

The descent is even more precipitous than the climb. You keep a firm foot on the brake all the way down, and much of the way you remain in low gear. Finally you bottom out on the valley floor and glide away northeast on the only road there is, through Kilcummin and Stradbally, on to Tralee and, some thirty minutes south on the N22, to Killarney. The Connor Pass run has cost you no more than half an hour, and you will remember it forever.

Top row, from left: Dingle Peninsula coastline; Ballyferrier. Middle row: beehive hut; a pub meal; the coast near Slea Head. Bottom: County Kerry's countryside.

WATERVILLE

The Ring of Kerry is a mixed blessing. Scenically, this road is a treasure—the sea, the jagged coastline, the hills, the sheer nonstop delight of it. But in season the two-lane N70 can also be slow and heavily traveled and maddening. Killarney to Waterville, only fifty miles, can take two hours.

The Waterville Golf Links, ranked twenty-first by *Golf World* among the top hundred courses in the British Isles, sits on a sand hills–dotted peninsula bound by the combers of Ballinskelligs Bay and the estuary of the river Inny. This is ideal linksland, and golf was first played here, on a rudimentary nine, in the 1880s, when the workers in the transatlantic cable station on nearby Valentine Island discovered entirely natural golf holes just waiting in the dunes.

In 1970 John A. Mulcahy, a successful New York businessman and a member at Winged Foot, who was born in Ireland and emigrated to America at the age of eighteen, returned to his native land and acquired the by then near-derelict Waterville nine, plus an additional parcel of linksland and Waterville House. He hired Eddie Hackett to collaborate with him in laying out an eighteen. Mulcahy himself, possessing a sound instinct for what constitutes a good golf hole, contributed much to the design, with the result that the attribution generally reads "Eddie Hackett/John A. Mulcahy." The new links soon took its place among Ireland's six or seven greatest courses. Almost 7,200 yards from the tips, it could challenge the game's best players.

ON THE COURSE

I remember coming to Waterville for the second time, in 1980. John Mulcahy, then seventy-four, walked the 2nd and 3rd holes with me and my two playing companions, explaining changes he had recently made in order to toughen them. That evening, at Waterville House, eight of us joined him for cocktails. He talked about having been a member at Knollwood, in the New York City suburb of Elmsford, where Willie Turnesa was also a member and Turnesa's brother Mike was head professional for more than forty years, beginning in 1943. Willie won the U.S. Amateur in 1938 and 1948 and

the British Amateur in 1947. Mike lost in the final round of the PGA twice, to Snead in 1942 and to Hogan in 1948. The other five brothers, all professionals (Jim won the PGA in 1952; Joe was runner-up in the U.S. Open in 1926 and the PGA in 1927) would assemble on the practice tee at Knollwood every Friday in the late afternoon to join Mike and Willie in hitting shots and fine-tuning their swings. According to John Mulcahy, plenty in the way of useful swing tips was bandied about. Then Mulcahy would take the seven Turnesas to dinner at a nearby Italian restaurant. More golf talk there, but anecdotal rather than instructional.

On hand that evening at Waterville House was a very elderly man who rarely participated in the conversation. Father Lynch, a Jesuit, formerly headed the physics department at Fordham University, where he had taught two of John Mulcahy's sons. He was eighty-six years old, stooped, slow, rheumy-eyed, but still keen of mind. He was wearing capacious black trousers, a dark blue sweater vest with a Fordham logo, and a Roman collar. For fifteen years he had been accompanying John Mulcahy to Waterville for the summer, though he himself did not play golf. Simply to be in Ireland was what counted. The warmth of their friendship was tellingly illustrated in our host's simple words about a key element in the daily regimen: "Every day Father Lynch says Mass here at the house, and I'm his altar boy." Then he added with a smile, "We make do all right together, the two of us."

In 2002 (with John Mulcahy now gone), the Waterville board of governors, having decided to add more contouring and test to the relatively flat first nine, commissioned Tom Fazio to undertake the changes. Long regarded as one of the world's two or three top golf architects, Fazio was especially admired for the beauty of his layouts. His golf holes are often little short of luscious. Some observers worried that he would beautify Waterville, that the simple, raw, natural charm of the linksland would sprout an artificial prettiness, as it were. This concern turned out to be unwarranted. Fazio's modifications were not simply sensitive and tasteful, they were marvelously right, with the result that this great course is noticeably greater. He created two entirely new holes (the 6th and 7th), and he radically altered five others.

Opposite: Waterville, 6th.

Now there is not a weak or prosaic moment on the course, which measures 7,309 yards from the tips, 6,781 yards from the middle tees, 6,237 from the daily markers, and 5,276 from the ladies' tees. Said Fazio at the completion of his task: "The overall objective was to enhance all the areas of the golf course that were not visually strong or dramatic in order to blend them into the natural dune settings. Now . . . you'll get that rush you expect from a great links on every hole."

Fazio's expertise is evident from the outset. On the 1st, 375 yards from the daily markers, 430 from the back tees, he fashioned low mounding along the left (covered with marram grass) to give the hole much needed definition and to separate it from the practice ground. The four Hackett bunkers that threatened the drive and the two at the green have been rebuilt, and the burn and boundary running along the right are a touch more in play than they were. A once dull hole now demands our respect.

At the 2nd, just under 400 yards from the regular tees, a series of low dunes have materialized, courtesy of Fazio's bulldozer, to line the left side of the hole; the number of bunkers that imperil the drive has been doubled (six now); the green has been reconstructed and moved left to bring the new dunes into play. The estuary of the Inny is a fetching backdrop for the green.

The two new holes are superb; the 6th, a downhill one-shotter (194 yards, 166, 134) through a dune-framed valley with a burn along the right, and the 7th, a 380-yarder bending gently right as it rises, perfectly framed by dunes at the left and a deep burn at the right, the angled green defended by sand and little falloffs. Both holes, in harmony with their surroundings, look as though they've been here for years.

Right: Waterville, 7th.

REMOTE, WINDSWEPT, WONDERFUL

- Play **Waterville**, not only a great links but also perhaps a perfect one.

- Keep **Payne Stewart** in mind here—the locals vow never to forget him.

- Stay at **Waterville House**, an exquisite seaside B&B with salmon fishing that beguiled Tiger Woods for hours.

- Dine at the **Butler Arms Hotel**, where the cooking and the ambience are both outstanding.

- Visit the rebuilt pre-Famine village of **Cill Rialaig**.

Waterville's second nine is of such distinction that it can be compared with the second nine on Ballybunion Old, which is the gold standard. What hole here is not at least arguably great as we foray into the tall, shaggy sand hills? The classic and merciless 10th, 405 yards from the daily markers, 475 from the tips, its sand-free green secluded in a dell of dunes, is followed by Tranquility, one of the 500 *World's Greatest*, a short par 5 (play it at 467, 477, or 506) that curves gracefully along a dune-framed corridor, the undulating fairway shrinking or expanding as the sand hills alternately bite into it or draw back. A dip just short of the green teases us on the little pitch. Gary Player has said that it may be the most beautiful and satisfying par 5 of all. Who, having played this hole, in sheltered isolation, would disagree?

The 12th (144–200 yards), swaddled in the sand hills, plays over a deep hollow to a broad, tabletop green. It is called the Mass Hole, and the hollow could fairly be called sacred ground: It was here during Oliver Cromwell's Penal Days, more than three hundred years ago, that the local population would attend Mass in hiding. The punishment for such "popish practices" was death.

The 13th, another short par 5, doglegs vigorously left and contains concealed burns right and left in the high rough to swallow the errant shot. Dunes all the way on both sides and a two-tier green make the 410-yard 14th demanding. The double-dogleg 15th (370–428 yards), threading through low dunes, has a lovely rhythm, gently up on the drive, gently down on the approach to a new and very long, heavily contoured Fazio green in an amphitheater of tangled mounds. Even more of Fazio is apparent on the medium-length two-shot 16th, a dogleg left with new dunes on the right all the way, the second shot uphill to a relocated green whose right edge is mere steps from a falloff to the beach. Terrific stuff!

The 17th (124–200 yards) is pure theater, doubtless one of the reasons it was chosen for *The 500 World's Greatest Golf Holes*. It is called Mulcahy's Peak, for not only did the founder particularly cherish this hole and all that it unveiled, but when he died, at the age of eighty-eight, the urn containing his ashes was buried in the teeing ground. Playing this hole is a five-step procedure. First comes the near-vertical ascent to the tee, the flattened summit of what is actually the tallest dune on the links. Second, we catch our breath. Next, revolving 360 degrees, we attempt to drink in the world that is Waterville: the rumpled and wooly links, Lough Currane, the estuary of the Inny, Ballinskelligs Bay blurring into the Atlantic Ocean, and, in the far northern distance, the mountain range

that has popped into view again and again ever since we reached Killarney, MacGillycuddy's Reeks. Fourth, we attempt to gauge the wind—the towering 17th tee bears the full brunt of it. Then, at last, we have no choice but to strike the golf ball. The green, looking smaller than it is and bunkered only at the left front, beckons. Between us and it lies a jungle of densest vegetation.

Whenever the 18th hole is an ocean-side par 5, Pebble Beach comes to mind. The 18th here at Waterville—594 yards from the tips, 556 from the middle markers, 522 from the daily tees—is a deserving companion,

almost as visually enthralling as Pebble's home hole and rather more difficult. Fazio has strengthened this great hole by judiciously siting five bunkers en route (there had been none) and constructing an angled green with a ridge running prominently through the heart of it. From the high tee—almost certainly in a high wind—we must trust our swing if we are to have any chance of avoiding the snarly rough and low dunes on the left or the beach on the right. The drive is the most important stroke on the hole. Following it comes the task of hitting the fairway on the long second shot, then holding the green on what can sometimes be a husky

Opposite, top: Waterville, 11th; bottom: 12th. Above: 15th.

approach shot. Three sound swings are needed. And keep in mind that from the tips, which means just under 600 measured yards, this hole, into the wind, can play 700 yards. Regardless of the tee chosen and regardless of the wind, this all-world hole is a summation of the splendid golf that has preceded it.

Long a great test and today clearly greater than ever, Waterville just may also be something even rarer—dare I say it?—a perfect course.

In 1998 Tiger Woods, Mark O'Meara, Payne Stewart, and Scott McCarron came here the week before the Open Championship, held at Royal Birkdale, to polish their links course games and do a little trout fishing. O'Meara captured the claret jug a week later. Prior to the Open the following year, Woods, O'Meara, and Stewart returned, bringing with them Lee Janzen, Stuart Appleby, and David Duval.

Payne Stewart, with not a drop of Irish blood in his veins, fell in love with Waterville, not just with the course but with Waterville House and the village and, above all, the people. His youthful charm triggered a powerful response. Wherever he went he was greeted affectionately, almost adoringly. And when it came to merrymaking, he even showed the locals a thing or two, playing the harmonica and singing in the pubs till the wee hours of the morning and, at the High Bar in the Butler Arms Hotel, personally pulling pints of Guinness and serving them. A non-Catholic, he nevertheless took his wife to Sunday Mass at St. Finian's, escorting her to a pew, then going back to stand with the men of the parish in the rear. The golf club named the two-time U.S. Open champion and 1989 PGA champion its honorary captain for 2000. And then, on October 25, 1999, this vital and outgoing man was gone, killed in the crash of his chartered plane. In November, when Catholics pray especially for the departed, Stewart's name was one of those posted before the altar at St. Finian's, between the names of Mary Carey and Eileen Murphy. As Jeff Williams wrote in *Links* magazine (May/June 2003), "At a memorial Mass for the dead, 9-year-old Caoimhe O'Mahony carried Stewart's candle to the altar. . . . Says Father Martin Sheean, the pastor, 'I suspect that light will always be here.'"

Opposite: Waterville, 17th.
Above, left: 15th; right: 18th.

In Waterville there are two outstanding places to stay:

- For years John Mulcahy's home but now owned by the small consortium of New Yorkers who own the golf links, **Waterville House** is an elegant, intimate eighteenth-century manor catering to small parties of golfers and anglers. It is set on forty acres beside the ocean. The twelve guest rooms, many with sea views and some with fireplaces, are spacious, handsomely appointed, thoroughly comfortable. The public rooms are also wonderfully inviting. Breakfast is the only meal served. An outdoor heated swimming pool, sauna, steam room, and private practice facility with

putting green are among the amenities. Literally at the front door is Butler's Pool, which many consider to be Ireland's single best spot for salmon and sea trout fishing. Tiger, Mark O'Meara, and Payne Stewart whiled away hours here prior to the British Open.

- In the heart of the village and overlooking the sea is the **Butler Arms Hotel**, which has been owned and operated by the hospitable Huggard family for four generations. The forty-two accommodations include twelve luxurious junior suites, some with fireplaces. Among the public spaces is the Charlie Chaplin Lounge, where photos on the walls call up the many

visits of the large Chaplin family; Butler's Pool was the little clown's favorite fishing haunt, but there is no record of his ever striking a golf ball. The beamed-ceiling restaurant boasts ocean views and, more to the point, excellent and imaginative cooking.

Waterville itself, a seaside resort with a year-round population of about six hundred, is neither pretty nor quaint, but, with its shops (the Waterville Craft Market specializes in pottery, textiles, and jewelry) and pubs and inns for holidaymakers, it has an animated quality. A few sightseeing attractions ought to be noted, if only to suggest that for the nongolfer there are things to do: the his-

Clockwise from below: Knightstown, on Valencia Island; Portmagee Harbor; the Portmagee Channel; inlet near Portmagee.

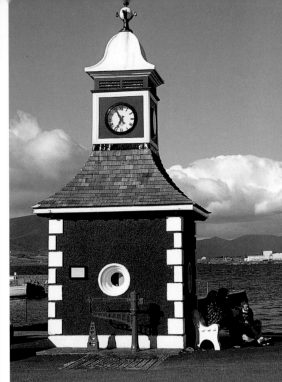

torical pre-Famine village of Cill Rialaig, rebuilt into an artist's retreat and set high on a cliff at the edge of Ballinskellings Peninsula; the Skelligs Chocolate factory, on St. Finian's Bay (sample the brandy-and-champagne chocolate truffles); Coomanaspig Pass, one of the highest points in Ireland accessible by car, affording breathtaking views north to the Dingle Peninsula; the captivating little fishing village of Portmagee, with over 80 percent of the area's fishing fleet based here; and Great Skellig, the site of two lighthouses as well as the ruins of a monastery, possibly founded by St. Finian in the seventh century.

Clockwise from top left: Skellig Islands, along the Ring of Kerry; lighthouse on Valencia Island; Ballinskelligs Priory, near Waterville; near Caherdaniel.

THE SOUTH: CORK AND KILKENNY,
WATERFORD AND CARLOW

OLD HEAD

For most of the last century, the Old Head of Kinsale was known—if it was known at all—for a horrific tragedy. In 1915 the British luxury liner *Lusitania* was torpedoed by a German submarine just off the Old Head, with the loss of 1,198 lives.

It was in 1989 that John O'Connor, a Cork man, and his brother Patrick bought the 220-acre Old Head from a farmer for $400,000. The start of course construction was long delayed by the protests of environmentalists, who decried in vain the proposed transformation of the Old Head's wild natural beauty into a man-made playground. I visited the site in the spring of 1995 and came away suspecting that there might not be enough room for 18 holes on this stark and treeless diamond-shape property ringed by the sea; it looked to me like a stage that had been propelled straight up out of the Atlantic depths. I got back two years later and was astonished at the legerdemain that had been worked here on a site like no other in the world of golf.

Five individuals participated in the design of Old Head: Ron Kirby (Nicklaus's right-hand man at Mount Juliet, etc.), Joe Carr, Paddy Merrigan (Australian-trained and Cork-based golf architect), Liam Higgins (Waterville's longtime head professional), and Eddie Hackett. Merrigan once said, "You're in a kind of Shangri-la out there and you have to pinch yourself to find your way back to reality." On a more practical note, John O'Connor told me that Eddie Hackett once counseled him to make sure that the greens would not be heavily contoured because they are so exposed to the wind and that the fairways should be generous for the very same reason.

Old Head is not a links course: It is not routed over sand-based linksland; there are no dunes; and there is no rippling or tumbling terrain. Like Pebble Beach, it is a headlands course, often clinging to the clifftops. A key difference between the two is the bluffs. Pebble's rise all of sixty-five to seventy feet above the beach. There is no beach at Old Head, where the cliffs soar two hundred to three hundred feet above the rock-thrashing seas. At Pebble Beach, six holes—seven counting the green of the par-3 17th—skirt the ocean. At Old Head, nine do. For sheer theatricality, Old Head is the world champion.

ON THE COURSE

Old Head measures 7,215 yards from the championship tees, 6,868 from the blues, 6,451 from the regular markers, and 5,550 from the forward tees. Par is 72. The layout is jam-packed with superior holes, including several of the "inside" ones, like the climbing short par-5 6th, with a boundary wall tight on the left all the way; and the thrilling dogleg left 18th, where we tee off in the lee of the 160-year-old black-and-white lighthouse, the sea at our back flailing amid the rocks far below, a forced carry over a ravine requiring a courageous driver swing, the sparkling clubhouse signaling from its perch beyond the sand-defended green and high above us. A home hole for all time.

Of the nine cliffhangers, no fewer than four are great. At the 415-yard 4th we play from a towering tee at the edge of a bluff, the markers no more than two paces from the brink, the broad fairway falling as it doglegs emphatically left around a rocky inlet, then rising on the long second shot to a green all but teetering more than two hundred feet above the water. The hole is called The Razor's Edge.

The 206-yard 13th (258 from the tips), with the cliff edge again tight on the left, climbs to an exquisitely sited plateau green with a single large bunker at the left that just may save us from a two-stroke penalty plunge to the roiling seas. A driver is often called for.

The back nine has three par 5s (it also has three two-shotters and three short holes), the first one a double dogleg "insider," the other two tip-toeing along the edge of a bluff from start to finish. These two are epic holes. For pure intimidation, the 12th (537 from the whites, 564 from the blacks, 11 teeing grounds all told!) is in a class very much of its own. The drive from the brink is a rising shot across a corner of the abyss (an enormous noisy cavern here is populated by thousands of roosting birds) to a generous fairway that doglegs sharply left in the landing area. The fairway grows progressively narrower, proceeding along the heights to a green that threatens to tilt left over the edge and collapse into the ocean far below.

The 17th heads in the opposite direction and has the sea on the right all the way. And "all the way" is a very long way—578 yards from the

Opposite: Old Head, 4th.
Previous spread: 1st.

There are those who insist that the course is showy, flamboyant, excessive, over the top, that its designers were determined to put Pebble Beach in the shade, even if that called for squeezing in perimeter holes over the sea. On one or two occasions, there may be merit in this contention. But the holes at Old Head are not only visually arresting, they are rigorously and fairly challenging.

At times we may wonder how, without risk to life or limb, some of them ever could have been built. "Haulie" O'Shea's heroics produced an imperishable moment in golf course construction. The 15th hole, called Haulie's Leap, is a very short par 4 perilously close to the cliff edge. Atop his four-ton excavator one day and negotiating an especially precarious stretch, Haulie suddenly felt the ground give way and his rig tipping over the bluff. Desperately abandoning ship, he flung himself to safety even as his mobile phone, mounted near the controls, started to ring. He heard three rings and then no more, the caller now to be greeted with Haulie's voice on the recorded message as the plummeting excavator finally came to rest at the base of the cliff on the sea-splattered rocks: "I'm sorry I can't take your call right now, but if you leave your name and number I'll get back to you as soon as possible."

NEARBY COURSES

Many well-heeled touring golfers make the trip from Waterville to the Old Head of Kinsale by helicopter; it takes thirty minutes. Harriet and I drive, twisting and turning and up-and-downing via Sneem, Parknasilla, Kenmare, Glengarriff, Bantry, Clonakilty, Balinspittle, and Kinsale; it takes four hours. There is golf in most of these small towns.

The original nine-hole course at **Parknasilla**, which I played in the early 1980s, had very few serious golf holes and a plethora of awkwardly hilly stances and lies. Dr. Arthur Spring, of Beaufort fame, came along in the mid-1990s to radically revise what he found here and, I have no doubt, to improve Parknasilla immeasurably. I regret to say I've not been back.

At **Kenmare** there was a pretty nine-hole course beside the broad estuary of the Kenmare River. As golf it was negligible, but as a walk it was an undiluted pleasure. Some fifteen years ago Eddie Hackett was called in to add nine holes, which turned out to be strenuously up and down.

It is the N71 that links Kenmare with Glengarriff, and the thirty-minute drive is one of the most memorable in Ireland for beauty and spectacle: steep ascents and descents, subtropical foliage and gardens,

whites, 632 from the blacks, the kind of mileage that nicely accommodates a gentle jog left, a gentle jog right, and a couple of downhill stretches that produce hanging lies, where any kind of a cut sails over the cliff and down onto the rocks. The green balances on a bluff. This hole was chosen for *The 500 World's Greatest* book, but it may actually be no greater than the 12th. No nine in the British Isles can point to two par 5s as strong and fine and pulse-pounding as 12 and 17 at Old Head. Indeed, it is possible that no nine on the planet can.

It is also likely that no course you've ever played will prepare you for Old Head. Beyond mighty and majestic, it is monumental, a triumph of seaside grandeur. Again and again we find ourselves taking a deep breath as we set up for the shot—not so much to inhale the intoxicating splendor of the moment as to quiet our unsteady nerves in order to summon a sound swing in these extravagant circumstances. The course ranks 61st in *Golf World*'s most recent list of the top 100 courses in the British Isles (far too low, in my judgment).

Above: Old Head, 3rd.
Opposite: 2nd.

moorlike terrain dominated by great rock outcroppings, three short rock-piercing tunnels, a gorgeous quilt of sectioned meadows, and eye-popping panoramas of Bantry Bay. The **Glengarriff** nine is all of 2,000 yards long, an unbroken series of exhausting ups and exhilarating downs punctuated by numerous blind shots and compelling water-and-mountain views. Actress Maureen O'Hara lived next door for years.

When I played it, more than twenty years ago, the 3,218-yard nine-hole course at **Bantry Bay** had one bunker, nine holes running up or down a big hill, and smashing views of Bantry Bay far below. Only moments away is Bantry House, an early-eighteenth-century Neoclassical structure that is one of the noblest mansions in Ireland. Its public rooms are there to be enjoyed by sightseers, and it also offers nine accommodations. Bantry House is not to be bypassed.

Clonakilty has a hilly, rocky nine-hole course south of town. The nine measures 2,230 yards against a par of 32. We may take it as gospel that the sea views are enthralling, though I'm afraid I've never played here.

Kinsale, a holiday town that in season (April into November) is thronged, has two courses. I played the 2,850-yard par-35 nine-holer long ago and enjoyed it. The clubhouse rests atop a high hill. We are either driving downhill, in which case our second shot will be a half-wedge, or driving up from the shore of the Bandon River estuary, in which case our second shot will be anything from a 5-iron to a 3-wood. The estuary view, narrowing through a gap in the hills covered with a patchwork of sheep-dotted meadows, is ravishing. The newer course at nearby **Farrangalway** measures just over 6,600 yards, par 71, and is reputed to be a stiff test. Alas, you cannot prove it by me.

Opposite: Old Head, 17th.
Above: 16th.

Lively little Kinsale has countless places to spend the night:

- One of our favorites is attractive and unpretentious **Old Bank House**, opposite the sailboat-filled harbor. Two Georgian townhouses, which used to function separately as a bank and the post office, have been combined to make a B&B with seventeen guest rooms, an antiques-filled sitting room with a fireplace, and a cozy breakfast room where Michael Riese and his wife, Marie, who own and run Old Bank House, provide a wonderful cooked meal to start the day: hot porridge, sausage, black pudding, scrambled eggs with salmon. The four-story house is blessed with an elevator, and the higher you go, the better the view.

- Just across the street is **Perryville House**, another upscale B&B, this one with twenty-two accommodations ranging from snug to roomy and including junior suites. All rooms are individually appointed in a traditional style. Many have harbor views, but at least as many do not. The sitting room and the drawing room are large. Breakfast features a comprehensive buffet.

- If simply looking down on the marina is not enough to satisfy your craving for seaside charm, you may want to book a room at the **Trident**, which, at the water's edge, gives the impression of being about to set sail. The thirty-four guest rooms are tastefully appointed, and the two suites have private balconies. Our room was so close to the water that we seemed afloat. The hotel's **Wharf Tavern**, with good bar food, is a traditional Irish pub that is as popular with locals as with hotel guests, and the **Savannah Waterfront** specializes in seafood brought in daily to the pier here. The Trident also has a leisure center with sauna, steam room, Jacuzzi, and gym. Massage therapy is available.

- **Ballinacura House**, a private residence converted into a country-house hotel in 2003, is reported to be the most luxurious place to stay in the Kinsale area. We've not yet had the chance. The house can accommodate as many as thirty in thirteen guest rooms. Among the ample public spaces are a bar, dining room, study, sitting room, living room, and a drying room for golf clothes and clubs.

Kinsale claims to be the "Gourmet Capital of Ireland," which Dublin may not be willing to concede, but there can be no denying the number of first-rate dining spots here:

- In season, **Le Restaurant D'Antibes** at The White House (there are also a bistro and a bar here) can be crowded and noisy, but the cooking and service are both first-rate, with fish and shellfish dishes leading the way.

- At the **1601 Restaurant** the emphasis is on stews and soups.

- For a highly informal bite, stop in at the **Kinsale Gourmet Store and Seafood Bar**, which offers a wider range of choices than you might expect.

- The same is true of **Crackpots**, where unusual artwork and pottery create the atmosphere.

Picture-postcard lovely and prosperous, Kinsale is probably the most sophisticated and cosmopolitan seaside spot in Ireland, attracting Irish and international visitors in

Views of Kinsale.

droves. A number of smaller houses from the nineteenth century, many of them faced in slate, have been sympathetically restored. Behind gaily painted masonry fronts are all manner of galleries (art, silver, ceramics) and shops (trinkets and wearables being the most prevalent offerings). There are three sailboat and yacht marinas, a deep-sea angling facility, sports centers, and countless pubs (music nightly in many of them). Kinsale is a sparkler.

It is also ancient, dating back more than eight hundred years to the barony of Kinsale. The town's position on the estuary of the Bandon can best be appreciated from Compass Hill. On the south bank is the ruin of Ringrone Castle. The village of Summer Cove, with its good bathing, is overlooked by Charles Fort (1677). Almost certainly the single most interesting structure in Kinsale itself is the church of St. Multose, parts of which date to the early thirteenth century. Nearby Desmond's Castle is a good example of a sixteenth-to-eighteenth-century townhouse.

Kinsale and the surrounding area.

CORK

The drive, due north, from Old Head first through Kinsale and then on up to the Cork Golf Club, outside the city at Little Island, takes more than an hour. This eighteen at Little Island, as the club is often called, is neither a links course nor a great course, but it may be a unique course. It might reasonably be dubbed a "3-in-1 course," as we shall see.

The club was formed in 1888 by a small group made up of leading Cork citizens, as well as a handful of officers of the then resident British army and navy. Its first two locations, Glanmire and Blarney, provided golfing ground that was deemed too rough and hilly. In 1898 the club put down permanent roots at Little Island (actually a peninsula) on a tract of land containing a limestone quarry. David Brown, an Edinburgher who was the club's first professional, teamed up with England's Tom Dunn, an exceptionally prolific golf architect, to lay out nine holes. In 1927 Alister MacKenzie remodeled the existing nine and added a second nine. Nearly eighty years later the course that delights us remains a tribute to the great man, though in 1975 Frank Pennink made some well-received changes.

Little Island has been the venue for such important events as the 1932 Irish Open, the 1941 Irish Professional Championship, and the 1965 Carrolls International. But it is still best known as the home club of Jimmy Bruen, who served as captain and then president following his great successes. He won the Irish Close Amateur in 1937 and 1938, the Irish Open Amateur in 1938, and the British Amateur in 1946. A three-time Walker Cupper, he had a pronounced loop at the top of his swing—the clubhead would fly so far past parallel that, like John Daly's, it would actually be pointing at the ground—that was the source of his enormous length, and also of his wildness.

ON THE COURSE

Par is 72 on this rolling and moderately bunkered eighteen, which has few blind shots. The course measures 6,740 yards from the back tees, 5,810 from the ladies' markers, and 6,270 from the daily tees. The 370-yard opener rises gently to start, then climbs to the green. Bruen actually drove it several times—with that now old-fashioned driver and ball! For the rest of us, it is not even a birdie hole. On the other hand, the 2nd, a short downhill par 5, and the third, a 275-yard par 4, give up more than their share of birdies.

Now, after this agreeable parkland start, we duck through a thicket behind the 3rd green and out onto a tee smack beside the shore of the River Lee's vast estuary. An unexpected and altogether delightful moment, and one made even more satisfying by the prospect of playing the truly great 4th hole. It stretches away, parallel to the water on our right, 425 yards from the shortest men's tee. The drive is a daunting forced carry over rough ground to a wrinkled fairway, the mouth of the Lee lurking to devour a fade. The gorse-splashed rough on the left is hardly a haven. Our long uphill second shot—we can see the flag but not the putting surface—seeks a green that is inclined to shunt the ball away, and any work called for from the humpy surrounds will be hard work. The green complexes at Little Island have spirit to spare, courtesy of MacKenzie.

And if the 4th is an authentic links hole, so is the equally great 5th, a 510-yarder pursuing the same direction and again close beside the water. Here the fairway dipsy doodles before bending right and showing the way to a green on a low, stone-banked promontory that noses into the estuary. The bold second shot aiming to get home is that of a riverboat gambler.

The 6th completes what is a marvelous trio, and with it we turn our back on the Lee and enter the realm of the quarry. We've tackled parkland golf and waterside golf, and now it is time for the land of limestone. The tee shot on the 300-yard 6th is blind, a forced carry over a wasteland of scrub to a hospitably broad—and hidden—fairway. We are left with what is an appropriately short pitch, for this green is not *on* a knob, it *is* a knob. Framing it at a respectful remove are the high gray rock walls of the long-abandoned quarry. The green is unreceptive. Our shot inclines to edge away from the refuge of the center and slide down the shaven banks at right, left, front, and rear into tenacious rough. There are no bunkers. Nor will a 7 or 8 ever materialize. But how disappointing to write down 5 when, as we stood beside our drive, a 3 seemed not too much to ask. A tantalizing hole and another great one.

Opposite: Cork Golf Club, 6th.

Following two more quarry holes, the 170-yard 7th (platform tee) and the 400-yard 8th (elevated two-tier green), the first nine closes with another superlative hole. It is a 185-yarder that plays from one low knob to another, the green an astonishingly convoluted surface that looks to be pure MacKenzie. Like the 4th and 5th, this hole would be thoroughly at home on any links course, so much is there of the seaside in its topography and turf and feel.

The second nine starts with a testing par 4 of 390 yards marked by a narrow, rumpled fairway that is difficult to hold. At the excellent 11th, a 500-yard par 5 curving right and gently rising, we say good-bye to the quarry. Here the green is sited on high ground just above the rock out-croppings. If an aggressive second shot or an indifferent third leans to the right, it is gone. On this hole Seve Ballesteros, playing an exhibition round in 1983, unleashed a thunderous drive of 411 yards (powerful tail-wind, rock-hard fairway). In commemoration, a Spanish chestnut tree

was planted just opposite where the ball came to rest, 89 yards from the center of the green. When I gained that point with two hits, it confirmed what I had long suspected: Seve was a club longer than I.

The last seven holes, traditional parkland, are not up to the standard of the eight-hole stretch that began beside the water at the 4th tee, but they are worthy. And we remember the 16th and 17th warmly. The former, from a tee in a pretty glade, is a short par 4 that plays out to a broad fairway, then, turning hard right, climbs abruptly to a plateau green with a deep bunker under its right flank. It is a cousin of the wonderful 14th at Loch Lomond. The 17th is a grand driving hole from a pinnacle tee down to a fairway sloping right to left, where a boundary awaits.

Little Island is the only course I've ever played that is mostly park-land, partly quarry, and has a soupçon of true links holes—an irresistible mix if ever there was one.

Above: Cork, 5th.
Opposite: 7th.

Loyal Goulding, long one of the club's outstanding players, intended to accompany me the second time I toured Little Island, but a bad back sidelined him, reducing him to hosting lunch for Harriet and me in the clubhouse lounge, with its distant views across the course to the estuary. The three of us ate smoked salmon on brown bread—delicious! He visited the United States annually, as a rule for the Masters. Thanks to his many friends here, he was able to tick off the American shrines—Merion, Pine Valley, Baltusrol, Winged Foot, Oakmont, Pebble Beach, Cypress Point, Olympic, and rather more—that he had played over the years.

When Harriet asked him if his home overlooked the sea, he said, "It does indeed. I could drop a boat in the water at the bottom of my garden and paddle my way to Boston."

NEARBY COURSES

Not fifteen minutes from Cork Golf Club and next door to the Fota Island arboretum and gardens is **Fota Island Golf Club**. The course, which opened in 1993, was designed by Christy O'Connor Jr. and two-time British Amateur champion Peter McEvoy. The Irish Club Professional Championship was played here in 1995, the Irish Close Amateur in 1995 and 1996, but it was the 2001 Irish Open that got Fota Island international exposure. Colin Montgomerie seized the lead with an opening round 8-under-par 63 and never relinquished it, coasting home comfortably with a 266 total, 5 strokes ahead of runners-up Padraig Harrington, Darren Clarke, and Nicholas Fasth.

The course is laid out on rolling parkland with views of Cork Harbour. The perimeter of the tract contains mature woodlands, but there is an open aspect to the holes themselves. The layout was extensively revamped in 1998 and 1999, when all eighteen greens were rebuilt and eight holes were redesigned. The very broad fairways were narrowed at this time. Water comes into play on five or six holes. Four sets of tees permit the course to be played at 6,927 yards, 6,488 yards, 6,111, and 5,520; par is 71. Among the many outstanding holes on what is now a genuinely stiff test—at least for the club player—are the 6th (down from an elevated tee, then up to a plateau green patrolled across the front by a nest of bunkers in the slope) and the 10th. A par 5 of only 487 yards, the 10th plunges between a grove of hardwoods on the left and a high bank of gorse on the right. We seem to be in a tunnel. The fairway turns abruptly

left beyond a stone wall at the bottom of the hill before proceeding to a green with water behind it. This is a highly unusual golf hole.

Like Cork Golf Club, the **Harbour Point Golf Complex**, with its twenty-one-bay driving range, has a Little Island address and enjoys similarly handsome views of the Lee estuary. The testing par-72 course, which opened in 1991, can play as long as 6,700 yards and as short as 5,650. The first seven holes are routed over mildly rolling terrain. The last eleven, by and large, are hilly. We ought to be able to play to our handicap because the bunkering is light and there are no water hazards. But the narrow fairways exact a toll. For example, on the par-5 9th, with its top-of-the-world tee, the steeply downhill drive is blind to a fairway that is all of 18 yards wide in the landing area. There must be many days, with the wind rampaging across these slopes, when hitting a fairway (or a green, for that matter) is purely accidental.

Less than thirty minutes east of Little Island and Fota Island, in the village of Shanagary, lies **Ballymaloe House**. It is the fountainhead of the outstanding cooking, once uncommon in Ireland, that we can now count upon enjoying wherever we roam. Established by Ivan and Myrtle Allen, the country-house hotel and attendant four-hundred-acre farm are operated today by their extended family. The point of view behind the success of Ballymaloe House—first its restaurant, then its lodgings—can be grasped from Myrtle Allen's words on the cover of the dinner menu: "We have always gone down to our own garden and glass houses, into our local butcher's shop and to the pier at Ballycotton to collect our produce. We write a new menu each afternoon when we see what we have got." Today there are Ballymaloe cookbooks (thirteen so far), a Ballymaloe cooking series on television, and a Ballymaloe Cooking School. Other country-house hotel owners have felt compelled to raise the standards of their own tables.

Dinner at Ballymaloe House is served in several small or medium-size rooms, which display a collection of modern Irish paintings, including canvases by Jack B. Yeats. The atmosphere is relaxed—nothing formal or stiff about it. There are five courses. You can start with fish soup and work your way through crab croquettes with two sauces, French casserole roast pork with a Normandy mustard sauce and carrots, a selection of Irish farmhouse cheeses, and a strawberry meringue for dessert.

The thirty-three guest rooms are in the main house (early nineteenth century, partially cloaked in lavender wisteria), in the annex across the cobbled courtyard, and in the sixteenth-century gatehouse. You may be surprised to find an outdoor heated swimming pool and a tennis court at Ballymaloe House, and perhaps even more surprised to find a seven-hole pitch 'n' putt course. It is just possible that the Allens have thought of everything.

Much closer to Cork City and on the N25 in Tivoli is **Lotamore House**, an eighteenth-century manor that is now an upmarket B&B. Set well above the highway in its own small park, it has twenty-one rooms, each with private bath and TV. Smartly appointed—mirrored armoires and beds with marquetry inlays—the accommodations are often quite spacious and, in many instances, look out over the top of a couple of bulky oil storage tanks far below to the Lee estuary. The flower-filled public spaces are richly furnished, particularly the sitting room, with its welcoming fireplace as the focal point.

Since Lotamore House serves only breakfast, it's good to know that a couple of minutes away is the **Barn Restaurant**, which prides itself on its authentic Irish cooking. The decor may be too vivid for some, and the cooking is not up to the Ballymaloe House standard, but, on balance, dinner here is enjoyable.

With a population of about one hundred forty thousand, Cork is the Republic's second-largest city. Its center is squeezed onto an island between two forks of the Lee. So whichever direction you take, you'll come to water, a bridge, and a waterfront street with "Quay" in its name. The Lee endows Cork with character, interest, and a modicum of charm. The charm, however, is sometimes counterbalanced by grim gray warehouses, not to mention tanneries and breweries and some derelict housing. There are very few structures of architectural distinction. St. Fin Barre's Cathedral, in the French Gothic style and completed in 1878, is somewhat of a landmark, but its interior does not please. St. Ann, Shandon, which was completed in 1726, is unusual in that two sides of its steeple are faced with white limestone, the other two with red sandstone. For many visitors, the covered Regency shopping arcade known as the English Market is more appealing than either of the two churches, and so are several of the steeply terraced Georgian streets away from the center.

Some six miles northwest of the city is the village of Blarney, where, at its fifteenth-century castle, you can kiss the Blarney Stone, thus gaining extraordinary powers of eloquence.

Below, from left: St. Fin Barre's Cathedral; Blarney Castle; Lotamore House, outside and in-. Opposite: Cobh, at dusk.

MOUNT JULIET

Driving from Cork to Thomastown, where Mount Juliet is located, takes about two hours: first east on the N25 through Youghal and Dungarvan (the bar at Lawlor's Hotel here, with its dark wood, stained glass, and convivial atmosphere, is a good bet for a sandwich and a beverage) to Waterford, then north on the N9 to the simple village of Thomastown. Here you'll see signs for Mount Juliet. May I suggest that you head not for the golf club but for the main entrance to the estate. Inside the wrought-iron gates, a lane swings away over lush, rolling meadowland for nearly a mile, finally revealing, with some distance still to go, the great manor house, nobly sited on the high ground above the banks of the River Nore. Pheasants flutter up from the underbrush, and peacocks strut across the lawn. It is bewitching, this long approach, and it is just one element in the mystique of Mount Juliet.

ON THE COURSE

This eighteen that Jack Nicklaus designed—his first and, thus far, only Irish venture—is a pleasurable experience. He was specifically requested to lay out a course that would be, above all, beautiful to look at and playable for the average golfer. The length for ladies is just under 5,500 yards. Men have a choice of the green tees (6,170 yards), the whites (6,640), or the blues (7,256). Par is 72.

In a very real sense, the course, which opened in 1991, is a reflection of the estate. There is a gentility about it, a decorous beauty, if you will, as it moves naturally over this lovely meadowland. The fairways are broad, the greens are generous (but bunkering and contouring make them *play* rather smaller than they are); old fieldstone walls contribute their share of pastoral charm; ancient oak and beech and lime trees impart a stateliness and serenity to the scene; and even the water hazards strike us first as pretty, then as perilous. And so excellent is the turf, in both texture and maintenance, that it singlehandedly raised the standard of Irish greenkeeping.

The undeniable charm of the golf course aside, many of the holes have real sting. Water unnerves us on the 2nd (our drive must carry a slit of a stream), 3rd (a 155-yard death-or-glory shot), and 4th (a pond all but

laps the right side of the green on this par 4). The 5th and 6th, 510 and 200 yards, respectively, are dry. In the 1994 Irish Open, John Daly started the final round with six straight 3s, including an eagle on the 5th (drive and a 9-iron), but he finished a stroke behind winner Bernhard Langer.

Among the outstanding holes on the second nine is the 518-yard 10th. At about a hundred yards from the green, the fairway splits. You must elect to hit your second shot left or right, because on the direct line to the green, standing implacably abreast, are three majestic beech trees. Go right and you bring into play a minefield of bunkers. Left is longer but safer.

Almost certainly the best hole on the course is 13, a great 412-yarder. Our drive finishes just over the crest of a low rise, and now Nicklaus asks us to unfurl what may well be a 4-iron (or a 7-metal) to an elevated green jutting into a pond. The hole that follows, 177 yards from a pulpit tee across a valley to a two-tier green ringed by sand, is another beauty.

Opposite: Mount Juliet, 4th.
Above: 2nd.

It ought also to be mentioned that Mount Juliet boasts a fascinating 18-hole putting course, plus the only David Leadbetter Golf Academy in Ireland and a superb 3-hole minicourse, along the Nore and created to the same level, in challenge and turf quality, as the regular eighteen.

The Irish Open was held here in 1993, 1994, and 1995. Mount Juliet ranked fifty-second in *Golf World*'s most recent list of the top hundred courses in the British Isles.

NEARBY COURSES

Less than an hour south, on the N9, is Waterford and, on a three-hundred-acre island in the estuary of the River Suir, **Waterford Castle Hotel & Golf Club**. The overall elevation change is less than 25 feet, and much of the play is over relatively level ground. The 210-acre tract was blessed with countless mature oak, elm, sycamore, and chestnut trees; and many hundreds of new trees were planted to help define the holes. The greens—spacious and imaginatively contoured—are excellent. From the championship tees, the course measures just over 6,800 yards; it is 6,400 yards from the regular markers (par 72) and nearly 5,600 from the ladies' tees.

Among the best holes are the 180-yard 2nd, played across a man-made lake to a narrow green angled to the line of flight; the 8th and 13th, a pair of shortish par 5s, where sand along the way as well as at the green demands unwavering accuracy; and the 190-yard 16th, another watery one-shotter, this one with a pond where we can least afford it, at the right front. Every once in a while a fox—of all things out here on this small island!—will lope lightly across the fairway.

Waterford Castle Hotel with its ivy-clad gray stone walls and its battlements, its Elizabethan oak paneling, and its massive stone fireplaces, dates to the 1400s. Today, in its rebirth as a hotel, the castle provides guest rooms that are big, comfortable, and full of character. The cooking on our most recent visit was very good.

Nine miles due south of the city of Waterford lies Tramore, a popular seaside resort. A paved promenade—boardwalks as we think of them are rare in Ireland—carries us along the beach.

Tramore Golf Club has a parkland course that was laid out by Colonel H. C. Tippet, of Walton Heath. It measures 6,600 yards from the championship tees (the Irish Professional Match Play Championship and the Irish Amateur Close have been contested here), 5,600 yards from the ladies' markers, and 6,100 yards from the regular tees; par is 72.

Right: Mount Juliet, 3rd.

Pine trees frame many holes on what is a flat and unadventurous layout. Bunkering is light, fairways are wide, gorse is a factor, water and boundaries are not concerns. There is no call for the gambling play. One hole, the 355-yard 4th, displays the kind of spirit that is all too rarely encountered here. On this dogleg right, the drive, a forced carry over rough and broken ground to a constricted landing area, is followed by a 6- or 7-iron over yet another hostile patch to a modestly raised green. Tramore's fairways, almost seaside in their springiness and a pleasure to walk, produce marvelous lies. And the greens are superlative—swift, true, silken.

Less than an hour's drive north of Mount Juliet on the N9 brings us to the **Carlow Golf Club**, which celebrated its centenary in 1999. The course we tackle today is mainly the 1937 handiwork of Tom Simpson. This par-70 measures only 6,470 yards from the tips. Still, it was once considered testing enough to host the Irish Amateur Open (1977) and, two years earlier, the Irish Professional Championship, won by Christy O'Connor.

Carlow is uncommonly spacious, routed over nearly 250 acres of fast-drying turf and ranging from rolling to hilly. Though there are countless species of deciduous trees, not to mention white birches punctuating the dark green firs and pines, rarely do trees constrict the shot. The fairways are broad, the greens generous and boldly contoured. Even on a blustery day, there is plenty of room to play.

And if it is a treat simply to be abroad on Carlow, with its splendid vistas (the views over the countryside from the soaring tees on 5 and 8 are exhilarating), the exacting nature of the golf holes will stake out an even stronger claim on our memory. Among the many top-notch two-shotters, three are particularly fine. At the tree-framed 8th, 430 yards, the endlessly falling tee shot from the highest point on the course is followed by a long second shot from a downhill lie to a sternly bunkered green; a rim of hills in the distance and the glint of water on a nearby pond add to the hole's appeal. On the 12th, a deep, grassy plunge at the left edge of the green makes this 370-yarder a little terror. And a high left-hand shoulder running the full length of the fairway gives the two-shotter 14th, a behemoth of 455 yards, a rare individuality.

On a course that yields birdies only grudgingly, the home hole may turn out to be our best chance to pick up a stroke. We are again at a lofty tee, this time with the hole curving gently left as it sweeps down a long hill. The card says 500 yards, but if the breeze is tailing, two aggressive swings will leave only a chip and a putt for a 4. Which is a lovely way to bid farewell to Carlow, one of Ireland's outstanding inland courses.

Left: Mount Juliet, 13th.

Dating to the seventeenth century, Mount Juliet's walled fifteen-hundred-acre property—probably the finest true sporting estate in Ireland—is more than golf. It is the home of the Ballylinch stud, breeding ground for champion Thoroughbreds. Here, too, is the Iris Kellett Equestrian Centre, which enables guests to enjoy not only dressage and arena jumping but trail riding, cross-country jumping, and riding to hounds with the Kilkenny Hunt. Mount Juliet is also host to one of Ireland's oldest cricket clubs, whose grounds overlook the Nore.

A particularly important amenity is the spa, with its wide range of traditional and alternative treatments (for example, La Stone Therapy, featuring waterheated basalt lava stones and frozen marble stones). Completing the fitness picture are an indoor swimming pool, gymnasium, steam room, and sauna.

Since both the Nore and its tributary, the Kings, flow through the estate, there are four miles of river fishing, including a dozen named pools, for salmon and trout. About it all is an atmosphere that calls up long weekends of country-house parties in the Edwardian Age. It

might, however, be noted that then there was no golf course outside the door to please the guests.

There are thirty-two accommodations, including nine suites, in **Mount Juliet House**, which was built by the Earl of Carrick more than two hundred years ago. Spacious and high-ceilinged, the rooms are individually decorated in a warm, traditional fashion that is luxurious but not ostentatious. Many rooms have delicate plasterwork designs on the ceilings, beautiful marble fireplaces, and window seats with idyllic views over the Nore to the meadows and the distant hills. Less grand but scarcely less comfortable are the Hunters Yard rooms and the Rose Garden suites, in the old stables courtyard near the clubhouse.

The public rooms in Mount Juliet House, with fireplaces reliably aglow when there is a nip in the air, are dignified yet relaxing. Dinner in the Lady Helen McCalmont Dining Room (the McCalmont family owned the estate from 1914 to 1986) could well be the high point (off the golf course, that is) of an Irish holiday. This is one of the country's exquisite period rooms: The carved plas-

terwork on walls and ceiling, in the Adam style, is of surpassing grace and delicacy, with classical figures in relief on medallions, and stylized vine tendrils lightly swagging the medallions. The ceiling is painted in five or six beguiling pastels. The Neoclassical fireplace, predominantly white marble, is elegant and warming. A table for two in one of the long windows looking down on the river, the horses grazing in the white-fenced paddocks beyond, will bring out the romance in the soul of even the most golf-obsessed individual. The cooking lives up to the setting and the view.

A dozen years ago, when Harriet and I visited Mount Juliet for the first time, Katherine MacAnn was the resort's director of sales and marketing (she serves as a consultant to the golf operation today). For some years she was one of Ireland's outstanding women amateurs. She told us that her thirtieth birthday occurred during the 1993 Irish Open and that, unknown to her, several of the players had got wind of it. "That night," she related, "at a big dinner with many of the well-known players, when it came time for dessert the room suddenly went quiet. I

Below: the Mount Juliet House and its grounds. Opposite: Jerpoint Abbey.

looked up and there, coming across the room toward me, were Seve Ballesteros and José Maria Olazabal, carrying a birthday cake with the candles all lighted and them leading everyone in singing 'Happy Birthday'! Can you imagine them doing that, for me?"

At Mount Juliet, yes. It is that kind of place.

Just outside Thomastown lie the ruins of twelfth-century Jerpoint Abbey, in a peaceful countryside setting. Jerpoint is one of Ireland's best examples of a Cistercian monastery. The cloister, which was restored in 1953, preserves some worthwhile carvings, including one of St. Christopher. There are five tombs, mostly from the fifteenth and early sixteenth centuries. The fifteenth-century tower has characteristic Irish battlements, and the chapter house contains objects found among the ruins. An interpretive center helps us make the most of our visit.

Not quite twenty minutes from Mount Juliet is the "medieval city of Kilkenny." Please don't expect to find the clock turned back six-hundred years, but do expect to enjoy a visit. This town of almost twelve-thousand bestrides the Nore on both low and high ground. Hundreds of years ago the Irish Parliament met here. The most important sights are eight-hundred-year-old Kilkenny Castle, all gray stone towers and battlements on a hill above the river, with an extensive collection of period art and furniture; the Cathedral of St. Canice, which the *Blue Guide Ireland* calls "one of the finest unruined churches in Ireland" (I'm smiling, but I'm not sure I should be); and Kilkenny College, where traces of the ancient town walls can still be seen. Among the pleasures of simply walking in Kilkenny are the occasional narrow winding lane that climbs and dips, an old cobbled passage here and there, streets with a number of attractive Georgian structures, a house or two that goes back to Elizabethan times, and the fetching river. On a more contemporary note, the Kilkenny Design Workshops (ceramics, fabrics, and much more), with studios and showrooms in converted stables across The Parade from the castle, well reward a visit. At No. 1 The Parade is **Rinuccini's Restaurant**, serving not only classic Italian dishes but modern Irish choices with the emphasis on seafood and game.

Half an hour's country drive from Kilkenny, and somewhat less from Mount Juliet, is Inistioge, a picturesque hamlet on the ubiquitous Nore, where scenes from the film version of Maeve Binchy's *Circle of Friends* were shot. A ten-arched eighteenth-century bridge spans the river here and seduces everyone who has a camera. The square is planted with lime trees. Two ancient towers, one of which is part of the beautiful parish church, St. Mary's, remind us that a friary was established here in the thirteenth century. The **Woodstock Arms**, a highly atmospheric pub (dark pine paneling, faded green velvet bar stools, a shaggy old dog wandering in and out) is a good place for a sandwich and a stout.

Waterford City, founded in 835, is widely considered to be the oldest Viking town in Europe. Remnants of the ancient city walls show the limits of the original Viking settlement, which is bordered on one side by the Suir. Today the waterfront is the liveliest part of this city of about forty-thousand. City Hall, an eighteenth-century structure, is home to memorabilia and the Waterford Show, an entertaining presentation of the town's history. An old stone grainstore has been converted into the interactive Granary Museum, dramatizing Waterford's Viking and Norman histories. A wave-tossed Viking ship that jump-starts the presentation is particularly appealing to children, and there's a lot more fun to follow. Adults are intrigued by the archaeological finds. In the heart of town are **Bianconi's Restaurant** (Italian-influenced dishes), in the **Granville Hotel**, and **The Olde Stand**, on Michael Street, a pub/restaurant that highlights steak and seafood and has twice won the Irish Pub of Distinction Award.

About a mile and a half out of town on the Cork Road (N25) is the Waterford Crystal factory. Visitors may tour it and observe certain stages in the manufacture of the pieces, especially cutting and polishing. They may also buy. Nowhere else is there such an extensive array of the Waterford line, everything in cut glass from a violin to the head of a driver (it makes a provocative paperweight). There is one service here that you may want to take advantage of: Purchase a gift, say, a cross, and have the recipient's initials engraved on it, free of charge. You can actually sit there opposite the engraver and watch him or her inscribe the letters on the glass. Do not expect "factory outlet" prices at this factory outlet.

Opposite: Kilkenny Castle.
Clockwise from above: Bridge at Inistioge; Waterford Castle; and Kilkenny Castle.

483

WICKLOW, "THE GARDEN OF IRELAND"

DRUIDS GLEN AND
DRUIDS HEATH

Newtownmountkennedy, where Druids Glen and Druids Heath are located, is some fifteen miles due south of Dublin, in County Wicklow. The best way to get there from Mount Juliet is to head north on the N30 (at New Ross) and then on the N11, via Enniscorthy, Arklow, and Wicklow. It's a run of just over two hours, and here await two of Ireland's very best inland courses.

The first to open, in 1995, was Druids Glen, which was designed by Pat Ruddy and the late Tom Craddock. Hugo Flinn, the owner of the four-hundred-acre property, hired them and served as the builder. Flinn had played the same role at St. Margaret's, where the three had collaborated six years earlier. St. Margaret's was the source of Tom Craddock's first big check, and so excited by it was he that he flew at once to Lourdes, there to give thanks to the Blessed Virgin. When Hugo handed him his second big check, at Druids Glen, the former Irish Amateur champion promptly took off for Minneapolis and the 1993 Walker Cup Match at Interlachen, saying, "I've played in a couple of Walker Cups [1967, 1969], but I've never *seen* one. This is my chance!"

A nongolfer, Flinn was inclined from time to time to chime in at Druids Glen with some decorative concepts—flower gardens, arched bridges—that rubbed Ruddy the wrong way. "Look," Pat said to him once, "what do you think Michelangelo would have said in the Sistine Chapel if he looked down from the ceiling and found the Pope painting one end of the hall and an altar boy painting the other end?"

ON THE DRUIDS GLEN COURSE

Druids Glen wanders over 175 acres of very beautiful countryside. We sense early on why County Wicklow is called The Garden of Ireland. What with the grand trees and the shrubs and the flowers and the water, we seem to be playing in a veritable arboretum. The par-71 layout, which ranges from rolling to hilly, measures 7,026 yards from all the way back, 5,590 from all the way up. Most players will choose either the 6,550 whites or the 6,215 daily markers. The routing plan is attractively unpredictable—we never know where the next hole is hiding.

A handsome par 4 of 425 yards is a no-nonsense starter that sweeps down over a soft swale (sand to starboard in the driving area), then edges right as it rises to a narrow green framed only by trees. The architects' inspiration for the par-3 2nd hole, 175 yards, was the long second shot on the infamous Road Hole at St. Andrews. To give the designers their due, the green *is* angled to the line of flight, there *is* a lone bunker tight to the putting surface at its left center, and off to the right and rear *are* a road and a wall. But whether the allusion registers with us or not, one thing is certain: This is a superb one-shotter. It is the first of a quartet of outstanding short holes, two more of which also pay obeisance to famous par 3s. The 8th, taking its cue from the 16th at Augusta National, plays 152 yards through a glade and across a lagoon to a cruelly contoured green—three-putting is common. Much the same length but playing shorter, the 12th plunges through the trees from a high tee to a generous green sealed off at the front and the right by a broad stream that the Irish insist on calling a river. We are now squarely in the druids glen. As we troop down toward the green, we observe in the woods on our right the remains of an authentic druid altar, a small cluster of boulders believed to date back roughly a thousand years. A player faced with a curling 3-foot putt here should, according to Pat Ruddy, look toward the altar and, arms upraised, invoke the pagan power: "Oh mighty druid, please let me hole this tiny teaser!"

The last of the par 3s is the island 17th, 180 yards from the whites, 203 yards from the tips, an intriguing combination of fun and ferocity. The green is defended by water and by a horseshoe of sand across the front and along the sides, thus blessedly enlarging the haven. But in an honest breeze, and considering the length of the hole (40–60 yards longer than the 17th at TPC Sawgrass), this is one of the most potentially lethal shots we will ever be called upon to play. So where, you might ask, is the prom-

Opposite: Druids Glen, 12th.
Previous spread: The European Club, 3rd.

Above: Druids Glen, 13th.
Opposite, top: 8th;
bottom: 18th.

ised fun? Ah, you cross to the putting surface by means of a stone weir. From the tee, the players in the following group would swear that you are actually walking on water, for they cannot make out the flat stones, two inches below the surface, that are supporting you. The illusion is perfect.

No tricks—and, in truth, no water—on a couple of par 4s of 330 yards, each rising to a smallish and well-bunkered green, the 3rd curving left, the 14th curving right. Both holes are gems. "The idea," says Ruddy,

"is to mix muscle calls with finesse calls. To reward a player's strength and then to punish him in a moment of mental or physical weakness."

One more hole demands to be described, the par-4 13th, 451–471 yards. It's not enough that, from tee to cup, this is the most arresting and rigorous hole on the course. It is also, at the start, a treat for the olfactory sense. A graceful stone bridge arches over a narrow "river" below the elevated teeing grounds. An aromatic herb covers the bed of the bridge, and the footsteps of the players crush the herb, releasing its exotic perfume. In view of the 13th's scented charm, we may be more than a little surprised at its unassailable greatness. Trees frame the entire hole, which is played from a nobly high tee down into a valley crossed, about 170 yards out, by that stream, which then ripples along beside the right edge of the fairway to the point, about 90 yards short of the green, where it blossoms into a full-blown pond squarely in front of the green. The drive is testing (with the hole doglegging right, it's all too easy to run out of mown grass on the left) and the unconscionably long second shot over the pond goes beyond unnerving to terrifying—there is no bailout left or right. The green is set among mature chestnuts and oaks. The 13th at Druids Glen is an awe-inspiring creation.

Exactly one year after it debuted, Druids Glen played host to the first of four consecutive Irish Opens. Colin Montgomerie won in 1996 and 1997 and looked likely to make it three straight until, in a sudden-death playoff with David Carter, he found the water on the first extra hole. In 1999 a nineteen-year-old won: Sergio Garcia, in his sixth tournament as a professional, scored his first victory, posting a 7-under-par 64 in the final round for an aggregate of 268 (69-68-67-64).

The clubhouse at Druids Glen is as outstanding as the course. Built by an Anglo-Irish aristocrat in 1760, this is a Georgian house of high ceilings, classical columns, long windows, and carved plaster decoration on walls, ceilings, and cornices. Flinn spent roughly $3 million to restore it to what just might be even more than its original glory. He also added a roof terrace, with panoramic views over the course to the Wicklow Mountains and to the Irish Sea.

In a conversation with Pat Ruddy after I had played Druids Glen for the first time, a dozen years ago, he said to me, "We have created a fun course with a great deal of beauty. From the championship tees we have built a lot of unreasonable shots into it on the basis that the charge was not to create commercial golf but good golf for good players. . . . We have been given the freedom, the grand site, and the money to do the job right. I hope we have succeeded so that I won't have to leave town."

ON THE DRUIDS HEATH COURSE

Well, he did not have to leave town. In fact, he was asked to design a course next door, called Druids Heath. It opened in 2003, and the only thing easy about the Heath is characterizing it in three words: *thrilling, scenic, hard.* How hard? A minimum of 2 to 3 strokes tougher than the Glen, it seems to

me. A significant element in its difficulty is length. Also a par 71, this course from the championship tees is more than 400 yards longer than its sister, 300 yards longer from the daily markers. A simple recitation of the lengths of the eleven two-shotters tackled from the tips makes our head spin: 404, 467, 466, 449, 439, 426, 492, 420, 513 (!!!), 447, and 415. Even from the daily markers there are five par 4s over the 400-yard mark.

Length is only the beginning. The Heath, it might fairly be said, has it all: dramatic elevation changes (the only level hole is a stout par 3 over water from tee to green); sand (109 pits, a number of them deep); water (Ruddy has demonstrated admirable restraint here—only four water holes); two natural rock quarry holes; gorse, trees, and innocent-looking rough that will throttle you; stunningly sited greens that are often very large, complex, and baffling; a fresh breeze off the Irish Sea, which is little more than a mile away and sometimes in view; and no fewer than six genuinely great holes. The other twelve range from good to terrific.

As at next door, there is no easing into the game here. The 406-yard opener (gently up, down, up) and the two water holes that immediately follow, a long downhill par 5 and a 185-yarder, make clear the sternness of the test. Perhaps the finest holes on the nine are consecutive par 4s. The story on the 6th, 450 yards and tumbling downhill all the way from a high tee, is sand and trees. Bunkers corset the driving area, and the long second shot must be threaded between a pair of sentinel trees and then must carry a big cross bunker blockading the green. Two perfect swings will do, nothing less. The same is true on the 409-yard 7th and for

Right: Druids Heath, 2nd.

"OH MIGHTY DRUID, LET ME HOLE THIS TINY TEASER!"

- Play **Druids Glen**, four times the site of the Irish Open.

- Relish the panoramic views to the **Wicklow Mountains** and the **Irish Sea** from the rooftop terrace of the clubhouse.

- Play **Druids Heath**, at least 2 strokes harder than the Glen and studded with great holes.

- Stay—and dine—at the sparkling and contemporary **Druids Glen Marriott Hotel**, with its excellent spa.

- Visit the village of **Avoca**, setting for the BBC-TV series *Ballykissangel*.

the same reasons—sand and trees—only this time the hole rises and doglegs left, the drive menaced by bunkers and trees, the long second shot by sand squeezing the front of the green. Another great and classic hole.

The second nine, where the land has even more feature, is another of those mighty back nines (Ballybunion, Tralee, Waterville, Old Head) that pop up with astonishing frequency in Ireland. Every hole is strong and sparkling, and in the 12th and 13th we encounter the rarest thing in the game: *original* golf holes. Just think of it: Two of them, indeed, back to back.

The 466-yard 12th climbs from a low tee into an uphill landing area with bunkers left and right. We can see nothing beyond the crest of the hill. The fairway there turns right and slopes away left to right as it moves downhill. It also shrinks to the vanishing point as it is replaced by a pond. This body of water, on a par 4 so long and contoured, comes as a considerable surprise. But it is not the only surprise. Jutting boldly in from the

left is a long shoulder of rough-covered ground beyond which sits the green, sand left and right, trees virtually lining the right side of the putting surface. The second shot on this hole is tension-ridden: more than 225 yards long for most of us, hit over this menacing shoulder to a concealed, narrow, unreceptive green, yet inclining, from the sloping stance and lie, to edge right, where the pond awaits. This is one of the most intimidating shots in my experience, and this is a hole that only world-class players—492 yards for them—can handle.

The 13th is only 345 yards long (420 from the tips). Hidden water on the right threatens the tee shot. Trees in the left side of the elevated driving area—not *at* it but *in* it—also menace the tee shot. Can we clear them or must we attempt to draw the ball around them? The hole now turns right for the second shot, which, from high ground, must carry water and sand while avoiding a big tree within feet of the putting surface that cuts

off access to the entire left side of the green. Sited on the far side of a dip, the green is sharply angled to the line of flight of the shot.

It is almost certain that no hole you've ever encountered looks or plays like either the 12th or 13th at Druids Heath.

This is a great contemporary course, designed and built to test today's accomplished players. Will the 15-handicapper also enjoy a game here? I believe so. The 12th and 13th holes aside, this is not a course where the average player spends the day losing balls. What he cannot expect is to play to his handicap or, in fact, anywhere near his handicap. The course is too hard for that, quite possibly the most difficult inland course in Ireland. But it is also invigorating, and, when we do manage to meet its stringent shot-making demands, immensely rewarding. Besides, as its author says, "Dull would he be of soul who would allow a few stray golf shots to spoil a day in such a beautiful spot."

OFF THE COURSE

Within two minutes' walk from the 18th green is the **Druids Glen Marriott Hotel**, which opened in 2002. It is chic, modern, inviting. There are 148 accommodations, including executive suites. All rooms are spacious, appointed to a high standard of style and comfort, and equipped with data port, voice mail, satellite TV, movie channel, and minibar.

There are three dining options: **Flynn's Steakhouse**, with its crackling fire and woodland vistas, is a particular treat. The emphasis is on char-grilled Irish beef, though there are also attractive seafood dishes. In **Druids Restaurant**, where a buffet breakfast is served daily, the dinner menu will almost certainly include traditional Irish lamb stew, fish and chips, and grilled tiger prawns. The **Thirteenth Bar** serves pub food throughout the day.

The centerpiece of the hotel's spa and health club is a fifty-five-foot-long indoor swimming pool. There are also a sauna, steam room, whirlpool and aroma steam room, gym, solarium, hydrotherapy room, and four cubicles for massage treatments.

THE EUROPEAN CLUB

In a profile published in *Golf Digest* in 2004, Jaime Diaz called Pat Ruddy "the happiest man in golf." Aye, and why shouldn't he be? It was in the mid-1980s that Ruddy, according to his own account, "surveyed the east coast of Ireland by helicopter in search of a home for my golfing obsession—to create and own a links of my own." He spotted exactly what he had dreamed of in County Wicklow, about an hour's drive south of Dublin, amid the soaring and tumultuous dunelands along the Irish Sea at Brittas Bay. And having found the land, he mortgaged his house to buy it. On the day of the auction Pat asked his bankers whether they were standing behind him if he should submit the winning bid.

"We'll let you know tomorrow," they replied.

"But the auction is today," he pointed out.

"We'll let you know tomorrow," they assured him. By tomorrow he owned it.

He proceeded to design the course and, with the help of his two sons, Jerry and Pat Jr. (Pat and Bernardine Ruddy have two boys and three girls) constructed the holes, guiding the bulldozer himself for days on end. Much of his shaping effort was applied to the fascinating green complexes.

It was at Christmas 1992 that Ruddy presented his gift to the golf world. He ran an ad in the Dublin newspapers on a Friday, saying that he was opening fourteen holes of a new links course down at Brittas Bay the following day and anyone with £10 was welcome to play. "By 8 A.M.," he told me, "the queue extended from the trailer—we had no clubhouse—out to the car park. It was the first new links course on the east coast of Ireland in the twentieth century, and I guess the golfers were hungry for it."

Permit me to mix a metaphor: The one-man band had hit a home run. He had found the duneland and acquired it, he had laid out the links and built it, and he had opened it to an enthusiastic public. Ever since, he has been running and refining it. This bear of a fellow, sixty years old and with a warm smile, a welcoming hand, and a ready wit, has loved "the beautiful golf" with an all-consuming passion for fifty years, and today he finds himself presiding over a personal fiefdom, The European Club, with its great and majestic links. No other individual in Britain or Ireland can claim a similar achievement.

The European Club is a humble place. The small, cheerful red-brick clubhouse is the soul of simplicity. There is no pro shop and no bar. In the roomy eating area you can have as little as a scone and a cup of tea, as much as a steak and a pint. There are no caddies, no yardages on sprinkler heads. The club owns three golf carts; shouldering your bag or pulling the trolley is the order of the day. The practice range is minimal, and you will be well advised to bring your own practice balls. You are expected to arrive, change your shoes, pay your green fee (rather higher today than 1992's £10), and head for the 1st tee. Recalling his boyhood in County Sligo, Ruddy has written: ". . . at Ballaghadereen the clubhouse was a one-room tin shack measuring 10 feet by 10 feet. You hung your coat on a nail in the wall and the Bishop of Achonry hung his on the next nail and everyone went golfing." This is the way it has always been in Irish golf. And if Pat Ruddy has his way—and at The European Club we can expect him to—this is the way it will continue to be.

What awaits here is a veritable feast of links golf: magnificent sand hills directing the line of play; an overall elevation change of about one hundred feet; unfailingly natural holes with superb shot values through the air and along the ground; marram grass, gorse, bracken, broom, and buckthorn framing the holes; *perfect*—the word is not used loosely—sand-based turf on fairways as well as on the beautifully contoured and silken greens; artfully deployed bunkers, all of them boarded, some of them deep; an unbroken skein of enthralling sea views; and a virtual absence of blind shots—fourteen holes present a complete tee-to-green vista, and on the other four the landing area for the drive is clearly visible.

Still, the sly Mr. Ruddy has a few tricks up his sleeve. Fairways often appear to be no more than thirty yards across when they are actually much wider (as they should be, considering the stiff sea breezes that regularly rake this site). This deception is achieved by hiding portions of fairways beyond hillocks, in valleys, behind reeds. Also, the clever use of what is sometimes called "dead ground" (dips, the extent of which cannot

Opposite: The European Club, 8th.

accurately be judged) conceals a club length or more on some shots to the green. On the other hand, the appearance of length is sometimes exaggerated by long corridors of tall dunes, which has the effect of "reverse telescoping" medium-length shots into challenges that look endless.

ON THE COURSE

This par-71 layout measures 7,323 yards from the tips ("I'm an old man with a big belly and a bad hip," says Ruddy, "and even I can reach the green on a 420-yard hole with a drive and a 6-iron"), 6,186 from the daily markers, 5,804 from the ladies' tees. No hole is less than very good, and the number of genuinely great holes is at least 8. A medium-length par 4, rising to an elevated dune-framed green fronted by sand, gets the game off to a promising start, followed by a 140-yarder from a pulpit tee to

another green bunkered in front. Next comes a lovely short par 5 spilling downhill toward Arklow Bay, the ground sloping emphatically from left to right, a trio of penal bunkers at the front of the green. Two superlative par 4s (the steep uphill drive to a spacious fairway on the 400-yard 4th calls to mind the tee shot on the 3rd at Lahinch) are succeeded by two so-called "river holes." The stream is tight at the left of the green on the falling 150-yard 6th (sand on the right) and tight at the right every foot of the way on the 380-yard 7th, a secluded beauty situated on a sand bank that runs through a reed bed. Along the left here are dunes covered with marram grass and a marsh filled with reeds. The marsh appears to be about 170 yards out from the tee but is really 270. The player's instinct is to drive with a fairway metal and aim conservatively left, away from the stream, but this leaves a long second shot that must clear the wetlands

Above: The European Club, 7th. Opposite: 12th.

and be angled dangerously right, toward the lurking stream. "The question is," says Ruddy, "can you hit the ball twice in a straight line while ignoring the straight line of the river hugging both the fairway and the green on the right?" Brittas Bay shimmers behind the green, and wild horses graze at the right of the putting surface. The hole was chosen as one of the top one hundred in *The 500 World's Greatest* volume.

We are now introduced to one of the eccentricities of this course: the first of two extra holes, 7A. You do not have to play it, but you will almost certainly want to, since it is a beguiling 115-yarder that Pat uncovered several years after the course opened. He simply could not resist fashioning a couple of tees and a shelf green flanked by dunes.

At the 380-yard 8th, with its serpentine fairway, we play along a dune-framed corridor and over a chasm to a green in a dell of sand hills. It is sublime.

The second nine brings us out to the sea, with the beach much in play along the right on the 12th and 13th. The 12th, 413 yards, begins on a high tee and ends on a long green—a scandalously long green, 381 feet long, to be precise! "I wanted to restore the great three-putt to the game," Pat explains, with a wicked grin.

Conveniently nearby is the second extra hole, 12A, another one-shotter, 160 yards from the regular markers, 205 from the back tees, across a dip to a raised green all but ringed by dunes. These bonus holes are stunning, as was obvious to the architect when he came upon them. Easily recognizing natural sites for tees and greens, he dropped half a dozen balls on the ground, selected clubs for the two shots, and executed his swing (he was for years a 2). The two holes turned out to be all he had hoped, and green-fee payers get more than their money's worth as a result.

The par-5 13th, open in aspect and with the sea skirting its right side, measures 489 yards from the regular markers and 596 from the championship tees. Two bunkers are cut into a low dune that runs along the left side of the hole for the last hundred yards. The firm turf slopes from left to right down to the water. "Talk about being between the devil and the deep blue sea," chuckles Ruddy. This hole and the following one were both included in *The 500 World's Greatest Golf Holes*.

We tuck back into the shelter of the dunes to play the brilliant 14th, which spans 160 yards, knob to knob. A deep bunker at the left front, bulwarked with railroad ties, and a less perilous bunker at the left rear incline us, willy-nilly, to head right, toward a high sand hill. Better to forget this cautious play and just try to make your best swing.

MAJESTIC SEASIDE GOLF IN WINSOME WICKLOW

- Play **The European Club** links, a bona fide masterpiece by any yardstick.

- Have a chat with its creator/owner/operator, the irrepressible **Pat Ruddy**.

- Enjoy a cup of tea or a pint of Guinness in the simple, **sunny clubhouse**.

- Spend the night—and be sure to have dinner—at **Tinakilly House**, with its comfortable period furnishings and classic Irish cooking.

- Visit unique **Glendalough**, an ancient monastic settlement on two lakes deep in the **Wicklow Mountains**.

The final four holes, all two-shotters, maintain the extraordinarily high standards of the first fourteen. The exhilarating 15th curves smoothly left as it skirts the sea and climbs higher and higher to a green at the cliff edge. The 370-yard 16th is a charmer, gently down, gently up, the fairway shrinking as the hole bends right. The 17th, 378 yards, is stunning. The backdrop for the hole is sea, sand hills, gorse, bracken, and mountains, with the drive falling endlessly into a deep valley. So tall are the framing dunes and so lofty is the tee that the fairway, punctuated by four separated thornbushes, appears narrow; in fact, it is 80 yards wide. No such generosity, real or illusory, on the home hole. The fairway offers little breathing room between the dunes for our drive on this level 400-yarder (445 from the tips), and the second shot must clear a burn snug across the front of the green and along its left side. The pressure on both swings is intense. You have not played the very best of Irish golf until you have played the links of The European Club.

Has Pat Ruddy finished tweaking and fiddling? I have to doubt it. Within the last couple of years he turned his back on a stretch of linksland just down the road from Royal Aberdeen because he wanted to confine his efforts to The European Club. "Some evenings, especially in the long days of summer," he told me, "I'll come out to the high dunes on the second nine, find a good spot where I can see a number of holes, and prop myself up with a Kit-Kat [chocolate bar] and a Coke—"

"Neither of which you need," I interjected.

"Neither of which I need." He laughed in agreement. "I find myself wondering whether a little change here or there, maybe adding a bunker or raising one side of a green or moving a tee, might not be a good thing to do. I will tell you this—I never think maybe I ought to leave well enough alone." Then a broad smile lit up his face. "How about a handful of fairways shaped like shamrocks, to accommodate the players who hook *and* the players who slice?"

Now open for nearly fifteen years, The European Club has made its mark in the rankings. The most recent poll of Irish courses finds only Portmarnock, Ballybunion Old, and the two royals—Portrush and County Down—listed above The European. In *Golf World*'s ranking of the top hundred courses in the British Isles, The European Club is number twenty-seven, bracketed by Nairn and County Louth (Baltray). In *Golf Magazine*'s listing of the world's top hundred courses, it is ninety-first.

There may be a deep-seated yearning in Pat Ruddy to host the British Open or the Ryder Cup or both. He would dearly love to see the best players in the world face off against his creation, which you will never hear him claim to be a masterpiece. In fact, it is a masterpiece and, like Waterville, very probably a perfect course as well as a great one.

In July 2002 Tiger Woods helicoptered into The European Club with three of his pals, Mark O'Meara, David Duval, and Scott McCarron. The four of them believed that a round here could be useful preparation for the British Open at Muirfield a week later. Playing from the tips, 7,323 yards, Woods returned a course-record 67, beating the 69 shared by Padraig Harrington and Eamon Darcy.

Ruddy walked along with the Americans, occasionally pointing out features and requirements of the holes. As the group stood on the tee of the 459-yard 12th, admiring the sea view, the Irishman turned to Woods, who had the honor. "What I think you'll want to do here," he said, "is set your drive out on the right, toward the bunker, with a little draw. That way—"

O'Meara cut him off. "Ah, Pat, just the hole. Tiger can handle the shot." O'Meara was smiling, as was Woods. And so was Pat Ruddy, who could be forgiven, because it's difficult not to be a little proprietary when you are the proprietor.

Above: The European Club, 14th. Opposite: 17th.

Ten minutes from The European Club is **Tinakilly House**, on the outskirts of the village of Rathnew. An oak-lined driveway curves up to the high ground where this substantial country-house hotel is situated. The gracious Victorian/Italianate structure is framed by seven acres of gardens. The public spaces can be opulent—the great reception hall boasts ceilings at least thirty feet high, with a broad and imposing staircase and, quite frequently, logs aglow in the marble fireplace. All fifty-two accommodations, including suites and junior suites, are appointed with antiques and period furnishings. A member of Small Luxury Hotels of the World, Tinakilly House is highly regarded for its food, and the kitchen garden inspires a number of dishes, including beetroot chutney and a beetroot and apple relish.

Five minutes from Tinakilly House, in Ashford, is the **Chester Beatty Inn**, an hospitable family-run enterprise with twelve guest rooms (spiffy, cheerful, and with pristine bathrooms), a traditional bar with fireplace, and cooking that satisfies.

From left: tower at Glendalough; Tinakilly House, outside and in-; the Gap of Wicklow.

Less than fifteen minutes up the N11 toward Dublin lies the **Glenview Hotel**, at Glen O' The Downs, in the foothills of the Wicklow Mountains. There is a nice warmth to public spaces and guest rooms. The total of seventy accommodations—many with captivating views up the glen itself—includes thirteen suites. The cooking is good, but don't expect an extensive menu.

The long Wicklow coast, stretching from Bray in the north, just outside Dublin, down to Clogga in the south, offers sailing and, below the county town of Wicklow, bathing at Silver Strand, Jack's Hole, Brittas Bay, and Clogga. Inland, marvelous attractions abound. Outside the village of Enniskerry is the Powerscourt Estate, whose forty-seven acres of gardens (Irish, English, Japanese, Italian), many of them terraced, are open to the public, but the great house itself is not.

Due west of Powerscourt is Russborough, one of the Republic's grandest stately homes. Dating from 1750 and built in the Palladian style, it is a treasure trove of antiques, tapestries, carpets, bronzes, and, most notably, Dutch, Flemish, and Spanish paintings.

To the southwest and just beyond Ashford are the gardens of Mount Usher, with some rare plants and an impressive collection of carriages and carts. Farther south are the thatched roofs of Avoca, better known to American viewers of the BBC-TV series as Ballykissangel, a fetching Irish village if ever there was one.

Essentially in the center of the county and probably Wicklow's most important attraction is Glendalough, an ancient monastic settlement that was home, during the Dark Ages, to at least one thousand monks and more than three thousand lay people studying under them. In all of Ireland there is nothing quite like Glendalough, which is situated on two lakes deep in the mountains. Here we find evocative ruins of a cathedral dating to the early ninth century, a very tall stone bell tower that is a thousand years old and in perfect condition, a twelfth century priest's house (partly rebuilt in the nineteenth century), a two-story oratory in good condition, and the

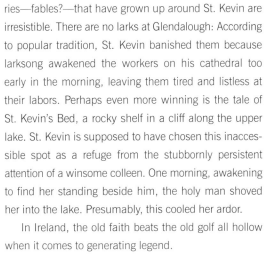

remnants of a number of other very early structures. Over it all hang the myth and mystique of Glendalough's founder, St. Kevin, who built a church on the upper lake in the first part of the seventh century. The pious stories—fables?—that have grown up around St. Kevin are irresistible. There are no larks at Glendalough: According to popular tradition, St. Kevin banished them because larksong awakened the workers on his cathedral too early in the morning, leaving them tired and listless at their labors. Perhaps even more winning is the tale of St. Kevin's Bed, a rocky shelf in a cliff along the upper lake. St. Kevin is supposed to have chosen this inaccessible spot as a refuge from the stubbornly persistent attention of a winsome colleen. One morning, awakening to find her standing beside him, the holy man shoved her into the lake. Presumably, this cooled her ardor.

In Ireland, the old faith beats the old golf all hollow when it comes to generating legend.

Top row, from left: Powerscourt Waterfall; statues and gardens at Powerscourt. Middle: countryside near Powerscourt and scenes of Arklow. Bottom: the town of Bray.

COURSES

Scotland

Alyth Golf Club
Alyth, Perthshire PH11 8JJ
Tel: 44-1828-632-411
www.alythgolfclub.co.uk

Anstruther Golf Club
Anstruther, Fife
Tel: 44-1333-310-956
www.anstruthergolf.co.uk

Arbroath Golf Links
Arbroath, Angus DD11 2PE
Tel: 44-1241-875-837
www.scottishgolfcourses.com
/heartland/arbroath.html

Auchterarder Golf Club
Auchterarder, Perthshire PH3 1DZ
Tel: 44-1292-313-471
www.aucherfieldgolf.co.uk

Barassie Links, Kilmarnock Golf Club
Barassie, Troon, Ayrshire KA10 6SY
Tel: 44-1292-313-920
www.kbgc.co.uk

Belleisle Golf Club
c/o S. Ayrshire Council, Burns House
Burns SQ, Ayrshire KA7 1UT
Tel: 44-1292-441-258

Blairgowrie Golf Club
Rosemount, Blairgowrie PH10 6LG
Tel: 44-1250-872-622
www.theblairgowriegolfclub.co.uk

Boat of Garten Golf and Tennis Club
Boat of Garten, Inverness-Shire
PH24 3BQ
Tel: 44-1479-831-282
www.boatgolf.com

Braid Hills–Braids No. 1
Edinburgh EH10 6JY
Tel: 44-1-31-447-6666
www.greenfeesavers.co.uk
/southeast/braidhillsone.html

Brora Golf Club
Brora, Sutherland KW9 6QS
Tel: 44-1408-621-417
www.broragolf.co.uk

Bruntsfield Links Golfing Society
Davidson's Mains, Edinburgh
EH4 6JH
Tel: 44-1-31-336-2006
www.sol.co.uk/b/bruntsfieldlinks

Carnoustie Golf Links
Carnoustie, Angus DD7 7JE
Tel: 44-1241-853-789
www.carnoustiegolflinks.com

Charleton Golf Course
Colinsburgh, Fife KY9 1HG
Tel: 44-1333-340-505
www.charleton.co.uk

Craigielaw Golf Club
Aberlady, East Lothian EH32 0PY
Tel: 44-1875-870-800
www.craigielawgolfclub.com

Crail Golfing Society–Balcomie and Craighead Links
Fifeness, Crail KY10 3XN
Tel: 44-1333-450-686
www.crailgolfingsociety.co.uk

Cruden Bay Golf Club
Cruden Bay, Peterhead AB42 0NN
Tel: 44-1779-812-414
www.crudenbaygolfclub.co.uk

Dalmahoy Hotel, Golf & Country Club
Kirknewton, Lothian EH27 8EB
Tel: 44-1-31-333-1845
http://marriott.co.uk/Channels/global
Sites/propertypage/UK/edigs

Downfield Golf Club
Dundee, Angus DD2 3QP
Tel: 44-1382-825-595
www.downfieldgolfclub.co.uk

Duddingston Golf Club
Duddingston Road West, Edinburgh
E15 3QD
Tel: 44-1-31-652-6057
www.golftoday.co.uk/clubhouse/course
dir/scotland/Midlothian/duddingston.html

Duke's Course, The
Craigtown, St. Andrews, Fife
KY16 89S
Tel: 44-1334-474-371
www.oldcoursehotel.co.uk

Dunaverty Golf Club
Southend, Argyll PA28 6RW
Tel: 44-1586-830-677
www.dunavertygolfclub.com

Dunbar Golf Club
East Links, Dunbar, East Lothian
EH42 1LT
Tel: 44-1368-862-317
www.dunbar-golfclub.co.uk

Edzell Golf Club
Edzell, Angus DD9 7TF
Tel: 44-1356-647-283
www.edzellgolfclub.net

Elgin Golf Club
Hardhillock, Morayshire IV30 8SX
Tel: 44-1343-542-884
www.elgingolfclub.com

Elie, The Golf House Club
Elie, Fife KY9 1AS
Tel: 44-1333-330-301
www.golfhouseclub.org

Forfar Golf Club
Forfar, Angus DD8 2RL
Tel: 44-1307-465-683
www.forfargolfclub.com

Fortrose and Rosemarkie Golf Club
Fortrose, Ross-Shire IV10 8SE
Tel: 44-1381-620-529
www.fortrosegolfclub.co.uk

Glasgow Golf Club–Glasgow Gailes
Glasgow Golf Club, Killermont,
Bearsden G61 2TW
Tel: 44-141-942-2011
www.glasgowgailes-golf.com

Gleneagles Hotel
Auchterarder, Perthshire PH3 1NF
Tel: 44-1764-694-469
www.gleneagles.com

Golspie Golf Club
Golspie, Sutherland KW10 6ST
Tel: 44-1408-633-266
www.golspie-golf.co.uk

Grantown-on-Spey Golf Club
Grantown-on-Spey, Morayshire
PH26 3HY
Tel: 44-1479-872-079
www.grantownonspeygolfclub.co.uk

Gullane Golf Club
Gullane, East Lothian EH31 2BB
Tel: 44-1620-842-255
www.gullanegolfclub.com

Irvine Golf Club, Bogside
Bogside, Irvine, Ayrshire KA12 8SN
Tel: 44-1294-275-979
www.theirvinegolfclub.co.uk

Kilspindie Golf Club
Aberlady, East Lothian EH32 0QD
Tel: 44-1875-870-358
www.golfeastlothian.com

Kingsbarns Golf Links
Kingsbarns, Fife KY16 8QD
Tel: 44-1334-460-861
www.kingsbarns.com

Kirriemuir, Golf Club
Kirriemuir, Angus DD8 4LN
Tel: 44-1575-573-317
www.kirriemuirgolfclub.co.uk

Lanark Golf Club
Lanark, Strathclyde ML11 7RX
Tel: 44-1555-661-456
www.lanarkgolfclub.co.uk

Letham Grange Golf Course
Colliston, Angus DD11 4RL
Tel: 44-1241-890-725
http://www.golfeurope.com/clubs
/letham_grange/index.htm

Leven Links Golf Club
Leven, Fife KY8 4HS
Tel: 44-1333-428-859
www.leven-links.com

Loch Lomond Golf Club
Luss, Dunbartonshire G83 8NT
Tel: 44-1436-655-555
www.lochlomond.com

Longniddry Golf Club, Ltd.
Longniddry, East Lothian EH32 0NL
Tel: 44-1875-852-141
www.longniddrygolfclub.co.uk

Luffness New Golf Club
Aberlady, East Lothian EH32 0QA
Tel: 44-1620-843-336
www.luffnessgolf.com

Lundin Golf Club—Lundin Links
Lundin Links, Fife KY8 6BA
Tel: 44-1333-320-202
www.lundingolfclub.co.uk

Machrie, The
Port Ellen, Islay PA42 7AN
Tel: 44-1496-302-310
www.machrie.com

Machrihanish Golf Club
Machrihanish, Argyll PA28 6PT
Tel: 44-1586-810-277
www.machgolf.com

Meldrum House Golf Club
Oldmeldrum, Aberdeenshire
AB51 0AE
Tel: 44-1651-873-553
www.meldrumhousegolf.co.uk

Monifieth Golf Links
Monifieth, Angus DD5 4AW
Tel: 44-1382-535-553
www.monifieth.co.uk

Montrose Links Trust
Montrose, Angus DD10 8SW
Tel: 44-1674-672-932
www.montroselinks.co.uk

Moray Golf Club
Lossiemouth, Morayshire IV31 6QS
Tel: 44-1343-812-018
www.moraygolf.co.uk

**Muirfield (Honorable Company of
Edinburgh Golfers)**
Gullane, East Lothian EH31 2EG
Tel: 44-1620-842-123
www.muirfield.org.uk

Murcar Golf Club
Bridge of Don, Aberdeenshire AB23
8BD
Tel: 44-1224-704-354
www.murcar.co.uk

Musselburgh Golf Club
Monktonhall, Lothian EH21 6SA
Tel: 44-1-31-665-2055
www.themusselburghgolfclub.com

**Musselburgh Links,
The Old Golf Course**
Musselburgh, East Lothian EH21 7SD
Tel: 44-1-31-665-5438
www.musselburgholdlinks.co.uk

Nairn Dunbar Golf Club
Nairn, Nairnshire IV12 5AE
Tel: 44-1667-452-741
www.nairndunbar.com

Nairn Golf Club
Nairn, Nairnshire IV12 4HB
Tel: 44-1667-453-208
www.nairngolfclub.co.uk

**North Berwick East Links
(The Glen)**
North Berwick, East Lothian
EH39 4LE
Tel: 44-1620-892-726
www.glengolfclub.co.uk

**North Berwick Golf Club
(West Links)**
North Berwick, East Lothian
EH39 4BB
Tel: 44-1620-892-135
www.northberwickgolfclub.com

Panmure Golf Club
Barry by Carnoustie, Angus DD7 7T
Tel: 44-1241-855-120
www.panmuregolfclub.co.uk

Peterhead Golf Club
Peterhead, Aberdeenshire AB42 1LT
Tel: 44-1779-472-149
www.peterheadgolfclub.co.uk

Prestwick Golf Club
Prestwick, Ayrshire KA9 1QC
Tel: 44-1292-671-020
www.prestwickgc.co.uk

Prestwick St. Nicholas Golf Club
Prestwick, Ayrshire KA9 1SX
Tel: 44-1292-473-900
www.prestwickstnicholas.com

Royal Aberdeen Golf Club
Balgownie, Aberdeenshire AB23 8AT
Tel: 44-1224-702-571
www.royalaberdeengolf.com

Royal Burgess Golfing Society
181 Whitehouse Road, Edinburgh
EH4 6BY
Tel: 44-1-313-339-2075
www.royalburgess.co.uk

Royal Dornoch Golf Club
Dornoch, Sutherland IV25 3LW
Tel: 44-1862-810-219
www.royaldornoch.com

Royal Musselburgh Golf Club
Prestonpans, East Lothian EH32 9RP
Tel: 44-1875-810-276
www.royalmusselburgh.co.uk

Royal Troon Golf Club
Troon, Ayrshire KA10 6EP
Tel: 44-1292-311-555
www.royaltroon.com

**St. Andrews Bay–Torrance and
Devlin Courses**
St. Andrews, Fife KY16 8PN
Tel: 44-1334-837-412
www.standrewsbay.com

**St. Andrews Links Courses–Old,
New, Jubilee, Eden, Strathtyrum,
Balgove**
St. Andrews, Fife KY16 9SF
Tel: 44-1334-466-666
www.standrews.org.uk

Shiskine Golf and Tennis Club
Blackwaterfoot, Isle of Arran, KA27
8HA
Tel: 44-1770-860-205
www.shiskinegolf.com

Skibo Castle, Carnegie Club
Dornoch, Sutherland IV25 3RQ
Tel: 44-1862-894-600
www.carnegieclub.co.uk

Stonehaven Golf Club
Stonehaven, Kincardineshire AB39 3RH
Tel: 44-1569-762-124
www.stonehavengolfclub.co.uk

Tain Golf Club
Tain, Ross-shire IV19 1PA
Tel: 44-1862-892-314
www.tain-golfclub.co.uk

**Turnberry Hotel–Ailsa and Kintyre
Courses**
Turnberry, Ayrshire KA26 9LT
Tel: 44-1655-334-135
www.turnberry.co.uk

Western Gailes Golf Club
Gailes, Irvine, Ayrshire KA11 5AE
Tel: 44-1294-311-649
www.westerngailes.com

Whitekirk Golf and Country Club
Whitekirk, East Lothian EH39 5PR
Tel: 44-1620-870-300
www.whitekirk.com

Wick Golf Club
Wick, Caithness KW1 4RW
Tel: 44-1955-602-726
www.wickgolfclub.com

Winterfield Golf Club
Dunbar, East Lothian EH42 1AU
Tel: 44-1368-863-562
www.winterfieldgolfclub.net

Ireland

Adare Manor Golf Club
Adare, Co. Limerick
Tel: 353-61-396204

Adare Manor Hotel & Golf Resort
Adare, Co. Limerick
Tel: 353-61-396566
www.adaremanor.ie

Ardglass Golf Club
Castle Place, Ardglass, Co. Down
BT30 7TP
Northern Ireland
Tel: 44-28-4484-1022
www.ardglassgolfclub.com

Ballybunion Golf Club
Sandhill Road, Ballybunion, Co. Kerry
Tel: 353-68-27146
www.ballybuniongolfclub.ie

Ballycastle Golf Club
Cushendall Road, Ballycastle, Co.
Antrim BT54 6PQ
Northern Ireland
Tel: 44-28-2076-2506
www.ballycastlegolfclub.com

Ballyliffin Golf Club
Ballyliffin, Co. Donegal
Tel: 353-74-937-6119
www.ballyliffingolfclub.com

Bantry Bay Golf Club
Bantry, Co. Cork
Tel: 353-27-50579
www.bantrygolf.com

Beaufort Golf Course
Churchtown, Beaufort, Co. Kerry
Tel: 353-64-44440
www.beaufortgolfclub.com

Bundoran Golf Club
Bundoran, Co. Donegal
Tel: 353-71-984-1302
http://www.bundorangolfclub.com
/contactpage.htm

Carlow Golf Club
Deerpark, Carlow, Co. Carlow
Tel: 353-59-913-1695
www.carlowgolfclub.com

Carne Golf Course
Belmullet, Co. Mayo
Tel: 353-97-82292
www.carnegolflinks.com

Carton House Golf Club
Carton, Maynooth, Co. Kildare
Tel: 353-1-505-2000
www.carton.ie

Castlerock Golf Club
65 Circular Road, Castlerock, Co.
Londonderry BT51 4TJ
Northern Ireland
Tel: 44-28-7084-8314
www.castlerockgc.co.uk

Ceann Sibeal Golf Club
Ballyferriter, Co. Kerry
Tel: 353-66-915-6255
www.dinglelinks.com

Connemara Golf Club
Ballyconneeley, Co. Galway
Tel: 353-95-23502
www.connemaragolflinks.com

Cork Golf Club
Little Island, Cork, Co. Cork
Tel: 353-21-435-3451
www.corkgolfclub.ie

County Louth Golf Club
Baltray, Co. Louth
Tel: 353-41-988-1530
www.countylouthgolfclub.com

County Sligo Golf Club
Rosses Point, Co. Sligo
Tel: 353-71-917-7134
www.countysligogolfclub.ie

Donegal Golf Club
Murvagh, Ballintra, Co. Donegal
Tel: 353-74-973-4054
www.donegalgolfclub.ie

Dooks Golf Club
Dooks, Killorglin, Co. Kerry
Tel: 353-66-976-8205
www.dooks.com

Doonbeg Golf Club
Doonbeg, Co. Clare
Tel: 353-65-905-5246
www.doonbeggolfclub.com

**Dromoland Castle Hotel &
Country Estate**
Newmarket-on-Fergus, Co. Clare
Tel: 353-61-368144
www.dromoland.ie

Druids Glen Golf Club
Newtownmountkennedy, Co. Wicklow
Tel: 353-1-287-3600
www.druidsglen.ie

Dunloe Golf Course
Gap of Dunloe, Killarney, Co. Kerry
Tel: 353-64-44578
www.dunloegc.com

Enniscrone Golf Club
Enniscrone, Co. Sligo
Tel: 353-96-36297
www.enniscronegolf.com

European Club, The
Brittas Bay, Co. Wicklow
Tel: 353-404-47415
www.theeuropeanclub.com

Farrangalway Golf Club
Kinsale, Co. Cork
Tel: 353-21-477-4722
www.kinsalegolf.com

Fota Island Golf Club
Fota Island, Carrigtwohill, Co. Cork
Tel: 353-21-883700
www.fotaisland.ie

Galway Bay Golf & Country Club
Renville, Oranmore, Co. Galway
Tel: 353-91-790500
www.lawrencetown.com/galgolf.htm

**Glasson Golf Hotel &
Country Club**
Glasson, Athlone, Co. Westmeath
Tel: 353-90-648-5120
www.glassongolf.ie

Glengarriff Golf Club
Glengarriff, Co. Cork
Tel: 353-27-63150

Harbour Point Golf Complex
Little Island, Cork, Co. Cork
Tel: 353-21-358-3094
www.harbourpointgolfclub.com

Island Golf Club, The
Corballis, Donabate, Co. Dublin
Tel: 353-1-843-6205
www.theislandgolfclub.com

Kenmare Golf Club
Kenmare, Co. Kerry
Tel: 353-64-41291
www.kenmaregolfclub.com

Kildare Hotel & Country Club
Straffan, Co. Kildare
Tel: 353-1601-7200
www.kclub.ie

Killarney Golf & Fishing Club
Killarney, Co. Kerry
Tel: 353-64-31034
www.killarney-golf.com

Kinsale Golf Club
Kinsale, Co. Cork
Tel: 353-21-477-4722
www.kinsalegolf.com

Kirkistown Castle Golf Club
142 Main Road, Cloughey, Co. Down
BT22 1JΛ
Northern Ireland
Tel: 44-28-4277-1004
www.linksgolfkirkistown.com

Lahinch Golf Club
Lahinch, Co. Clare
Tel: 353-65-708-1003
www.lahinchgolf.com

**Laytown & Bettystown
Golf Club**
Bettystown, Co. Meath
Tel: 353-41-982-7170
www.landb.ie

**Limerick County Golf and
Country Club**
Ballyneety, Co. Limerick
Tel: 353-61-351881
www.limerickcounty.com

Malone Golf Club
Upper Malone Road, Dunmurry, Co.
Belfast BT17 9LB
Northern Ireland
Tel: 44-28-9061-4917
www.malonegolfclub.co.uk

Mount Juliet
Thomastown, Co. Kilkenny
Tel: 353-56-77-73000
www.mountjuliet.com

Mullingar Golf Club
Belvedere, Mullingar, Co. Westmeath
Tel: 353-44-48366
www.mullingargolfclub.com

Narin & Portnoo Golf Club
Portnoo, Co. Donegal
Tel: 353-75-45107
www.narinportnoogolfclub.ie

Old Head Golf Links
Old Head of Kinsale, Co. Cork
Tel: 353-21-477-8444
www.oldheadgolflinks.com

Parknasilla Golf Club
Parknasilla, Co. Kerry
Tel: 353-64-45233
www.sneem.net/parknasilla

PGA National Golf Club
Johnstown, Co. Kildare
Tel: 353-45-906901
www.palmerstownhouse.com

Portmarnock Golf Club
Portmarnock, Co. Dublin
Tel: 353-1-846-2968
www.portmarnockgolfclub.ie

**Portmarnock Hotel and
Golf Links**
Strand Road, Portmarnock, Co. Dublin
Tel: 353-1-846-0611
www.portmarnock.com

Portsalon Golf Club
Portsalon, Co. Donegal
Tel: 353-74-915-9459
www.golfeurope.com/clubs/portsalon/

Portstewart Golf Club
117 Strand Road, Portstewart, Co.
Londonderry BT55 7PG
Northern Ireland
Tel: 44-28-7083-2015
www.portstewart.co.uk

Roganstown Golf & Country Club
Swords, Co. Dublin
Tel: 353-1-843-3118
www.roganstown.com

Rosapenna Hotel & Golf Links
Downings, Co. Donegal
Tel: 353-74-915-5301
www.rosapenna.ie

Royal County Down Golf Club
Newcastle, Co. Down BT33 0AN
Northern Ireland
Tel: 44-28-4372-3314
www.royalcountydown.org

Royal Dublin Golf Club
Dollymount, Dublin 3
Tel: 353-1-833-6504
www.theroyaldublingolfclub.com

Royal Portrush Golf Club
Dunluce Road, Portrush, Co. Antrim
BT56 8JQ
Northern Ireland
Tel: 44-28-7082-2311
www.royalportrushgolfclub.com

St. Patrick's Golf Links
Carrigart, Co. Donegal
Tel: 353-74-915-5114
www.stpatricksgolflinks.com

Seapoint Golf Club
Termonfeckin, Co. Louth
Tel: 353-41-982-2333
www.globalgolf.com/seapoint

Strandhill Golf Club
Strandhill, Co. Sligo
Tel: 353-71-916-8725
www.strandhillgc.com

Tralee Golf Club
Barrow, Co. Kerry
Tel: 353-66-713-6379
www.traleegolfclub.com

Tramore Golf Club
Newtown Hill, Tramore, Co. Waterford
Tel: 353-51-386170
www.tramoregolfclub.com

**Waterford Castle Hotel &
Golf Club**
The Island, Waterford, Co. Waterford
Tel: 353-51-878203
www.waterfordcastle.com

Waterville Golf Links
Waterville, Co. Kerry
Tel: 353-66-947-4102
www.watervillegolflinks.ie

Westport Golf Club
Carrowholly, Westport, Co. Mayo
Tel: 353-98-28262
http://homepage.eircom.net
/~westportgolf/

HOTELS

Scotland

Ardell House
Machrihanish, Argyll PA28 6PT
Tel: 44-1586-810-235
www.milford.co.uk/go/ardellhouse.html

Auchendean Lodge
Dulnain Bridge, Inverness-Shire
PH26 3LU
Tel: 44-1479-851-347
www.auchendean.com

Auchterarder House Hotel
Auchterarder, Perthshire PH3 1DZ
Tel: 44-1764-663-646

Balcomie Links Hotel
Crail, Fifeness, Fife KY10 3TN
Tel: 44-1333-450-237
www.balcomie.co.uk

Balmoral Hotel
1 Princes St., Edinburgh EH2 2EQ
Tel: 44-1-31-556-2414
www.thebalmoralhotel.com

Bayswell Hotel
Dunbar, East Lothian EH42 1AE
Tel: 44-1368-862-225
www.bayswell.co.uk

Blenheim House Hotel
North Berwick, East Lothian
EH39 4AF
Tel: 44-1620-892-385
http://www.blenheimhousehotel.com/

Boat Hotel
Boat of Garten, Inverness-Shire
PH24 3BQ
Tel: 44-1479-831-258
www.boathotel.co.uk

Boath House
Auldearn, Nairn, Nairnshire IV12 5TE
Tel: 44-1667-454-896
www.boath-house.com

Burghfield House Hotel
Dornoch, Sutherland IV25 3HN
Tel: 44-1862-810-212
www.burghfieldhouse.com

Caledonian Hilton
Princes Street, Edinburgh EH1 2AB
Tel: 44-1-31-222-8888
www.hilton.com

Cameron House Hotel
Alexandria, Dunbartonshire GH3 8QZ
Tel: 44-1389-755-565
www.devere.co.uk/hotels/cameron

Carlogie House Hotel
Carnoustie, Angus DD7 6LD
Tel: 44-1241-853-185
www.carlogie-house-hotel.com

Carnoustie Golf Course Hotel & Resort
Carnoustie, Angus DD7 7JE
Tel: 44-1241-411-999
www.carnoustie-hotel.com

Cartland Bridge Hotel
Lanark, Strathclyde ML11 9UE
Tel: 44-1555-664-426
www.cartlandbridge.co.uk

Channings
South Learmonth Gardens, Edinburgh
EH4 1EZ
Tel: 44-1-31-623-9302
www.channings.co.uk

Craigsanquhar House
Cupar, Fife KY15 4PZ
Tel: 44-1334-653-426
www.craigsanquhar.com

Crusoe Hotel
Lower Largo, Fife KY8 6BT
Tel: 44-1333-320-759
www.crusoehotel.co.uk

Culloden House
Culloden, Inverness-Shire IV2 7BZ
Tel: 44-1463-790-461
www.cullodenhouse.co.uk

Culzean Castle Apartments
Culzean Castle, Maybole, Ayrshire
KA19 8LE
Tel: 44-1655-760-274
www.informationbritain.co.uk
/showPlace.cfm?Place_ID=1210

**Dalmahoy Hotel,
Golf & Country Club**
Kirknewton, Lothian EH27 8EB
Tel: 44-1-31-333-1845
http://marriott.co.uk/Channels/global
Sites/propertypage/UK/edigs

Delnashaugh Inn
Ballindalloch, Banffshire AB37 9AS
Tel: 44-1807-500-255
www.delnashaugh.co.uk

Dornoch Castle Hotel
Dornoch, Sutherland IV25 3SD
Tel: 44-1862-810-216
www.dornochcastlehotel.com

Five Gables House
Arbroath, Angus DD11 2PE
Tel: 44-1241-871-632
www.hotelsandguesthouses.net/500468

Glebe House
North Berwick, East Lothian EH39 4PL
Tel: 44-1620-892-608
www.glebehouse-nb.co.uk

Glenaveron House
Brora, Sutherland KW9 6QS
Tel: 44-4108-621-601
www.glenaveron.co.uk

Gleneagles Hotel
Auchterarder, Perthshire PH3 1NF
Tel: 44-1764-662-231
www.gleneagles.com

Golf View Hotel
Nairn, Nairnshire IV12 4HD
Tel: 44-1667-452-301
www.swallow-hotels.com

Golf View Private Hotel
Prestwick, Ayrshire KA9 1QG
Tel: 44-1292-671-234
www.golfviewhotel.com

Greannan House, The
Blackwaterfoot, Isle of Arran
KA27 8HB
Tel: 44-1770-860-200
www.thegreannan.co.uk

Greywalls Country House Hotel
Gullane, East Lothian EH31 2EG
Tel: 44-1620-842-1444
www.greywalls.co.uk

Harford House
26 Harling Drive, Troon, Ayrshire
KA10 6NF
Tel: 44-1292-679-401
www.harfordhouse.com

Howard, The
Great King Street, Edinburgh
EH3 6QH
Tel: 44-1-31-623-9303
www.thehoward.com

Kilmarnock Arms
Cruden Bay, Aberdeenshire
AB4 7ND
Tel: 44-1779-812-213
www.kilmarnockarms.com

Kilmichael County House
Brodick, Isle of Arran KA27 8BT
Tel: 44-1770-302-219
www.kilmichael.com

Kinloch Hotel
Blackwaterfoot, Isle of Arran
KA27 8ET
Tel: 44-1770-860-444
www.bw-kinlochhotel.co.uk

Kinloch House Hotel
Dunkeld, Perthshire PH10 6SG
Tel: 44-1250-884-237
www.kinlochhouse.com

Lochgreen House Hotel
Troon, Ayrshire KA10 7EN
Tel: 44-1292-313-343
www.costley-hotels.co.uk

Lundin Links Hotel
Lundin Links, Fife KY8 6AP
Tel: 44-1333-320-207
www.lundin-links-hotel.co.uk

Machrie Hotel, The
Port Ellen Islay PA42 7AN
Tel: 44-1496-302 310
www.machrie.com

Mansion House Hotel
Elgin, Morayshire IV30 1AW
Tel: 44-1343-548-811
www.mansionhousehotel.co.uk

Marcliffe at Pitfodels
Aberdeen, Aberdeenshire AB15 9YA
Tel: 44-1224-861-000
www.marcliffe.com

Marine Hotel
Crail, Fife KY10 32Z
Tel: 44-1333-450-207

Marine Hotel
North Berwick, East Lothian
EH39 4LZ
Tel: 44-1620-892-406
www.macdonaldhotels.co.uk

Marine Hotel
Troon, Ayrshire KA10 6HE
Tel: 44-1292-314-444
www.paramount-hotels.co.uk

Meldrum House
Oldmeldrum, Aberdeenshire
AB51 0AE
Tel: 44-1651-872-294
www.meldrumhousegolf.co.uk

Myres Castle
Auchtermuchty, Fife KY14 7EW
Tel: 44-1327-828-350
www.myres.co.uk

Newton Hotel
Nairn, Nairnshire IV12 4RX
Tel: 44-1667-453-154
www.swallow-hotels.com

North Beach Hotel
Prestwick, Ayrshire KA9 1QG
Tel: 44-1292-479-069
www.northbeach.co.uk

Old Aberlady Inn
Aberlady, East Lothian EH32 0RF
Tel: 44-1875-870-503
http://www.aberlady.org/Hotels.html

Old Course Hotel
St. Andrews, Fife KY16 9SP
Tel: 44-1334-474-371
www.oldcoursehotel.co.uk

Open Arms Hotel
Dirleton, East Lothian EH39 5EG
Tel: 44-1620-850-241
www.openarmshotel.com

Park Hotel
Montrose, Angus DD10 8RJ
Tel: 44-1674-663-400
www.montrosepark.co.uk

Parkstone Hotel
Prestwick, Ayrshire KA9 1QN
Tel: 44-1292-477-286
www.parkstonehotel.co.uk

Piersland House Hotel
Troon, Ayrshire KA10 6HD
Tel: 44-1292-314-747
www.piersland.co.uk

Red House Hotel
Cruden Bay, Aberdeenshire AB4 7ND
Tel: 44-1779-812-215

Rosslyn Castle
Roslin, Lothian
c/o Landmark Trust
Tel: 44-1628-825-925
www.landmarktrust.org.uk

Royal Golf Hotel
Dornoch, Sutherland IV25 3LG
Tel: 44-1862-810-283
www.swallow-hotels.com

Royal Marine Hotel
Brora, Sutherland KW9 6QS
Tel: 44-1408-621-252
www.highlandescapehotels.com

Rufflets Country House Hotel
Strathkinness Low Road
St. Andrews, Fife KY16 9TX
Tel: 44-1334-472-594
www.rufflets.co.uk

Rusacks Hotel
St. Andrews, Fife KY16 9JQ
Tel: 44-1334-474-321
www.macdonaldhotels.co.uk

St. Andrews Bay Golf Resort & Spa
St. Andrews, Fife KY16 8PN
Tel: 44-1334-837-000
www.standrewsbay.com

Scores Hotel, The
St. Andrews, Fife KY19 9BB
Tel: 44-1334-472-451
www.bestwestern.com

Shore Cottage
Saddell, Argyll
c/o Landmark Trust
Tel: 44-1628-825-925
www.landmarktrust.org.uk

Skibo Castle, Carnegie Club
Dornoch, Sutherland IV25 3RQ
Tel: 44-1862-894-600
www.carnegieclub.co.uk

Stotfield Hotel
Lossiemouth, Morayshire IV31 6QS
Tel: 44-1343-812-011
www.swallow-hotels.com

Tigh Fada
Brora, Sutherland KW9 6QS
Tel: 44-1408-621-332
www.tighfada.fsnet.co.uk

Trevose Guest House
Dornoch, Sutherland IV25 3SD
Tel: 44-1862-810-269
www.sutherland-business.co.uk
/business.php?id=206

Turnberry Hotel
Turnberry, Ayrshire KA26 9LT
Tel: 44-1655-331-000
www.turnberry.co.uk

Udny Arms Hotel
Newburgh, Aberdeenshire AB4 0BL
Tel: 44-1358-789-444
www.udny.co.uk

Waldon House
St. Andrews, Fife KY16 9JB
Tel: 44-1334-472-112

White Hart Hotel
Campbeltown, Argyll PA28 6PT
Tel: 44-1586-552-440
www.whiteh.com

Ireland

Aberdeen Arms
Lahinch, Co. Clare
Tel: 353-65-708-1100
http://www.a1tourism.com/ireland
/lahinch-aberdeen-arms.html

Adare Manor Hotel &
Golf Resort
Adare, Co. Limerick
Tel: 353-61-396 566
www.adaremanor.ie

Aherne's Seafood Bar
163 N. Main Street
Youghal, Co. Cork
Tel: 353-24-92424
www.ahernes.com

Albany House
Harcourt Street, Dublin 2
Tel: 353-1-475-1092
www.holidaycityeurope.com
/albany-house-dublin/index.htm

An Tintean Guest House
Doonbeg, Co. Clare
Tel: 353-65-905-5036
http://homepage.eircom.net
/~antintean/

Hotel Ard Na Sidhe
Caragh Lake, Killorglin, Co. Kerry
Tel: 353-66-976-9105
www.killarneyhotels.ie/ardnasidhe

Ardtara Country House
8 Gorteade Road
Upperlands, Co. Londonderry
BT46 5SA
Northern Ireland
Tel: 44-28-7964-4490
www.ardtara.com

Ashford Castle
Cong, Co. Mayo
Tel: 353-94-954-6003
www.ashford.ie

Atlantic Hotel
Lahinch, Co. Clare
Tel: 353-65-708-1049
www.loguehotelgroup.com/atlantic

Ballinacurra House
Kinsale, Co. Cork
Tel: 353-21-477-9040
www.ballinacurra.com

Ballyliffin Hotel
Ballyliffin, Co. Donegal
Tel: 353-77-76106
www.ballyliffinhotel.com

Ballymaloe House
Shanagary, Co. Cork
Tel: 353-21-4652-531
www.ballymaloe.ie

Berkeley Court Hotel
Lansdowne Road, Ballsbridge, Dublin
Tel: 353-1-661711

Boyne Valley Hotel
Stameen, Drogheda, Co. Louth
Tel: 353-41-983-7737
www.boyne-valley-hotel.ie

Brook Manor Lodge
Fenit Road, Tralee, Co. Kerry
Tel: 353-66-712-0406
www.brookmanorlodge.com

Bruckless House
Bruckless, Co. Donegal
Tel: 353-74-973-7071
www.brucklesshouse.com

Bushmills Inn
9 Dunluce Road
Bushmills, Co. Antrim BT57 8GQ
Northern Ireland
Tel: 44-28-2073-3000
www.bushmillsinn.com

Butler Arms Hotel
Waterville, Co. Kerry
Tel: 353-66-947-4144
www.butlerarms.com

Caragh Lodge
Caragh Lake, Co. Kerry
Tel: 353-66-976-9115
www.caraghlodge.com

Cashel House Hotel
Cashel, Co. Galway
Tel: 353-95-31001
www.cashel-house-hotel.com

Chester Beatty Inn
Ashford, Co. Wicklow
Tel: 353-404-40206
www.hotelchesterbeatty.ie

Coopershill House
Rivertown, Co. Sligo
Tel: 353-71-916-5108
www.coopershill.com

Croaghross Guest House
Portsalon, Co. Donegal
Tel: 353-74-915-9548
www.croaghross.com

Cromleach Lodge
Castlebaldwin, Co. Sligo
Tel: 353-71-916-5455
www.cromleach.com

Doonbeg Golf Club
Doonbeg, Co. Clare
Tel: 353-65-905-5246
www.doonbeggolfclub.com

**Dromoland Castle Hotel &
Country Estate**
Newmarket-on-Fergus, Co. Clare
Tel: 353-61-368144
www.dromoland.ie

Druids Glen Marriott Hotel
Newtownmountkennedy, Co. Wicklow
Tel: 353-1-287-0800
http://marriott.com/property
/propertypage/DUBGS

Dunraven Arms Hotel
Adare, Co. Limerick
Tel: 353-61-396633
www.dunravenhotel.com

Enniscoe House
Castlehill Ballina, Co. Mayo
Tel: 353-96-31112
www.enniscoe.com

Hotel Europe
Killarney, Co. Kerry
Tel: 353-64-7130
www.killarneyhotels.ie

Fitzwilliam, The
41 Fitzwilliam St., Dublin 2
Tel: 353-1-662-5155
http://reservations.accommodation.ie
/avlcheckprem.asp?PremisesCode
=GAS07406

Four Seasons Hotel Dublin
Simmonscourt Road
Ballsbridge, Dublin 4
Tel: 353-1-665-4000
www.fourseasons.com

Glassdrumman Lodge
Mill Road
Annalong, Co. Down BT34 4RH
Northern Ireland
Tel: 44-28-4376-8451
www.glassdrummanlodge.com

Glasson Golf Hotel & Country Club
Glasson, Athlone, Co. Westmeath
Tel: 353-90-648-5120
www.glassongolf.ie

Glenview Hotel
Glen O'The Downs, Co. Wicklow
Tel; 353-1-287-3399
www.glenviewhotel.com

Glin Castle
Glin, Co. Limerick
Tel: 353-68-34173
www.glincastle.com

Great Southern Hotel
Killarney, Co Kerry
Tel: 353-1-214-4800
www.greatsouthernhotels.com

Gregans Castle Hotel
The Burren, Co. Clare
Tel: 353-65-707-7005
www.gregans.ie

Gresham Hotel
O'Connell Street, Dublin 1
Tel: 353-1-874-6881
www.gresham-hotels.com/htm
/dublin_i.htm

Harvey's Point Country Hotel
Lough Eske, Donegal Town,
Co. Donegal
Tel: 353-74-972-2208
www.harveyspoint.com

Highfield House
Baltray, Co. Louth
Tel: 353-41-982-2172

Kildare Hotel & Country Club
Straffan, Co. Kildare
Tel: 353-1601-7200
www.kclub.ie

Killarney Golf & Fishing Club
Killarney, Co. Kerry
Tel: 353-64-31034
www.killarney-golf.com

Killeen House
Killarney, Co. Kerry
Tel: 353-64-31711
www.killeenhousehotel.com

King Sitric Fish Restaurant and Accommodation
East Pier, Howth, Co. Dublin
Tel: 353-1-832-5235
www.kingsitric.ie

Links Lodge
Doonbeg, Co. Clare
Tel: 353-65-905-5600
www.irishprogolftours.com
/linkslodgedoonbeg.asp

Liscannor Hotel
Liscannor, Co. Clare
Tel: 353-65-708-6000
http://www.hotelclub.net/hotel
.reservations/Logues_Liscannor
_Hotel.htm

Lotamore House
Tivoli, Co. Clare
Tel: 353-21-482-2344
www.lotamorehouse.com

Marine Links Hotel
Golf Links Road, Ballybunion, Co. Kerry
Tel: 353-68-27522
www.marinelinkshotel.com

Meadowlands Hotel
Oakpark, Tralee, Co. Kerry
Tel: 353-66-718-0444
www.meadowlandshotel.com

Merrion Hotel
Merrion St., Dublin 2
Tel: 353-1-603-0600
www.merrionhotel.com

Mount Juliet
Thomastown, Co. Kilkenny
Tel: 353-56-77-73000
www.mountjuliet.com

Moy House
Lahinch, Co. Clare
Tel: 353-65-708-2800
www.moyhouse.com

Mustard Seed at Echo Lodge, The
Ballingary, Co. Limerick
Tel: 353-69-68508
www.mustardseed.ie

Old Bank House
Kinsale, Co. Cork
Tel: 353-21-477-4075
www.oldbankhousekinsale.com

Perryville House
Kinsale, Co. Cork
Tel: 353-21-477-2731
www.perryvillehouse.com

Portaferry Hotel
Portaferry, Co. Down
Tel: 44-28-427-28231
http://www.portaferryhotel.com

Portmarnock Hotel and Golf Links
Strand Road, Portmarnock, Co. Dublin
Tel: 353-1-846-0611
www.portmarnock.com

Rathmullan House
Rathmullan, Co. Donegal
Tel: 353-74-915-8188
www.rathmullanhouse.com

Rock Glen Hotel
Clifden, Connemara, Co. Galway
Tel: 353-95-21737
www.westirelandholidays.com
/galway/rockglen.htm

Roganstown Golf & Country Club
Swords, Co. Dublin
Tel: 353-1-843-3118
www.roganstown.com

Rosapenna Hotel & Golf Links
Downings, Co. Donegal
Tel: 353-74-915-5301
www.rosapenna.ie

St. Ernan's House Hotel
Donegal, Co. Donegal
Tel: 353-74-972-1065
www.sainternans.com

St. John's Country House & Restaurant
Fahan, Co. Donegal
Tel: 353-74-936-0289
www.ireland.ie/things_2_do_results_
single.asp?sID=246

Shelbourne Hotel
St. Stephen's Green, Dublin 2
Tel. 353-1-663-4500
www.shelbourne.ie

Slieve Donard Hotel
Downs Road, Newcastle, Co. Down
BT33 0AH
Northern Ireland
Tel: 44-28-4372-1066
www.hastingshotels.com

Stella Maris Hotel
Ballycastle, Co. Mayo
Tel: 353-96-43322
www.stellamarisireland.com

Strand Hotel
Ballyliffin, Co. Donegal
Tel: 353-74-937-6107
www.ballyliffin.com/strand/index.htm

Tinakilly Country House & Restaurant
Rathnew, Co. Wicklow
Tel: 353-404-69274
www.tinakilly.ie

Trasna House Hotel
Ballyliffin, Co. Donegal
Tel: 353-74-937-8688
www.trasnahouse.com

Trident Hotel
Kinsale, Co. Cork
Tel: 353-21-477-2301
www.tridenthotel.com

Waterford Castle Hotel & Golf Club
The Island, Waterford, Co. Waterford
Tel: 353-51-878203
www.waterfordcastle.com

Waterville House
Waterville, Co. Kerry
Tel: 353-66-947-4102
www.watervillegolflinks.ie

Westbury Hotel
Grafton Street, Dublin
Tel: 353-1-679-1122
www.jurysdoyle.com

Yeats Country Hotel
Rosses Point, Co. Sligo
Tel: 353-71-917-7211
www.yeatscountryhotel.com

GREAT ITINERARIES, GREAT SITES,

Scotland

SHORT WEEKENDS (2 GOLF DAYS)

Fly to Edinburgh or Glasgow
GOLF: St. Andrews Old Course, Kingsbarns, Elie
LODGING: Rusacks or The Scores
DINING: Peat Inn, Grange Inn

Fly to Aberdeen
GOLF: Royal Aberdeen, Murcar, Cruden Bay
LODGING: Marcliffe at Pitfodels (Aberdeen) or Udny Arms (Newburgh)
DINING: Same as Lodging

Fly to Edinburgh
GOLF: Gullane No. 1, North Berwick (West Links), Dunbar
LODGING: Golf Inn (Gullane) or Open Arms (Dirleton)
DINING: Same as Lodging

Fly to Glasgow
GOLF: Turnberry Ailsa and Kintyre, Prestwick
LODGING: Turnberry Hotel or North Beach Hotel (Prestwick)
DINING: Turnberry Hotel, Lochgreen House (Troon)

LONG WEEKENDS (4 GOLF DAYS)

Fly to Edinburgh or Glasgow
GOLF: St. Andrews Old and New Courses, St. Andrews Bay (Devlin Course), Kingsbarns, Crail (Balcomie), Carnoustie
LODGING: St. Andrews Bay Hotel or Rufflets Hotel
DINING: St. Andrews Links Clubhouse, Vine Leaf Restaurant, Balaka Bangladeshi, Craigsanquhar House (outside St. Andrews), The Cellar (Anstruther)

Fly to Edinburgh
GOLF: Muirfield, Gullane No. 1, North Berwick (West Links), Dunbar, Whitekirk, Longniddry
LODGING: Greywalls (Gullane) or Glebe House (North Berwick) or Marine Hotel (North Berwick)
DINING: Greywalls, Open Arms, Old Clubhouse (Gullane), Waterside Bistro (Haddington)

Fly to Glasgow
GOLF: Turnberry Ailsa and Kintyre, Prestwick, Western Gailes, Irvine/Bogside, Royal Troon
LODGING: Turnberry Hotel or Harford House B&B (Troon) or Lochgreen House (Troon) or Parkstone Hotel (Prestwick)
DINING: Same as Lodging except for Harford House

Fly to Inverness
GOLF: Nairn, Tain, Carnegie Club at Skibo Castle, Royal Dornoch, Brora, Golspie
LODGING: Culloden House (near Nairn), Newton Hotel (Nairn), Skibo Castle (Dornoch), Royal Golf Hotel (Dornoch), Trevose Guest House (Dornoch)
DINING: Boath House (Nairn), Culloden House, Skibo Castle, Burghfield House (Dornoch), Dornoch Castle Hotel

Dozen Best 36-Hole Days

Royal Aberdeen and Cruden Bay
Muirfield and North Berwick
St. Andrews Old Course and Crail (Balcomie Links)
Prestwick and Western Gailes
Kingsbarns and Leven
Gleneagles King's and Queens's
Royal Dornoch and Brora
Carnoustie Championship Course and Carnoustie Burnside Course
Turnberry Ailsa and Royal Troon
St. Andrews Bay (Devlin Course) and Lundin
St. Andrews New Course and Elie
Gullane No. 1 and Dunbar

Dozen Best Par 3s

St. Andrews Old Course–11
Kingsbarns–15
Crail (Craighead)–17
Carnoustie–16
Gleneagles King's–5
Cruden Bay–4
Carnegie Club, Skibo Castle–3
Royal Dornoch–6
Royal Troon–8
Turnberry Ailsa–6
North Berwick–15
Muirfield–13

Dozen Best Par 5s

St. Andrews Old Course–14
St. Andrews Jubilee Course–12
St. Andrews Bay (Devlin Course)–13
Kingsbarns–12
Carnoustie–6
Gleneagles PGA Centenary Course–16
Royal Aberdeen–2
Carnegie Club, Skibo Castle–18
Machrihanish–12
Loch Lomond–6
Prestwick–3
Gullane No. 1–3

Outstanding Seaside Courses with Numerous Sea Views

St. Andrews Bay (both eighteens)
Kingsbarns
Crail (Balcomie Links)
Elie
Lundin
Murcar
Cruden Bay
Peterhead
Moray Old Course
Nairn
Royal Dornoch
Brora
The Machrie
Shiskine
Prestwick
Royal Troon
Western Gailes
Turnberry (both eighteens)
Gullane No. 1
North Berwick (West Links)
Dunbar

AND GREAT GOLF

Dozen Best Clubhouses

Setting, or exterior, or interior

Royal & Ancient
St. Andrews Links
St. Andrews Bay
Crail
Elie
Cruden Bay
Carnegie Club at Skibo Castle
Rossdhu House (Loch Lomond G.C.)
Western Gailes
Royal Musselburgh
Bruntsfield Links
Muirfield

Dozen Best Restaurants

Old Course Hotel
Peat Inn (outside St. Andrews)
The Cellar (Anstruther)
Andrew Fairlie (Gleneagles)
Boath House (Nairn)
Culloden House (near Nairn)
Skibo Castle
Loch Lomond
Cameron House (Alexandria)
Turnberry Hotel
Greywalls (Gullane)
Open Arms (Dirleton)

Old Tom Morris Courses

*Original layout and/or remodeling
and/or expansion*

St. Andrews Old Course
St. Andrews New Course

Crail (Balcomie Links)
Elie
Leven
Carnoustie
Montrose
Alyth
Moray Old
Royal Dornoch
Tain
Machrihanish
Prestwick
Lanark
Royal Burgess
Luffness New
Dunbar
Muirfield

James Braid Courses

*Original layout and/or remodeling
and/or expansion*

St. Andrews Old Course
St. Andrews New Course
Elie
Downfield
Carnoustie Championship Course
Carnoustie Burnside Course
Edzell
Forfar
Alyth
Kirriemuir
Blairgowrie (Rosemount, Wee Links)
Gleneagles (King's and Queen's)
Murcar
Boat of Garten
Nairn
Fortrose & Rosemarkie

Golspie
Brora
Irvine/Bogside
Prestwick
Royal Troon
Belleisle
Bruntsfield Links
Royal Burgess
Dalmahoy (East and West)
Royal Musselburgh
North Berwick (East Links)

Castle Hotels

Myres Castle (outside St. Andrews)
Meldrum House (outside Aberdeen)
Culloden House (outside Nairn)
Skibo Castle (Dornoch)
Dornoch Castle Hotel
Culzean Castle (near Turnberry)
Rosslyn Castle (Edinburgh)

Worthy B&Bs

Five Gables House (Arbroath)
Trevose Guest House (Dornoch)
Glenaveron (Brora)
Greannan (Isle of Arran)
Harford House (Troon)
Golf View Private Hotel (Prestwick)
The Howard (Edinburgh)
Glebe House (North Berwick)

Appealing Villages

Kilconquhar
Falkland
Lower Largo

Corris
New Lanark
Dirleton
Preston
East Linton
Garvald
Morham

Attractive Harbors

St. Andrews
Crail
Anstruther
Pittenweem
Lower Largo
Cruden Bay
Campbeltown
Brora
Dunbar
North Berwick
Eyemouth
Cove

Castles near Courses

St. Andrews Castle (Old Course)
Falkland Palace (Old Course)
Kellie Castle (Elie)
Glamis Castle (Gleneagles)
Slains Castle (Peterhead)
Cawdor Castle (Nairn)
Dunrobin Castle (Golspie)
Brodick Castle (Shiskine)
Culzean Castle (Turnberry)
Edinburgh Castle (Braids No. 1)
Holyrood Palace (Braids No. 1)
Tantallon Castle (North Berwick)

Churches near Courses

St. Andrews Cathedral (Old Course)
Holy Trinity Church (Old Course)
Collegiate Church of St. Mary (Crail)
Elie Parish Church (Elie)
Tullibardine Chapel (Auchterarder)
St. Andrew's Cathedral (Royal
  Aberdeen)
The Round Church (The Machrie)
Crossraguel Abbey (Turnberry)
Rosslyn Chapel (Braids No. 1)

Ireland

SHORT WEEKENDS (2 GOLF DAYS)

Fly to Dublin
GOLF: Portmarnock, The Island, The European Club
LODGING: King Sitric Restaurant or Four Seasons Dublin
DINING: King Sitric, Seasons Restaurant (Four Seasons)

Fly to Belfast
GOLF: Royal County Down, Ardglass, Malone
LODGING: Slieve Donard Hotel or Glassdrumman Lodge
DINING: Same as Lodging

Fly to Londonderry
GOLF: Royal Portrush (Dunluce and Valley Links), Portstewart
LODGING: Ardtara Country House or Bushmills Inn
DINING: Same as Lodging

Fly to Londonderry
GOLF: Rosapenna (Morris-Ruddy Course and Sandy Hills Links) and Portsalon
LODGING: Rosapenna Golf Hotel or Rathmullan House
DINING: Same as Lodging

Fly to Knock
GOLF: County Sligo (Rosses Point), Enniscrone, Carne
LODGING: Enniscoe House or Stella Maris
DINING: Same as Lodging

Fly to Shannon
GOLF: Lahinch, Doonbeg, Dromoland Castle
LODGING: Doonbeg G. C. or An Tintean (Doonbeg) or Dromoland Castle
DINING: Doonbeg G. C., Morrissey's Seafood Bar & Grill (Doonbeg), Dromoland Castle

Fly to Shannon
GOLF: Ballybunion (Old and Cashen Courses), Tralee
LODGING: Glin Castle (near Limerick) or Marine Links Hotel (Ballybunion) or Meadowlands Hotel (Tralee)
DINING: Same as Lodging

Fly to Cork
GOLF: Old Head, Cork Golf Club, Fota Island
LODGING: Old Bank House (Kinsale) or Ballymaloe House (outside Cork City)
DINING: Ballymaloe House or Le Restaurant D'Antibes (Kinsale)

LONG WEEKENDS (4 GOLF DAYS)

Fly to Dublin
GOLF: Portmarnock, The Island, The European Club, K Club (Palmer and Smurfit Courses), County Louth (Baltray)
LODGING: King Sitric Restaurant or K Club
DINING: King Sitric, Byerley Turk Restaurant (K Club), Seasons Restaurant (Four Seasons)

Fly to Belfast
GOLF: Royal County Down, Ardglass, Royal Portrush (Dunluce and Valley Links), Portstewart, Castlerock
LODGING: Slieve Donard Hotel or Glassdrumman Lodge; Ardtara Country House or Bushmills Inn
DINING: Glassdrumman Lodge, Ardtara, Bushmills

Fly to Londonderry
GOLF: Ballyliffin (Old and Glashedy Links), Portsalon, Rosapenna (Morris-Ruddy Course and Sandy Hills Links), Donegal G. C.
LODGING: Rosapenna Golf Hotel or Rathmullan House; St. Ernan's Country House
DINING: Rosapenna Golf Hotel, Rathmullan House, St. Ernan's

Fly to Shannon
GOLF: Lahinch, Doonbeg, Dromoland Castle, Adare Manor, Ballybunion (Old and Cashen Courses)
LODGING: Moy House or Doonbeg G. C. or Dromoland Castle or Adare Manor or Glin Castle
DINING: Same as Lodging

Fly to Shannon
GOLF: Tralee, Ballybunion Old, Killarney (Killeen and Mahony's Point Courses), Dooks, Waterville
LODGING: Europe Hotel or Killeen House, both in Killarney
DINING: Same as Lodging

512 APPENDIX III

Dozen Best 36-Hole Days

Lahinch and Doonbeg

Ballybunion Old and Cashen

Enniscrone and Carne

Royal Portrush (Dunluce) and
    Portstewart

The European Club and Druids Heath

Rosapenna: Morris-Ruddy Course
    and Sandy Hills Course

Portmarnock and The Island

K Club: Palmer and Smurfit Courses

Royal County Down and Ardglass

Old Head and Cork Golf Club (Little
    Island)

Tralee and Killarney Golf Club's
    Mahony's Point Course

Ballyliffin Glashedy and Portsalon

Dozen Best Par 3s

Portmarnock–15

The Island–13

Royal County Down–4

Royal Portrush–14

Rosapenna's Sandy Hills–7

Donegal G. C.–5

Lahinch–8

Doonbeg–14

Ballybunion Old–15

Ballybunion Cashen–12

Waterville–12

The European Club–14

Outstanding Seaside Courses with Numerous Sea Views

Royal Dublin

Portmarnock

Portmarnock Golf Links

County Louth (Baltray)

Royal County Down

Ardglass

Royal Portrush

Castlerock

Ballyliffin Glashedy

Portsalon

Rosapenna: Sandy Hills

Narin & Portnoo

County Donegal

County Sligo (Rosses Point)

Enniscrone

Carne

Lahinch

Doonbeg

Ballybunion (Old and Cashen)

Tralee

Dooks

Waterville

Old Head

The European Club

Dozen Best Clubhouses
Setting, or exterior, or interior

Portmarnock

K Club: Smurfit Course

Royal County Down

Ardglass

Portstewart

Portsalon

County Sligo (Rosses Point)

Tralee

Waterville

Old Head

Fota Island

Druids Glen

Dozen Best Restaurants

Seasons Restaurant (Four
    Seasons Dublin)

King Sitric

Byerley Turk (K Club)

Ardtara Country House

Coopershill

Cromleach Lodge

Enniscoe House

Dromoland Castle

Adare Manor

Glin Castle

Ballymaloe House

Mount Juliet (Lady Helen Dining Room)

Eddie Hacket Courses
*Original layout and/or remodeling
    and/or expansion*

The Island

Mullingar

Castlerock

County Sligo (Rosses Point)

Strandhill

County Donegal

Enniscrone

Carne

Westport

Connemara

Ashford Castle

Ballybunion Old

Ceann Sibeal

Dooks

Waterville

Kenmare

Parknasilla

Bantry

Castle Hotels

Gregans Castle

Dromoland Castle

Adare Manor

Glin Castle

Waterford Castle

Worthy B&Bs

Albany House (Dublin)

Highfield House (Baltray)

Links Lodge (Doonbeg)

An Tintean (Doonbeg)

Lotamore House (outside Cork City)

Attractive Harbors

Howth

Baltray

Newcastle

Ardglass

Ballintoy

Portstewart

Killybegs

Portnoo

Donegal

Portmagee

Cork City

Appealing Villages

Portbraddan

Cushendall

Westport

Adare

Portmagee

Inistioge

Castles near Courses

Dublin Castle (Royal Dublin)

Dunluce Castle (Royal Portrush)

Carrieabragh Castle (Ballyliffin)

Glenveagh Castle (Rosapenna)

Donegal Castle (County Donegal)

Newtown Castle (Lahinch)

Desmond Castle (Adare Manor)

Bunratty Castle (Dromoland Castle)

Ross Castle (Killarney G. C.)

Ringrone Castle (Kinsalc)

Kilkenny Castle (Mt. Juliet)

Churches near Courses

Christ Church Cathedral (Royal Dublin)

St. Patrick's Cathedral (Royal Dublin)

St. Brigid's Cathedral (K Club)

St. Peter's (County Louth)

Millifont (County Louth)

Moyne Abbey (Enniscrone)

St. Mary's Cathedral (Adare Manor)

Oratory of Gallarus (Ceann Sibeal)

St. Multose (Kinsale)

St. Ann, Shannon (Cork G. C.)

Jerpoint Abbey (Mt. Juliet)

Cathedral of St. Canice (Mt. Juliet)

St. Mary's, Inistioge (Mt. Juliet)

INDEX

Page numbers in *italics* refer to illustrations

D

Dalmahoy, 216
    East Course, 216
    West Course, 216
Daly, John, 469, 475
Danure, 207
Darcy, Eamon, 498
Darwin, Bernard, 24, *137*, 144, 162,
    194, 215, 247–48, 302, 311, 376,
    396
Davaar Island, 170
David Leadbetter Golf Academy, 475
Da Vinci Code, The (Brown), 220
Deane, John and Kay, 335
de Burgh, Chris, 93
Defoe, Daniel, 61
de Gaulle, General and Madame, 389
Delnashaugh Inn, 123
de Savary, Peter, 133, 135, 163, 443
Desmond Castle, 408, 467
de Vicenzo, Roberto, 51–52
Devlin, Bruce, 31, 32, 33
Diaz, Jaime, 495
Dickinson, Gardner, 114
Dingle Peninsula, 430, 432, 434, 444,
    446, *446, 447*, 457
Dingle Town, 446–47, *446*
Dirleton (village), 231, 235, 252
Dirleton Castle, *231*
Discovery, 73, *73*
Doagh Visitors Centre, 331
Doak, Tom, 110, 393
Dobson, James, 237
Donald, Luke, 125, 289
Donard Park, 304
Donegal Castle, *354, 355*
Donegal Golf Club, *350*, 351–55, *352,
    353*
Donegal Town, 351, 354, 355
Dooks Golf Club, *443*, 444, *444*, 445

Doonbeg (village), 415
Doonbeg Castle, 415
Doonbeg Golf Club, 255, *410*, 411–15,
    412, 413, 414, 417
Dooncarton Stone Circle, *381*
Dormy House, 93
Dornoch Castle Hotel, 141
Dornoch Cathedral, *141*
Dorothy Draper & Co., 401
Doune Castle, *99, 220*
Dow, Professor, 41
Dowager Marchioness of Lansdowne,
    81
Downfield Golf Club, 72, *72*
Downings (village), 344
Doyle, Kevin, 252
Doyle's Seafood Bar, 447
Dreel Tavern, 53
Drogheda, 293
Dromoland Castle, 382–83, 385, *400,
    401*–3, *401, 402*
    hotel, *403, 403*
Druids Glen Course, *486*, 487–89, *488,
    489, 490*
Druids Glen Marriott Hotel, 490, 493
Druids Heath Course, 487, 489–93,
    490–91, 492, 493
Druids Restaurant, 493
Drumcliff, 365, *365*
Drumcliff Churchyard, 358, 365
Dublin (city), 259, 262–63, *262, 263*
Dublin Castle, 263
Dublin CPA, 269
Dublin Spire, 263
Duel in the Sun (Corcoran), 201
Dulnain Bridge, 123
Dunaverty, 169, 170
Dunbar (town), 235, *235*
Dunbar Golf Club, *232*, 233–35, *233*
    Winterfield, 234

Dunbar Golfing Society, 233
Duncan, George, 15, 137, 265
Dundee, 73
Dundonald Golf Club, 269
Dunes Golf and Beach Club, 405
Dunfanaghy, *345*
Dunkeld (town), 85
Dunkeld Castle, 85
Dunloe Golf Course, 443
Dunlop International, 87
Dunlop Masters, 265
Dunluce Castle, 307, 308, *313*
Dunn, Tom, 224, 469
Dunnottar Castle, 79
Dunraven Arms Hotel, 409, *409*
Dunrobin Castle, 145, *145*
Dunvegan Hotel, 21, 28
Duval, David, 265, 417, 455, 498
Dye, Pete, 39, 118, 138, 194, 275

E

Earlesferry (village), 49
Earlesferry & Elie Golf Club, 49
East Fortune, 235
East Linton, 235
East Lothian, 16, 44, 234, 235, 237
East of Ireland Amateur Championship,
    290–92
East of Scotland Amateur
    Championship, 57
Eby, Stan, 269
Edinburgh (town), 75, 216, 219, 220,
    220, 263
Edinburgh Burgess (Royal Burgess
    Golfing Society of Edinburgh),
    103, 215, 216–19
Edward I, King of England, 235
Edward VII, King of England, 103, 133,
    223, 253, 269, 297, 307

Edzell (village), 78, 79
Edzell Castle, 79
Edzell Golf Club, 9, 78, 209
Eisenhower, Dwight, 206
Electric Brae, 207
Elgin (town), 125, 130
Elgin Golf Club, 129
Elie (village), 47, 49, 50, 53
    see also Golf House Club, Elie, The
Elie & Earlesferry Ladies Golf Club, 49
Elizabeth, Queen Mother, 99
Els, Ernie, 149, 185, 247, 249, 417
Elysium Health and Leisure Centre,
    304
Emerald Gems: The Links of Ireland
    (Lambrecht), 329, 357
Engh, Jim, 377–78
English Ladies' Championship, 289
Ennis, *415*
Enniscoe House, *372, 372, 373*, 377
Enniscrone Golf Club, *366*, 367–73,
    367, 368, 369, 370, 371
Enniskerry, 500
Erskine, Wilma, 307
Esperante, 33
European Club, The, 255, 375,
    484–85, 494, 495–501, *496, 497,
    498, 499*
European Open, 276
European Ryder Cup, 31
European Tour, 83, 149, 292
Europe hotel, 445
Evans, Clive and Joan, 354
Evans-Lombe, Brian, 250–51
Ewing, Cecil, 357–58
Eyemouth (town), 235
Eyemouth Museum, 235

PHOTO CREDITS

All golf course photographs are by Laurence C. Lambrecht, except for page 49.
All photographs in "Off the Course" sections are by Tim Thompson, except for those listed below:

Scotland

P. 28—top, courtesy of Myres Castle
P. 33—right, courtesy of St. Andrews Bay Hotel
P. 49—courtesy of the Golf House Club, Elie
P. 98—right, both courtesy of Gleneagles Hotel
P. 119—lower right, courtesy of Udny Arms
P. 123—bottom right, courtesy of Boat Hotel
P. 130—center, P. Tomkins/Visit Scotland/Scottish Viewpoint
P. 131—middle row, center and right, courtesy of Boath House
P. 135—both courtesy of Carnegie Club
P. 145—top left, courtesy of Royal Marine Hotel
P. 157—top right, courtesy of Rossdhu House
P. 170—center, top, courtesy of the Landmark Trust
P. 207—bottom row, center, Allan Devlin/Scottish Viewpoint
P. 220—bottom left, courtesy of the Landmark Trust
P. 253— courtesy of Greywalls Hotel

Ireland

P. 262—left, courtesy of Dublin Four Seasons
P. 282—left, both courtesy of the Kildare Hotel & Country Club
P. 304—left, courtesy of Slieve Donard Hotel
P. 313—bottom, courtesy of Northern Irish Tourist Board
P. 321—right column, second from top, courtesy of Ireland's Blue Book
P. 344—bottom, courtesy of Ireland's Blue Book
P. 354—right, both courtesy of Ireland's Blue Book
P. 372—center, courtesy of Enniscoe House
P. 390—upper left, courtesy of Ireland's Blue Book
P. 398—upper right, courtesy of Ireland's Blue Book
P. 403—center, both courtesy of Dromoland Castle
P. 409—center right, both courtesy of Dunraven Arms Hotel
P. 427—left and center, all courtesy of Glin Castle
P. 445—left, courtesy of Great Southern, Killarney
P. 447—middle row, center, courtesy of Ireland's Blue Book
P. 472—right, both courtesy of Lotamore House
P. 483—lower right, courtesy of Waterford Castle
P. 500—center, both courtesy of Tinakilly House